T0313530

THE UNIVERSITY OF MICHIGAN
CENTER FOR CHINESE STUDIES

MICHIGAN MONOGRAPHS IN CHINESE STUDIES
NO. 49

LABOR AND THE CHINESE REVOLUTION

CLASS STRATEGIES AND CONTRADICTIONS OF CHINESE COMMUNISM, 1928-48

S. BERNARD THOMAS

Ann Arbor
Center for Chinese Studies
The University of Michigan
1983

*Open access edition funded by the National Endowment for the Humanities/
Andrew W. Mellon Foundation Humanities Open Book Program.*

Library of Congress Cataloging in Publication Data

Thomas, S. B. (S. Bernard), 1921–

Labor and the Chinese revolution.

(Michigan monographs in Chinese studies; no. 49)
Bibliography: p.
Includes index.
1. Communism—China—History—20th century. 2.
Labor and laboring classes—China—History—20th century. 3. Peasantry—China—History—20th century. I.
Title. II. Series.
HX417.T495 1983   335.43'0951   83–19045
ISBN 978-0-89264-049-2

Jacket photograph: PLA troops entering Shanghai, 25 May 1949.
Museum of Revolutionary History, Peking.

Printed and bound by CPI Group (UK) Ltd, Croydon, CR0 4YY

ISBN 978-0-89264-049-2 (hardcover)
ISBN 978-0-472-03841-1 (paper)
ISBN 978-0-472-12824-2 (ebook)
ISBN 978-0-472-90224-8 (open access)

To Ruth, John and Ira

CONTENTS

CONTENTS

ACKNOWLEDGMENTS

In preparing this study I have had the support and assistance of many people and institutions. I am grateful to the staffs of the Hoover Library at Stanford University, the Harvard-Yenching Library at Harvard University, the China Documentation Center at Columbia University, the Kresge Library at Oakland University, and the Universities Service Centre in Hong Kong. I especially thank Mr. Wei-ying Wan and the staff of the Asia Library at the University of Michigan for their unfailing courtesies and help through the years of my research on the book. I have also been assisted by a number of grants and stipends from the Oakland University Research Committee, and I am particularly grateful to Professor Lewis N. Pino, former Director of Research and Academic Development at Oakland University for his many kindnesses and aid in facilitating my work and furthering the publication of this book.

Many friends and colleagues in the China field, as well as anonymous readers from the University of Michigan Center for Chinese Studies, read earlier drafts of the manuscript, and I have benefitted greatly from their suggestions and criticisms. Any remaining errors of fact or interpretation are my responsibility. Professor Robert C. Howes of Oakland University gave unstinting help in translating Russian sources, and my former colleague Mr. Shih-chen Peng gave generously of his time and linguistic skills in working with me on Chinese-language materials.

The late Marian P. Wilson, editorial assistant of the College of Arts and Sciences at Oakland University, working on the initial draft of the manuscript, and as a good friend and sharp critic did much to improve it. Her able successor, Anne H. Lalas, has been an invaluable editorial counsellor in taking the manuscript through further revisions and drafts. I am also indebted to Barbara Congelosi, former editor for the Center for Chinese Studies Publications, for her unsparing efforts in editing and preparing the manuscript for publication; to her successors Janis Michael and Janet Opdyke who so ably and efficiently took charge of all final editorial and production details; and to Diane Scherer, who typed and processed the copy for the printer.

I wish also to give my special thanks to Dr. Harvey A. Lincoff, a most distinguished retinal surgeon, whose extraordinary skills and concern have literally given me the gift of sight, without which this book and much else would have been impossible. My wife Evelyn, as always, has been an indispensable source of loving help and encouragement.

S. Bernard Thomas
Oakland University
Rochester, Michigan
August 1983

ABBREVIATIONS*

ACFL All China Federation of Labor
CAL   China Association of Labor
CBSA Central Bureau of the Soviet Areas
CCP   Chinese Communist Party
CI   Comintern (Communist International)
ECCI Executive Committee, Communist International
ILO   International Labor Organization
KMT   Kuomintang (Nationalist Party)
NCNA New China News Agency
PLA   People's Liberation Army
RILU Red International of Labor Unions (Profintern)
WFTU World Federation of Trade Unions

* Note. While the *pinyin* romanization system adopted by the
People's Republic of China is now becoming the standard system
for transcribing Chinese, I have somewhat reluctantly continued
to use the older Wade–Giles form. I do this because my study
deals with a period for which virtually all the English-language
sources and translations cited and quoted use the latter system.
However, for all Chinese names and places listed in the index, the
pinyin equivalent has been provided in brackets. *Pinyin* romanization has also been used for current citations of journal titles now
known in that form: *Beijing review, Renmin ribao,* [People's
Daily], *Gongren ribao* [Worker], *Guangming ribao* [Bright Daily],
and for the news service, Xinhua [NCNA].

INTRODUCTION

The two decade period from 1928 through 1948 witnessed a remarkable reversal of fortune for the Chinese Communist revolutionary movement. It began in the wake of the enforced retreat of the shattered Communist remnants from the countryside and ended with the final triumphant return to those cities by the Communist-led peasant forces of the People's Liberation Army (PLA). The once powerful left labor movement of the mid-1920s had suffered an all but fatal blow in the succession of disasters that befell the CCP in the 1927 dissolution of the first KMT-CCP united front. But though the Communist-led labor movement never recovered its former momentum and influence during the subsequent twenty years of revolutionary struggle, the party's assessment and handling of labor's role in the revolution remained an important and often crucial ingredient in CCP doctrinal, strategic, and policy formulations in those years, as well as in the leadership conflicts which developed from these formulations.

The above issues and conflicts were evident in the agrarian revolutionary line of the party, in its rural-urban strategic concepts and class policies, in united front issues, in questions of revolutionary stages and class leadership, and in the economic and developmental policies pursued in Communist-controlled areas. The role assigned to labor continued to be a critical touchstone, whether in the efforts to accentuate and reinforce the party's proletarian base and character in the decade following 1928 or, conversely, in the moves during the subsequent ten years to forge new policies and strategies which in effect restructured and redefined the class contours of Chinese Communism. One may indeed question whether

1

labor's "narrow" class interests were compatible with those of a peasant-based social revolution or with the developmental needs of the massive and poverty-stricken rural society that was China.

The proletarian themes and issues underlying the party's ideological utterances were shrouded in rhetoric designed, perhaps, as much to disguise as to chart actual class strategies. Rhetoric notwithstanding, a careful analysis of such pronouncements is vitally important in following and evaluating the party's changing lines during this key revolutionary period. The function of the "proletariat" in the complex of policy issues and leadership struggles which developed under the precarious circumstances of those years had an importance out of all proportion to labor's relatively minor role in the post-1927 Communist-led revolution. This may be noted, for example, both in Maoist criticism of the urban and proletarian bias of the Comintern-sponsored (Internationalist) leadership wing of the CCP in the 1930s for its dogmatic misunderstanding of the rural-peasant realities of the Chinese revolution[1] and in Soviet Russian analyses which view the Chinese party's long-term isolation from proletarian centers before 1949 as the root cause of the party's "agrarianization" and the social basis of "petty bourgeois" Maoist nationalism.[2]

In the early, primarily urban-based phase of its existence, the CCP gave top priority to organizing and leading a mass labor movement and to mounting labor struggles built around both economic and political issues. The Communist-led All-China Federation of Labor (ACFL), formally organized in 1925, claimed to represent some 2.8 million workers at its Fourth National Labor Congress in June 1927, though this high-water mark was even then eroding rapidly under the relentless and ruthless suppression of the left labor movement in much of China.[3]

It was during 1927 that the CCP-led labor movement reached both its zenith of strength and influence and its nadir of defeat, destruction, and demoralization. This shift in fortunes is largely the tale of three cities: Shanghai, Hankow (Wuhan), and Canton. The

Communist-organized Shanghai general strike and workers' uprising in March 1927, on the eve of Chiang Kai-shek's entry into the city, was followed by Chiang's coup of 12 April against the left, which effectively liquidated the red labor movement in China's leading industrial center. The high tide of the Hankow-based labor movement was in evidence at the Fourth ACFL Congress held there in June, but was quickly dissipated with left-wing KMT leader Wang Ching-wei's split with and suppression of the Communists soon thereafter. And finally, the party's powerful Canton labor organization, which had functioned during the famous Canton-Hong Kong strike of 1925-26 as a de facto second government in that originating center of the Nationalist revolution,[4] was destroyed in the aftermath of the ill-fated Canton uprising of December 1927, the party's last desperate effort to reverse the counterrevolutionary tide.[5] In the bleak aftermath of these developments a May 1928 internal notice of the Party Center on the labor movement acknowledged that "the Red labor organizations of the working class across the country have been smashed to pieces [so] that it is impossible to restore them immediately."[6]

Under these unpromising circumstances, the Party Center, now underground, continued to operate primarily from Shanghai until late 1932 or early 1933. It sought to retain and expand its links with the urban labor movement by organizing surviving left elements into secret red trade unions and by trying to counter the growing role of the legal, KMT-controlled ("yellow") unions. The ongoing KMT "white terror" against the Communist underground in the cities effectively impeded the progress of the sectarian red labor movement. According to Communist sources, the Fifth ACFL Congress of the red trade unions, meeting secretly in Shanghai in late 1929, represented only some sixty-five thousand workers, three-fifths of whom were located in the rural soviet areas.[7] In a September 1930 report to the Third Plenum of the CCP Central Committee, Chou En-lai acknowledged that industrial workers numbered little more than two thousand in a party which had by then grown to one

hundred twenty thousand members.[8] By 1932, the Central Council
of the Moscow-based Red International of Labor Unions (RILU, or
Profintern) conceded that the red trade unions in the nonsoviet areas
were "extremely weak" and lagged far behind "the growing militancy
and struggle of the masses."[9] Despite efforts after 1931 to promote
a "strike-struggle" movement focused on countering Japanese imperialism, the constantly reiterated Communist projections of an
impending new urban revolutionary upsurge which would reinforce,
coordinate, and ultimately lead the rural movement remained unrealized as the post-1927 soviet era moved to a close with the Long
March of 1934-35.

However, the revolution did regain vitality after 1927 in
scattered rural areas of south central China by means of a strategy
that incorporated armed struggle, agrarian revolution, and the
organization of soviets. The Communist task now was to fulfill the
antifeudal (agrarian) and antiimperialist (nationalist) goals of the
aborted "bourgeois-democratic" revolution, which would, in turn,
provide the foundation for a final revolutionary transition to socialism and proletarian dictatorship. The political and strategic guidelines for this new phase of the struggle were outlined by the Sixth
CCP Congress, held in Moscow during the summer of 1928, and were
summed up in the oft-repeated phrase, "a peasant war led by the
proletariat." The urban component of this line was the effort to
revive Communist influence in the urban labor movement so that the
cities could once again become active arenas in a rising revolutionary tide. This strategy was espoused most forcefully from
January 1931 on by the youthful, Russian-returned student leadership of the party and was implemented on this faction's authority in
the Chinese Soviet Republic, which was established in the Kiangsi-
Fukien central soviet area in November 1931. The party sought to
proletarianize soviet area party, army, and government organs with
a view to giving local labor a favored economic and political status,
raising proletarian consciousness through anticapitalist struggle, and
promoting "class" trade unions as "the pillar of soviet power." These

unions were to assume a leadership role over the poorer elements of the peasantry and to forge closer links with them. They were to function as struggle instruments for accentuating and advancing the class interests of both agricultural and nonagricultural workers at the expense of the "rural bourgeoisie" (rich peasants and capitalists).[10]

Mao's policy-making role as chairman of the Kiangsi-based soviet republic after 1931 remains ambiguous. But it appears evident that his efforts to foster a broader base of support among the peasantry and to focus on economic construction issues operated within the overall constraints of the class strategies formulated by the Comintern and the CCP leaderships. Moreover, while the mobilization techniques promoted by Mao in Kiangsi provided models and experiences for the later Yenan years,[11] it was only in the latter period that the new class strategies and content of the Maoist mass line fully unfolded.

Just as the urban proletarian component of the party's strategy remained frustrated during the 1928-35 soviet period, so, too, did the effort to promote more directly proletarian leadership in the rural revolution founder on an unreal assessment of the significance of both proletarian and capitalist forces in the Chinese countryside and on the inevitable difficulties and contradictions that such class war policies encountered under conditions of a protracted, isolated, and increasingly beleaguered peasant-based struggle for survival.

Problems of class line remained largely unresolved as the Kiangsi base was abandoned in late 1934. However, new possibilities for a KMT-CCP national anti-Japanese united front after 1935 seemed once again to open opportunities for the CCP to return to and revive its urban labor roots. The advocates of this new united-front proletarian line focused their efforts on rebuilding and fortifying the party's links to a national labor movement centered principally in the cities, which would serve as the key Communist political bases under the overall "bourgeois" leadership of the KMT in the national resistance war against Japan. The influence of this line was

felt also in the northern Shensi Communist base, which the deci-
mated Long March forces had reached in late 1935 and which
became the Shensi-Kansu-Ninghsia (Shen-Kan-Ning) Border Region
(the famed Yenan) in 1937 under the new united front arrangements
with the KMT. This was evident in the policy trend (to about 1940-
41) which gave priority to the development of a necessarily modest
state-sponsored and advantaged industrial and proletarian nucleus in
the Border Region.

This policy line, which was identified with the Moscow-
oriented faction of the CCP led by Wang Ming (Ch'en Shao-yü), was
by no means an urban revolutionary strategy as opposed to a Maoist
rural revolutionary strategy.[12] It was rather an abandonment (for at
least the duration of the war) of a Communist-led revolution, urban
or rural, in favor of a collaborative joint bloc against Japan, in
which the "proletariat," linked to its Communist vanguard and
retaining its class identity, would subordinate itself to the leadership
of the national government for the "bourgeois nationalist" resistance
war. But, again, these proletariat-oriented policies contained intrin-
sic difficulties and contradictory aspects, and the actual course of
military and political developments in the early war years seriously
undermined this line and led to the political eclipse of its Internationalist proponents within the party.

Although Mao had been in a leading (though not commanding)
position in the CCP since 1935, a Maoist line did not fully emerge
until the eve of the Mao-initiated party rectification movement
(cheng-feng) of the early 1940s, a movement which brought an end
to the remaining political power of the Wang Ming group. In contrast to the latter's wartime program, Mao stressed overwhelmingly
the CCP's primary commitment to the rural base areas. He advanced a broad range of rural-oriented, populist (mass line) policies
in which the previously advantaged status of the Border Region's
nascent state industrial sector and its managerial, union, and worker
constituencies was downgraded. The party at the same time accelerated its mobilization of the peasantry, increased its pressure on

the landlords, and moved more forcefully to affirm an independent Communist role in the resistance war based on its expanding base areas and peasant armies. These strategies were expressed politically in the party's assertion of direct and long-term leadership over a new-democratic coalition of classes in which both labor and capital were constituent, but subordinated, elements. Thus, as the Maoist leadership moved toward fuller and broader mobilization of the peasantry (its major constituency) on an antifeudal basis, it proclaimed a mutual-benefits theme for labor and capital which sidestepped the issue of worker (farm and industry) mobilization through class interest appeals or policies. At the same time, a "lie low" strategy for the urban centers under KMT or Japanese control concentrated on a broad political approach to a multiclass bloc in which "narrow" labor class interests and struggles were played down.

The civil war years after 1945 brought a more radical revolutionary CCP line and a more intricate interplay of interests and forces as the Communists moved more directly and massively into the national political arena. New responsibility for running the economies of Communist-occupied urban centers and direct contact with larger labor constituencies led to more complex wage policies and to some resurgence of proletarian-line attitudes and policies among party cadres. Yet the fundamental outlines of the conciliatory Maoist labor-capital strategy predominated as the rural peasant revolution escalated and, indeed, were strongly reiterated as the party prepared to enter the cities in 1948.

In dealing with the policy issues and policy variations in Chinese Communism over these two decades of war and revolution, it would be overly simplistic to juxtapose an urban to a rural revolutionary strategy as continuous and discrete entities. The urban labor standpoint had its significant rural concomitant, and the rural peasant line had its important urban counterpart as well. Each of the various urban-rural approaches had its specific class content and strategy. The ultimately successful Maoist strategy no longer found it necessary to view the cities as crucial revolutionary struggle centers which could generate the reliable proletarian base needed to ensure final revolutionary victory and the socialist future of the revolution. To the contrary, Mao was able to fashion a CCP-led united front strategy which not only facilitated peasant mobilization and revolutionization in a protracted rural resistance struggle, but also provided the party with its first really viable urban political strategy as well. By no longer linking the party's urban base and destiny primarily with labor, Mao succeeded in shaping a broadly based urban approach in which the cities became passive but increasingly receptive and still crucial targets as the rural revolution moved on to final victory in the 1946-48 civil war period.

The Sixth CCP Congress in 1928 had seen the proletarianization of the agrarian revolution as a necessary step toward the ultimate creation of a "workers' government" which would "inaugurate a collective-village economy under the leadership of large state-owned urban industries" and which would unite (through cooperatives) "the rural economy of several hundreds of millions of peasants with the urban socialist industrial economy." [13] In the actual event, the massive Chinese agrarian revolution, though successfully led by a Communist Party committed to socialist goals, was not and could not be kept within the proletarian parameters set by the 1928 program. The prerequisites for the kind of "workers' government" projected at that time had not been fulfilled. A primary commitment to an organized and "class-conscious" proletariat militantly defending and advancing its class interests proved unsuited (in both Communist-controlled and Nationalist-ruled areas) to the basic interests and necessary class strategies of the ultimately successful Chinese revolution. And the appropriate role and status of industrial labor in postliberation China, relative to other class forces and to overall developmental priorities and goals, have continued to be a source of political controversy and conflicting policies. The latter point will be briefly addressed in the conclusion to this study.

CHAPTER I

A Peasant War Led by the Proletariat:
The Class Line for the Post-1927 Soviet Era

The focus on the agrarian problem as the major task of the uncompleted presocialist phase of the revolution was, on the ideological level, a pragmatic reflection of the 1928 scene in China, where the scattered beginnings of rural soviet enclaves were the sole evidence of active Communist-led struggle. The ECCI Ninth Plenum had acknowledged in February 1928 that after "the terrible defeats" of the previous year, there was "no mighty upsurge of the revolutionary mass movement on a national scale."[1] Pointing to the uneven development of the Chinese revolution, it declared that "whereas in some provinces the peasant movement develops further, in some industrial centres the labor movement is bled white and subjected to unexampled white terror and is experiencing a certain degree of depression."[2] Overall party membership had reportedly declined from over fifty-seven thousand to perhaps ten thousand within six months of Chiang's April 1927 coup, with the major blow falling on party organizations in the large proletarian centers.[3] The "core of the revolutionary movement—the base and the main ramparts—the core of the proletariat," Comintern head Nikolai Bukharin told the Sixth CCP Congress in June 1928 "up till now still has not been able to cure its wounds in the aftermath of serious defeat."[4]

While Comintern and CCP pronouncements continuously and expectantly pointed to trends which supposedly presaged an urban resurgence, it was the fact of the growing disparity between the reviving peasant struggle and the persisting urban "depression" which Communist policy makers had to deal with throughout the post-1928 soviet period. But in according primary emphasis to the agrarian revolution and the rural soviet movement, appropriate rural class strategies and policies were seen as essential to prevent the land revolution from leading merely to the victory of a "small-holding" (petty-bourgeois) peasantry whose instincts and aspirations were viewed as anything but socialistic   Bukharin thus also observed to the Sixth CCP Congress that the peasants as small private owners "think to get rich from that plot of land of theirs. This is their ideology. This is their endeavor."[5]   Only by proletarianizing the Communist-led rural struggle could the land revolution transcend its innately small-holder character and not merely topple the "feudal" (landlord-gentry) forces of the countryside, but also advance the struggle against the bourgeoisie. The latter class had, since the 1927 KMT-CCP break, been consigned by the Communists to the enemy camp, together with landlord, militarist, and imperialist forces, and all were now identified with the KMT regime. The final guarantee against Communist submergence by the peasantry was to be a reactivated left-led urban labor struggle movement, which would be linked to an urban-based Party Center and would focus on a new urban-rural revolutionary upsurge as the ultimate key to victory (under proletarian-Communist leadership) in at least a substantial portion of the country.[6]

While viewing the existence of "several hsien" (counties) with soviet regimes as harbingers of a renewed revolutionary advance, Bukharin still stressed to the Sixth CCP Congress that "a regime covering no cities absolutely cannot last very long."[7]   Chinese party leader Ch'ü Ch'iu-pai. in also taking note of these initial rural revolutionary successes, nonetheless declared to the Sixth Comintern Congress in July 1928 that without a victorious insurrection of the proletariat, a victory of the Chinese revolution, at least in several provinces, was unthinkable. Ch'ü stressed the need for "more energetic mass work in the trade unions" to enable the working class to assume its revolutionary leadership.[8] While the key role of the city was unmistakably asserted. it was equally clear that the immediate revolutionary arena was the countryside and that the immediate revolutionary task was on the agrarian front. But a proletarian class-struggle line, both rural and urban, was seen as the fundamental link between the emerging rural movement and its essential, though now increasingly eclipsed, urban connection and leadership.

Thus, under the differing circumstances and opportunities of the rural and urban settings—the one an expanding center of armed revolutionary struggle and the other an increasingly peripheral arena of slow, painful underground rebuilding and preparation—the role of proletarian forces and their mobilization and organization loomed large in the party's strategic calculations and policies. But the two key circumstances of the Chinese revolution pinpointed by Bukharin in 1928—the principal role of the "petty-bourgeois" peasant masses[9] on the one hand and the extremely tenuous Communist presence in the cities on the other—remained the irrefutable realities with which these calculations and policies had to contend.

The Class Line of the Sixth CCP Congress

The Sixth Congress of the CCP, held under Comintern supervision in Moscow from 18 June to 11 July 1928,[10] spelled out the class strategies and revolutionary projections for the new soviet era of the Chinese revolution and remained the ideological and programmatic base[11] from which (with some later modifications) the party's class line of the post-1928 years stemmed. While clearly focusing on the rural peasant struggle and its agrarian program as the central issue, the Sixth Congress documents also reveal the determination of the Communists to foster the interests and enhance the role of those elements viewed as proletarian and semiproletarian forces in the Chinese countryside. The congress's resolution on the peasant movement projected a basic alliance of hired farm laborers, poor peasants, and middle peasants[12] (all of whom were expected to be beneficiaries of, or at least not harmed by, a land confiscation and redistribution program), with a leading role assigned to the hired hands. High priority was given to organizing agricultural labor and promoting its class struggles, preferably through a separate union of hired farmhands. The farmhands were to play a leadership role in the poor peasants' associations, either through cells within these associations or through a separate union, and to maintain close contacts with nonagricultural workers' unions. The hired farmhand union was also to be accessible to workers in rural handicraft industries.[13] The leadership role of the rural labor movement and of the Communist Party (the latter not viewed merely as a surrogate proletariat) vis-à-vis the peasant movement, it was emphasized, was "a prerequisite to the success of the agrarian revolution."[14] Elements from the workers' movement were to be drawn into the peasant movement and its leading organs. Village party organizations, the key to local working-class leadership, were to be based on the rural proletariat and "progressive elements of the semiproletariat (handicraftsmen, hired farmhands, and poor peasants)" and to remain organizationally separate and distinct from the peasant associations and the soviets.[15]

While landlords were unmistakably prime targets of the land revolution, the congress took a more ambivalent position toward the rich peasants, evidently the result of a Stalinist compromise at that time with the more right-leaning Bukharin forces.[16] However, in their Communist-defined role as rural capitalists, the rich peasants were an obvious and even essential target of a rural proletarian class line. Ch'ü Ch'iu-pai thus told the congress that "the rich peasant is an element of the peasantry that exploits the labor of hired farm laborers. He is a capitalist, a rural entrepreneur. He is no different from a factory owner."[17] The hired farmhands, he continued, were "the agricultural proletariat, and they are juxtaposed against the rich peasants."[18]

The resolution on the peasant movement spelled out a complicated, if not contradictory, line on the rich peasants. Wherever the latter retained a revolutionary potential, they should be absorbed into the struggle against the feudal (warlord, landlord-gentry) forces; where they "wavered" between revolution and counterrevolution, the aim should be to neutralize rather than to push them into the enemy camp; but where they had already become counterrevolutionary, the struggle against them should be mounted simultaneously with that against the landlord-gentry class.[19]   Yet, at the same time, the resolution noted that as the peasant movement developed, a class conflict between the rural proletariat and the rural bourgeoisie would arise "extremely rapidly."   The rich peasants "usually engage in exploiting hired labourers in agricultural as well as in industrial and commercial enterprises; or at the same time [they] rent out a part of their land to exploit the tenants in the usual cruel manner, or else exploit the poor peasants through usury."   Thus, it was assumed that the rich peasants would "inevitably join" the counterrevolutionary camp.   Even where the resolution counselled against intensifying the struggle against wavering rich peasant elements, it carefully qualified this by adding, "so far as the struggle of poor peasants and hired farmhands is not handicapped."[20]   The struggle against rich peasants was thus seen as the natural concomitant of an intensified rural class conflict.

The congress's resolution on the land question further elaborated agricultural class divisions and policies.   Declaring that "the method of exploiting hired farmhands has begun to become an essential economic characteristic of the rich peasants,"[21] it sketched out its picture of the emerging proletarian and semiproletarian forces of the Chinese countryside.   First were the "agricultural workers," described as contract workers hired by the "capitalist agricultural economy" and by the various related processing industries (tea, oil, sugar, etc.).   In this category, the sale of labor power was the sole source of livelihood.   The "poor" peasant class was divided into two groups: "small" peasants, those barely able to eke out a living on their land; and "smallest" peasants, those who tilled a minimal plot of land (their own or rented) but earned the major portion of their income as contract (hired) labor.   This latter group comprised the semiproletarian class, with the distinction between it and the agricultural proletariat acknowledged to be "often very unclear."[22] The "middle" peasant was described as the "small private landowner," who in good years might accumulate a small amount of capital and who often required the services of hired labor.[23]

The emphasis on hired labor as part of an agricultural proletariat created some confusion and differences of opinion at the congress as to whether they, too, should be allotted land. A number of delegates feared that such laborers, if given land, would lose their proletarian identity and become "petty owners" reinforcing the capitalist-oriented forces in the countryside.[24] Li Li-san, for example, while avoiding a definite stand on the issue, saw the question of protecting contract labor's interests as one to be solved by the labor movement rather than the peasant movement.[25] But despite the fuzzy differentiations between poor peasant "semiproletarians" and hired hand "proletarians," it was to become evident that both groups aspired to petty-owner status and that any attempt to deny land to the latter could only result in their alienation from the Communist camp.[26]

The land resolution further acknowledged that the democratic-agrarian phase of the revolution would necessarily constitute "a starting point in the advance along the capitalist path" (for which the small family farm economy of the middle peasant was presumably the agricultural prototype). However, the resolution added, "It will, during the revolutionary process, transform itself into a preliminary step toward socialist development."[27] The key factors promoting the latter transformation would be the establishment of worker-peasant political power, the "bankruptcy" of bourgeois leadership and the enhancement of proletarian class-consciousness, and the links forged by a revolutionary peasantry with the proletariat of the Soviet Union and of "various advanced countries and of China itself."[28] The firm establishment of soviet political power in China, it added, would then be followed by the end of private ownership of land. And, as has already been noted in the Introduction, all of these developments would enable "a workers' government" to institute a collective village economy under the leadership of an urban socialist industrial economy.

Thus, according to the resolution, organized village workers (both nonagricultural and agricultural), together with the "immense numbers" of the rural semiproletariat and under the leadership of organized urban workers, would "struggle against the rural and urban bourgeoisie for the future triumph of the socialist revolution." The CCP, it declared, "will lead the Chinese revolution towards the development of this line."[29] The importance of and commitment to a rural proletarian as well as an antilandlord line was therefore clearly underscored, as was the ultimately crucial leadership role of the urban labor movement.

The nonagricultural (essentially urban) labor policies of the Sixth Congress were outlined in its resolution on the trade union movement. This document reviewed the history of the labor movement and its past weaknesses as well as the repressions and destruction it had suffered since 1927. Noting that, as a result, the "workers' movement was at a lower level than the peasants' movement," it added that this was "a great and special danger in the Chinese revolution at the present stage."[30] It summed up the party's basic organizational tasks in the labor area as follows:

> to lead the proletariat in its daily economic and political struggle, to oppose reactionary trade unions, to organize revolutionary trade unions, to promote the class consciousness of the broad working masses by means of propaganda and agitation. Only thus can the Party accelerate the arrival of a revolutionary high tide, on the one hand, and ensure that the Chinese proletariat will lead the revolutionary masses, on the other.[31]

Declaring that "the broad economic struggle of the working class will inevitably be transformed into political struggle," the resolution emphasized the need to mount well-organized economic struggles as the path to successful political struggle. It called for a strike strategy based on the economic platform of the 1927 (Fourth) ACFL Congress, which was built around the core demand for an eight-hour work-day and a six-day work-week.[32] Individual strike struggles were to focus on those portions of the 1927 platform that were of immediate relevance and concern to the workers involved, with the red labor unions adopting a low profile and operating through workers' strike and factory committees and a variety of cover organizations.

The workers were called on to "engage in severe struggle" against both foreign and Chinese capitalists, who were described as being "all alike in their cruel exploitation of the Chinese working masses and are all our class enemies."[33] The urban petty bourgeoisie (small businessmen) were divided into an upper stratum (employers of labor) against whom the same antagonistic class stance as for the bourgeoisie in general should prevail, and a lower stratum (those who did not employ outside [nonfamily] labor) whose interests should be supported. Once again, however, the overriding principle was the unhindered development of the class struggle and the unimpeded promotion of the workers' class interests.[34] These policies toward the petty bourgeoisie were to have particular relevance for the soviet areas, where the promotion of nonagricultural worker interests and struggles had as their only "capitalist" target the petty-bourgeois merchant-shopkeepers and small enterpreneurs of the rural towns and villages in the Communist-controlled areas.

The trade union resolution noted that the newly formed anti-Communist KMT unions utilized both repressive and "reformist" methods to win over "part of the backward workers." Consequently, in the struggle against these unions the "backward ideology of some workers" would also have to be fought. Toward the non-Communist unions in general, the party should work among the masses within these unions, exposing their leaders (but abjuring the use of "terrorist" methods), winning over their members, and "thoroughly destroying the reactionary unions."[35] The resolution further emphasized the need to foster worker activists, pointing to the continuing pattern of "too few workers and too many members of the intelligentsia" in the party-led labor movement.[36] The key importance of forging links with production workers in large enterprises was stressed and underlined again in the resolution on organization. The latter emphasized the need to place "the center of gravity" of the labor movement in the large industries and called on the party to pay close attention to developing its organizations in key centers of the country, i.e., "the great industrial cities, the military strongholds, and cities and villages along ocean transportation routes, railways, and large rivers."[37] The red union organization (ACFL) was also directed to maintain close links with the peasants through *hsien*-level unions which would assume responsibility for organizing agricultural and nonagricultural (transport, construction, and handicraft) workers in the villages. The urban-based ACFL, however, was to remain the guiding force for this rural labor movement.

In sum, the party's 1928 urban labor guidelines reflected the severe organizational and political weaknesses, problems, and repressions the CCP faced in this aspect of its work, combined with a strongly expressed determination to proletarianize the already predominantly peasant party membership (then estimated to be seven times greater in number than proletarian members)[38] and transform it into a party again substantially based in the urban industrial proletariat.[39] These policies sought to promote worker struggles along strongly anticapitalist lines; to foster economic strike actions and work to develop them into larger, party-led political struggles; and to work primarily (though often indirectly) through underground red labor unions in opposition to the government-sponsored, legal labor movement. An increasingly worker-based urban Party Center was to maintain and reinforce close leadership links to the (Communist-led) peasant movement, whose class organizational and struggle line would help ensure overall proletarian hegemony in a newly rising urban-rural revolutionary tide. Such were the essential prerequisites for advancing along a noncapitalist path of development to the higher, socialist stage of the revolution.

Alterations in the Class Line and the Shifting Focus to the Soviet Areas, 1929-31

As has been noted, the Sixth Congress's line on rich peasants was not fully consistent with the "class contradiction" concepts of the rural proletarian line. But a Stalin-promoted Comintern directive in June 1929 (which reflected his defeat of and break with the Bukharin rightist forces in the Soviet party and the Comintern) resolved this ideological conflict by outlining an unequivocally anti-rich-peasant policy. The directive criticized the Sixth Congress's "inexact formulations" on this issue and set a harsher line based on the rich peasant's status as semilandlord or rural capitalist.[40] While taking care to note that the landlord-gentry class remained the chief target of the land revolution, it emphasized that the rural proletarian line demanded an unequivocal struggle against the rich peasant as well. "If it pursues the line of alliance with the kulak (rich peasant), or even if it fails to intensify the struggle against the kulak," the directive declared, "the communist party will be unable to take the lead in the class struggle of the village poor, it will dull the edge of their activities to the benefit of the exploiting kulak strata in the Chinese village." Instead, it continued, the party should be moving more than ever "to expand the movement of the rural proletariat, [to] organize the village poor."[41] The impact of this new, virtually liquidationist line on not only the rich peasants, but also the more well-to-do middle peasants (as incipient rich peasants and "exploiters" of hired labor),[42] created difficulties for building the necessary broad peasant base of support in the expanding land revolution. The pressures to develop and enhance a divisive "class consciousness" and struggle in the soviet areas were not easily compatible with the primary, "antifeudal" objectives of the agrarian revolution.[43] But the Comintern and its Chinese Communist spokesmen forcefully emphasized the central importance of organizing hired agricultural labor as a basic test of the party's proletarian character and vanguard role in leading the peasant struggle and criticized the soviet areas' initial failure to move effectively on this score.[44]

The Comintern line in the early soviet years was summed up in the July 1930 ECCI resolution on the Chinese question, dispatched as a letter to the Li Li-san-dominated party leadership in Shanghai at that time.[45] The letter reiterated the above themes in accord with its overall concept of implementing "proletarian hegemony" in the rural revolution. The task of the land revolution in the soviet areas, it stated, "is inseparably linked with that of organizing hired hands' unions and unions of the rural proletariat, as well as with that of organizing poor peasant corps."[46] On labor policy generally, it repeated the need to legislate a basic program of labor benefits and protection for the soviet areas; improvements beyond this to be based on concrete local conditions, would be attained through "class struggle and union work."[47] And again, in pursuit of overall proletarian leadership of a "daily rising" (though not yet "high") revolutionary tide, the ECCI resolution called on the party to develop the strike movement of the (urban) workers, linking economic and political struggles and building toward general political strikes in the major industrial centers.[48]

But it was already apparent (as the fiasco of the Li Li-san urban-oriented revolutionary line in the summer of 1930 underscored) that the center of gravity of the revolution had firmly shifted to the countryside. "The center of the Chinese revolution is the land revolution," with the revolution developing in the form of a proletarian-led peasant war, as the July 1930 ECCI letter had affirmed.[49] These assessments were accompanied by directives during 1930 to unify the central soviet areas under an overall soviet regime and were also reflected in the convening of a preliminary soviet areas' delegates conference in Shanghai at the end of May 1930.[50] Various political and military contingencies and circumstances, however, delayed the holding of the First National Soviet Congress in Juichin, Kiangsi, until November 1931.

With the accession of the youthful "Twenty-eight Bolshevik" group to party leadership in January 1931, the political stage was set for the establishment of the new rural-based soviet republic along the class lines outlined in this chapter. While the CI-CCP leadership continued to set its sights on the mobilization and organization of the urban workers' movement, the latter's primary function was now clearly viewed as one of supporting the rural soviet areas which were then becoming targets of the KMT's extermination campaigns. The new CCP leadership in January 1931 thus put its continued commitment to an urban labor line in this revised context, declaring that

> The workers, under the violent attack of the capitalists, are yearning for the leadership of our party and Red labor unions, whereas the Soviet Areas and the Red Army are yearning for urban support and assistance. Revolutionary responsibility demands the whole party to lead tens of millions of people to resist the all-out offensive now under preparation against the Soviet Areas.[51]

And an August 1931 ECCI resolution on the tasks of the CCP emphasized that a "central Soviet Government must be set up as quickly as possible in the safest area" and stated that the "immediate aim" of the party's work in non-soviet areas was "the organization of a powerful mass movement in defense of the Soviet areas, and to give all help to defeating the KMT's military campaign against the workers' and peasants' Red Army."[52] These 1930-31 measures and formulations, a recent Soviet Russian analysis observes, represented "bold new conclusions" by the Comintern, based on the actual circumstances of the revolutionary struggle at that time; that is, continued urban weakness and growing rural strength.[53] In the context of these new perspectives and circumstances, however, Communist pronouncements underscored the continued importance of promoting a revolutionary urban labor movement.[54] The bleak prospects for and the further failure of such efforts after 1931 are detailed in the next chapter.

The realities of the Chinese revolutionary scene by 1928 or soon thereafter essentially resolved the issue of urban versus rural strategic primacy; and, as recent Western and Soviet Russian scholars have emphasized, the 1928-31 CI-CCP guidelines reflected this fact in their charting of much of the course of the Communist-led rural-peasant revolution.[55] But the party's perception of the meaning and content of its role as proletarian vanguard gave the developing rural-centered struggle in the years after 1928 a class line and an urban focus that strongly influenced and often distorted and impeded the basic land revolution. In pursuing the concept of a proletarian-led peasant war, Communist policy makers overlaid the "antifeudal" peasant struggle for land with class analyses and policies, rural and urban, which greatly accentuated the role of proletarian forces and the importance of the anticapitalist class struggle[56] In the ultimately successful unfolding of the Chinese revolution, neither proletarian nor capitalist class forces (urban and rural) could or did play the major roles assigned to them in the class line strategy described above.

It was the later Maoist strategy (under the opportunities and circumstances of the anti-Japanese war) which unequivocally focused on and successfully harnesssed, in C. Martin Wilbur's words, the "two dynamic forces, rural discontent and Chinese nationalism."[57] Mao was thereby able to avoid the pitfalls and impracticalities of worker-capitalist class contradictions and to move instead to subordinate and incorporate both of these forces under Communist ("proletarian") leadership in a new rural-urban strategic revolutionary design. In promoting the rural agrarian revolution after 1928, the CI-CCP leadership sought, in the orthodox Leninist approach, "to be able to go among the peasantry without becoming lost among them."[58] To this concept Mao later juxtaposed his view of the role of the Communist Party and army as "fish" swimming in the sea of

people's (peasant) war.   These differing standpoints marked the
transition from the urban-related rural line of the post-1928 years to
the indigenous rural strategy of the 1940s, from which developed
what could be called a rural-related urban line as well.

CHAPTER II

The Quest for a Revolutionary Upsurge:
Urban Labor and the CCP, 1928-35

In its efforts to rebuild a party-led urban labor movement during the post-1927 soviet years, the CCP operated on the assumption (particularly in the initial years) that, while in the "uneven development" of the Chinese revolution the peasant movement had for the time outdistanced the workers' movement, a future revolutionary "high tide" called for a coordinated struggle in which the cities and the workers would again play a major part. The continued underground location (probably until late 1932) of the Party Center in Shanghai—China's leading proletarian center—attested at least symbolically to these projections. Under its declared aim of preparing for armed insurrection, the party sought to build a politicized and revolutionary labor movement. And even when the party began to stress a more supportive role for urban labor in helping to defend the rural soviet areas and in the antiimperialist struggle focused on defense of the Soviet Union, political-revolutionary objectives remained uppermost.

This approach was in large degree a grafting on to the Chinese scene of Leninist concepts of the relationship of the trade union movement to the pre-1917 revolutionary socialist goals of the Russian Bolsheviks. Lenin had vigorously attacked the so-called "economist" approach, which placed greater emphasis on economic over political struggle, on the trade unions over the party, and on practical, day-to-day problems rather than ideological issues.[1] According to an analyst of these views, for Lenin "the economic struggle might serve as an important support for the political struggle, but the political fight was the main one." The trade unions' economic struggle should be utilized primarily to advance the revolutionary cause and should come under close party control, thereby avoiding the pitfalls of a nonrevolutionary, "reformist" path.[2]

But the conditions of counterrevolutionary terror in China, as well as the searing memory of 1927, encouraged instead a worker focus on more immediate and less dangerous economic and other issues of daily concern, for which the legal "yellow" unions could to a certain extent become channels.[3] While a segment of the Shanghai-based party leadership did attempt to set the party's sights more directly on the more basic trade union issues and to promote greater contact and cooperation with the legal labor unions, such policies were attacked as examples of "economism" and "right opportunism" which failed to keep uppermost the party's political-revolutionary goals. Urban labor in many ways became a political abstraction—the "proletariat" whose destined "vanguard" revolutionary role remained an orthodox principle for an increasingly harried and isolated urban party underground.

Before turning to specifics of the party's urban labor policies during the rural soviet era, it may be useful to describe briefly the Chinese industrial labor scene in the 1930s prior to the anti-Japanese war. Official estimates for 1933 by the Nanking government Ministry of Industries gave varying figures (from roughly half a million to more than two million) for the number of "factory" workers in China, with all such totals admittedly based on incomplete and often unreliable data and on greatly differing definitions of a factory.[4] There were probably little more than two thousand enterprises that met the government's Factory Act definition of a factory (a plant using mechanical power and employing more than thirty workers), with the majority of these located in the Shanghai-Wuhsi area. Most workers labored in thousands of small workshops and factories employing fewer than thirty workers. Feuerwerker, utilizing the various studies and data available for those years and broadening the definition of a factory to include any manufacturing establishment using mechanical power regardless of size, has derived the following breakdown of China's nonagricultural work force in 1933: 1,130,000 factory workers; 770,000 miners; 40,000 utilities workers; and 12,130,000 employed in handicraft industries.[5] The total output of these four categories accounted for 10.5 percent of China's net domestic product in 1933, with factory industry accounting for only one-fifth of this total.[6] According to official estimates, there were also some 112,000 communications workers manning the state-run railways and postal and telegraph services in KMT China as of 1936.[7]

While the average size of factories was very small, particularly Chinese-owned enterprises, there was a comparatively heavy concentration of workers in some five hundred larger factories. The cotton textile industry, the most important, employed nearly a quarter of a million workers in 143 mills in 1937, while other comparatively large factories engaged in silk reeling, oil pressing, printing, and other light industries. Although 95 of the 143 cotton mills were Chinese-owned, approximately half the looms and spindles and one-third of the workers were employed in foreign mills, mostly Japanese-owned.[8] A similar situation existed in other industries, with British and Japanese capital predominating in the foreign sector. Many of the industrial enterprises, Chinese as well as foreign, were located in the foreign concessions. The marginal, though geographically concentrated character of modern industry in China is evident from the figures given above, indicating that in 1933 such industry accounted for little more than 2 percent of China's net domestic product. The combined total of women and children employed equalled or outnumbered adult male workers.[9] Working hours were long, varying (according to locality, industry, and ownership) from nine to twelve or more hours daily, with perhaps two rest days per month. Chinese textile mills before 1937 generally operated on two twelve-hour shifts, with eleven-hour shifts in the more capital-intensive Japanese-owned mills.[10] Workplaces were mostly substandard and wages, with the exception of certain skilled fields, were generally at or below family subsistence levels.[11] These hardships were further compounded by the evils of the prevailing use of recruiting agents (contractors) in the hiring of labor. Factory workers frequently retained close ties to their agricultural villages, which they had been forced to leave under arrangements made by labor contractors with their families. This constant reservoir of contract labor (generally young women and children) from the depressed countryside helped maintain the status quo of low wages and harsh working conditions and injected an element of instability into the urban labor force.[12]

A year-long study, conducted by the Bureau of Social Affairs of the Shanghai city government, of income and expenditures of over three hundred Shanghai worker families in 1929-30 confirmed the situation described above. The study indicated that average annual income from the earnings of *all* family members was $121.23 below average annual family expenditures of $454.38, with the deficit made up through the help of friends or relatives or by borrowing, peddling, or subletting rooms. The gap between these subsistence-level family outlays and the income of the principal wage-earner in the family was greater still.[13] Writing in 1932, the English social historian R. H. Tawney concluded that, with very few exceptions, "the conditions generally obtaining in factory employment [in China] recall those of the first, and worst, phase of the Industrial Revolution in England."[14] The working conditions of mining labor (over 200,000 of them coal miners) in these years were at least equally deplorable. A 1933 survey called miners' wages "pitiably low," their hours "unusually long," and their work environment "generally unhygienic."[15] The mining industry was also character-ized by insecurity of employment, unfair practices of labor con-tractors, and the predominance of foreign ownership in the modern sector.[16] The Kailan Mining Administration coal complex, located at Tangshan in northern China, was a case in point. Organized as a joint Sino-British enterprise in 1912 (with the British playing the dominant role),[17] it employed over 30,000 miners in the early 1930s and was the largest coal producer in China, excluding Manchuria.[18] The contract labor system prevailed here, and on its account the Kailan mines became an important center of labor organizing activity from the 1920s on.[19] These miners were relatively militant in the early 1930s, with Communist organizers continuing to play a role.[20] Later, after the mines fell under Japanese control, many of the miners took an active part in the anti-Japanese resistance struggle.

In the wake of its ruthless suppression of the left trade union forces in 1927, the new KMT-led Nanking government in 1928 moved to "readjust" and "reorganize" a purged labor movement under its firm political control.[21] The Labor Union Act of October 1929, with later amendments and supplementary regulations and laws up to 1935, provided the legal basis and framework for the KMT-sponsored (yellow) unions during the Nanking decade.[22] Under this legislation, unions could be formed only with government consent: registration and the submission of lists of union officers and members for approval was required. Staff members of government agencies, institutions, and enterprises (civil and military) were not allowed to unionize. All union elections and deliberations came under direct government supervision, and the government had the authority to dissolve unions on a wide range of grounds. Paralleling governmental "supervision," local KMT party bureaus were given "direction" authority over the unions.[23] The right to strike, though still legally sanctioned in private industry, was hedged with so many restrictions and built-in conciliation-arbitration devices that, according to a 1938 account, "the legal exercise of the right has been made almost impossible."[24] The 1929 act also forbade the formation of regional or national labor organizations, restricting unions to their own city or district boundaries and thereby ensuring a lack of coordination, unified action, and national direction in the labor movement.[25] Thus, efforts in the 1928-29 period to reestablish a Shanghai General Labor Union to replace the dissolved CCP-led Shanghai labor federation were disallowed under the Labor Union

Act, despite the fact that the projected organization was sanctioned and directed by the Shanghai KMT organization.[26] A similar situation prevailed in Hankow, China's second major labor center.[27] Interestingly, in terms of the dynamics of even the highly circumscribed KMT labor movement, the government in 1934 and 1935 finally acceded to the open establishment of such federations in both cities, though their legal status apparently continued to be uncertain and subject to arbitrary governmental decree.[28]

The June 1928 Act Governing the Settlement of Labor Disputes (amended in 1930 and 1932) outlined detailed labor-management-government conciliation and arbitration boards and procedures. Government and employer representatives were clearly the dominant forces on the boards; "labor" members were often the nonworker officials of the government-sponsored unions. The government's Bureau of Social Affairs branches in the major cities were subsequently given responsibility for administering these procedures, which often resulted in direct mediation by bureau officials without regard for the formally outlined legal procedures. Actually, labor disputes tended to be settled by a multiplicity of agencies, with little direct reference to the labor disputes act.[29]

The Nanking government in December 1929 promulgated a Factory Act, which was to take effect in 1931. A supplementary Factory Inspection Act was passed in 1931, with additional regulations, administrative measures, and amendments promulgated through 1935.[30] Though these enactments provided for sweeping and ambitious reforms and were designed to protect workers in matters of wages, hours, working conditions, safety and health, rest days and vacation time, women's and children's labor, and education, this body of legislation was essentially just another example of the KMT's propensity for advanced but unenforced (and largely unenforceable) reforms. A 1933 study of labor issues in China noted that "the problems involved in the enforcement of labor laws are much more difficult than the task of drafting them, and unless the National Government of China can tackle these issues satisfactorily its legislative efforts will become entirely meaningless and futile."[31] And Augusta Wagner, in her informative 1938 study of labor legislation in China, concluded, "It is now almost ten years since the [Factory] Act was promulgated. Little has as yet been achieved."[32]

Total membership in the KMT-reorganized labor movement declined considerably in the years following the 1929 Labor Union Act. The Nanking government reported a total of 738 unions with a membership of 1,224,855 in 1929; by 1932 the number of unions had increased to 872, but total membership had declined to 743,764.[33] By 1935 the official total had shrunk even further to 469,240 members in 823 unions, with Shanghai accounting for 65,618 of this number in 119 unions.[34] With only a few exceptions, [35] these unions were "little more than nominal associations of workers" set up in individual plants by government organizers under the close scrutiny and control of KMT party bureaus.[36] In addition, labor bosses (contractors) and gang leaders exercised strong influence on the labor unions. With each of the hundreds of unions having its separate organization, a 1933 study noted, "There is no bond that unites all of them into one single whole and no effective co-ordination in their working programs."[37]

Yet, despite these facts, the KMT after 1927 did retain at least a formal commitment to labor organization and protection, and the still substantial (though greatly reduced) membership in the government-sponsored or approved unions was not without significance. Notwithstanding the regime's intent to curb labor militancy and strikes, large numbers of disputes occurred, many of them leading to strikes. In the five-year period from 1928 to 1932, 1,491 labor disputes and 517 strikes were reported for Shanghai alone, most of them related to wage, employment, and collective contract issues.[38] With labor difficulties in the 1930s accentuated by depressed conditions in many enterprises (though evidence defining the impact of the depression on overall industrial production is conflicting),[39] disputes and strikes were often of a "defensive" nature, seeking to avert wage cuts and layoffs.[40] Over 128,000 workers were involved in 41 of 104 reported strikes in 1932; in 1933, more than 187,000 participated in 168 strikes and lockouts; and smaller but still sizable numbers were recorded in 1934.[41] (There was another strong upsurge of strikes in the 1935-37 period; see Chapter V.) And, as pointed out above, by 1934-35 labor federations were again operating in Shanghai and Hankow, presaging the establishment of a government-sanctioned national labor association by the time of the war of resistance against the Japanese.

Especially in the Shanghai area, with its strong foreign business presence and international political jurisdictions and its remaining core of Communist labor activists, the role of the KMT government and of the yellow unions in labor struggles was complex indeed. Some trends and forces within KMT ranks sought to control and lead the "reorganized" unions as authentic mass organizations, which necessitated some degree of responsiveness to labor grievances and demands. At the same time, Chiang Kai-shek's Nanking government had a strong and growing preoccupation with maintaining "social order," conciliating business interests, and inhibiting mass movements and strikes which could increase leftist influence.[42] These latter considerations naturally promoted a more coercive and repressive government stance toward labor.

The powerful foreign business and political role in Shanghai added other complications. On the one hand, the political and police power of the foreign-ruled International Settlement and French Concession could be useful to the KMT in putting down strikes directed at foreign enterprises; on the other, however, the strong antiimperialist overtones and sentiments involved in such labor struggles made it both necessary and expedient for the KMT to give them some measure of support. But the overriding tendency of the government in major strike situations was to mediate and bring them to an end, usually at the expense of the workers.

Major and prolonged strikes in the early 1930s by the workers and unions of the British-American Tobacco Company (BAT) and the

French Electric Company are key examples of how all of these conflicting forces and interests came together.[43] In detailing the prolonged and complex (and largely unsuccessful) 1933-34 struggles of the BAT workers against work cutbacks and factory closings, Edward Hammond has observed that the BAT yellow union "worked best when there was pressure from below [the workers] and permission from above [the government]."[44] The strikes (of the BAT plants in both the International Settlement and adjacent Chinese-controlled P'utung), reflected the convergence of virtually all the forces involved in the 1930s Shanghai labor scene: rank and file militancy, the initially active role of Communist elements, the increasing involvement of yellow union leaders, the powerful and effective resistance of the British-supported BAT Company, and the generally opportunist stance of the KMT government. The latter, its prestige and nationalist image challenged by the BAT struggles, gave some support to the union while concurrently moving to mediate and end the strikes, with only minimal results for the workers.[45] Yet, even though the BAT union used delaying tactics and had to act cautiously in this complex situation and to operate within the legal constraints set by the government, "within the bounds of legality the union was active, organizing, protesting and petitioning."[46]

The strong Shanghai Postal Union's 1932 struggle against corrupt practices in the government-run postal service and the union's involvement in the growing anti-Japanese resistance movement after 1931 were other signs of yellow union activism in this period.[47] Clearly, the legal unions could and did serve, however inadequately, corruptly, and repressively, as vehicles for labor's economic demands and grievances.[48] This role of the unions was to become an even more important feature of the labor movement in KMT China in the period between 1945 and the Communist victory in 1949.

Begun in 1927, the KMT's anti-Communist "purge" dealt a particularly crippling blow to the CCP's urban labor leadership forces and organizations. The party-led ACFL (more literally, the

National General Staff-Workers' Union) had claimed to represent up to three million organized workers at its peak in the early part of 1927.[49] In this same period, 53.8 percent of the party's reported membership of nearly 58,000 was said to be workers, virtually all of them activists in the urban labor movement.[50] By the end of 1927 (after the defeat of the Canton Commune in December), Liu Shao-ch'i later told Nym Wales, "the power of the [red] workers' unions was completely destroyed. Only the Shanghai workers still had hidden power, so after this Shanghai was the center of the labor movement of China."[51] In an October 1929 report to the ECCI Tenth Plenum, famed CCP labor leader Teng Chung-hsia stated that the red unions (organized under the now illegal ACFL) had "a relative stronghold only in Shanghai and Hong Kong. . . . When we had to go over from legality to illegality, combined with the reign of terror, many of our trade unions collapsed completely." As a result of the party's inability to cope effectively with these new circumstances, Teng added, "the red trade unions have not yet been reconstructed" and, under the continuing terror, "are in a very precarious condition."[52] According to Communist historian Ho Kan-chih, some 80 percent of the workers with "experience in revolutionary struggle" had been murdered or fired; the urban labor movement, he added, had passed "from a high tide to a low ebb, from the offensive to the defensive."[53]

In June 1929 the Shanghai-based Kiangsu Provincial Committee of the party reported 6,800 members, 591 of them industrial workers.[54] Other sources cite lower figures, with a total party membership in all industrial centers in 1929 of less than 4,000, with 1,300 in Shanghai.[55] Chou En-lai disclosed in September 1930 that industrial worker members numbered little more than 2,000 in a party of some 120,000.[56] The vast majority of the party members were, of course, located in the rural soviet areas; by early 1931, there was reportedly a total of some 6,000 party members in nonsoviet (KMT) China, with only 500 in Shanghai.[57] Wang Ming, in his report to the ECCI Thirteenth Plenum in December 1933, claimed that the CCP then had a total of 60,000 members in KMT China (though only half of them were regularly paying dues and doing "steady party work"), with "workers" making up 25 to 30 percent of this number.[58] These figures are clearly overblown, however, and hardly accord with the general picture of continued erosion of the party's urban and labor base after 1931.

The ACFL held its Fifth Congress in November 1929 secretly in Shanghai and at that time claimed to represent 64,381 red union members, 60 percent of them in soviet-area unions.[59] Communist sources report that in late 1930, Shanghai had 2,100 red unionists, Hong Kong 900, Wuhan (Hankow) 200, Tientsin 500, and the north China mining center of Tangshan 840.[60] Given the imminent dangers facing the underground Communist urban organizations and the party's increasing focus on the soviet areas, the ACFL virtually ceased its activities in the KMT-ruled cities (chiefly Shanghai) after 1931, and its Central Bureau moved to the Kiangsi soviet area.[61] Liu Shao-ch'i left the "white" areas for the Kiangsi soviet republic in the fall of 1932, where he became chairman of the ACFL.[62] However, an underground Shanghai ACFL headquarters was probably maintained until the anti-Japanese war in 1937.[63] The Party Center itself found it necessary to relocate gradually to the central soviet area in Kiangsi over the period from late 1931 to early 1933.[64] Though the party leadership continued to overstate the range of its labor activities, influence, and strength in the urban areas after 1931,[65] it was evident that the red labor organizations in the KMT areas had all but collapsed.[66]

A CCP summary report on the red labor movement for 1931 acknowledged that only some 3,000 workers then had links to Communist labor organizations, with little more than one-third of them actual members of red unions and 666 of these in Shanghai.[67] While it claimed leadership in five strikes, it conceded that all but one (of Shanghai cold-storage workers) had failed. The report observed that efforts to establish red union organizations in such major labor centers as Tientsin, Peking, and Hankow had been unsuccessful. It duly noted the dearth of effective cadres in industry and the party's inability to establish factory committees or mass union organizations. The party's scanty publications had few readers and little influence. The red unions (in nonsoviet areas), the report concluded, lagged behind the masses and had been unable to lead the latter's struggles.[68]

The CCP, in summing up party history in 1945, noted that after 1931 the party's work in the cities had "shrunk even further."[69] A recent Soviet source describes the situation rather more forcefully, stating "anything resembling real [party] organization in the cities had been crushed."[70] The CCP, under Mao, however, viewed these developments as confirmation of the errors and fallacies of the post-1930 "third left line" in the party, which then still dreamed of imminent urban rising tides and the seizure of key cities. The Soviet analysts, on the other hand, conclude that the destruction of the party's base in the major proletarian centers "was a real tragedy for the CCP."[71] In these contrasting retrospective assessments, one clearly sees the divergent Chinese and Soviet views on the necessary role of labor in the revolution.

The party's determination to build its own "revolutionary unions" and to concentrate on a highly politicized class-struggle strategy was unsuited to the realities of the urban political and labor scene outlined above. The party's stance led also to an impatience with "reformist" trade union work and an underestimation of the growing role of the legal unions, which further weakened the party's already tenuous links with urban labor. Even though "trade unionist" leaders did emerge in the red labor movement, their role was undermined first by the urban revolutionary adventurism of the Li Li-san line in 1930 and subsequently by attacks from the youthful new Twenty-eight Bolshevik leadership, which saw in the Communist labor movement continuing "right opportunist" and "economist" trends that undercut the political-revolutionary goals of the party's urban labor line.

In the 1930 Shanghai strike against the French Electric Company, for example, the yellow union forces were effectively led by a covert Communist labor leader Hsü A-mei, who was later jailed. But while all Shanghai labor was rallying to the union cause and the antiimperialist connotations of the strike, the Li Li-san party leadership was denouncing the union as "nothing but a tool of the Kuomintang for deceiving the working masses" and labeled Hsu himself a "rightist."[72] Such attacks on Hsu and the union proved highly counterproductive and merely led to further defections from the Communist Party's dwindling ranks in Shanghai.[73] The ambiguous and often contradictory nature of CI-CCP labor policy guidelines, coupled with a tendency to make inflated claims of influence, further compounded these problems. The necessarily conspiratorial, ingrown, and dangerous circumstances under which the underground party apparatus operated in the cities added significantly to these internal tensions and conflicts.[74]

In his 1929 report to the ECCI Tenth Plenum, CCP labor leader Teng Chung-hsia had strongly attacked the idea of a reformist path for the Chinese labor movement.[75] In his view, the social and economic basis which had been present in Europe for such a movement did not exist in China. But even though the yellow unions could not be expected to take on a credible reformist role, Teng acknowledged that anti-Communist terror, combined with "some concessions" to workers' demands by the KMT, had placed the red unions in "a very precarious condition."[76] He warned of an actively developing "right opportunist" tendency in the party, which favored working within the yellow unions at the expense of forming separate red unions. In outlining Communist tactics for countering the influence of the legal unions, he called for the formation of factory and strike committees under Communist leadership and the creation of clandestine red union nuclei within the yellow unions as a "revolutionary opposition." While endorsing efforts to win over the rank and file of these unions, he thoroughly rejected any notion of cooperating with their leaders. Any Communist activity within the yellow unions, he reiterated, should not be pursued "unconditionally," i.e., at the expense of developing, particularly among industrial workers, an independent red labor leadership. Finally, he stressed the importance of taking immediate steps to organize the rural proletariat as a "strong ally" of the urban industrial workers.[77]

A resolution on CCP trade union work adopted by the ECCI Tenth Plenum brought the policy ambivalences evident in Teng's report even more sharply into focus.[78] Though it stressed the need to put "life" into the red unions and condemned any "liquidationist" attitude toward them, it also called for the dissolution of such unions in places where they could maintain only a shadow existence and competed directly with mass legal unions. It attacked "the remnants of sectarianism" in the party and acknowledged that Communist work within the yellow unions had been made imperative by the very existence of such mass unions, on the one hand, and by "the extremely weak Red trade union organizations" on the other.[79] However, it added, Communists and revolutionary workers should join yellow unions only where the latter had already taken on a "mass" character. And wherever conditions were "objectively favourable," red unions ("the basis of the revolutionary labour movement") should be organized to parallel the mass yellow unions; these would work covertly within the legal unions "with the object of capturing the masses on the basis of revolutionary policy, with a view to the ultimate liquidation of these organizations."[80] The resolution reemphasized the role of Communist-organized factory committees as vehicles for party leadership of the workers' economic and political struggles, with these committees serving both as conduits for channeling workers into the red labor movement and as nuclei for future mass red unions to be set up "when the labor movement revives."[81]

A Communist report on the results of the Fifth Congress of the ACFL was also indicative of the difficulties of fashioning clear-cut tactics toward the KMT-sanctioned labor movement and of coordinating legal and illegal activities. The congress, which convened secretly in Shanghai on 7 November 1929, apparently leaned more in the direction of combatting the yellow unions.[82] The yellow unions "must be fought both from within and without and supplanted by militant [red] unions." The report acknowledged, however, that "under the Kuomintang dictatorship no one had any illusion about the legality of class [red] unions"; the consensus was that "legal and semi-legal work must be maintained" if the party were to develop mass influence.[83]

The tactical lines reviewed above obviously constituted a serious dilemma for the urban party. How was a policy to carry on work within the yellow unions and simultaneously seek to rebuild a separate revolutionary labor movement to be implemented? How were red elements supposed to foster and lead "legal" worker economic struggles and win over the yellow union masses without thereby enhancing the influence and credibility of the "reformist" union movement and subordinating the party's larger revolutionary political objectives? These and related questions understandably exacerbated the divisions and dissensions in the underground urban party of the early 1930s.

In summing up the shortcomings in the party's urban labor work and influence, a December 1929 ECCI letter to the CCP Central Committee touched on problems that prevailed in the cities until the close of the soviet era in 1935.

> Few of the red trade unions are mass organizations, while the influence of the yellow KMT unions is still great. . . . The Communist party is far from having rallied to its side the revolutionary cadres of the industrial workers; still less has it accomplished the task of winning the majority of the working class, or, what is of cardinal importance at the present moment, winning the leadership of the spontaneous economic and political struggles of the proletariat. The party has not yet become the pioneer, organizer, and leader of the direct revolutionary struggle of the broad masses.[84]

Deposed party leader Ch'en Tu-hsiu, in a 1929 valedictory critique of party policy ("A Letter to All Party Comrades"), pointed to the superrevolutionary stance and authoritarian tactics of the party in ordering strikes as key reasons for the distance between the party and the workers. "Every small daily struggle," he wrote, "is forcibly expanded into a big political struggle, causing the worker masses and worker comrades to further separate themselves from the Party."[85]

Intense factional struggles in the Shanghai-based Party Center during 1930-31 further weakened the party's influence in the labor movement. Ho Meng-hsiung, a young Communist labor organizer in Shanghai and a leading figure in the key Kiangsu Provincial Committee of the party, clashed with the Li Li-san leadership over the latter's 1930 urban revolutionary line. Ho Meng-hsiung, along with Lo Chang-lung, Wang K'e-ch'üan, and other dominant figures in the Shanghai-based Kiangsu party apparatus and the ACFL in 1930, opposed not only Li Li-san but also the subsequent takeover of the Party Center by the returned-student group under their Russian mentor, Pavel Mif, at the party's Fourth Plenum in January 1931.[86]

The Li Li-san line of 1930 had carried to its extreme the view of the party's urban labor policy as designed primarily to spark the expected revolutionary upsurge. The Li Li-san line reflected also the impatience of some Party planners with the painfully slow and very limited progress of the red labor movement and with the more mundane trade unionist emphasis on labor's day-to-day economic interests and struggles. This outlook was evidenced in Li's ambitious plans for escalated political strikes and worker-based armed insurrections in the major cities of China, which were to be coordinated with Red Army assaults on the key interior cities of Changsha and Wuhan. Li's summary approach was also demonstrated in his moves to replace urban party and red union organizations with newly formed "action committees" to spearhead his insurrectionary plans.[87]

In venting their opposition to the Li Li-san line, the trade union party faction led by Ho Meng-hsiung sharply refuted Li's overblown assessment of red labor strength and attacked his ultra-revolutionary approach to the labor movement. In a September 1930 letter to the Party Center,[88] Ho stressed the still weak links between the party and the labor movement, and he disputed the leadership's claim that the party had already "politically" won over the majority of the workers despite the lack of a numerical majority organized in the red unions. Such reasoning, Ho argued, belied the importance of the CCP's organizational work. To rely chiefly on revolutionary slogans to mobilize the workers undermined the significance of economic issues and their pivotal role in building an effectively politicized strike movement.[89]

Ho Meng-hsiung further complained that Li's action committees exemplified an exclusively political approach to the labor movement and an authoritarian style of work which further separated the party from the workers. He challenged the Party Center's contention that the yellow unions' influence among the workers had already become "bankrupt" and called for intensified work among the labor masses, with joint strike tactics and Communist participation in all unions of a mass character. Only by identifying with and resolutely struggling for worker interests, Ho asserted, could the party isolate and expose the yellow union leadership.[90]

The ECCI, in a November 1930 letter to the CCP Central Committee, sent after the collapse of Li's line, also criticized Li's exaggerated assessment of the urban labor movement and acknowledged that the party still "had been unable to become the organizer and director of large-scale economic and political strikes."[91] In stating that the peasant movement had "considerably outstripped in tempo and volume the workers' movement," the ECCI indicated its approval of the new line, which called for concentrating party resources on the consolidation and expansion of the rural soviet areas and the Red Army. However, though backing away from the notion of imminent urban insurrection, the post-1930 CI-CCP stance nonetheless continued to link a firm proletarian class line in the soviet areas with a similarly firm urban class-struggle policy.

Moreover, party leaders still talked in terms of imminent revolutionary upsurges and emphasized the key importance of taking industrial centers, but these events were now predicated on the political and military consolidation and fortification of the soviet districts.[92]

Thus, the trade union faction found itself involved in what turned out to be another losing leadership and policy struggle, this time, as noted above, with the Twenty-eight Bolshevik group at the January 1931 Fourth Plenum. Despite the shared anti-Li Li-san outlook of the two sides, the faction led by Ho Meng-hsiung and Lo Chang-lung inevitably clashed with the highly politicized leftist line of the Russian-returned students.[93] In the wake of the January plenum, Ho Meng-hsiung and his supporters moved to organize a rival Kiangsu Provincial Committee of the party.[94] But their arrest while meeting secretly in a Shanghai hotel, and the subsequent execution of Ho and over twenty others by the KMT at the notorious Lunghua execution grounds outside Shanghai, dealt a mortal blow to the opposition forces.[95] The new "Bolshevik" Party Center then launched a final struggle against the still active Lo Chang-lung forces in both the ACFL and the party. By the end of January they had unseated Lo's "rightist" leadership faction in the ACFL, and Lo himself was expelled from the party.[96] Lo continued his oppositionist activities until his arrest by the KMT in 1933.[97] The Party Center's intensive campaign against rightist forces in urban party and labor organizations in east and north China further eroded the extremely tenuous CCP links to the urban labor movement.[98]

Meanwhile in these years, other key leaders in the Shanghai red labor movement were relocating to the central soviet area in Kiangsi, another indication of the decline in the party's urban labor organizations and activities. Hsiang Ying, a major party figure and labor leader of proletarian background who had been elected chairman of the ACFL at its 1929 congress, relinquished that post in 1930 and went to Kiangsi.[99] There he played a key role in the party's Central Bureau of the Soviet Areas (CBSA), set up in January 1931 by the newly installed, returned–student party leadership. Hsiang, then also active on the Revolutionary Military Council which supervised the Red Army, was subsequently appointed Minister of Labor and one of the two vice–chairmen under Mao of the Chinese Soviet Republic in November 1931.[100] Liu Shao–ch'i, another major figure in the party's urban underground who was active in Shanghai party work in 1930-31, went to Juichin, the soviet-area capital, in 1932. There he served as chairman of the ACFL, whose headquarters and activities were by that time concentrated in that soviet area.[101] As party and labor headquarters gradually shifted to Juichin during 1932 and early 1933, a caretaker Bureau of the Central Committee was set up in Shanghai in 1933.[102]

The ongoing castigation of "right opportunism" in the urban red labor movement, manifested in charges of revolutionary pessimism and liquidationism and of replacing political with economic struggle,[103] did nothing to bolster the parlous state of that movement in the post-Fourth Plenum period. The April 1931 arrest of Ku Shun-chang, head of the CCP's Special Service Department, and his defection and disclosures to the KMT accentuated the dangers to and pressures on the underground party apparatus.[104] The Shanghai arrest and execution in June 1931 of party secretary–general Hsiang Chung-fa, a labor organizer of worker background,[105] was a graphic example of the escalating risks party organs in the cities faced. The arrest, also in June 1931, of the Noulens couple, who reportedly ran the Comintern's Pan–Pacific Trade Union office in Shanghai, further impaired Communist labor operations (and financing) in Shanghai.[106] In the early months of 1933, the arrests of a number of underground leaders of the Shanghai ACFL delivered another blow to the remaining red union apparatus in the cities, and a KMT raid on the Central Committee's Shanghai bureau in June 1934 further reduced the party's Shanghai organization.[107] The dispirited state of the remaining urban party ranks at that time was later described to Nym Wales in Yenan by a Korean Communist who had been active in the Chinese urban party underground until 1935. It was a time, he told her, when party members "were unscrupulously fighting for supremacy, both on the basis of personal rivalry and political problems." He described the period as one of "general demoralization," in which "Party work became weaker and weaker on the outside, and morale within broke down."[108]

Wales's informant described the increasing isolation of the white (urban) areas from 1931 on: "One by one most of the good Marxist leaders went [to the soviet areas], while those left behind were imprisoned or killed." The soviet-area party's "information about us in the White areas was very limited, and ours was the same about them."[109] It is evident from party documents and statements on the labor movement that an "opportunistic" (i.e., realistic) pessimism toward and criticism of the party's urban labor prospects and policies continued to permeate the Communist labor apparatus despite the Party Center's 1931 moves against rightist opposition elements. A report on the 1931 red labor movement by the party labor department, for example, clearly reflected such attitudes and was subsequently attacked for its "opportunist" stance.[110]

The same report also focused on policy deficiencies and orientations which, in effect, called into question the revolutionary assertions and assumptions of the Bolshevik party leadership. It noted that the majority of newly established factory party branches (to replace those which had collapsed during the Li Li-san period) had failed to aid or lead worker economic struggles. The training of industrial cadres by the party and union had been neglected, which placed severe limitations on the party's efficacy in production enterprises. Basic union organizational work was inadequate: little that had been achieved in building organizations was geared to the needs and demands of the masses. In belittling the influence of party publications among the workers, the report impugned the relevance and effectiveness of the party's heavily politicized printed material. The party had failed to reach the worker masses with its program; its sweeping slogans on eliminating KMT influence in the labor movement remained empty talk even among the cadres themselves. The party strategy for infiltrating the yellow unions while concurrently building independent red unions had been poorly understood and applied by the cadres, with the result that the party had still not been able to develop effective revolutionary opposition organizations within the major yellow unions.[111] A June 1932 party document, published by the CCP's Central Bureau for the Soviet Areas (CBSA), attacked both the 1931 report and an apparently inadequate criticism of it that had appeared in the party's Shanghai journal *Red Flag*.[112] The June statement assailed the "opportunist" red labor movement for its miscalculations, pessimism, rightist tendencies, negativism, and capitulationism in forsaking the red unions and "surrendering" to the yellow unions.[113]

A March 1932 "Letter to Labor Union Comrades" from the Party Center had also focused on right opportunism in the urban red labor movement with much the same catalogue of complaints.[114] It attacked sharply what it termed "pure syndicalism" (trade unionism) and "pure economism," i.e., attempts to separate economics from politics and to avoid involvement in political struggle.[115] But such attacks served only to call attention to the abstract nature of the party's urban line and also highlighted a reality which no amount of revolutionary rhetoric and polemic could obscure—that of small and isolated red forces seeking ways to reach the workers and compete with the legally sanctioned unions under the harsh conditions of anti-Communist repression.

In the wake of the Japanese invasion of Manchuria in September 1931 and the attack on Shanghai in January 1932, Communist urban policy focused increasingly on promoting the anti-imperialist movement.[116] The ongoing attempts to transform the red unions into mass organizations and to strengthen the Communist role in the growing, "spontaneous" strike actions were now linked to the political mobilization of labor behind the antiimperialist issue. This, in turn, was coupled with slogans for the defense of the USSR against the growing Japanese threat and with support of the rural soviet areas' struggle against the KMT extermination campaigns.[117] The major Shanghai strike against Japanese-owned cotton mills in early 1932, the Kailan miners' strikes in north China, and other key labor struggles of that year were welcomed as significant signs of a growing labor militancy and heightened political consciousness. [118] Pavel Mif, the Comintern's China specialist, hailed the rising strike tide of 1932 as a "struggle which impels the Chinese working class forward to its position at the head of the anti-imperialist movement." He pointed to "the considerable number of strikes . . . of a clearly political and anti-imperialist character," and, while acknowledging that "economic motives continued to remain the basis of the strike struggle," he emphasized that "nevertheless the struggle was becoming more political."[119] Under a "united-front-from-below" strategy, the CCP sought to take leadership of this strike movement and direct it against the imperialist powers (chief among them Japan), the KMT regime, the foreign and domestic (national) bourgeoisie, and the yellow union organizations. "Unless the present-day anti-imperialist movement is provided with a proletarian background," the party journal *Struggle* [*Tou-cheng*] wrote in mid-1933, "unless we have revolutionary organizations of the broad proletarian masses (mass Red trade unions, strike committees, anti-imperialist leagues, workers' pickets, workers' volunteer detachments, etc.) it is impossible to bring about a really revolutionary united front, and impossible to bring about the hegemony of the proletariat in the national revolutionary struggle."[120]

This comprehensive China labor policy line was outlined in some detail by the Comintern's red labor international (Profintern) in a late 1931 resolution of its Central Council.[121] It too hailed the rising and "for the most part spontaneous" strike struggle as a "fresh upsurge" in the Chinese labor movement. It acknowledged the increased strength and influence of the yellow unions, adding that to "a certain extent" the more active role of these unions reflected "the desires of the working class to improve its material and legal standards, to organize and unite." But this made it all the more imperative to mount red opposition activities within these unions.

As for the red unions, the Profintern added, they had failed as yet to become mass organizations and consisted in most areas of an "apparatus" and small groups (with extremely "fluid" memberships) or else of quasi-legal auxiliary organizations.[122]

The labor international's resolution exhorted the red unions to mobilize labor through graduated escalation of economic, political, and ultimately revolutionary struggles. At the same time, the Communists should work more effectively within the yellow unions to achieve the latter's disintegration and to win over their members. Favorable conditions existed for this effort, the resolution contended, and the red unions "must realize once and for all that the breach between the masses and the leadership of the yellow unions will be deepened and widened the more speedily, the better the Red Unions carry on their work among the working masses." The united-front-from-below tactic was seen as a particularly effective strategy against the yellow union bureaucrats and the KMT.[123] The resolution admitted, however, that the current status of the red unions "does not at all ensure the required leadership for the growing working-class struggle in China."[124]

The Profintern resolution's lengthy final section, which dealt with the soviet areas' labor movement, attested to the shift in the revolutionary center of gravity to those areas. Labor in relation to the soviet movement was now seen as assuming a dual role: as the proclaimed "pillar" of the newly established soviet republic in Kiangsi on the one hand, and as the vanguard support of that movement in the "white" urban centers on the other. The "revolutionary T[rade] U[nion] movement of China," the resolution thus concluded, "must subordinate its work to the task of actively assisting the soviet movement," winning over and organizing the proletarian and semiproletarian masses in the struggle for the triumph of that movement throughout China.[125]

At the same time, the increasing number of strikes after 1931 was cited by Communist spokesmen as evidence of growing labor militancy and red influence. K'ang Sheng, who had been sent to

Moscow from the Shanghai party underground in 1933 as a CCP representative to the Comintern, thus detailed some achievements in red leadership of strikes in a December 1933 report to the ECCI Thirteenth Plenum. He asserted that the "revolutionary opposition" within the yellow unions had "grown tremendously" and that red union membership had "lately more than doubled."[126] K'ang also stressed the growing militancy of labor struggles (worker sit-ins, seizure of plant managers and directors, and worker resistance to troops, police, and yellow union bureaucrats) as a sign of "a higher, more determined" form of struggle in response to KMT terror and "the offensive of capital." *"Economic strikes,"* he declared, *"frequently pass into political strikes."* [127]

However, though strike actions were taking on a more combative character, they continued to be overwhelmingly concerned with such basics as wage, employment, and dismissal issues. In making this point in an examination of labor disputes in China in 1933, Lowe Chuan-hua, who was active in Chinese labor affairs as the YMCA's industrial secretary, observed that "disputes caused by political factors have been of almost negligible importance."[128] The growing hardships facing Chinese labor in these years as a result of rising unemployment and wage cuts were reflected in both the specific strike issues and the increasing militancy of labor conflicts; the politicization of the strike movement along the lines so strongly pressed by the Communists was far less manifest.[129] Indeed, as Wang Ming conceded to the Seventh Comintern Congress in 1935, the rigidly anticapitalist and antireformist proletarian line of the CCP itself conflicted with the more broadly based needs of an antiimperialist national front.[130]

Thus, despite the comparatively optimistic picture he painted to the ECCI Plenum, K'ang Sheng was nonetheless compelled by reality to recite the usual litany of Communist organizational and leadership weaknesses in the overall strike movement, in linking labor struggles with the antiimperialist movement, and in countering the influence of the yellow unions.[131] Wang Ming's acknowledgment to this same plenum that the party in the KMT areas had thus far failed "to create an organized proletarian framework in the widely developing anti-imperialist movement" was further confirmation of both the importance assigned to and the continuing frustrations of the CCP's work in the urban labor movement.[132]

The importance of mobilizing urban labor was again emphasized at the Central Committee's Fifth Plenum, which met in Juichin, the soviet-area capital, in January 1934 under the aegis of the Bolshevik group. In a major resolution on union work in the KMT areas, the plenum declared that worker struggles had reached a previously unsurpassed level and had become a key factor in advancing the Chinese revolution.[133] This statement was offered as proof of the vanguard role of the working class in the antiimperialist struggle and its attainment of leadership in the battle for China's independence and unity—a rhetorical stance hardly in keeping with Wang Ming's ECCI statement quoted above.

The resolution described current strikes in the Tangshan and Fushun (Manchuria) coal mines and along north China railways and in seaports and credited the workers in the major industrial centers of Shanghai, Tientsin, and Wuhan with leading the developing national strike movement. It stressed the role of labor in the struggle to defend the soviet areas and affirmed the party's determination, despite all obstacles, to lead the workers' daily struggles and to organize and participate in strikes and in antiimperialist and anti-encirclement (of the soviet areas) mass movements. The party, it claimed, had established many factory bases in Shanghai and in north China, built some mass unions in textile and tobacco enterprises, and "overthrown" several yellow unions.[134] It attributed these achievements to post-Fourth Plenum policies; that is, to the period of Bolshevik leadership since 1931.

Yet the plenum resolution recognized that there remained a great gap between the degree of leadership the party had been able to assume and the speed and scope of the developing proletarian struggle. This leadership lag was most evident in such major industrial centers as Shanghai and Tientsin, where labor conflicts lacked an adequate degree of political consciousness and coordination with the soviet movement. In other major cities—Wuhan, Changsha, Nanchang, and others—the red labor movement was not only "extremely weak" but had been unable even to regain previously held positions (an apparent reference to the consequences of the Li Li-san line). The plenum was thus forced to conclude that white-area union work was "the weakest sector of the party's overall work."[135] The call went out once more to muster all available resources in promoting the red labor movement through firm identification with labor interests and struggles, particularly in railway, mining, maritime, and textile enterprises. Renewed efforts to strengthen the movement were seen as a key component in the battle against the KMT's fifth soviet encirclement campaign, then underway.

Ch'en Yün, who had long been involved in Communist labor work in Shanghai before going to the central soviet area to head the labor federation there, authored the report on which the resolution of the Fifth Plenum was based.[136] He apparently continued to maintain contact with and "responsibility" for KMT-area labor work at that time,[137] a symbol of the party's continued interest in linking the two arenas through the labor movement. In a follow-up May Day article published in 1934 in the party journal in Kiangsi, Ch'en sought yet again to foster the image of a resurgent white-area revolutionary labor movement acting in coordination with the central soviet forces in their now desperate battle against the KMT. Increased aid to and support for the workers' struggle in the white areas, he declared, was crucial to the soviet republic's battle for survival.[138]

Reality notwithstanding, assertions of the revolutionary significance of urban labor's growing militancy continued to be proclaimed. A July 1934 Comintern article acclaimed the rising strike tide in China as more solid evidence of Chinese labor's revolutionary and vanguard character.[139] Again, the emphasis was on the increasingly militant and revolutionary nature of strike actions, the growing influence of the red unions, and the intensified "disintegration" of the yellow unions. The strikes were declared to be "an indestructible revolutionary link in the development of the Chinese Soviet revolution;" they were "vanguard fights which are preparing a broad field for the great political clashes of the near future." The article went on to affirm that the "Chinese proletariat has proved to the world proletariat by its heroic struggles and by the successes which it has achieved that it is one of the powerful vanguard detachments of the world revolution."[140]

Despite the courageous and occasionally effective role of Communist activists in the upsurge of labor strikes in the early 1930s and the theoretical exhortations of the CCP's labor pronouncements, the party's efforts to rebuild a solid urban labor base were clearly unsuccessful. The attempt to mobilize and lead a militantly anticapitalist, anti-KMT labor movement as the vehicle for a new urban revolutionary upsurge which could ultimately lead the rural soviet movement had foundered under insurmountable obstacles: the complex, demoralizing, and destructive impact of the white terror; the political circumspection of labor and its focus on issues of economic immediacy; the organizational weaknesses and factional infighting of the urban CCP; and the party's sectarian tactics and overly abstract political approach to labor problems and interests. China's workers and the organized labor movement, particularly in Shanghai, had by no means been quiescent in attempting to defend labor interests. And since many strikes represented challenges to the KMT authorities and were also often directed against foreign enterprises, they inevitably took on some limited political and antiimperialist colorations.[141] Though there was often Communist input in such struggles, the CCP's projected role for urban labor in the post-1927 "peasant war led by the proletariat" had remained essentially unrealized. Instead, the implementation of this strategic formula rested increasingly on efforts to enforce the "class line" in the rural soviet areas, a task the CCP's Bolshevik leadership turned to vigorously after taking power at the Fourth Plenum. However, in turning to the central soviet area in Kiangsi as prime territory for advancing a proletarian line, the Party Center came up against different, but no less compelling, realities and difficulties, which we will consider in the next chapters.

A new opportunity to resolve the contradictions of a rural-based proletarian line and for a Communist return to the cities would present itself later, in the volatile post-1935 political climate of an emerging anti-Japanese national front. Wang Ming, rallying behind the Comintern's new united-front line at its Seventh Congress in 1935, presaged the beginnings of a class collaboration policy in his call to "the entire Chinese people, to all parties, groups, troops, mass organizations, and all prominent political and social leaders" to join with the CCP "in organizing an All-Chinese united people's government of national defense."[142]   Under the conditions of the gradually unfolding KMT-CCP united front after 1935, the proletarian-oriented Internationalist (Bolshevik) wing of the party, led by Wang Ming, sought once more to build an urban labor political base under the more opportune circumstances of Communist legality and CCP support of the KMT-led resistance war against Japan. But the contradictions and weaknesses inherent in an appeal to labor based on a collaborative, united-front strategy, as well as the conse-quences of the loss of the major cities to Japan in the early wartime period, spelled doom for this new urban proletarian line and helped lead to the final defeat of its Internationalist protagonists in the party leadership.

CHAPTER III

Labor and the Kiangsi Soviet: Problems of the
Proletarian Line, 1931-32

As has been noted in Chapter I, from 1930 on the Comintern
had been calling for the organization of a central soviet government
as a top priority task for the Chinese Communists.[1] Though a
preparatory conference of delegates from the soviet areas to promote this step had been convened in Shanghai on 31 May 1930 under
Li Li-san's somewhat reluctant direction, the activation of the
latter's urban-oriented line immediately thereafter and its attendant
complications delayed further progress on the matter until after the
Russian-returned student takeover of the Party Center at the
January 1931 Fourth Plenum. Thus, reviewing Li Li-san's errors, the
plenum resolution stated that Li had "completely neglected the
establishment of a strong Soviet political regime."[2] A March 1931
Comintern article in support of the new "Bolshevik" course of the
CCP listed as the first two of the party's three fundamental tasks
the formation of an "authoritative Soviet Government" and of a
"regular disciplined Red Army" firmly based in soviet territory.[3]

The class policies for the soviet areas outlined in CI and CCP
pronouncements and directives of the 1929-31 period strongly
emphasized the organization and mobilization of the rural proletariat and the escalation of the struggle against rich peasants, in
which hired agricultural labor and the poorer peasantry would be the
vanguard forces. Wang Ming, writing in the party's Shanghai paper
in March 1930, inveighed against the continuing influence of rich
peasant elements and a "rich peasant mentality" in the soviet districts; he called for reliance on hired labor and the poor peasantry,

51

which he viewed as the "pillar" in the battle against the rich peasants and as the core of soviet party and mass organizations.[4] In an article published later that year, Wang criticized comrades in the soviet areas who blamed peasant opposition for their own failure to organize agricultural labor. "Shall we fail to organize the agricultural laborers for fear of the rich peasants?" he queried. "Then we are absolutely not the party of the proletariat."[5] Wang also decried the slow progress in organizing soviet-area shop employees and handicraft and small enterprise workers, noting that these efforts suffered unduly from a fear of undercutting the economic interests of middle and small merchants.[6]

The ECCI, in its July 1930 resolution on China, had emphatically stated: "The task of the land revolution in the Soviet Areas is inseparably linked with that of organizing hired hands unions and unions of the rural proletariat, as well as with that of organizing poor peasant corps."[7] And in late November of the same year, a CI directive to the CCP on land and peasant problems again listed the organizing of the farmhands and coolies and the poor peasants as a high priority task of the party in the soviet area.[8] Yet despite these repeated exhortations, it was only after the takeover of the party by the Bolshevik group in early 1931 that such organizational steps were more vigorously promoted.

To establish their political dominance in the soviet areas and to implement the class line there more effectively, the new Party Center in Shanghai moved quickly in January 1931 to set up the Central Bureau for the Soviet Areas (CBSA), a body which had apparently been authorized by the September 1930 Third Plenum.[9] Hsiang Ying, the former head of the ACFL in Shanghai, was named secretary, and soviet-area leaders Mao Tse-tung and Chu Te were included in its nine-member standing committee. The dynamics of power and leadership in the CBSA remain somewhat obscure, though it does appear likely that Chou En-lai (another member, who arrived from Shanghai during 1931) assumed a major and characteristically mediating and balancing role. There is little doubt, however, that the bureau's purpose was to project the authority and line of the Party Center in the soviet districts, a key preliminary step in establishing a unified soviet regime based on the Kiangsi-Fukien central soviet area.[10]

The Rural Class Scene in the 1930s

The official statement of the soviet government in Kiangsi on rural class categories, adopted in October 1933, asserted that the main form of exploitation practiced by rich peasants was their hiring of long-term (regular) labor to help farm their land (though they might also be renting out part of their land and engaging in money-lending and commercial activities).[11] For landlords, who generally did not engage in productive labor, the main form of exploitation was the collection of land rents. Middle peasants were those who either entirely or mainly derived their income from their own labor on their own land, though in some cases they might be renting all or part of the land they tilled. The wealthier middle peasants, however, hired some labor (and thus practiced exploitation), though farming was their regular or principal source of income. In subsequent elaborations on these class definitions, it was stipulated that a peasant could remain in this upper middle peasant category if the proportion of income derived from exploitation did not exceed 15 percent of total family income. Under certain circumstances, the proportion could even rise to 30 percent without the peasant falling into the rich peasant category, "if the masses have no objection."[12]

These class analyses and decisions evolved over the course of the first phase of the Land Investigation Movement (1933), and Mao, in his capacity as chairman of the soviet government, clearly had a strong hand in their formulation. The definitions reflect some of the issues which were debated by Mao and the class line party leaders during 1933 and 1934. There was obviously a fine line between "rich" and "middle" peasants (and an even finer one between "new-rich" and "old-rich" peasants), and the difficulties of interpretation grew as the campaign against rich peasants mounted in intensity.

The strong promotion of hired labor interests inevitably undercut to some degree the interests of many middle peasants as employers—a particularly significant issue under post-land-reform conditions in the soviet areas, when considerably more peasants achieved middle peasant status or emerged in some cases as "new-rich" peasants.[13]

The same set of analyses defined poor peasants as those who rented all or part of the land they cultivated and who were thereby exploited by the landlords or rich peasants to whom they paid rent and interest. Their role as temporary or seasonal hired labor was another aspect of their exploitation by their wealthier neighbors. As for farm laborers, they owned neither land nor farm implements as a rule, and their livelihood derived primarily from the sale of their labor.[14] This definition was applicable also to nonagricultural workers in the rural soviet districts.

Mao's October 1930 investigation of a district of Hsingkuo County, in the south of the Kiangsi soviet area, analyzed the pre-land-reform character of the population and landholding patterns in terms of class. The population broke down as follows: landlords (excluding absentee landlords), 1 percent; rich peasants, 5 percent; middle peasants, 20 percent; and poor peasants, 60 percent. The remaining 14 percent was comprised of handicraft workers (7 percent), small businessmen-merchants (3 percent), farm laborers (1 percent), and various "declassed" elements (yu-min) (2 percent). Land ownership, not surprisingly, broke down much differently: landlords, 40 percent; rich peasants, 30 percent; middle peasants, 15 percent; and poor peasants, 5 percent. Land managed by public welfare organizations (usually dominated by landlords and rich peasants) accounted for the remaining 10 percent.[15]

Though Mao's rural survey was based on limited sources from a single area (eight Red Army informants from the Yungfeng district of Hsingkuo County) and used imprecisely defined class categories, it nonetheless roughly corresponded to non-Communist surveys and thus painted a reasonably credible picture of rural society and the polarized landholding patterns in South-Central China, the primary base of the soviet movement. The survey exemplified Mao's tendency to base policy decisions on concrete class analyses, a stance that apparently brought charges of "narrow empiricism" from the more doctrinaire Internationalist party leaders after 1930.[16] A number of independent surveys conducted in various regions of China during the same period indicated that 30 percent of all farm families owned no land at all and found that tenancy rates were generally considerably higher in central and south China (33 to 41 percent for Kiangsi) than in most of north China.[17] In its breakdown of the data for one of the villages studied, Gamble's 1926-33 survey of a north China rural county reported that the lower 62.3 percent of the farm families owned some 22 percent of the farm area, while the upper 3.5 percent owned 20.9 percent of the land.[18] Again, it should be kept in mind that landholding patterns were more polarized in the southern and central rice-producing regions of China than in the northern wheat-producing regions. It should also be pointed out, however, that the more extreme tenancy and landholding conditions in the rice-producing regions did not in itself mean greater rural impoverishment there than in the north. And tenancy per se was not always to be equated with poverty.[19]

The results of Mao's rural survey underscored the considerable importance of the middle peasant group as well as the small role of full-time hired hands in the farm economy, though the latter group was augmented by the part-time labor status of many of the poor peasantry. Tawney, in summing up the results of a number of comparable studies of China during this period, also emphasized that nonlandholding farm laborers formed only "a small minority" of the rural population.[20] Wage workers "do not form a distinct class differing sharply in economic position from the farmers for whom they work. . . . The typical figure in Chinese country life is not the hired labourer, but the land-holding peasant."[21] Hired farm laborers, and particularly those who were only seasonally or temporarily employed, were not proletarian in outlook but rather aspired to become landowners or tenant cultivators themselves. A Chinese analyst thus wrote in the 1930s that

it is highly important to remember that in general the
hired agricultural labourers in China are at the same
time poor peasants who cultivate land either owned or
leased, and in intervals are also hired out as coolies. . . .
One day they do field work on their own land or the land
they have leased, the next day they work as hired
labourers in someone else's field; and the day after that
they work as coolies transporting goods from the shops in
the city.[22]

Communist sources in the early 1930s cited not only the dearth of
full-time agricultural laborers but also their wide dispersion among
individual farm families as obstacles to their effective
organization.[23]

The category of nonagricultural labor was comprised of a
diverse grouping of handicraftsmen-artisans, apprentices, shop
employees, and coolies. According to Gamble's survey, the number
of workers in the various shops (enterprises) in Ting County in Hopei
Province averaged 4.0 to 4.8 per shop.[24] Tawney described this
"small-master system" in China's rural towns and villages as follows:

The traveller who explores the streets of any Chinese
town passes between rows of houses open to the streets,
at once workshops and homes, in which small groups of
artisans are hammering metal, fashioning wood, or
making clothing and shoes, side by side with their employers, whose meals they share, and with whom, when
apprentices, they normally lodge. In the more pre-
tentious establishments, and more delicate crafts, like
fan-making and lantern-making, the front serves as a
shop where wares are displayed; the rooms and courts
behind it are the workshops where materials are stored,
work is carried on from dawn to dusk, and food is prepared. There is little sub-division of labour or speciali-
sation of functions, and in the majority of cases, no

machinery or power. Work is heavy; craftsmanship fastidious; methods patient, laborious and slow; discipline slack or absent. Relations are human, not mechanical.[25]

The central soviet area, based largely in the more remote areas of southern Kiangsi and western Fukien provinces, was, of course, predominantly agricultural, with an "industrial" economy which generally conformed to the above pattern. A sympathetic contemporary account of the soviet districts gave this description: "No large industries are found there, but the manufacture of textiles, paper and camphor—not to mention the mining industry—is carried on after a primitive fashion in the form of small enterprises."[26] Small merchant shops, cartage, and ultimately some modest soviet-owned arsenals, printing plants, and other enterprises, comprised the remainder of the nonagricultural scene. The attempt militantly to advance labor interests in this primitive industrial setting brought further problems for the class line.

The Post-Fourth Plenum Labor Line in the Soviet Areas

The newly established CBSA moved quickly under the Party Center's direction to outline and propagate a firmer proletarian line in the soviet districts and to clarify the role of organized labor there. One of its first notices in late January 1931 focused on problems of the relationship between the soviets as organs of government and the unions as mass-struggle organizations.[27] This notice was probably directed in good part at the Li Li-san forces in the soviet areas, which had attempted to juxtapose their asserted labor leadership role against Mao's peasant movement.[28] In attacking such an approach, the CBSA moved in the mainstream of post-Li Li-san CI-CCP policy, which stressed both the centrality of a soviet movement based on the land revolution and the importance of instilling it with a strong and integral proletarian core. Thus, while emphasizing the distinct spheres of activity of the soviets and the unions, the CBSA sought to refute any notion of a conflict of interest between the two; the notice insisted that the demands and goals of the unions coincided with the interests and goals of the soviet movement as a whole, which represented workers as well as peasants and the poor and stood for their liberation. The notice observed that in some soviet districts "in the past," this fundamental correspondence had been misunderstood, leading to the idea that "the unions are working class organizations and the soviets are the peasant masses' organizations."[29] This misapprehension wholly invalidated not only the concept of proletarian hegemony within the soviets but also the role of the working class as a mass base of soviet power. The document went on to state that this kind of interpretive error could only create antagonisms and divisions between the proletariat and the toiling peasantry in their joint struggle for the soviets. Neither the soviets nor the unions should coopt the functions and responsibilities of the other but rather should focus on their mutually reinforcing relationship. The unions were thus affirmed to be a pivotal and integral mass organizational base of soviet power, with the promotion of labor interests and struggles strongly endorsed as a key element both in advancing the soviet movement and in fulfilling the vanguard revolutionary role of the proletariat.

A subsequent major CBSA notice (1 March 1931) laid out the "correct" line for the soviet-area labor movement and elaborated on the problems mentioned in the January notice.[30] It indicated as well how far removed the soviet-area unions then were from being the activist, authentically proletarian vanguard force the party aspired to build. It called on the unions to help realize worker goals by fully implementing soviet labor-protection laws and welfare provisions and further stressed the importance of proletarian leadership in all aspects of the soviet movement: the land revolution, the Red Army, the soviet government, and the mass organizations. It acknowledged that, lacking major cities, the soviet districts contained few industrial workers; even handicraft workers and hired laborers were in short supply. This only served to highlight labor's crucial role, however; despite their diminutive ranks, soviet-area labor forces, through their heightened class consciousness, could readily be linked to and guided by the industrial proletariat—presumably of the cities outside the soviet zones. It was thus vital to organize and strengthen these class elements and give them a key role in all campaigns and movements.

There was a serious impediment to success on this front, however. Labor's vanguard role was undermined by the impure class composition of the soviet unions, whose ranks included shop-owners, independent handicraftsmen, and even Taoist priests. The always perplexing problem of maintaining proletarian consciousness among hired laborers who had been given land was also raised. Land ownership tended to transform laborers into peasants who no longer perceived a struggle target. A successful transition to the socialist revolution theoretically required intensification of the class struggle and proletarian leadership of the peasant masses; but how could this come about if the proletariat became part of the peasant masses? Though the document offered no solution to this problem, it is significant that the "impure" class nature of the unions was singled out in this context. If the unions were unable to instill a clearcut class consciousness in their members (difficult indeed, given the latter's diverse economic circumstances), then whatever else they might achieve, they were not fulfilling their primary function.[31]

In reviewing asserted past mistakes in union work, the CBSA statement articulated some of the problems of building a labor movement in a rural setting. Organizational formalism with "non-class, non-struggle" unions functioning as "empty shell" bureaucratic "yamens"; inadequate numbers of dues-paying members; infiltration into responsible posts of "riffraff"; and the prevalence of corrupt practices were among the charges leveled against the existing soviet union organizations. These unions had pursued only their own narrow and separate interests and allowed worker-peasant separatism and antagonism to build, the CBSA declared. These shortcomings were identified as having stemmed from the party's failure to give adequate attention and proper guidance to union work as a central party task in the soviet areas, to which only the most reliable comrades should be assigned.

The CBSA document concluded with a listing of the priority tasks and correct line for the union movement "from now on." This included the expulsion of all union members who were not part of the wage-earning labor force (thereby creating genuine "class unions"), the establishment of farmhand unions and poor-peasant corps, and the liquidation of bureaucracy, thus turning the unions into mass organizations. The unions were urged to take a stronger leadership role in the forefront of all soviet revolutionary struggles. They were instructed to pay attention to all worker demands and to plan and promote a variety of struggles designed to advance worker interests. The CBSA cautioned against relying solely on the soviet government to enforce the capitalists' compliance with labor-protection statutes and worker demands, stressing the importance of building worker consciousness and of employing such labor tactics as direct union negotiations and strikes. While any tendency toward "narrow economism" which focused on worker interests without regard to those of the soviet movement as a whole must be avoided, the notice also warned against "right opportunism" which would abandon all worker struggles on the pretext that this was necessary in the name of such overall interests. This dual formulation side-stepped the problems and contradictions involved in mobilizing labor as the revolutionary vanguard. Yet, the fact remained that the militant expression of labor interests and demands inevitably conflicted with the larger economic and political interests of the peasant-based, small enterprise economy of the soviet districts.

In line with the ongoing concern to link soviet labor with the ultimately more crucial urban proletarian forces, the CBSA notice also disclosed that a central executive bureau of the ACFL for the soviet areas was being established both to unify the soviet labor movement and to help establish, through the ACFL organization, close relations with the white-area workers' movement. The two movements were admonished to keep abreast of developments on both fronts.

In keeping with the labor line of the CBSA, the organizational regulations for hired farmhand unions and for poor peasants' associations, or corps (in which hired hands and other rural proletarian elements were to play a major part), had been drawn up in February 1931.[32] The hired hands' union was to be an organ of class struggle with a leadership role in the soviet movement. Only those who hired out their labor as the principal source of livelihood were eligible for membership; those formerly in this category who had been allotted land no longer qualified unless they continued to do hired labor on a regular (long-term) basis.[33] The determination to utilize the hired hands as the proletarian vanguard of the peasant movement was dogged by ambiguity. To begin with, there was always a fine line between the poor peasant and the hired agricultural laborer, and the allotment of land to laborers rendered it even more obscure. What constituted "long-term" hiring out, and should that continue to be a requirement for union membership? Who among the peasantry were legitimate class-struggle targets after land redistribution? These were some of the problems party policy makers continued to grapple with throughout the remaining Kiangsi years.

The hired hands' union was to be structured hierarchically: the lowest levels would be comprised of small groups of three or more members, and these would be integrated into branch, district, county, and provincial or soviet special-area unions. Congresses were to elect administrative organs at all levels under the guiding Communist principle of democratic centralism. The union was enjoined to lead its members in struggles against exploitation and oppression of the hired hands, to rally poor and middle peasants around the union, and to carry out "all struggles for the consolidation and expansion of the Soviets."[34] The union was to direct schools, clubs, publications, and other activities in an effort to raise the political and cultural level of the workers.

The poor peasants' corps were to organize the poor rural masses and to promote their interests by carrying out the land revolution, practicing class struggle (their particular target was the rich peasantry), allying with the middle peasants, and expanding and intensifying all revolutionary struggles "in order to make it possible for the Chinese revolution to head for socialism."[35] It was evident from the membership criteria that the term "poor peasant" included not only the poorest peasant cultivators but virtually the entire range of the rural proletariat (wage-earners) as well: farmhands, laborers hiring out to shop proprietors or contractors, transport coolies, and handicraftsmen with their own tools (but with no assistants or apprentices) who hired out to employers.[36] While it was stipulated that poor peasants' corps were to be organized only at the village *(ts'un)*, township *(hsiang)*, and district *(ch'ü)* levels,[37] subsequent organizational regulations issued by the Southwest Kiangsi Special Area Committee of the party further limited the upper level of corps organization to the township. For the corps to organize at the district and upper levels, these latter regulations declared, would create a rival leadership to that of the working class and would thereby deny the latter's vanguard role in the Chinese revolution.[38] These same regulations now also restricted corps membership to the more specifically agricultural categories of poor peasants (excluding those who hired labor), farmhands, coolies, and poor women.[39] In all of the above organizational arrangements, the aim clearly was to accentuate the concept of proletarian leadership of the peasant movement by organizationally subordinating the latter to the labor movement and by ensuring that the poor peasants' corps would be tempered by a rural proletarian presence (farmhands and coolies). Thus, it was also stipulated that the chairman of the township poor peasant corps (the highest organizational level) must be a hired farmhand. Also emphasized was the role of the corps in uniting the poor peasantry and the rural proletariat (while "rallying" the middle peasants around the corps) against the rich peasants; this would assure the party of "a proletarian basis" in the "clear-cut class line of battle" in the rural districts.[40] The design, therefore, called for the poor peasant corps to gather in the poorer peasant masses at the village level and to assert proletarian primacy within the corps through rural labor leadership. The overlap in membership between the corps and the hired hands' unions would serve to integrate the corps under the district and soviet-area (or provincial) union organizational structure.

Despite the efforts to stimulate organization of poor peasants' corps at the village level, progress on this front apparently continued to lag in many soviet districts. Corps organization was propelled forward only in conjunction with the Land Investigation Movement's escalated class war against landlord and rich peasant elements in mid-1933.[41] Further organizational principles were issued at that time to emphasize the corps' broad representation of all poor rural class elements and to reaffirm the leading role of rural labor elements. The village-township organizational structure of the corps was also reiterated.[42]

An April 1931 notice of the Southwest Kiangsi Special Area Committee stressed again the crucial mass organizational role of the hired hands' union in a soviet movement which thus far lacked major urban (proletarian) centers.[43] The document outlined the union's tasks in militantly promoting agricultural labor interests. It called for the intensification of the anti-rich peasant struggle and the training of hired hands as cadres in the soviet movement.

There can be little doubt that the labor policies enunciated during the early months of 1931 conformed in essentials to the proletarian line of the post-Fourth Plenum Party Center and its Comintern supporters. At the same time, there was always the question, particularly in this initial period when the Party Center itself remained based in Shanghai, of how completely and firmly the party organs in the central soviet area were under returned-student control. The precise nature of the balance of forces and the relationship among the party, soviet government, and the Red Army there were also in question. In addition, the actual social, economic, political, and military circumstances of the soviet districts played their part in determining the extent to which proclaimed policy lines could effectively and practically be carried out. Thus, the Maoist faction in the central soviet area, with its strong positions in soviet government organs and the Red Army and rich experience in the rural soviet struggle, undoubtedly continued to have a significant impact on policies, and even more on policy implementation. Ilpyong Kim's 1973 study of the Kiangsi Soviet supports this view in the discussions of agrarian and economic policies and organizational techniques and of the Maoist role in the 1933 phase of the Land Investigation Movement.

It is important to emphasize that none of the above observations should obscure the point that the proletarian line so vigorously propagated from early 1931 on stemmed primarily from the returned-student leaders, no matter what the degree of actual support for or expedient concurrence in these policies may have come from the indigenously based Mao forces. This is clear from the center's repeated attacks (probably aimed at the proponents of both Li Li-san and Mao) on past mistakes and defects of the soviet-area labor policies and on the "rich peasant mentality" in the soviet areas, which was seen as an impediment to a firm and militant class stance. Whatever the shifting balances of power and personalities within the CBSA, the fact remains that its majority elements and its first secretary, Hsiang Ying, represented the Bolshevik group, whose "mission," as it were, was to create a party structure in the soviet area responsive to the authority and line of the Shanghai Party Center. The unassailable orthodoxies of the proletarian line and the line's direct link to both the Party Center and the Comintern were surely factors which contributed to the Maoist inclination to "live with" the Bolshevik line in the post-1930 Kiangsi years. But this did not preclude Mao's efforts to modify or soften the harsher and more intractable aspects of the center's policy; indeed, some of the more obviously counterproductive consequences of the class line became matters of concern for the party leadership as a whole toward the end of the Kiangsi period.

Whatever the problems of the initial Bolshevik efforts through the CBSA, the Party Center was able in the latter part of 1931 to tighten significantly its control over the central soviet-area party in conjunction with the formal establishment of the Chinese Soviet Republic at the First National Soviet Congress in November 1931. These developments were accompanied by the first stages in the relocation of the Party Center to Juichin, the new soviet capital in Kiangsi, and by the convening of the First Party Congress of the central soviet area, also in November, under the aegis of the Bolshevik leadership.[44] The line on the labor movement that came out of that congress and the labor law adopted by the First National Soviet Congress were clearly in accord with the policies outlined in the early months of the year by the CBSA and other soviet-area party organs.

The November party congress's resolution on the soviet-area union movement again stressed the latter's vital role in the revolution despite its nonindustrial handicraft worker, coolie, and farmhand constituency.[45] It noted as well the special problems of handicraft enterprises in the soviet districts which, under the impact of the KMT's military encirclement and economic blockade, were suffering widespread unemployment among their workers. It also remarked somewhat cryptically on the question of the changing status of hired farmhands who had been allotted holdings through the land redistribution program. The past mistakes of the soviet labor movement were dredged up once again with specific reference being made to the "false" (or "non") class line which had resulted in unions that became tools of the bosses and protectors of the interests of independent craftsmen rather than of genuine (wage-earning) workers. While some corrective action had been taken under party pressure, authentic "class unions" had yet to be established, the resolution complained. In criticizing economist tendencies in some areas, manifested by excessive wage increases that were detrimental to the soviet economy, the document noted that such increases had been mainly in the interests of master craftsmen and "bosses" (apparently self-employed elements), offering little or no advantage vis-à-vis regular workers. The unions were again accused of failing to lead genuine worker struggles and of doing little to increase wages and improve livelihood for the worker masses. The resolution dwelt further on problems in relations between the unions and the soviet government, stating that the correction of the earlier errors of separation of interests, etc., had led to a reverse situation in which unions had become subordinate organs of the soviet government. This was probably a criticism of the Mao-dominated soviet government apparatus which, in the context of the campaign against Li Li-san's separatist labor forces, may well have moved to gain control of the unions. Developing the appropriate and necessary leadership role for the unions, one which would also encompass the various struggles of the peasant masses, was a task still awaiting completion, the resolution noted. It went on to criticize the policy of disallowing membership in the hired hands' union to those who had been allotted land, a policy that in effect abolished such unions. It was not clear whether this was a criticism of the stipulation that only hired hands who continued to do "regular" hired labor were eligible for membership or if it was meant rather to reinforce that provision, though other policy documents, some of which shall be reviewed below, tend to support the first of these suppositions.

Other criticisms included the fact that the unions still lacked close links with the worker masses and were monopolized by a minority; they functioned, on the whole, with a strong flavor of commandism and lacked vigor. The resolution called the soviet party's role in union work "extremely weak" and blamed this neglect on past misinterpretation of the class line and proletarian hegemony, which had led to a general inability to appreciate the central and fundamental character of union work.

In calling for immediate correction of the above deficiencies, the party congress document insisted that proletarian leadership called for the fullest development of the union movement (especially of the hired hands) so that organized labor could become the core, or "heart" (ho-hsin), of all mass campaigns and of the soviet movement as a whole. The realization of this goal, which was predicated on the building of class unions to develop and lead the workers' struggles, was "the most fundamental practical task" of the party in the soviet areas. In this connection, the document urged the accelerated recruitment of workers, and particularly unemployed artisans, farmhands, and coolies, into the Red Army and the election of activist elements to soviet government organs.

The resolution stressed again the need thoroughly to eliminate nonproletarian elements from the unions and to improve working conditions and livelihood through worker struggles. Special mention was made of the previously projected conflict that would unite the poor and middle peasants under the leadership of the hired hands against the rich peasants. Though the twin deviations of narrow economism and opportunist abandonment of worker interests were warned against and the coordination of labor interests with the development of the "state economy" was called for, the document's chief emphasis was clearly on the key importance of mobilizing labor through struggle tactics.

It is evident that the November party congress's labor policy resolution essentially reaffirmed all of the key points in the earlier 1931 documents. Moreover, it reflected strong dissatisfaction with the degree of progress since then, with the soviet-area leadership bearing the brunt of the criticism. But there were, in fact, more fundamental and intractable obstacles in the way of the Party Center's labor line. Genuine proletarian elements in the small-scale, nonagricultural handicraft economy were difficult to define, identify, and organize, and the ailing condition of that economy posed special difficulties for a militant anticapitalist class line. It was also apparent that the existing soviet unions were far from being vital, responsive, and responsible mass organizations; on the contrary, their proclaimed leadership role in the peasant-based soviet movement had often taken an adversary form which clashed with the movement's overall political and economic interests. There was also the crucial and continuing question of the agricultural proletariat: how to develop and maintain a rural proletarian consciousness in the peasant movement's vanguard, the unionized farmhands. The ambiguous nature of this issue was only too apparent: the farmhands constituted only a small minority of the rural population, to begin with, and they themselves aspired to full landholder status, which was, ironically, being bestowed upon them by the Communists' own land redistribution program.

A major Comintern source on the Chinese soviet movement also pinpointed the key importance of mobilizing and organizing the worker masses in class organizations to fight for their demands rather than relying on governmental authority and orders to achieve them. This source called the January 1931 Fourth Plenum and the subsequent struggle against deviationist tendencies in labor policy and against opportunist elements the "turning point" in the development of the soviet labor movement. As a result, soviet efforts on behalf of worker organization and workers' interests had been strengthened; and this, in turn, acted to reinforce the role of workers in the soviet movement as a whole, "without which there can be no talk of the hegemony of the proletariat in the agrarian peasant revolution."[46]

The constitution of the now formally established Chinese Soviet Republic and the labor law passed by the First National Soviet Congress in November 1931 affirmed the party leadership's interest in both organizing labor and promoting its interests as the "pillar" of the new soviet state. This state was described by its constitution as a "democratic dictatorship of the proletariat and the peasantry," whose mission was to carry out the antifeudal and anti-imperialist revolution in China, to foster an increasingly class-conscious and united proletariat, and to lead the poor peasant masses in effecting the transition to a dictatorship of the proletariat.[47]

The constitution stated that "since only the proletariat can lead the broad masses to socialism," that they were to be allowed a disproportionately greater number of deputies in elections to the worker-peasant-soldier soviets at the various levels of government.[48] The constitution also included the soviet republic's commitment to improve worker living conditions, adopt labor legislation, introduce the eight-hour workday, set a minimum wage, institute social insurance and unemployment benefits, and grant workers the right to supervise production.[49]

The labor law, which went into effect in January 1932, was based in all essentials on a draft submitted to the congress by the CCP Central Committee.[50] Comprised of seventy-five articles pertaining to worker rights and benefits (many of which seemed only marginally applicable to a rural soviet setting), the law covered all wage workers in industrial, workshop, and other productive enterprises, and in state, cooperative, and private organizations (the military was excluded).[51] Specific conditions of labor for agricultural, forestry, and communications workers, coolies, domestic workers, seasonal workers, and other special labor categories were to be dealt with in supplementary governmental regulations. All existing and future contractual labor agreements were required to conform fully to the provisions of the law.

All employment was to take place through the unions and state labor exchanges; private contracting, exchanges, and payment of employment fees by workers were expressly prohibited. Working conditions were to be spelled out either in annual collective agreements between unions and employers or in labor contracts between one or several workers and an employer that would have to accord with prevailing collective agreements. The law set a maximum eight-hour day, with correspondingly reduced hours for youth (16-18) and child (14-16) workers and for those on night shifts or in dangerous occupations. Employment of persons under age fourteen was forbidden. A weekly rest period of forty-two continuous hours, annual paid vacations of at least two weeks (four weeks for those in potentially injurious occupations), eight additional paid holidays, rest days, and sick leave were also mandated. Overtime and holiday work (if permitted by the unions and the workers' supervisory bodies) was to be paid at double rates.

A minimum wage was to be fixed by the Ministry of Labor and reviewed every three months, with actual wage scales (paid in cash, not in kind) set by union-employer collective agreements. Women and youth workers were to receive equal wage rates for equivalent work, and special safeguards regarding their working conditions were to be instituted. Moreover, all those who worked reduced hours were to be paid for a full day's work at the prevailing rates. Piecework rates were to be fixed by union-employer collective agreements. The law also provided for paid maternity leaves (six to eight weeks, to be paid for by social insurance or by the employer) and day-care and child-nursing arrangements financed by the enterprises. Factories and workshops were required to upgrade the skills of young workers (ages 14-18) at employer expense; the "old system" of apprenticeship was prohibited, and all apprentice labor contracts were required to adhere to the labor laws. Elaborate safety and inspection provisions were written into the law, as were disability and workmen's compensation payments. Workers were not to be docked for absences related to union or political activities. Enterprises were required to provide either communal housing for their employees and families or a rent allowance.

Workers and staff were to be organized under the overall leadership and control of the ACFL through its new executive bureau for the soviet areas. The unions were empowered to organize strikes and to negotiate collective agreements, which would be implemented through union factory or shop committees. They were to participate directly in management of state and cooperative enterprises and through supervisory bodies in private undertakings. Employers were to contribute a sum equal to 3 percent of their wage package for union expenses and worker cultural needs. State, cooperative, and private enterprises were also obliged to set aside from 10 to 15 percent of their total wages for a social insurance fund. This fund was to provide all workers and their families with medical care, sick benefits, unemployment compensation, special childbirth expenses, funeral costs and survivors' payments to needy families, and old age and disability pensions. The insurance funds were to be administered by the union under the supervision of the Ministry of Labor.

Workers could be discharged only with union consent. Disputes between workers and capitalists and alleged violations of the labor law or of collective agreements were either to be brought before the people's courts or to be adjudicated by worker-capitalist grievance committees or by the arbitration commission of the Ministry of Labor. Violations of the labor law or of subsequent labor regulations were to be considered criminal offenses.

A resolution on economic policy adopted by the First National Soviet Congress further stipulated that while capitalist (private) enterprise would continue, production would be under the supervision of workers' councils and factory committees. The resolution warned capitalists against violations of soviet law, counterrevolutionary activities, or deliberate interference in or stoppages of production; the penalty for these actions would be confiscation of their enterprises, which would be placed under the management of either workers' cooperatives or the soviet government.[52] In addition, under a newly instituted "progressive tax" system, the capitalists would be made to carry the major tax burden; workers, Red Army men, and the "impoverished masses" (p'in-k'u ch'ün-chung) in cities and the countryside were to be exempted.[53]

Hsiang Ying, Minister of Labor in the new soviet government and one of its two vice-chairmen under Mao, delivered a detailed exposition and endorsement of the labor law's many provisions to the First Soviet Congress.[54] According to Hsiang, the function of the labor law was to protect workers by restricting capitalist exploitation and oppression. He declared that the law should not be viewed as suitable only for urban and factory workers; at the same time, however, he pointed to the need to work out the specifics of its applicability to farmhands, coolies and other special labor categories.[55] Hsiang stressed the urgency of setting minimum wage requirements, which should be periodically readjusted as living standards improved, and he reemphasized the status of the unions as "the most important mass organization" under the soviet government.[56] In hailing the new law as a beacon for the capitalist-oppressed workers in the KMT areas and looking forward to the day when it would be enforced throughout China under a Soviet regime, Hsiang underscored its broader political symbolism and urban perspectives.[57]

The May 1930 Soviet Areas Delegates Conference had adopted a draft "labor protection law" (lao-tung pao-hu fa) from which the 1931 law stemmed. It is noteworthy how closely in accord the two documents were, given the fact that the 1930 conference was held under Li Li-san's strongly urban-proletarian leadership. Both laws were in keeping with advanced industrial conditions which were hardly present in Shanghai, let alone in the Kiangsi soviet region. To be sure, some of the modifications which turned up in the 1931 law did reflect rural realities. For example, the 1930 conference had stipulated a 40-yuan minimum monthly wage (well above the Shanghai average), had prohibited overtime, and had forbidden employment of those under sixteen. The 1931 law avoided a specific minimum wage figure, was more flexible on the issue of overtime, and allowed employment of fourteen- to sixteen-year olds.[58] The 1930 draft was apparently concerned only with industrial labor, while the 1931 law included nonindustrial labor in its general purview, calling for supplementary regulations to serve the specific requirements of that sector's diverse constituency. Somewhat less realistically, the 1931 labor law spelled out certain worker benefits and union prerogatives that the earlier document had not addressed as explicitly.[59] All in all, as Hsiang Ying's comments above indicate, the labor law was more representative of the larger proletarian aspirations of the party leadership than of the realities of the soviet areas to which it pertained.

Promulgation of the labor law was accompanied by a Party Center resolution on the soviet labor movement which served to make two key political points.[60] The first was of a self-congratulatory nature; and the second sharply criticized past and present errors in the soviet-area labor line (criticism apparently directed principally at the central soviet-area leadership), while setting out the correct line and key tasks for the period ahead. In listing the "undeniable achievements" of the past year, the resolution noted that hired hands' unions and industrial union branches had been widely established. Moreover, total union membership now exceeded 100,000, with union organizations in virtually all soviet localities and levels. Several soviet regions outside the central soviet area (particularly the O-yü-wan (Hupei-Honan-Anhwei) base area) where the unions had played a "fairly large" leadership role in the land revolution, improved workers' livelihood, and led economic struggles were specifically singled out. The document noted more generally that the soviet unions had channeled outstanding worker elements into Red Army leadership work and that great numbers of workers had helped to repel the KMT's third encirclement campaign. Progress had also been recorded (here the central soviet area, as well as O-yü-wan and other bases, was included) in the expulsion of rich peasants, shop owners, counterrevolutionaries, and A-B League elements[61] from the unions; in selecting "genuine" worker cadres for the union movement; and in convening some union congresses and promulgating struggle programs.

Such successes, however, should not be exaggerated or allowed to cover up serious defects and mistakes, the most important of which was summed up as the absence of "a clear-cut class line" and "opportunist passivity."[62] It noted the continuing presence of alien class elements, and the failure to promote worker economic struggles, improve livelihood, and thoroughly implement labor legislation.[63] There was still the tendency to rely on governmental authority rather than on the "struggle power" of the worker masses. At the same time, there was inadequate cohesion between the worker and peasant movements, which led to mutual antagonisms and conflicts of interest ultimately detrimental to one side or the other. The eight-hour workday had yet to be implemented in many areas, and union work in surrounding white industrial districts had not been intensified. There was still inadequate recognition of the "foundation" role of the unions for the soviet government, reinforcing estrangements between the two. The tasks before the soviet unions were, therefore, as before: to overcome the problems which impeded the unions' effective mass-leadership role. The resolution concluded by stating that progress thus far lagged far behind objective struggle requirements.

A 1931 report by the party's Shanghai labor bureau assessed soviet-area work in much the same terms as the Party Center resolution.[64] It gave a figure of over 97,000 union members for the major central (Kiangsi and western Fukien) and O-yü-wan areas and estimated the total for all soviet bases at from 100,000 to 150,000. Hired hands' unions were thought to be among the best, with unions in the O-yü-wan and Hunan base areas better than elsewhere.

The labor bureau acknowledged its lack of concrete information on soviet labor developments, and specifically on the extent to which the soviet unions had been able to set up formal mechanisms for dealing with such issues as wages and hours, social insurance, housing, and unemployment relief. In the face of this data gap, and while conceding the special economic difficulties created by wartime conditions, it nevertheless chided the soviet labor movement for failing thus far to move expeditiously on these issues.

The leadership role assumed by the urban-based party and ACFL headquarters was indicated in the labor bureau's observation that the soviet unions should be assisted in solving their problems by the urban industrial workers and the ACFL. It noted that the party labor bureau and the ACFL were in the midst of an investigation of social insurance, cooperatives, and economic struggle questions, the results of which would be forwarded to the soviet areas. The guidance offered, one can surmise, undoubtedly continued to mirror predominantly urban labor concerns and preoccupations transplanted to the countryside.

The major Profintern resolution on the Chinese Communist labor movement during this period naturally touched on similar overall policy themes for the soviet areas. In calling on the soviet unions to overcome "all narrow and 'trade-unionistic' tendencies," it too emphasized that these unions "must at the same time most resolutely develop work to defend day to day economic interests of the working class."[65] Notions of neglecting or devaluing union work on the pretext of soviet wartime conditions were to be mercilessly combatted. The resolution targeted as a "fundamental" union task the complete and universal realization of the labor law provisions, as well as of demands not articulated in the law, such as wage increases and other benefits and safeguards. It underlined the importance of an activist worker struggle role in achieving these aims against the resistance of the capitalists, "particularly the numerous small exploiters."[66]

The peasant-agrarian revolution to eliminate "feudal and semi-feudal forms of exploitation" (land tenancy and usury) was thus to be interlaced with and intensified by a concurrent struggle to restrict "capitalist exploitation" (wage labor in agriculture, commerce, and industry). The whole struggle would be led by a Communist Party which, by means of increasingly proletarianized worker-peasant-soldier soviet power, would guarantee the transition to socialism. That a proletarian core was an integral part of the agrarian revolution was fundamental to this design. As summed up in a key Comintern exposition on the soviet movement: "In the very process of intensifying agrarian revolution, the poor and middle peasantry stand closer and closer around the proletariat; they are continually leaving the bourgeoisie and the kulaks in the enemy camp."[67] This was even more graphically expressed in another major Comintern source, Soviets in China, which declared that the Chinese revolution, which continued to be "a bourgeois-democratic and anti-imperialist" one, "simultaneously turns its dagger against the national bourgeoisie, and against the rich peasants in the villages."[68] Yet it was the very process of injecting sharpened proletarian struggle into the agrarian-based soviet revolution that was to have a divisive rather than a cementing impact, as the new soviet republic moved to implement its labor line.

1932 Labor Developments

In February 1932 a Kiangsi-Fukien worker representatives' congress was held under the auspices of the ACFL to establish a two-province general labor union for the central soviet area.[69] It provided for a hierarchical structure from the township *(hsiang)* to the province *(sheng)*, took up the question of a "struggle program," and elected a chairman (Ch'en Shou-ch'ang) and a twenty-one member presidium. It also named as honorary chairmen central soviet-area leaders Mao, Chou En-lai, Hsiang Ying, Chu Te, and Liu Shao-ch'i as well as a number of international Communist figures including Stalin and Profintern head Lozovsky.[70]

In connection with the opening of the congress, an article by Chou En-lai in the soviet organ *Red China* affirmed the growing role of labor in the revolutionary war.[71] Chou linked this with the importance of capturing "central cities" (the so-called "forward and offensive" strategy), expanding the revolutionary war beyond the soviet boundaries, and advancing the national leadership role of the workers in the anti-KMT, anti-imperialist struggle. He called on the Red Army to take Kanchow, a major southwest Kiangsi center on the Kan River, and make it the pivot of soviet power. The working class must become the central force in soviet governmental and military organs, with the unions as the organizational core of all work and activities.

The "Kiangsi Workers' Struggle Program," a March 1932 document of the newly formed Kiangsi provincial union organization, apparently stemmed from the program and line formulated at the February congress.[72] The program's outline of the unions' leading role and tasks in the soviet movement was essentially a repeat of the major points already addressed by the February congress. Its economic program enumerated the worker benefits and rights contained in the labor law, including the special needs of women and young workers. On minimum wages, it specified (as did the labor law) that these should be reviewed every three months in the context of changes in the cost of living in the soviet area. Wang Ming would later cite the practice of paying wages in silver instead of soviet paper currency as an example of a "leftist" labor demand in this period.[73] The program called for the establishment of a piecework wage system which would link base pay to an established production norm and allow for increases as workers exceeded that norm. Other provisions were equally in line with the labor law: wages were to be paid semimonthly and in cash, and there were to be at least twenty paid holidays per year (apparently two weeks of vacation time plus legal holidays). Workers who participated in any union or soviet conference, military training, jury duty, etc., were to be paid at their regular rate; those who joined the Red Army were to receive three months wages from their employers.[74] Employers could hire labor only through the unions and could not lay off workers without union assent, and the employer was required to pay three months wages as severance pay.

In a section on agricultural workers, the Kiangsi program listed the key land and property redistribution provisions of the land law adopted by the First Soviet Congress and laid particular emphasis on the law's stipulation that rich peasants were to receive allotments of poorer land. It called also for confiscation of rich peasants' farm equipment, to be distributed to hired hands and poor peasants, and mandated the allocation of surplus rich peasant and landlord housing to these poorer elements. The hired hands were assigned the task of aiding the government in collecting land taxes and grain from the rich peasants.[75]

Though viewed as the crucially important rural proletarian force, agricultural labor posed special difficulties for those attempting to fit these workers into a clear-cut class category and struggle role. The Profintern labor policy statement cited above alluded to some of these difficulties in its discussion of union tasks in that area. It instructed the unions to employ different approaches to rich peasant employers (as "systematic" exploiters of labor) and to middle peasant employers ("who have recourse to the employment of auxiliary labor power") in pressing the demands of farm workers.[76] In addition, it stipulated that the farmhands' union must allow the "semi-proletarians" (defined as those who possess land but are still compelled, "systematically from year to year," to hire out their labor) to join their ranks. However, poor peasants who hired out only for the purpose of supplementing their primary source of income were ineligible for membership. The Profintern statement additionally and separately stated that farm laborers who received land in the agrarian revolution "must also be drawn into the unions," yet it did not clarify whether such former laborers would also have to continue "systematically" to hire out. It added finally that in districts where the working class was especially small and only farmhands' unions were present, the latter unions must be predominantly "proletarian" in composition.[77]

The issues and ambiguities outlined above were much more fully explored in a resolution of the Comintern's International Farm Laborer Committee on the policies of the soviet-area farmhands' union.[78] This statement (probably dating from late 1932 or early 1933), which circulated as an internal CCP document, made reference to a report to the committee's secretariat by Wang Ming that apparently served as its basis. It declared the establishment of the farmhands' union to be "one of the most important events" in the Chinese labor movement and noted approvingly the unions' reported membership of 100,000 in the soviet areas.

The resolution pointed to past errors in working with the hired hands, errors which, it asserted, were largely traceable to the pre-1931 ACFL leadership that had supported Li Li-san's view that farm labor should not be given land but ought rather to be utilized to create a soviet collective and state-farm system. It also criticized the tendency to "overly oppose" the middle peasants in defending farm labor's economic interests. This constituted a "mechanical" application of industrial labor rules to the soviet areas which failed to take into account the special conditions involved in applying the wage system to agriculture. Thus, the worker-peasant alliance had been weakened, and poor and middle peasants had been driven back into the arms of rich peasants and landlords. Despite these apparent problems in application, however, this document too stressed the importance of organizing agricultural labor (on which only a beginning had been made), emphasizing that this sector was an integral part and constituted an absolute majority of the Chinese working class and the proletarian vanguard in the villages.

To exercise its paramount role in the peasant land revolution it was necessary for agricultural labor to be alloted land, but this should in no way diminish the importance of the hired hands' unions nor lead to the notion that their establishment was unnecessary. These unions should rather become "struggle organs" for the purposes of advancing the farmhands' welfare and status on the one hand, and integrating agricultural labor into the broader ranks of the working class in the overall revolutionary movement on the other. In calling for the drafting of concrete guidelines to promote these goals, the document once again emphasized the importance of a differential approach, one that would gear labor demands to the employers' class background. While endorsing the principles of the labor law, it conceded the necessity of modifying it to take into account differences between industry and agriculture. Hired hand labor regulations should therefore be promulgated to reflect all of these points and at the same time continue to ensure the basic protection of such workers in terms of wages, working conditions, and treatment. It underscored the important responsibility of the more experienced and organized industrial workers in helping to resolve problems in hired hands' union work and recommended setting up a special industrial workers' committee under the ACFL to help organize (in the white areas as well as the soviet regions) "proletarian" agricultural workers' unions.[79]

In at least some recognition of rural agricultural realities, the soviet regime in June 1932 issued "provisional regulations on rural labor" which modified some aspects of the labor law.[80] It permitted the agricultural workday, for example, to be extended to a maximum of eleven hours during the busy season and allowed for wages (adequate to sustain the workers' livelihood) to be paid in kind. These arrangements were to be based on individual labor contracts rather than on overall collective agreements.[81] Although not entirely clear from the sources, we can assume that these more pliable provisions were designed to apply primarily to middle or poor peasant employers rather than to rich peasants. The individualized labor contract arrangements would allow for such differential treatment of employers much more readily than would more uniformly negotiated collective labor agreements. And evidently in accomodation to small village handicraft and shop enterprises, the new regulations also permitted more flexible apprenticeship arrangements.[82] Yet it was obviously not easy (if at all practicable) to set up differential wage and hour arrangements for agricultural labor (with lower wages and longer hours when working for poor or middle peasants); nor was it conducive to strengthening the "worker-peasant alliance" to promote the hired hands' class struggle under post-land redistribution conditions where the bulk of peasant employers began to move into a substantially expanded middle peasant category and even become "new-rich" peasants. The continuing difficulties in advancing rural labor interests and organization were apparent in a June 1932 commentary in the new labor organ of the soviet-area ACFL, *Soviet Worker*, which complained that average labor livelihood in the rural areas had not improved. The article further criticized the unions for failing to provide leadership for the hired hands' struggle against the rich peasants.[83]

The first Chinese agricultural workers' congress, held in Juichin in April 1933 under the auspices of the CCP and the soviet ACFL executive bureau, emphasized the supportive "proletarian backbone" responsibilities of rural labor in the Red Army and the soviet government at a time of heightening military and economic pressures in the central soviet area.[84] This continued to be linked to the union role in advancing and protecting the everyday interests and welfare of agricultural workers and to calls for including all such labor elements in the union, making it a truly "mass class union." But that the class status of now propertied farmhands continued to be a bedeviling issue was shown in the congress's expressed determination to deal a "severe blow" to the notion that once farmhands had been given land there was no longer need for the union.[85]

The place of agricultural laborers in the larger revolutionary scheme was thus seen as crucial. They were expected to be the proletarian wedge and handle for the mass peasant movement, and they could in turn be organized and integrated into broader soviet working class ranks. Once organized, they could then be linked to and guided by an increasingly prominent national revolutionary labor movement in which the urban industrial workers would finally come to the fore. But the successful integration of the rural proletariat into the soviet peasant movement as a key vanguard element was quite a different matter.

It was to the "urban" centers of the central soviet area (such towns as Juichin, T'ingchou, Huich'ang, and Ningtu) that the labor law seemed most readily applicable in this initial period. A December 1931 organizing congress of the Huich'ang city general labor union (representing fourteen unions), for example, had drawn up a "struggle program" in the spirit of the labor law.[86] It provided for increased wages retroactive to 1 November 1931, spelled out arrangements for worker supervision, and outlined union safeguards and prerogatives in worker hiring and firing. But even in this non-agricultrual setting, proletarian-minded commentaries expressed dissatisfaction at the slow progress being made, particularly in regard to raising labor struggle consciousness.

A June 1932 editorial in *Soviet Worker* thus inveighed against continuing "right opportunist" trends in the labor movement.[87]

Noting that four months had elapsed since the February Kiangsi-Fukien labor congress attack on earlier rightist errors of the soviet labor movement, it asserted that only minimal progress had since been made on this score. It acknowledged that there had been some improvement in workers' livelihood in the larger soviet towns, but it criticized the fact that such advances had not been accompanied by "torrential, bubbling and boiling struggles" (hsiung-yung, fei-t'eng-ti tou-cheng) of the masses. The editorial was especially critical of the lack of progress on the rural labor scene and in providing relief for the unemployed. In this connection, it maintained that the significance of the proletariat's overall revolutionary leadership function had still not been adequately grasped by union cadres, which accounted for the unions' failure to play a mobilizing role in the soviet movement.[88] In a similar vein, an April 1932 article in *Red China* had sharply criticized the inadequacies of the Ningtu soviet government's labor work.[89] Noting that Ningtu had earlier supported over 2,000 workers (mostly in textile enterprises), it reported that the majority of them were now unemployed. It complained that the Ningtu soviet neglected such labor problems and had even neglected to implement the eight-hour workday. The article added that notably little concern had been voiced on worker livelihood questions and that the various levels of the Ningtu labor bureau were merely "empty structures."[90]

The importance of promoting a militant and effectively organized soviet labor movement which could advance to a more politically conscious awareness of its larger revolutionary vanguard role and responsibilities was articulated theoretically in Wang Ming's major treatise *The Two Lines*. Originally published in 1931 as an attack on the Li Li-san line, the work was reissued by Wang in 1932 from his Moscow base on the ECCI. with a new postscript that took up the key question of the worker-peasant relationship in the Chinese revolution.[91] Wang criticized "some individual comrades among us" who disregarded the primary role of the working class while overstating that of the peasantry, thereby elevating the latter to a leadership position and relegating the former to a subordinate, supportive status. Though he recognized the major role of the peasantry and the agrarian revolution, Wang affirmed the crucial importance of proletarian leadership to the overall revolutionary cause and its socialist objectives. This leadership was reflected in the guiding role of the CCP itself and in the policy lines of the soviet republic. Wang emphasized also such substantive factors as the growing numbers and increasingly influential role of workers in the soviet party organs and the Red Army, in the numerous towns already under soviet control, and in the proletarian core of soviet mass organizations.[92] He added that all of this was, in turn, linked to and supported by the labor movement in the major white-area urban centers.

An intensified labor movement was thus viewed as a concrete manifestation of proletarian primacy and was linked to the preoccupation with a more aggressive "forward and offensive" soviet military strategy (also stressed by Wang Ming), which would bring larger urban centers and many more workers into the soviet fold. But the increasingly beleaguered position of the central soviet area and the counterproductive impact of labor demands on its hard-pressed economy led to further problems and frustrations for the proletarian line during 1933. These problems, and the alterations in labor policy which attempted to deal with them, are the focus of the next chapter.

CHAPTER IV

Labor and the Kiangsi Soviet: Problems of
the Proletarian Line, Phase Two, 1933-34

The central soviet area found itself in 1933 under growing
KMT military pressure, accompanied by economic and financial
stringencies and a consequent need for intensified military and
economic mobilization measures.[1] The KMT's fourth encirclement
campaign, under way since mid-1932, was terminated in the spring
of 1933 in the face of Nationalist setbacks and of renewed Japanese
challenges to the Nanking government in north China. This respite,
however, was soon ended with the onset of the massive fifth and
final campaign against the Kiangsi Soviet in the fall of 1933. These
drives were accompanied by a tightened economic blockade of the
soviet area. Two other important south-central soviet bases (O-yü-
wan and Hsiang-o-hsi) had collapsed under KMT pressure in the fall
of 1932, leaving the central soviet area in an even more isolated and
precarious position than before. These developments, in turn, led to
further debates on labor and economic policies. It was in this context that the Party Center, now wholly located in Kiangsi (amalga-
mating there with the CBSA), sought to adjust and accommodate
(but by no means to abandon) its proletarian line to the soviet area's
circumstances. While the initial response of some of the leaders
formerly based in Shanghai to these exigencies veered toward intensified class struggle, the view that prevailed in the Party Center by
late spring of 1933 moved in the opposite direction—apparently
reflecting the Center's increasing awareness of the realities in the
soviet region. Thus, though the dominant note in the very early part
of the year was to assert even more vigorously the labor struggle

and mobilization line of the 1931-32 period, this was soon superseded by a line which sought to backtrack from an overly militant labor stance. This new line stressed instead the soviet area's transcendent military, economic, and political interests and priorities and tried to steer a middle course between the more extreme and economically unmanageable "leftist" labor demands and struggle tactics and a "right-opportunist" forfeiture of labor's class interests and vanguard revolutionary role.

In accord with the earlier position, a 7 February 1933 keynote editorial in *Red China* took the line of strong proletarian leadership and struggle in emphasizing wartime mobilization needs.[2] It called for absorption of large numbers of workers into the Red Army as "backbone" elements in the newly intensified campaign to expand the soviet military forces. It declared that it was equally important to increase the number of worker cadres at all levels of the soviet government. Inveighing against those who would ignore or abandon union work responsibilities, it reaffirmed the necessity "resolutely" to carry out the labor law, to organize and lead workers' struggles, improve workers' livelihood, and build a broad mass union organization.

The editorial stressed also the importance of drawing a great many worker cadres into party leadership work and of stepping up the proletarianization of all party units. Newly recruited worker cadres must be constantly and continuously educated in their tasks and tempered in struggle, with new leaders of the masses nurtured from among such cadres as a prime requirement for the further development of soviet work. It voiced opposition to "those elements who fear and refuse" to promote worker cadres and to those who did so "formalistically" but without giving such workers the educational basis necessary for leadership tasks.[3]

The themes stressed in the *Red China* editorial, and the article's concluding summons to strengthen proletarian hegemony, had been given fuller elaboration in a major statement that had appeared only days earlier in the first issue of the Party Center's new soviet-area organ, *Struggle* [*Tou-cheng*].[4] The article was written by Teng Ying-ch'ao, Chou En-lai's wife and an important figure in the CCP in her own right, who had worked for years in the Shanghai party underground before coming to Kiangsi in 1932.[5] The article summed up the results of her investigations as head of a commission which had looked into the implementation of the labor law in the central soviet area, and it reflected the stronger urban and proletarian outlook of many of the newly transplanted party leaders in Kiangsi at that time. It revealed also the very substantial efforts being made in the soviet area genuinely to promote labor interests and power, as well as the obstacles such efforts faced as a result of the rural socioeconomic setting itself.

Citing a July 1932 directive from the Party Center, Teng Ying-ch'ao affirmed the importance of reinforcing proletarian leadership as the primary party task and the key to revolutionary victory and socialist transformation. This was linked to the struggle against those forces in the party whom she characterized as right opportunist and imbued with a "backward peasant consciousness," which impeded thorough and vigorous execution of the "forward and offensive line." A strong proletarian stance was thus a wartime task of the utmost urgency.[6] It was within this political-strategic framework that Teng Ying-ch'ao reviewed the results of her investigations.

In the latter part of 1932, the Red Army had instituted emergency mobilization measures and begun an expansion drive in response to the fourth KMT encirclement strategy. This was followed by a call in February 1933 to increase Red Army forces to one million troops.[7] In this connection, Teng noted that the percentage of workers and hired hands recruited into the Red Army in late 1932 had increased 24 percent for the eight counties surveyed in the July-September period; and 26 percent for the twelve counties examined in the October-December period. Despite the improved percentage, however, there had actually been a decrease in the absolute number of worker recruits in the latter months (presumably reflecting an overall drop in expansion totals). Recruitment of workers and hired hands into the party had risen from 20 percent of new members (in eleven counties) in the July–September period to 29 percent (in seventeen counties) in October–December. Though the increase was significant, the goal set by the CBSA and the Kiangsi provincial party committee of at least a one–third proportion of workers and hired hands among new members had not been met. To this observation Teng added that, in any case, it was not merely a matter of numbers but rather of transforming these new labor elements into genuine "leadership material." On this score she sharply criticized the absence of signs that the party had in fact mounted an educational and training program to achieve that goal.[8]

In turning to soviet governmental bodies, she expressed even greater dissatisfaction. The city of Juichin's soviet executive committee, for example, included only thirty-five workers and hired hands—something less than 25 percent of the committee as a whole. In the new soviet election campaign in Kiangsi (in line with a September 1932 soviet government decree to reorganize all local soviet regimes),[9] some eight or nine counties had drawn in a fairly large number of workers and rooted out alien class elements, but the lack of more complete information on these developments in itself was indicative of their neglect by party branches and soviet organs at all levels. Teng noted that from the limited data at hand it was evident that efforts to strengthen proletarian hegemony were still insufficient.

Teng further observed that despite CBSA efforts to expose and correct earlier mistakes in labor movement work, the soviet-area party's labor leadership role was, on the whole, still very weak. Provincial-level labor committees held few or no meetings; CBSA policy documents received scant attention from higher levels, resulting in a lack of central guidance, involvement, and support for local anticapitalist labor struggles. In some areas the party people were even saying that "the workers' struggle enthusiasm is not as high as the peasants' " ("struggle enthusiasm" referring primarily to their response to wartime mobilization and production appeals). Teng disputed this remark, citing the substantial percentage of union members joining the Red Army and the recent increases in production achieved by the state-owned mint and printing plant.

On the subject of the labor law, Teng pointed derisively to the "novel theories" of some comrades that the eight-hour workday could not be implemented due to the absence of clocks in the rural areas and also because it would evoke peasant resistance. These arguments, in her view, were "smoke screens" designed to conceal a downgrading of the labor movement. Even more serious were the antiworker tendencies apparent among some party elements.

Teng declared that the one significant accomplishment in remolding union work was the expansion in membership, with union totals in Kiangsi rising from 34,799 in August 1932 to 67,034 by the end of that year.[10] Despite this achievement, however, union work still lacked vigor and effectiveness; contract struggles were conducted "mechanically" and educational work was being neglected. The election movement to increase proletarian representation in government organs at all levels had been carried out spottily and without adequate propaganda work among the masses. As a result, there were still antagonisms between the unions and the soviets and instances of antiworker sentiments and actions on the part of soviet administrative personnel.[11] She further charged that party-building efforts did not adhere to an "open door policy" toward workers and hired hands and seemed hesitant to draw in worker cadres. Moreover, there was a lack of understanding in regard to the role of the hired hands' unions and a reluctance to undertake poor peasant corps' work. Teng viewed all of these problems as deficiencies in the struggle to strengthen proletarian hegemony.[12]

Teng then proceeded to outline a program for overcoming these shortcomings. A "merciless struggle" against the antiworker tendencies and opportunist elements and an educational campaign within the party and among the worker-peasant masses were considered vital components. The central importance of fostering worker struggles as the basis for developing labor's consciousness and generating activists among them for the party, government, and Red Army was stressed again. Teng concluded her essay by again linking an offensive military line with efforts to strengthen proletarian leadership, describing this as "the party's current fighting task which cannot be neglected for a single moment."[13]

Though focused on inadequacies in party and soviet labor work, Teng's article also pointed up the considerable efforts of the Bolshevik-dominated party leadership to build worker power in the soviet areas. Her criticisms reflected less the lack of a strong party labor line than the inherent difficulties of achieving proletarian primacy in the rural-based soviet government and party organs and on the peasant backlash such efforts might provoke. And her call for greater labor militancy and fuller benefits (as later moves in a reverse direction revealed) was apparently reflected in union-negotiated contracts for 1933 which included increased wages and what was subsequently to be criticized as the "mechanical" insertion in these contracts of numerous benefits taken verbatim from the labor law.[14] Although the party's response to the soviet area's crisis situation ultimately veered away from the more aggressive anti-capitalist stance taken by Teng, the determination to strengthen proletarian hegemony politically and organizationally remained a primary consideration in the consensus on party policy that emerged later in the year.

As an important part of the escalated war mobilization efforts in the central soviet area, areawide congresses of the major labor constituencies (agricultural workers, shop employees, and handicraft workers) were convened in April 1933.[15] The primary emphasis was now on wartime tasks and responsibilities (including support of the campaign to donate back to the government previously purchased soviet bonds), particularly a stepped-up drive to draw large numbers of workers into the Red Army, the government, and the party.[16] These goals continued to be linked by the congresses with the defense of their members' economic interests and the strengthening of their union organizations. The handicraft workers' and shop clerks' congress, in emphasizing the party enlistment drive, vowed that it would not permit a single politically conscious handicraft worker or clerk "to stand outside the Communist party's door!"[17] The party's new recruitment campaign was further publicized in the CBSA's May Day appeal to "workers, hired hands, coolies, Red soldiers, and all the laboring masses" to join the CCP and make it "the party of the advanced elements of the working class millions."[18]

It was becoming increasingly evident, however, that the effort to link greater labor organization and mobilization to an escalated class struggle and benefits strategy continued to be unrealistic. Officially sanctioned, organized, and unimpeded labor militancy could make a shambles of the fragile and hard-pressed small handicraft and mercantile economy and create serious rifts and problems on the agrarian front. The antisoviet suspicions and hostility of local capitalists and merchants were undoubtedly compounded and confirmed by such labor policies, as party spokesman Chang Wen-t'ien acknowledged in mid-1933. All this led many to close their businesses entirely or to flee the soviet areas with their capital, thereby significantly contributing to soviet wartime difficulties.[19] Costly worker benefits spurred such moves and aggravated the problems of the remaining entrepreneurs, leading to increased unemployment, commodity shortages, and rising prices. Soviet government moves to distribute land to many of these unemployed workers in response to worsening conditions apparently had the effect of increasing peasant resentment and friction between the two groups.[20] Thus, in keeping with shifting their focus to economic construction and mobilization issues by mid-1933, the party moved openly to acknowledge the impracticality for the soviet areas of many provisions of the 1931 labor law (leading to its formal revision in October 1933) and to counter the earlier demands for greater worker aggressiveness by pointing up the negative economic and political consequences of such "ultraleftist" policies.[21]

Labor Line Difficulties and a Turn to Moderation

Chang Wen-t'ien (Lo Fu), a leading member of the returned-student group, assumed direction of the CCP's propaganda department in Juichin in 1933, moving there from Shanghai. He also became a key member of the People's Commission for National Economy, formally organized under the soviet government at the end of April 1933 and charged with the task of developing the economy and countering the enemy blockade. In line with these objectives and in his role as party spokesman, Chang argued for a moderated labor policy in major articles appearing in mid-1933 in *Struggle* (of which he was the editor). In the first of these articles, he reviewed the impact of the 1931 labor law and presented persuasive arguments for its revision and for greater flexibility in its overall implementation.[22]   Chang cited specific (and probably extreme) examples of the "mechanical" and impractical application of the law, focusing on the problems that "by-the-book" interpretations created for middle (and poor) peasant hirers of labor and for master craftsman-apprentice and small entrepreneur-employee relationships.   He also hinted at the law's inapplicability to the fledgling state-owned enterprises. Chang stressed as a basic principle that implementation of the labor law should be in line with the fundamental interests of the soviet regime.   The latter, in turn, required maintaining a firm worker-peasant alliance and vigorously developing the soviet economy.   In a point-by-point analysis which drew on numerous examples, Chang argued that many provisions of the 1931 law, as carried out in union-negotiated collective agreements and labor contracts, had had adverse effects on both of these fronts.

Turning first to the agricultural sector, Chang enumerated examples of poor peasants employing youth workers who, under labor contracts conforming to the labor law, worked only four-or six-hour days (depending on their ages), were barred from heavy work, and received wages more than double those prevailing in the past. The unworkability of such an arrangement was proved by "common sense": either the peasant was forced to hire a number of such youths to compensate for their shorter working day at (for the poor peasant) an astronomical combined annual wage, or he refrained from employing younger people. These alternatives were bound to result in either peasant dissatisfaction or youth unemployment or both. While utilizing such poor peasant examples, Chang made clear that he was primarily addressing the larger problem of hired hands' wage and hour benefits as they impinged on broader middle-peasant interests. He insisted that the middle peasants, who now comprised a majority among peasant employers, should be treated as allies, not enemies. Apparently referring to Teng Ying-ch'ao's argument, he criticized those who tried to cover up these serious problems by suggesting that they sprang from a "backward peasant conscious-ness."[23] In pinpointing some of the more obvious and dire conse-quences of giving inordinate emphasis to labor interests and to the promotion of a proletarian leading core in the peasant movement, Chang merely articulated, more candidly and concretely than ever before, a problem that Communist policy-makers had been wrestling with for quite some time.

Chang turned next to the independent craftsmen and itinerant handymen, groups which had been regarded with suspicion in earlier labor policy documents. He observed that, despite a degree of apprentice exploitation on their part, the majority were essentially laborers and should also be treated as allies. Here he provided examples of labor contracts between master workmen and appren-tices that rigidly applied labor law provisions on working hours, holidays, overtime pay, fringe benefits, etc. "Common sense" again showed the impracticality of this sort of application: the result was master workers who could not afford apprentices and apprentices who lost their jobs and the opportunity to acquire necessary skills. In calling for more evenhanded regulations (a "reasonable" profit earned on apprentices could be considered a form of "tuition" for skills learned), he added that master workers should not be excluded from the unions, a point somewhat at variance with the usual party stress on "class unions."

Chang then took up the broader question of the development of the soviet economy. Here he brought up the effects of similarly unrealistic contracts on small merchants and entrepreneurs. In addition to excessively high wages and overtime remuneration, rigidly restricted hours, and paid holidays, he noted such employer burdens as the provision requiring three months' extra pay for employees joining the Red Army and the stipulations that compelled employers to pay full wages to workers who, on company time, attended soviet meetings or participated in other political or union activist work. He caustically raised the example of a T'ingchou shop employee who, as a result of a continuous round of such activity, had never done a single day's work for his employer yet continued to receive his full wage of twenty silver dollars per month plus other costly fringe benefits (including the New Year's double-wage payment).[24]

The consequences for this important sector of the economy were equally detrimental: many small enterprises were folding, causing economic dislocation and unemployment. Chang observed that while many of the employers who were shutting down their businesses and fleeing the soviet areas were motivated by antisoviet animus, the policies of the government and the unions toward them only provided the latter with further grounds for doing so. It was impossible, he contended, to build the soviet economy without fully utilizing private enterprise, and this required that the latter be permitted to earn some profit. Certain articles of the labor law were clearly unsuited to the small-scale nature of most businesses in the soviet area, particularly the 8-6-4 workday stipulations.

Chang painted much the same bleak picture in regard to the cooperatives. Full enforcement of the labor law by party and union leaders had given rise to serious economic difficulties and business failures in this sector also. Unless such policies were modified, all talk of developing the cooperative movement would be so many "empty slogans." The worker members of producer cooperatives should extend their hours, raise productivity, lower costs, and thereby strengthen their businesses, the ultimate key to improving their livelihood. Chang also called on workers in state enterprises to extend hours and reduce wages "voluntarily." In addition, Chang recommended that their enterprises adopt cost-accounting techniques, increase productivity, and cultivate a disciplined "Communist labor attitude." These latter points were later stressed much more forcefully in the growing war emergency of 1934.

These necessary revisions in the labor law, Chang concluded, would not only strengthen the worker-peasant alliance and the soviet economy but would also benefit labor by reducing unemployment. The current attitude, which he characterized as one of "let's eat up the capital and then we'll see," had precisely the opposite effect and was a reflection of the thinking of some "backward workers" imbued with "petty bourgeois consciousness."[25] Chang cautioned that even a revised labor law would have to be applied flexibly and should provide for a realistic assessment of the ability of individual enterprises to respond to workers' demands. All of this was finally coupled with warnings against right opportunists who would seize upon these difficulties to oppose the basic provisions of the labor law and who spoke of having to sacrifice labor interests to bolster the soviet regime. He deftly argued that unrealistic leftist demands played directly into the hands of such rightists, thereby obstructing effective struggle against this element.

In arguing against extreme labor demands and benefits on obviously pragmatic economic and political grounds, Chang touched on many of the dilemmas confronting the proletarian line in the soviet areas. It was considered axiomatic that the promotion of labor class interests through militant struggle was the key to effectively mobilizing and organizing this group and to the crucial objective of raising its anticapitalist class consciousness and activist political commitment—all deemed vital to ensuring labor's vanguard revolutionary role. Though it was true that the "vanguard" forces would ultimately have to be based primarily on the more advanced urban industrial workers, it was considered essential that the latter be able to establish close links and identify common interests with the emerging proletarian forces in the countryside. While labor policy pronouncements of 1931 and 1932 had taken note of some of the problems now explicated by Chang Wen-t'ien, these points had been wholly subordinate to the overriding goal of implanting an effective, and enduring, class line. A limited perception of the socioeconomic realities of the rural soviet scene on the part of the Party Center, still operating primarily out of Shanghai, probably further obscured the true nature of the difficulty. In any event, what we see developing by mid-1933, with the party leaders now firmly ensconced in Kiangsi, is a greater awareness of rural realities and at least a partial acknowledgment that an urban-oriented class line could not be mechanically transplanted to the soviet districts. Yet this by no means implied a jettisoning of the class line. It was rather an attempt to modify the more counterproductive aspects of anticapitalist struggle and at the same time to revitalize the drive for overall proletarian political primacy and organizational vigor; in this respect it was time to stress more sharply the class war in the peasant land revolution.

In June 1933, Chang Wen-t'ien published a sequel to his earlier piece, this time a two-part policy statement which dealt with some of the larger implications of the labor line he had expounded before.[26] The article began by affirming the central place of class struggle in the soviet revolution, extolling its violent and merciless character when directed against landlords and "counter-revolutionary capitalists," yet adding that such struggles could take more complex and peaceful forms as well. In elaborating this first point, Chang wrote that even though the soviet regime was, in political terms, a worker-peasant dictatorship, labor continued to be an exploited class economically in that capitalism still remained. Workers must therefore engage in class struggle for the improvement of their livelihood.

Chang then outlined the orthodox Communist class-struggle thesis: that only an ever-widening class struggle could improve labor's economic condition and further unite the working class in terms of a heightened class consciousness and a strong revolutionary commitment to the future move to socialism. To oppose the labor-capital struggle and the advancement of labor livelihood thus represented a right-opportunist, antiworker defense of capitalist and rich peasant interests. This stance, Chang declared, would inevitably undermine proletarian leadership and even hand its power over to the bourgeoisie. It was therefore undoubtedly "the present main danger."[27]

Having affirmed the validity of the standard Marxist formula, however, Chang went on to argue, carefully and rather tortuously, that the labor-capital struggle took a different form and content under soviet power than it did in the KMT-ruled areas. The ultimate aim in the latter case was the overthrow of KMT rule, while in the former it was the reinforcement of already established soviet political power. To confuse these two very different situations, to raise unlimited and unrestrained labor demands in the soviet areas, and to rely on force and governmental intervention to compel capitalist acceptance of worker demands represented an ultraleftist position of "some comrades" which would weaken, rather than strengthen, soviet power—a point already made explicit in his earlier article. Chang specifically noted the adverse effect of unbridled ("narrow guildist") worker demands on the peasant majority, for example, by creating shortages and pushing up prices of everyday commodities; the disenchantment of the peasants would undermine the worker-peasant alliance and proletarian hegemony would be forfeited. Again, his argument appeared to directly challenge the position outlined in Teng Ying-ch'ao's February article.

Chang took care to shore up both sides of the issue, however. The fundamental notions of labor-capital class conflict were not to be abandoned. He noted the continuing importance of a struggle orientation in negotiating contracts, advocating full participation on the part of the worker masses in the process. "Struggle committees" elected to press labor demands and the efforts made to expose the facts of capitalist exploitation and of basic class contradictions were also necessary measures. Yet the "backward" notions of many workers additionally required that this struggle for economic improvement be linked to tempering and educating labor; otherwise, labor was likely to undergo "petty bourgeoisification" *(hsiao tzu-ch'an chieh-chi hua)*. Chang here quoted Lenin on the "labor aristocracy" of the advanced capitalist countries; ironically, however, Chang was underscoring a different but nonetheless significant point: it was in the context of largely preindustrial peasant societies that the promotion of proletarian interests created a relatively advantaged labor class; this had the effect of widening the gulf between labor and the still mostly poor peasant masses. These issues, first confronted here in the soviet areas, were to be faced in more basic terms in the Yenan period; and they would surface yet again as the Communists drew in an increasingly substantial urban labor constituency during the 1946-48 civil war years.

Thus, according to Chang, while strikes remained one of labor's weapons in the soviet zones, there were alternative means to advance worker welfare and to discipline, unite, and educate the working class. He called for government mediation and arbitration in cases where prolonged labor-capital conflicts proved damaging to soviet political and economic interests. Such intervention should not always be for the purpose of forcing capitalist acceptance of labor demands; where necessary, it should also be able to persuade workers to make concessions. Chang lashed out sarcastically at leftist "verbal revolutionaries" who denounced this formula as compromising labor interests. In his view, "labor-capital compromise" *(lao-tzu t'o-hsieh)* that promoted the economy, jobs, and the circulation of goods was not a surrender to the capitalists but was rather an advancement of overall soviet (hence labor) interests.

Chang offered examples of some of the necessary accommodations to private enterprise. Soviet-area merchants who traded with the white areas were making greater supplies of needed commodities available at lower prices. In that they were attempting to counter the impact of the KMT blockade, such merchants should be given special dispensations and allowed to earn substantial profits. To wage an all-out anticapitalist struggle against them would be "stupid" and, moreover, a manifestation of Trotskyism. In addition, Chang noted that private capitalist investment in the exploitation of soviet mines and other resources had been thwarted not only by hostility on the part of capitalists but also by ultraleftist economic struggle tactics. The policy of "prematurely" liquidating capitalists had been a mistake, he asserted. While forcible means were an essential option in dealing with "counterrevolutionary" capitalists, for those abiding by soviet rules, compromise methods were more in keeping with soviet and worker interests.[28]

Turning to the class struggle on the agrarian front, Chang Wen-t'ien took a noticeably different tack. He issued a call for promoting the new Land Investigation Movement, one with sharply intensified class war aspects. Before examining in detail this extremely important new stage of the land revolution, which lasted from mid-1933 to the final months of the Kiangsi Soviet in 1934, we ought first to consider the continued evolution of the labor and economic policy line expounded by Chang in his May and June articles.

A September 1933 Comintern article by Wang Ming on the newly evolving soviet-area economic policies provided further illumination of the rationale for a modified labor-capital line.[29] It also showed that the position outlined by Chang Wen-t'ien, and the new economic measures being put into effect in the soviet zone, represented the official stance of the Party Center and had Comintern sanction as well. That the Comintern had conferred its blessing on these policies was further confirmed in a piece published simultaneously by Pavel Mif, the Comintern's leading China policy spokesman.[30] Wang wrote that the dire circumstances facing the soviet republic could not have been foreseen at the time of the First Soviet Congress in November 1931. The cumulative impact of war and blockade, the steady evaporation of special sources of revenue and supplies (e.g., confiscated property of class enemies, and supplies captured from KMT troops), and the problem of raising funds through taxation in a soviet economy already in precarious circumstances had all combined to create a new situation. The worsening financial condition of the soviet areas, it may be noted, was evidenced at this time in the virtual disappearance of silver money and its replacement by increasing amounts of depreciating soviet paper banknotes.[31]

Wang stated that even though the soviet area was now larger and more consolidated, its economy was still a backward agricultural one. He observed that this was in direct contrast to the assumptions and expectations of the 1931 congress, which had envisioned the expansion of soviet power to encompass numerous industrial and commercial centers. In light of the fact that this had not happened, the Party Center had been obliged to reassess the situation and formulate another series of economic policy measures.[32]   The factors necessitating a change were clearly perceived in negative terms by Wang Ming: the "backwardness" (from a Marxist perspective) of the soviet area, the failure to take major industrial centers, and the unavoidable realities of the wartime crisis.

Wang explained that it had been necessary to clarify misunderstandings of basic policies and principles among some party personnel, misunderstandings that had led to both left and right deviations.   On the left, he noted, were those who prematurely advanced socialist goals and pushed for "a life and death [liquidationist] struggle" against the rich peasants and their economy, a point also forcefully articulated by Pavel Mif.[33] On the other hand, however, there was a rightist tendency in the party which, based on the fact of the continued role of capitalism in the soviet economy, regarded the question of socialist transition as one for the distant future and thus completely ignored the struggle against the bourgeoisie, particularly the rich peasants (rich peasants were to be "opposed" but not "liquidated"). Wang delineated the three basic economic forms in the soviet area, starting with the capitalist forces represented by the rich peasants, middle and small merchants, handicraft factory (shop) owners, and independent craftsmen who employed labor. Next were the petty individual peasant and handicraft producers who comprised the majority of the population and included the now predominant middle peasant strata. Though small-scale commodity production of this second group was a major spawning ground of capitalism, it was not itself to be considered part of that capitalist economy. And finally, there were the socialist economic forces, comprised of state enterprises and consumer and producer cooperatives which, though still very weak, were the forerunners of all future economic development. Wang declared that, for the present, the soviet government would not "waste its strength" on what could not now be accomplished—ridding the soviet economy of capitalism—but would instead utilize the latter to the advantage of that economy.

Wang assailed both those who advanced "the theory of unlimited class struggle" in the soviet area and red labor unionists who advocated strikes as the principal means of defending soviet, as well as KMT-area, worker interests. At the same time, he reasserted the role of soviet unions in protecting labor's everyday concerns and livelihood and the importance of "suitable" forms of class struggle. Turning specifically to the 1931 labor law, Wang made much the same points as Chang Wen-t'ien had on the need for revisions. He noted that the new policy directives and resolutions of the Party Center spoke to the economic realities of the soviet districts and to its overriding military priorities. Wang's delineation of a party program for expanding agricultural and industrial production was fully in accord with the new economic construction and mobilization measures being adopted in the soviet republic.[34]

In regard to the industrial sector, Wang Ming pointed to the problems and discontents of craftsmen, artisans, and "independent laborers" (tu-li lao-tung-che). These groups were generally excluded from labor organizations and unions and their dissatisfactions frequently led to a negative or even hostile attitude toward the soviet government. Wang's concern vis-à-vis these elements was in keeping with his call to develop local private and cooperative handicraft enterprises and workshops, all of which were heavily dependent on the often self-employed skilled workers and artisans. These crafts-men generally worked with assistants or apprentices whose interests were protected by the labor law, usually at the expense of the employer. The ambiguous and blurred nature of "capital" and "labor" (and, in many instances, of "worker" and "peasant") in the small handicraft, artisan, and rural peasant household enterprises was, indeed, only tenuously related to the "clear-cut class line" stance of the earlier years of the soviet republic. These rural strata for the most part fell more readily into the Marxist "petty bour-geois" category (small independent producers and middlemen), who were supposed to be vacillating between the bourgeoisie and the proletariat, not becoming candidates for labor-capital adversary roles.[35]

The difficulties of fitting a labor mobilization and struggle strategy to the new economic and military priorities were evident in Pavel Mif's concluding guidelines: "Of course, the local [soviet] party and trade union organizations should develop the mass working class movement and carry on work in defence of labour. But this should be combined with the general economic conditions, with the interests of the Red Army's struggle." Not every conflict need lead to strikes; "there are many forms of struggle which can be used." Mif recommended that whenever the basic soviet economic and military interests were involved, government-employer-union mediation/arbitration procedures should take over.[36]

The revised labor law promulgated by the soviet government in October 1933 formally implemented the party's modified labor line, thereby conceding the law's inapplicability to a substantial segment of employed labor in the soviet region.[37] Seasonal labor hired by poor and middle peasants, small boat owners, small handicraft enterprises, and handicraft production cooperatives were exempted (pending the consent of the workers and unions concerned) from the provisions of the law and were to be covered instead by special regulations. Application of the law could be temporarily suspended during wartime and other emergency situations. Wage arrangements were made more flexible and could now include payment in kind. While there were only minor changes in work-hour provisions, such provisions no longer applied to the labor categories noted above.

The 1933 law also modified the union role in hiring and firing procedures and spelled out more fully the mediation processes for resolving labor disputes. It dealt more realistically with apprenticeship arrangements, allowing for a three-month training period (after which "adequate" wages would have to be paid) and wage increases based on seniority, skills, and productivity. It stipulated, however, that the work assigned to such apprentices had to be related to the skills they were to master. The new law reduced or eliminated some of the more burdensome employer obligations: for enterprises with less than fifty employees, the owner was no longer required to pay workers for time spent on union work; and severance pay for laid-off workers was reduced from the equivalent of three months' wages to up to one month's pay. In addition, provisions in the 1931 law that mandated continued wage payments to employees doing governmental work and a bonus equivalent to three months' pay for those joining the Red Army were eliminated from the 1933 law. While showing a greater accommodation to soviet-area realities, the new law reaffirmed the basic labor-capital dichotomy and the worker benefits and protections of the 1931 document. Though it was now acknowledged that the latter provisions could not be easily or widely applied in the "backward" and ailing soviet economy, they remained in principle the Communist model for the KMT-ruled urban centers. In addition they were still supposedly suited to the (rare) larger capitalists, merchants, and rich peasants in the soviet districts, as well as (ironically) to the few soviet-owned enterprises.

Regulations for the prosecution of labor law violators, issued with the October 1933 revised law, further highlighted the now more differentiated approach to the various employer categories and also demonstrated the soviet regime's continued commitment to labor interests.[38] The regulations called for graduated fines (or equivalent compulsory labor or detention) for violators of the labor law or of collective contracts. These ranged from minimal penalties (at least three silver dollars or three days' detention) for those employing no more than three workers, up to a maximum of at least one hundred silver dollars or three months' detention for those hiring more than seven workers and whose violation had affected all or a majority of their employees. Antiunion actions on the part of employers were also to be considered labor law infringements. Where state or cooperative enterprises were involved, violations were to come before the state labor or economic bureaus or a union-organized committee to resolve the problem. If these procedures were unsuccessful, these cases would have to go through the legal channels and punitive measures outlined in the regulations. Those employer categories not explicitly covered under the 1933 labor law's provisions (middle and poor peasants, handicraftsmen and boat owners hiring supplemental [seasonal] labor) were exempted from liability under these regulations for union-sanctioned noncompliance with labor law stipulations.[39]

Charting an Uncertain Course Between Left and Right

The summer months of 1933 evidently brought a movement for renegotiating that year's union contracts in line with the new approaches described above. From information available on developments in the city of T'ingchou, the new "temporary" contracts (to be revised again when and if business conditions improved) cancelled the 1933 wage increases that had been provided for in the collective contracts negotiated for T'ingchou workers in early 1933.[40] These mid-year modifications took a less rigid approach to work-hour and rest-day arrangements and exhibited an equally pliable attitude in dealing with the full array of labor law protective benefits.

As described by Ch'en Yün, the central soviet-area labor head, in a July report on the T'ingchou situation, the contract revisions required intensive discussion with and persuasion of the workers, evidently over the protests of unenthusiastic local union cadres.[41] Describing his role in the renegotiation of contracts for T'ingchou fruit trade workers Ch'en complained that the original 1933 labor contracts included numerous articles that had been mechanically copied from the 1931 labor law and the 1932 "struggle program" of the soviet unions. These identically written contracts had been produced by the union cadres without prior consultation with the workers and without taking into account variations in local conditions and the particular characteristics of the enterprises involved. As a result, Ch'en continued, it had not been possible to implement many of the terms stipulated in these contracts. He noted specifically the problems shop-owners had in attempting to adhere to the rigid 8:00 A.M.-4:00 P.M. eight-hour shift and the Sunday rest-day for their employees and in meeting unrealistic wage demands. The busiest times for many shops came before or after the eight-to-four shift; and the only alternative to closing down on Sundays was to pay the workers double wages for that day. Moreover, many shop-owners had fallen in arrears on workers' wages; a number of them had had to substitute government bonds (which they presumably had been obliged to purchase from the soviet regime) for cash wages.

Ch'en then recounted his experiences in drawing up the new contracts, which had attempted to resolve the above and other difficulties. He told of his intensive discussions with workers, undertaken in an effort to convince them to relinquish excessive demands. The outcome of these discussions formed the basis for new contracts which had proved acceptable to the employers involved. Describing one such contract, Ch'en reported that it had settled on monthly wages of twenty yuan (a reduction of ten yuan from the original 1933 agreement). And though the workday was held to eight hours, these no longer had to be continuous but could be selected to include other periods of peak business activity. This

arrangement in effect recognized the traditional Chinese rural shop
pattern of an extended but not necessarily uniformly pressured
workday punctuated by numerous breaks. The six-day week was to
be staggered; with Sunday no longer the designated rest-day, double-
pay arrangements for that day were no longer valid.

The new contracts described by Ch'en retained provisions for
worker supervisory committees, payment of sick-leave wages and
medical expenses (up to a maximum of three months), and for fixed
employer contributions to unemployment insurance, union expenses,
and cultural-educational activities. Employer obligations in these
areas, however, were scaled down from those contained in the 1931
labor law. Ch'en Yün emphasized that these contracts did not
include the full array of labor law benefits and protections, but only
those considered suitable and practical for the particular workers
and enterprises concerned. He added assurances that as business
improved for an individual enterprise, the union could demand partial or complete revision of the contracts; and he called on worker
vigilance to thwart capitalist exploitation of the current situation
("exploitation" that took the shape of layoffs and enterprise
shutdowns).[42]

Ambiguities in the soviet labor line, the result of conflicting
forces and goals, remained essentially unresolved in the latter part
of 1933. The moves to reduce labor benefits and deemphasize
economic struggle tactics in order to accommodate new production
priorities clashed with the commitment to strengthen labor's vanguard role, to intensify the rural class struggle, and to retain an
adversarial stance toward capital. This led, in turn, to further
debate on whether the main danger was from the left or the right.
Apparently in response to growing labor discontent over cutbacks in
the face of commodity scarcities, rising prices, and mounting unemployment, the emphasis came down on the dangers of right opportunism.[43] Already in July 1933 Chang Wen-t'ien had felt obliged to
point out that the criticism of leftist deviations should not be con-
strued as a "surrender" to the capitalists or an abandonment of
worker interests.[44]

In line with such considerations, Ch'en Yün himself, in a lengthy article appearing in August, stressed the importance of mobilizing the workers for active participation in and leadership of such major campaigns as the Land Investigation Movement and the Red Army expansion drive as well as soviet government bodies at all levels.[45] Ch'en observed that in correcting earlier leftist tendencies in the economic struggle area, the unions had veered to the right in ignoring everyday worker interests. They neglected the pressing problems on unemployment, food shortages, and the decline of real wages in the face of rising prices for scarce necessities. These difficulties were due not only to enemy attack and blockade but also to business interruptions and shutdowns by capitalists. The unions had performed inadequately in promoting welfare work and resolving workers' difficulties.

Ch'en claimed that union personnel openly reflected "capitalist thinking" in some areas by asserting that "workers now should no longer have economic struggles."[46] In signing new contracts, these unions often reduced workers' wages automatically, without regard to the specific circumstances of the enterprises involved (some of which were, in fact, doing well), on the mistaken notion that all contract revisions must begin with such reductions. Rightist tendencies, and particularly those that would ignore the protection of worker interests, were now "the main danger in the labor movement," Ch'en declared. The consequences would be union inability to mobilize labor for an activist leadership role in current major movements, which would forfeit the unions' opportunity to be "the most important pillar of the worker-peasant democratic dictatorship."[47]

Significantly, Ch'en returned to the problem of worker-peasant antagonism, which had been a matter of concern in party labor pronouncements during 1931. That such sentiments had apparently flared up again now, as the soviet regime moved to reduce labor benefits, is made clear by his observation that soviet organs were viewed by some union bodies as a "peasant regime" (nung-min cheng-ch'üan). Ch'en declared that this attitude had been openly expressed by the Juichin city labor leadership, which had taken a "worker-peasant adversary standpoint" *(kung-nung tui-li-ti li-ch'ang)*. Moreover, ACFL publications had "more than once" adopted an antagonistic tone toward the soviet government.[48]

Ch'en called on the unions to overcome bureaucratic inertia, apply maximum effort to protect worker economic interests, promote unemployment relief measures, oppose capitalist "assaults" *(chin-kung)*, strengthen basic-level government organs, and lead the economic construction and land investigation movements. He offered a delicately balanced formula on which labor contracts were to be based: the workers' demands, prevalent living standards, and careful assessment of an enterprise's capacity to pay. And while reaffirming the two-front struggle against both left and right deviations, he reemphasized, in closing, the right danger and exhorted the unions to stand at the head of the worker masses in striving for the latter's vital interests and in the battle against the KMT.

The stronger assertion of worker interests and of a firmer line toward capitalists seemed part of a complex response to the growing economic and military crises. While it was advisable to tamp down labor demands and benefits, the increasingly difficult situation of the soviet republic tended to escalate class tensions and to increase suspicions of capitalist economic sabotage and foot-dragging.[49] This in turn led to greater emphasis on raising proletarian awareness and activist identification with the soviet regime and on upholding labor's interests. This progression was clearly apparent in a December 1933 article in the ACFL's *Soviet Worker* which, returning again to the T'ingchou fruit trade workers, dwelt on their most recent experiences in labor contract revision.[50] In contrast to Ch'en Yün's July report, the December article advocated revising wage scales upward in the face of demonstrated improvement in local business conditions. Noting that the union had convinced these workers to "temporarily" reduce wages in line with earlier business adversity, the writer reported that the union had just negotiated a wage increase in response to a sharp upturn in the fruit business.

The ACFL paper declared that this was an example of dynamic protection of worker interests. Also noted were capitalist attempts to use current economic difficulties and the new KMT encirclement campaign as an excuse to carry out work stoppages and shutdowns, which created unemployment and privation. The example of a T'ingchou fruit merchant who secretly shipped his capital out of the soviet area—a "direct assault" on the workers—was cited. The merchant had been uncovered due to the workers' supervisory role and turned over to the soviet authorities for punishment. The article called for even more vigilant worker supervision to thwart similar capitalist plots.

At the same time, as pressures mounted in the early months of 1934 under the fifth (and final) KMT encirclement campaign, greater concern was shown for labor efficiency and production problems in the largely defense-related state enterprises in the central soviet area. According to Liu Shao-ch'i, the party leader apparently most directly involved in this sector of the economy, there were by 1934 thirty-three "national" (soviet-run) factories in the Kiangsi Soviet employing over two thousand workers and mostly engaged in the production of war materiel: munitions, uniforms, bedding, and other necessities for the Red Army.[51] Nym Wales, in 1937 interviews in Yenan with former Kiangsi state enterprise workers, was told that "wages were very high and Soviet factory conditions infinitely better there [in Kiangsi] than in the Northwest [the north Shensi base area]." Even so, she commented, the wage scales of these Yenan workers were "much higher than the average income of the local people."[52]

These "national" enterprises were now being pressed to increase both the quantity and quality of their output for the war effort. In major articles in the party press in March and April 1934 that exhorted these factories to improve their efficiency, Liu Shao-ch'i revealed the difficulties of creating a disciplined "industrial" labor force in the rural soviet region and discussed the efforts then being made to instill a "new attitude" among these workers.[53] It was evident from Liu's reports that these goals were to be accomplished by applying management, competitive production, and incentive policies derived from the Soviet Russian model.

In his March article Liu voiced alarm over production shortfalls, defective and often unusable products, accidents due to carelessness, and other problems. Not a single state factory could be considered well managed, he complained, a condition that went uncorrected by the state economic organs. Particularly in regard to the defense enterprises, there were serious problems with counterrevolutionary, gangster, and backward elements which resulted in sabotage, indolence, and work stoppages. Bureaucratic management methods had allowed this situation to persist without enforcing labor discipline; in addition, there was no evidence of production planning or delegation of responsibilities, and quality-control procedures were lacking. Liu strongly reaffirmed the authority of the factory head (within the framework and scope of the labor law) in all production and administrative matters. Elaborating on this point, Liu asserted that factory heads had the final word on wages, work hours, production quotas, personnel shifts, and on penalizing or firing workers. He added that before making such decisions, the factory head, in the interests of consensus and joint implementation, should consult with the factory party-branch secretary and the union head. In cases of disagreement, however, the authority and views of the factory head were to prevail.

Liu dwelt also on specific labor problems in the state factories: excessive absenteeism, tardiness, fraudulent sick leaves, and unauthorized breaks during work hours. These were evidently examples of a more informal, rural work-style that was unsuited to factory production and discipline. He called for carefully structured regulations on managerial responsibilities and authority and increased labor discipline; violators would be subject to wage reductions and other penalties. Liu took care to add that all such regulations must conform to the labor law and collective contracts and should have the approval of the union and the labor bureau.

Concentrating on the importance of raising labor productivity, Liu called for careful recruitment of the most activist and enthusiastic workers and party members to serve as "production shock troops" (sheng-ch'an t'u-chi tui) that would set a standard for the rest. Any extension of work hours should be completely voluntary, temporary, and restricted to the completion of specific tasks. Moreover, planning, cost accounting, and production norms were all vital to improved efficiency.

Turning to the wage system, Liu endorsed a piece-work arrangement in which payment would be geared to the number of products turned out, not to the time involved in producing them. He advocated reckoning wages on the basis of daily norms: those exceeding the target would receive additional pay, while those who fell behind would receive less. He outlined a bonus system for workers who adhered fully to factory regulations and labor discipline and who regularly met or exceeded production quotas. Alien class elements, "riffraff," and saboteurs among factory workers and administrators were to be rooted out.

In a follow-up article, Liu pursued the theme of fostering a "new attitude" among state workers, one which would reflect their special status as employees of the soviet government. He complained that some of the workers still acted as if state and cooperative enterprises were owned by capitalists. They exerted minimal effort, did an inferior job, appropriated supplies for their own use, and ruined public property. Liu declared that such "old attitudes" were aided and abetted by hostile elements who incited the workers to carry out stoppages and strikes. Age-old habits linked to the old society could not be easily or quickly eradicated; extensive education and determined struggle were required and the worst offenders had to be publicly denounced, expelled from the factories, or even imprisoned as "enemies of the people."

The themes and policies outlined in Liu's articles were reiterated in the soviet-area ACFL's 1934 May Day resolutions and by a congress of the state enterprise workers' union in July of that year.[54] The resolutions and tasks adopted by that congress were based on a political report to that body by Liu.[55] Though the congress characterized the workers of soviet state and cooperative enterprises as "one of the most disciplined and organized industrial proletariat and a model for all the laboring masses," it made clear that in their day-to-day functioning, these workers were something less than the fully dedicated vanguard force they were supposed to be.[56]

The concept of developing a "new attitude" on the part of labor was to come up again as part of the Maoist reassessment of class forces and policies in the Communist rural base areas during the *cheng-feng* (rectification) movement of the Yenan years. These latter developments, however, unfolded in a very different political context which moved decisively away from the perception of labor as the vanguard force in the base areas. Yet, in many respects, the seeds of Yenan economic and labor policies were being sown in the closing phases of the Kiangsi Soviet, the inescapable responses to the realities of a crisis-ridden and beleaguered rural economy and society. By the second half of 1933, the shifting focus to more broadly based and flexible economic construction measures, strongly promoted by the Mao forces, apparently represented a basic (if in some cases reluctant) consensus of the party leadership. It was thereby acknowledged that earlier attempts to enhance labor's leadership role through class struggle, linked to untenable demands and unmanageable benefits, had inevitably clashed with overall rural peasant interests, with the maintenance and development of a small-scale, nonagricultural, private economy, and with the production priorities and cost-accounting considerations of the modest state and cooperative sector.

Despite the growing recognition of these inherent problems, however, they were not to be resolved as the Kiangsi Soviet entered its final struggle for survival. The notion of proletarian leadership retained its dominant place, with the emphasis on labor's special status and a continued adversarial stance vis-à-vis local capitalists and merchants. Indeed, the developing Land Investigation Movement in the countryside at the time accentuated this line more than ever before.

The difficulties involved in affirming labor's clearly advantaged status under soviet rule while concomitantly pressing for greater moderation on labor's part were evident in Liu Shao-ch'i's report on the soviet labor movement to the Second National Soviet Congress in January 1934.[57] The report began by routinely taking note of the problems encountered earlier under the struggle line, the modifications made in that line during 1933, and the growing pressures on labor for greater contributions to the soviet economic and military effort. It soon became apparent, however, that Liu's overriding concern was the dualistic nature of the labor issue. There was, on the one hand, a need for pragmatic recognition of economic construction and military priorities and of the soviet economy's inability to sustain extreme labor demands. On the other hand, however, remained the goal of proletarian leadership, still linked to an enhanced economic, as well as political status.

Thus Liu noted the "extreme left mistakes" committed earlier in labor economic struggles, mistakes that had allowed wage and other demands to be met "without restriction." This had placed an intolerable burden on the small entrepreneurs, who thus "fell into a miserable plight." Since May 1933, he noted, such mistakes had been "generally rectified," as had been the error of "mechanically carrying out" the labor law.[58] Liu touched briefly on measures to raise labor discipline and productivity in state enterprises and drew attention to the pressures being placed on state workers to put in more than their required work time "on their own initiative." He also pointed to labor's subscribing at least two weeks' wages to a new government bond campaign for economic construction. (Such subscriptions were, in effect, direct contributions to the government; there had been a drive the year before to donate a previous issue of bonds back to the government without demanding repayment).[59]

At the same time, however, Liu pointed to the recent improvements in worker living conditions, lauding the effective work of the

unions in bringing workers under labor and collective contracts and
asserting that "on the basis of these contracts most of [the workers]
are receiving treatment higher than conditions stipulated in the
labor law."[60] He cited the now widespread standard labor benefits—
the eight-hour workday, the six-day week, paid holidays, annual paid
vacations of at least two weeks, and the full array of social insurance protection. He emphasized, too, the very substantial wage
increases over presoviet days, supplying a table of comparative
monthly wages (in yuan) for T'ingchou workers (table 1).

TABLE 1

Comparative Monthly Wages of Workers in Tingchow
(unit: yuan)

Trades	Wages before the revolution	Wages in 1933
Cakes and foodstuffs	2–10	28–32
Paper	3–10	31–35
Oil	3–6	12–18
Medicine	2–6	26–30
Cigarettes	3.5–7	30–36
Printing	5–15	28–36
Metalwork	6	14–18
Wooden boats	14	46
Dyestuffs	3–5.5	18–20
Oil-paper	2–5	17–20
Wine	3–6	18–20
Cotton cloth	2–10	31–35

Source: Liu Shao-ch'i, "The Trade Union Movement in Soviet Areas
during the Past Two Years," in CWLS, p. 50.

Liu stated that these increases had been duplicated in other soviet-area towns and further claimed that virtually all workers also received free living quarters. Monthly wages in the state-owned arsenal and mint ranged from 11 yuan to a high of about 32 yuan per month.

Liu reported a union membership of 229,000 for the central soviet area and neighboring soviet bases (the Hunan-Kiangsi and Hunan-Hupei-Kiangsi areas), with some 90 percent of all workers in the central soviet area in unions.[61] As part of the Red Army expansion and proletarianization drive, a Workers' Division had been formed, and the ACFL had set a goal of recruiting 20 percent of trade union members into the army. Liu pointed also to the growing role of labor in the soviets: worker representatives in provincial-level soviet congresses in some cases now exceeded the election-law requirement of 35 percent and this was true for some county soviets as well. Some 10 percent of all union members in the twelve counties of the central soviet area were serving in soviets or other government bodies, the majority of them engaged in "responsible work." One-third to one-half of the members of soviet executive committees at all levels were now workers.[62] Yet Liu also brought up the problems between the soviet and the workers on a number of important issues, saying that union branches had generally not "fully exercised leadership over and given support to the poor peasant associations." Among other shortcomings he cited the union movement's remaining inadequacies in fulfilling worker demands and safeguarding benefits. He acknowledged that the unions had "not yet aroused the revolutionary enthusiasm of the masses to the utmost extent."[63]

Though many of the points made by Liu seem hardly more than a pro forma expression of the party's labor line, they nevertheless illustrate some of the truly troublesome features of the class line in Kiangsi. How was labor's leadership of the peasantry to be effectively implemented when the former's "narrow" class interests often clashed with those of the peasant majority and of the soviet area as a whole? And, on the other hand, how was labor's "revolutionary enthusiasm" to be sustained and its class consciousness intensified when it had been necessary to curb the more militant and activist assertion of worker interests?

A policy directive to the Second Soviet Congress from the Fifth Plenum of the CCP Central Committee (meeting in Juichin on the eve of the congress), promulgated by the Bolshevik group,[64] provides a concrete example of the leadership's ambivalent approach to the problem.[65] At the same time that it emphasized economic construction needs, the need to overcome a critical grain shortage, and the need to encourage local capitalists and merchants, the directive reaffirmed the anticapitalist struggle, the full protection of worker interests, the rooting out of alien class elements, and the key foundation role of mass "class" trade unions.[66]

Mao's keynote report to the Second Soviet Congress reflected a similar stance. Speaking in his capacity as chairman of the soviet republic, Mao's report adhered to the guidelines of the Party Center and of its Fifth Plenum. Its exposition of soviet labor policy paralleled that of Liu Shao-ch'i's report, emphasizing the leading role of labor and the unions, the great improvement of worker livelihood (particularly since 1931), and the protections of the labor law, all achieved, Mao noted, through struggle against capitalists and rich peasants.[67] That Mao's primary concern was focused on the question of economic development, or, more specifically, on the role of broad mass mobilization and of cooperatives and small-scale private enterprise in effecting economic development, can be inferred from the fact that only the segment of his report that dealt with these issues finds a place in his *Selected Works*.[68]

The resolution on economic construction adopted by the Second Soviet Congress also indicated the presence of conflicting pressures. Though it emphasized economic priorities and necessities, it seemed preoccupied with the counterrevolutionary activities of merchants, capitalists, and remnant landlord elements in the soviet area.[69] It called for a determined crackdown against such capitalist offenses as price gouging, speculation, and business closures, instituting punishments that ranged from fines all the way to execution.[70] The same set of concerns appeared in the May Day slogans for 1934, which stressed worker supervision of the capitalist enterprises and opposition to capitalist shutdowns and which reiterated the call for full implementation of the labor law and for increased wages.[71]

These concerns, and the still strongly propagated tenets of the class line, were also evident in contemporary Red Army political indoctrination materials.[72] These were compiled under the auspices of the General Political Department of the Red Army, whose director was Wang Chia-hsiang, one of the leaders of the Bolshevik group.[73] These materials were aimed at promoting a proletarian standpoint in the Red Army and in countering "misunderstandings" among the red soldiers who could not see why it was not the peasants (rather than the workers) who led the army and the revolution.

The Land Investigation Movement

Undoubtedly the most striking example of the attempt to combine economic construction measures with sharply intensified class struggle was the Land Investigation Movement launched in June 1933.[74] This fierce struggle, directed against the remaining landlord and rich peasant elements in the countryside, sought also to promote a poor peasant revolutionary vanguard in the countryside (led, of course, by the proletariat) and to mobilize the rural masses to develop the agricultural economy and the consumer and producer cooperative movement.[75] Pavel Mif, writing in the Comintern journal in 1934, emphasized that in addition to its antilandlord, antirich peasant (kulak) character, the movement's purpose was to advance agricultural techniques, extend cultivated acreage, improve cultivation techniques, and increase yields.[76] It aimed also to mobilize fighters for the Red Army and to provide for them and their families.

The movement sought to uncover "disguised" landlords and rich peasants who had managed to avoid the consequences of the land revolution and had contrived to work their way into positions of influence and authority in the local soviets and mass organizations. Those identified as landlords were subject (under the provisions of the 1931 land law) to total confiscation of land and property; rich peasants would be deprived of their good land (exchanged for an allotment of poor land) and "surplus" property. The confiscated land, possessions, and implements would be distributed to the poorer peasantry, farm laborers, unemployed workers, and the families of Red Army men, while fines and special cash levies would go into the coffers of the financially hard-pressed soviet state.[77] At the same time, soviet institutions would be cleansed of these alien class elements. Through this means, the movement sought to mitigate rural economic distress and to develop the productive capacity and enthusiasm of these agricultural forces. Moreover, the retreat from a more aggressive class line in the nonagricultural sector served to concentrate the party's efforts more on strengthening proletarian leadership in the countryside, now an even more vital aspect of the soviet revolution.

In his careful study of civil government in the Kiangsi Soviet, Lötveit includes among the movement's objectives "class struggle, partial land redistribution, raising of funds, economic and cultural reconstruction, and military mobilization."[78] Yet, as Lötveit also notes, "the hard core of [the movement] was a class war," in which the farm laborers and other workers in the countryside were to be the revolutionary leaders, relying heavily on the support of the poor peasants.[79]

The heightened concentration on the land revolution seemed in keeping with the fuller recognition among the Kiangsi leaders that the agrarian sector was indeed the central core and foundation of the soviet movement. The Land Investigation Movement thus further symbolized the greater policy convergence that began to develop in mid-1933 between the Mao group and the Bolsheviks. The latter, however, in moving to such economic (primarily agricultural) development and peasant mobilization policies, clearly attempted to use these to advance class line objectives more forcefully. Mao's commitment to the broader mobilization and production aspects of the movement, based, as it was, on a more pragmatic view of the revolution, ultimately clashed with the Bolshevik leaders, who emphasized the movement's harsher, class war character. By the final months of the Kiangsi Soviet, the incompatibility of these two approaches would no longer be in doubt.

Party spokesman Chang Wen-t'ien had propounded the basic line and rationale for the Land Investigation Movement in his June 1933 articles on the new shape of labor and economic policy.[80] In so doing, Chang revealed the problems involved in implementing the dual developmental and struggle objectives noted above, particularly as these two goals related to the crucial middle-peasant stratum of the rural population.

Chang strongly reaffirmed the party's rural class strategy: an agricultural labor leadership, relying on the poor peasants and allied with the middle peasants, would wipe out the landlords and oppose the rich peasants. He noted that while the latter objectives had already been largely attained in the central soviet area, there still remained the important task of rooting out landlord and rich-peasant elements who had escaped the land revolution by hiding their true class identity and posing as ordinary peasants (in this way, some had even received land allotments). Some of these elements had "sneaked" into soviet and party organs and thereby continued to exercise authority at the village level. Chang thus declared that carrying on with the class struggle in the countryside was the party's "central task."[81]

Chang stated that it was necessary to distinguish classes among the peasantry, identifying brothers, friends, and enemies. The hired hands were the party's proletarian representatives in the villages; furthermore, on a national scale they made up an absolute majority of the Chinese working class. This observation again reflected the greater concentration on the peasant movement and on the corresponding need to build the party's "class base" within it. The agricultural worker masses, Chang continued, had to be organized and mobilized to exercise their leadership through struggle, with the hired hands' unions serving as the mass organizational "pillars" of the village soviets. These "pillars" were to act as the vanguard of the poor peasantry through the poor peasant corps. Chang complained, however, that both the union and the corps had only been superficially organized in the past and had yet to play their proper roles. The current Land Investigation Movement was bringing to the fore activist union and corps elements and, with these new cadres, was reconstituting many soviet government and local party branches cleansed of landlord and rich peasant elements. A "deeply penetrating rural class struggle," he emphasized, was therefore dependent on mobilizing agricultural worker and poor peasant forces. A tranquil countryside did not signify peasant contentment; rather, it indicated a stagnating situation in which the full objectives of the land revolution remained unrealized and the land demands and post-land-reform livelihood needs of farmhands and poor peasants remained partially unmet. Without escalated class conflict, unifying and raising the class consciousness of the latter two class forces—prerequisites to the future socialist revolution—would not be possible.

Having stated the basic line, Chang then focused on the thorny problem of the middle peasants, sternly criticizing those in the party who dismissed these peasants' feelings and demands as "peasant backwardness."[82] He reiterated that middle peasants were now the majority in the soviet area (many of them former poor peasants); to sacrifice or ignore their interests could only bring grief to the revolutionary cause. Even though this stratum of the peasantry had gained from and given its support to the soviet movement, its members were often swayed by landlord and rich-peasant elements who ridiculed their material aspirations and hard work on the grounds that the soviet government would ultimately deal with them as it had with the *t'u-hao* ("local bullies").[83] Chang wrote that it was up to the soviet government to reassure even the more prosperous middle peasants that they would not be subjected to land redistribution; they should be encouraged instead to "cherish" their land and make it even more productive.

In conjunction with this appeal for a firmer alliance with the middle peasantry, however, Chang warned against their "dual" character. Though themselves laborers on the land, middle peasants were also often speculators and exploiters who aspired to become rich peasants. Such tendencies must not be countered by force, but rather by education and encouragement to join producer and consumer cooperatives. These efforts notwithstanding, Chang conceded that "new-rich" peasants would inevitably emerge in the soviet villages and that these elements should not be treated as the rich peasant class had been treated in the land revolution; this would constitute a severe disincentive to middle-peasant production. The problem could best be dealt with by means of the progressive tax system[84] on the one hand (clearly less discouraging than land confiscation) and, on the other, by mobilizing and organizing agricultural labor in the struggle against the "old-rich" peasants. In this way, the laborers, as a constantly growing class-conscious force, could rally the poor and middle peasants to their side in the struggle for future socialist transformation that would provide the ultimate solution to the rich-peasant problem. The emphasis on fostering rural proletarian leadership was further evidenced in the new electoral regulations of August 1933, which stipulated that in elections for the basic *hsiang*-level soviets there would be one delegate elected for every fifty peasant electors, whereas the ratio for workers was to be one delegate for every thirteen electors.[85]

Yet, as Chang's exposition made clear, an intensified rural class war was at least as complex as the concurrent attempt to steer a modified struggle course between left extremism and right opportunism in labor-capital relations. The former objective called for promoting agricultural labor activism and organization, while simultaneously moderating labor's demands against the middle-peasant employer majority. Such laborers were to be more firmly directed toward land ownership (through the Land Investigation Movement) concurrently with the effort to raise their proletarian consciousness. And although class war against rich peasants required intensification, the more prosperous middle peasants had also to be reassured in order to stimulate production efforts. That these conflicting policy goals raised difficult questions was evident in Chang Wen-t'ien's attempt, in successive August issues of *Struggle*, to allay doubts expressed in regard to the rural class line projected in his June articles.[86]

Addressing first questions that pertained to the changing economic status of hired hands and poor peasants after land redistribution, Chang argued that in spite of such changes, these elements could still retain their original class standpoint, join the hired hands' union or the poor peasants' corps, and serve as the vanguard force in the agrarian revolution.[87] As to the sensitive problem of emerging "new-rich" peasants, Chang again emphasized the importance of maintaining careful class distinctions in these cases so as not to demoralize the middle peasants and thereby damage soviet agricultural output and wealth.[88] These were clearly the more outstanding of the difficulties and contradictions that plagued the Land Investigation Movement's various stages.

Mao, as chairman of the soviet republic and its Council of People's Commissars, had a major role in the initial phase of the Land Investigation Movement. He sponsored a number of key directives, wrote articles, and made reports to special conferences. These activities seem to indicate that Mao was indeed party to the new consensus that focused more directly on economic priorities, rural mobilization, and further intensification of the land revolution. At the same time, however, he was constrained to act within the framework of a sharpened rural class struggle line, a line which, as has been noted, conflicted in important respects with his own emphasis on agricultural development goals predicated on the broadest possible peasant base. It is noteworthy that Mao attempted to limit the movement's more extreme struggle tendencies and to stress its mass mobilization aspects. In so doing, he moved to define class categories more strictly in order to differentiate clearly between landlord and rich-peasant targets and to keep the movement from engulfing the more prosperous middle peasantry as well.

In an August 1933 summary of the results of the movement to date, Mao spelled out his own reservations.[89] As might be expected, the article began by acclaiming the great successes achieved in striking down class enemies, redistributing land, promoting Red Army enlistments, and advancing construction activities. Mao soon got to the point, however, stressing the importance of prudently investigating class and land status, of directly involving the peasant masses in this process, and of proceeding carefully on this basis to actual confiscation of land and property, which would also be carried out with the full participation of the masses. He seemed particularly concerned that middle-peasant interests be given adequate protection and that there be a clear differentiation between landlords and rich peasants. He cautioned against the indiscriminate application of "reactionary" and "counterrevolutionary" labels to rich peasants as a basis for total expropriation of their land and properties. Mao went on to stress the mass organizational aspects of the movement (adhering here to the party's line on the poor peasants' corps) and the importance of utilizing the enthusiasm generated by land redistribution to steer the masses into economic and cultural construction work, cooperatives, bond purchases, military mobilization, and so on. That Mao saw the protection of middle-peasant interests as the key to broad peasant mobilization was evident in his concluding warning that the violation of such interests was "an extremely serious danger" in the movement. Any "misconceptions about the rich peasants" could have an adverse impact on the middle peasants, and all "arbitrary behavior based on 'commandism' could be a very great menace to our alliance with the middle peasants."[90]

These concerns came up again in a review of the movement undertaken by the soviet government under Mao's direction in October 1933. It was then that the criteria for determining class status, adopted under Mao's leadership by a June conference on the movement, were approved by the Council of People's Commissars as an official government document.[91] These guidelines served to define the rural classes and to differentiate more explicitly among landlord, rich-peasant, and middle-peasant elements. A decision made simultaneously by the Council of Commissars dealt with the problems that had so far arisen during the Land Investigation Movement. This document stipulated that in cases where expropriation of land and property had been based on erroneous class determinations, whatever had been seized should be restored to the original owners.[92] These instructions (apparently also drafted by Mao) elaborated on how to determine class status and demonstrated, in Lötveit's words, "Mao's search for detailed rules in the class struggle."[93]

Thus, the documents adopted by the Council in October delineated in very specific terms the differences between landlord and rich peasant households and took note of a variety of special circumstances that called for flexibility. The directive additionally stipulated that well-to-do middle peasants (who were entitled to the same protections as ordinary middle peasants) could earn up to 15 percent of their total family income from "exploitation" (mostly the hiring of labor, the collection of small rents, and interest earnings) and, under certain circumstances (including family problems such as sickness, death, and inadequate labor power or natural calamities), even up to 30 percent, "if the masses have no objection."[94] The document noted that these well-to-do middle peasants (a "considerable proportion" of the rural population) had been treated as rich peasants in a number of localities during the course of the Land Investigation Movement and called for immediate rectification of this error. It warned against improper confiscation of rich-peasant property on the basis of erroneous "reactionary" or "counterrevolutionary" labels, and further remarked that the term "reactionary capitalist" had been "stretched so much beyond its proper limits that some commercial firms were illegitimately confiscated."[95] Limits were set on the degree to which the "surplus" properties of rich peasants could be confiscated; any attempt to go beyond such bounds would be considered an incorrect tendency to "annihilate" this class. The directive also differentiated between the compulsory labor required of rich peasants and the much more harsh assignment of landlords to hard-labor corps.[96] In an important provision intended to safefuard private mercantile interests, it was stated that property or wealth linked to the commercial enterprises of landlords or rich peasants was not to be confiscated, nor were merchants to be assigned to the hard-labor corps. Debts incurred to commercial firms as a result of business transactions were to be honored. Earlier provisions annulling all prerevolutionary debts of workers, peasants and poor people to landlords, rich peasants, or capitalists were not to apply to such cases.[97]

Mao's efforts at moderation and at "reversing verdicts" during the latter months of 1933 highlighted the difficulties of combining an intensified rural class war with broad mobilization and construction objectives. For example, Mao had observed in his August article that the land investigation process had stirred panic among the middle peasants, even causing some of them to flee to the mountains. He pointed specifically to the situation in the Juichin area, where some middle peasants had even approached the local soviet to request that their class status be changed to poor peasant since it seemed to be "dangerous" to be a middle peasant—only one step removed from a rich peasant.[98] The move now to curb excesses and redress wrongs undoubtedly permitted many "borderline" landlords and rich peasants to gain a reversal of status and recover their property. In some cases, local soviets apparently undertook to reverse what were presumed to have been errors in class determination that predated the Land Investigation Movement.[99] Restoring land and property that had been wrongly confiscated also proved very difficult, since those who had benefited from the redistribution were understandably loath to give up their gains.[100]   Thus the primary goal now of expanding a broader and more secure protective umbrella over the intermediate elements in the countryside and to limit and define the targets of struggle was beset with many difficulties and inevitably conflicted with the imperatives and priorities of class war.

The Central Committee's Fifth Plenum in January 1934 castigated Mao for his "right opportunist" and "rich peasant" line and sharply criticized the October decisions made under his supervision as an example of this line and as a violation of party policy.[101]   Mao was then apparently dropped from the Political Bureau elected by the Fifth Plenum and was later replaced as chairman of the Council of People's Commissars (though not as chairman of the central soviet government) by the Second Soviet Congress.[102]   The new chairman of the Council, Chang Wen-t'ien, quickly proceeded to reverse the October line and put the emphasis back on intensification of rural class struggle. A directive of the Council, issued under Chang's signature on 15 March 1934, called for reopening the Land Investigation Movement and criticized the October decisions for having opened the way for landlords and rich peasants to "counterattack" and to "recapture their previously lost land and property."[103]   It virtually forbade any changes in the status of those who had been classified as landlords or rich peasants before the Land Investigation Movement; reversals of status in decisions made during that movement were limited to cases where such decisions were being "doubted or criticized by the masses." The latter, however, was probably an unlikely occurrence, since many among "the masses" had been gainers from such decisions. The directive declared all those changes already made (presumably from October 1933 on) to be null and void. In those cases where land was to be restored to those who had been wrongly classified as landlords or rich peasants, the directive stipulated that land allocated to workers during the Land Investigation Movement could not be taken back. In an obvious attack on Mao's approach, the March directive inveighed against

"the substitution of 'class calculation' for class investigation, [and]
the substitution of percentage figures for class struggle."[104] And
while reaffirming the policy of alliance with the middle peasants, it
proclaimed that "unfolding the land investigation drive is still the
central task of the present. Right opportunism is the main danger
today."[105] The overriding demands of revolution as "the highest
manifestation of bitter class struggle" were plainly indicated by
Chang Wen-t'ien's call for a "life and death struggle between revolution and counter-revolution." Such a struggle might produce cases
of "injustice," but "this sort of 'injustice' is unavoidable in every
rebellion."[106]

The new phase of escalated rural class war was augmented by
a campaign of "red terror" against all "counterrevolutionary" class
enemies, a response to the increasingly desperate war situation, and
which was targeted principally against landlords and rich peasants.[107] It soon became apparent, however, that unlimited class
struggle had brought with it inevitably counterproductive consequences. By the end of June, Chang Wen-t'ien himself (whose pronouncements since mid-1933 had been virtually an embodiment of
the policy ambivalences of this period) called a halt to "ultraleftist"
excesses. In major articles written in June 1934, only months before
the final evacuation of the central soviet area by the Red Army,
Chang, though still affirming the party's class line, sought sharply to
curb what had become an indiscriminate policy of total confiscation,
mass conscription into hard-labor corps, concentration camps for
dependents, and even the physical destruction of landlords and rich
peasants.[108] Chang now warned that such policies only reinforced
the resistance of these classes and created a "united front" of landlords and rich peasants against the soviet regime; even more danger-
ously, they put these elements in "a favorable position to deceive
the masses." In terms reminiscent of Mao's October 1933 criticisms,
Chang stated that the ultraleftist trend would not only "create a
panic among all landlords and rich peasants but also create a panic
among the masses." Panic would allow the masses to be "deceived"

by class enemies; this could result in some, "primarily the masses of middle peasants," fleeing to the mountains, there to be utilized by landlord and rich peasant elements for antisoviet activities.[109] Chang significantly concluded that "only the correct implementation of both the class line and the mass line is the really revolutionary Bolshevik method. The revolution of the ultraleftists is a pseudo revolution, and gives a helping hand to the class enemy."[110]

It is apparent that by mid-1934 Chang Wen-t'ien was moving toward a position that was quite close to Mao's; and, indeed, at the historic Tsunyi Conference in January 1935, at which Mao finally emerged the victor over the Bolshevik group, Chang was evidently counted among Mao's supporters.[111] But Chang's attempt to link the class line and the mass line in June 1934 was no solution: the inherent contradictions between the two had been amply manifested throughout the Kiangsi years. It is true, as Ilpyong Kim has shown, that the Kiangsi Soviet period saw the emergence of mass mobilization techniques and organization that were strongly advocated by Mao. It is also evident that the outlines of many subsequent Maoist policies are discernible in the final Kiangsi phase, during which the soviet-area leaders genuinely tried to base their policies on the rural environment and to grapple with the economic and military crises that seemed daily to grow worse. This response was manifest in the move to tamp down labor economic struggles and shore up private enterprise; the attempt to strengthen labor discipline and productivity in state enterprises; and the promotion of the cooperative movement and agricultural development measures. But the mass line (as can be seen through its development in the later Yenan years) additionally required important changes in class content and strategies, changes that would prove indispensable to the development and implementation of the Yenan line some years hence.

The Kiangsi Soviet played a historic role as a major proving ground both for the Communist strategy of rural armed struggle and for a land revolution in the interests of the "poor and miserable" peasant masses. However, its more narrowly conceived class strategies, based on the concept of a "peasant war led by the proletariat," eventually became a major obstacle to broad rural mobilization and to the effective marshalling of the productive capacities of its small peasant, mercantile, and handicraft economy. In this connection, Wang Ming's advocation in 1930 of agricultural labor organization in the soviet regions comes to mind: adherence to a line which demanded a vanguard role for organized farmhands and a determined struggle against the rich peasants was seen as the true test of the soviet-area party's proletarian credentials.[112] Comintern directives supported this proposition, and the line was thus maintained through the final year of the soviet republic, culminating finally in the Land Investigation Movement. It was only the decisive defeat of those leaders still cleaving to a labor line that generated the full range of political, economic, and cultural policies associated with "Yenan Communism." Yet, despite Mao's emergence as the dominant party leader during the Long March in 1935, there remained serious challenges from the still powerful and Comintern-supported Bolshevik faction.[113] The issues dividing the two sides would not be thoroughly resolved until the party rectification movement initiated by Mao in the early 1940s, which brought the final defeat of the Internationalist group.

The impact of the Bolshevik leaders on the Kiangsi Soviet had been apparent on many fronts. The forward and offensive military line had sought to capture urban centers and thereby secure for the soviet area a more solid and reliable proletarian base. The land revolution, and particularly its final phase in the Land Investigation Movement, was intended to eliminate not only the "feudal" landlord class, but ultimately the "capitalist" rich peasant strata as well; the latter struggle was seen as especially vital to the advancement of proletarian primacy and consciousness in the rural areas. Despite the changes in the strongly asserted anticapitalist labor struggle line of the 1931-32 period that had been brought about by recognition of the socioeconomic realities and difficulties of the rural soviet regions, the ongoing and enhanced determination to "proletarianize" the soviets, the army, and mass organizations and to build the unions into the most important mass organizational pillars of the soviet regime remained a notable feature of soviet policy and created pressures for continued defense of labor interests and for a hostile class outlook toward local capitalists and merchants. As the Kiangsi republic girded for its final struggle against the KMT fifth encirclement in 1934, the class line sharpened further and was accompanied by expanded and harsher repression of "counterrevolutionary" enemies. As peril to the regime mounted, suppression in the soviets intensified. And this action undoubtedly served to increase active opposition to the soviets, as Chang Wen-t'ien acknowledged in June 1934. Such opposition by then encompassed not only landlord-gentry elements, rich peasants, capitalists, and merchants, but a major segment of the middle peasants as well.

In the final analysis, as Wang Ming had already concluded in September 1933, the "backward" soviet areas had not proven congenial to the effective promotion of the proletarian line, and the anticipated early capture of cities had not materialized. As new united-front possibilities began to open up in 1935 and 1936, prospects for a return to the cities as the centerpiece of Communist strategy offered new opportunities to the Internationalists to revive and develop the party's links to the urban labor movement. Ironically, this would be attempted not through intensified class struggle, but rather by means of an anti-Japanese national front strategy of class collaboration. The contradictions inherent in this new line and the obstacles it faced in the early resistance-war years from 1937 on will be considered below.

CHAPTER V

The Anti-Japanese National Front and CCP
Urban Labor Policy, 1936-44

As the CCP and the Nanking government edged toward a "united-front-from-above" policy in 1936-37 on the basis of national resistance to Japanese aggression, the Communists, now situated in their new base in northern Shensi, began gradually to modify their revolutionary class policies of the Kiangsi period.[1] While the land revolution continued in the northwest soviet area, the CCP at the close of 1935 made major changes in the way that policy was implemented vis-à-vis the rich peasants; the latter's property was now exempted from confiscation, "except that portion of it in feudal exploitation."[2] Through the first half of 1936 the CCP further modified its land policies, severely limiting the scope of further confiscation in a move to build the broadest possible anti-Japanese front. In another move reflecting the now more positive stance toward capitalist economy, the party stipulated in July 1936 that landlord-merchants, though still subject at that time to land confiscations, could continue to engage freely in trade.[3]

These measures, motivated by united-front considerations, represented a consensus of the Internationalist and the Maoist factions within the party leadership.[4] Ironically, the Moscow-based spokesman for the Internationalist group, Wang Ming, in keeping with his single-minded and unqualified commitment to the Comintern's new united-front line, apparently took a position somewhat to the right of the Mao-led Party Center in 1935-36 on the issue of moderating the party's land expropriation policies.[5] Under the united-front arrangements finally agreed upon by the CCP and

131

the KMT during 1937, the Communists formally abandoned their land confiscation policy and dropped the soviet and Red Army designations; the soviet area was to be reorganized as a "special region" of the Republic of China.[6]

It was in the context of an increasingly conciliatory united-front stance that the party moved to restructure its labor-capital policies also, both urban and rural. In the fall of 1936, Mao delineated what was presumably the current labor-capital line of the party in response to questions addressed to the CCP by leaders of the All-China Federation of National Salvation Unions.

> We do not confiscate the properties and factories of all big and small merchants and capitalists; we protect their enterprises and help them develop their business to increase the anti-Japanese material supplies of the Soviet districts. . . . Concerning the labour-capital problem, in the Soviet districts we have formulated the minimum conditions for the improvement of the living conditions of the workers; labour and capital have concluded agreements in accordance with the practical situation of their respective enterprises and all unnecessary strikes and sabotage are avoided. Former laws providing for superintendance and management of enterprises by workers have been repealed. The workers are advised not to press demands beyond the capacity of the enterprise. In the non-Soviet districts, though we support the improvement of the living conditions of the workers, we similarly do not wilfully intensify the anti-capitalist struggle. . . . While imperialism is intensifying its aggression neither the capitalists nor the workers can expect the improvement of their respective conditions. The joint interests of capitalists and workers are built on the foundation of struggle against imperialist aggression.[7]

To this statement Mao added, "Our slogan in the united front is: All parties and all classes, unite under the aim of fighting against Japan and traitors!"[8]

In a similar declaration in mid-1936 ("We are not opposed to the development of capitalism in China, but [are] against imperialism"), Mao had also noted that while the land confiscation policy could be negotiated as part of a united-front agreement, the "anti-Japanese program cannot be realized without relief to the peasantry. Agrarian revolution is of bourgeois character. It is beneficial to the development of capitalism."[9]

The themes advanced by Mao constituted a departure from an anticapitalist class line and from any overcommitment to labor's narrow "economist" interests. Mao stressed the mutual anti-imperialist interests of both labor and capital and the positive role of capitalism in the economy. At the same time, he continued to emphasize the importance of peasant mobilization through agrarian reform. The latter (whether in the form of land confiscation or the more moderate wartime rent and interest reduction policy), however, was now to be specifically directed at "antifeudal" aspects; rural capitalist forces (including the richer peasants who employed labor) were to be shielded from the full impact of these rural mobilization measures. It is important to note that while agrarian policy moved from confiscation to rent and interest reduction after 1937, the land revolution in the northwest soviet areas—renamed the Shensi-Kansu-Ninghsia (Shen-Kan-Ning) Border Region in the fall of 1937—had already been widely implemented.[10] In addition, in the early 1937-38 formative stage of the major Shansi-Chahar-Hopei (Chin-Ch'a-Chi) base area, a more revolutionary land program was effected in which the lands left behind by landowners who had fled were redistributed.[11] There was also the declared policy of confiscating the land of traitors and redistributing it to peasants who had little or no land.[12] These Communist policies, which also imposed heavy taxes and requisitioning of supplies on the gentry, in effect constituted a continued, if modified, agrarian social revolution and played a vital role in wartime peasant mobilization.[13]

The policy outlined above constituted a markedly differentiated approach to labor and to the peasantry. On the one hand, it stressed the need to moderate worker demands and protect capitalist interests; on the other hand, it gave strong support to the poorer peasants at the expense of the gentry. But this duality was not yet so clearly perceived within the party, nor was there full agreement on the role of the urban labor movement in overall party policy and strategy. Urban-centered forces remained important in the early war years, and the party leaders identified with them saw in the developing anti-Japanese united front a new opportunity to build a strong urban labor constituency and base.

Emergence of a New Urban-Proletarian Line

The political crosscurrents within the CCP in the period immediately prior to and during the first years of the war were reflected in the approach of the party to the labor movement and to the role of the movement in the developing resistance struggle. In the spring of 1937, for example, the party media strongly affirmed its support of urban labor economic struggles and carefully depicted such struggles (many of which were in fact directed against Japanese-owned enterprises) as significant milestones in the growing anti-Japanese movement. This was in line with the party's renewed attention to the major cities as primary centers of the developing national salvation movement, which, supported by the Communists, exerted strong pressure on the Nanking government in 1936-37 for internal peace and unity, democracy, and resistance to Japan. It also appeared to reflect the Internationalist view that the Communists should now return their attention to the cities and reinforce their ties with the working class, which was, once again, seen as the key national political base for the party's emerging united-front role in the resistance war led by the KMT. This was an approach most strongly espoused by the Wang Ming group,[14] and it had its inevitable ambiguities and ambivalences.

The depressed conditions in many enterprises in the early 1930s continued through 1935, with wage cutbacks and increased unemployment further aggravating the already difficult conditions under which Chinese workers labored.[15] The general economic picture apparently improved substantially in 1936 and in the prewar months of 1937, bringing a more favorable situation for labor. But such improvement by no means resulted in a significant amelioration of labor's lot. There was a partial restoration of earlier wage reductions and retrenchments, but these advances were largely cancelled out by increases in the cost of living in virtually all major Chinese cities after 1935.[16] Approximately half of the industrial disputes reported for the 1935-37 period led to strikes or lockouts that involved some 300,000 to 400,000 workers in each of those years.[17] In the majority of cases, the controversies centered around wages, worker treatment, working hours, and layoffs.[18] Many of the strikes were directed against Japanese enterprises, reflecting to some extent the growing impact of the anti-Japanese national salvation movement.[19] The National Salvation Association in Shanghai, for example, held rallies and collected funds to support strikes against local Japanese-owned cotton mills in late 1936.[20]

A major article by Wang Ming, written shortly after the start of the war and before his return to China from Moscow in late 1937, seemed clearly to express the urban-oriented, united-front point of view within the party. Wang focused on the party's new national role in the struggle for "the All-China democratic republic," stating this meant that the CCP "must devote tremendous effort to the education and organization of the working class millions," who, as "the most advanced . . . detachment of the entire Chinese people," were again beginning to take an active and open part in the anti-imperialist national liberation struggle. He noted that the Communists' efforts among workers and trade unions in the major cities had been "extremely weak in the previous period." But now, he added, "as a result of the growing class consciousness and organization of the working class and its activity and initiative, the mass influence and the base of the Communist Party grow and strengthen and the nationwide struggle against the Japanese aggressor will become more and more powerful."[21] Wang also noted that the majority of the CCP forces had been trained and tempered in armed struggle against the KMT: "Many of them are of peasant origin [and they] utterly lack experience in the struggle for the masses under conditions where there is neither a Soviet power nor a Red Army and have not the remotest concept of the working class movement in the big cities." The education of old party forces for these new conditions and methods of work "is a far from easy matter," he declared.[22] According to a Soviet Russian source, the Comintern had earlier criticized the "open-door" party recruitment policy, contained in the December 1935 Wayaopao (North Shensi) Political Bureau resolution on anti-Japanese, united-front policy, on grounds that it further diluted the party's miniscule proletarian base. The ECCI, this source states, expressed "grave anxiety" at the decision to admit into the party "all those who wished to enter regardless of their social origin, and continuously stressed the necessity of strengthening the proletarian nucleus of the CCP."[23] The subsequent wartime growth of the CCP, this Soviet source adds, came "exclusively from non-proletarian elements (peasants, kulaks, petty landowners, bourgeois and petty-bourgeois intelligentsia), and was accompanied by the strengthening of nationalistic tendencies in the CCP leadership."[24]

Other Communist sources reflected Wang Ming's orientation, stressing the opportunities offered by the new united front for urban labor movement work. One such account during the initial stages of the war described CCP activities as focused "primarily on organizing the broad masses" throughout China, and noted that

At the present time the Communist Party is giving special attention to consolidating its mass work among the workers and to extending the influence of the national united front to the trade union organizations. The Red trade unions are now joining the Kuomintang trade unions and the Communists are carrying on much agitation and explanatory work to recruit new members for these unified trade unions.[25]

The view that it was crucial to mobilize urban labor in order to develop the anti-Japanese struggle was reflected in a 1937 May Day editorial in *Liberation* [*Chieh-fang jih-pao*], the CCP's journal in Yenan, and was further amplified in a major article in the following issue.[26] The May Day commentary focused on a few key points. Through its recent anti-Japanese strike actions, the working class had manifested its "vanguard role" in the resistance struggle. The task of involving the working masses even more effectively in the cause of national liberation required an improvement in their miserably low living standard; thus worker demands for wage increases were just, and the exploiters who insisted that "workers eat less and work more" should be resolutely denounced by all. The editorial further recommended that the (Nanking) government extend full democratic freedoms, including the workers' right to organize and that the labor unions, in striving for the common goal of national salvation *(ch'iu-kuo)*, should become unified, democratized, and genuinely representative of workers' interests. Only in this way could the working class fully develop its potential and exert its great strength in the anti-Japanese struggle. The Chinese working class, the commentary concluded, tempered by its incomparably complex and difficult experiences, had now "taken up the great historic mission of national liberation leadership." While the level of rhetoric in these and subsequent assertions of labor's leading or vanguard role in the resistance struggle was undoubtedly high, such statements reflected (as their context made clear) a stronger labor-oriented standpoint, not merely the ritual adherence to orthodox political formulas.

The subsequent article, in elaborating at great length on those points, was revealing of the problems the party faced in pressing for a labor mobilization policy, and it pointed up particularly the difficulties involved in supporting the urban strike movement within the context of the party's new united-front policy.[27] Again there was stress on the working class as a central element in securing a victory in the impending resistance war. The united strike of some 10,000 workers during the winter of 1936-37 against Japanese-owned cotton mills in Shanghai and Tsingtao was cited as a key example of a politically significant anti-Japanese action, despite the fact that the strike focused on purely economic issues. That struggle, the article stated, had sparked the strike movement of the early spring of 1937, which included a citywide strike against more than 130 silk factories in Shanghai. The article clearly indicated that these strikes were directed not only at the Japanese, but also at other foreign enterprises and at Chinese firms as well. Chinese-owned silk mills, in fact, were major strike targets at that time.

The workers, it was emphasized, acted in simple "self-defense" in these strikes: they were responding to unjustified dismissals, refusals of severance pay, lockouts, employer and police violence, etc. The article also stressed that in many cases, including that of the over 15,000 striking silk workers, the strikers acceded to the (KMT) authorities' promises of mediation and pleas to "take the whole situation into account" and, "enduring their pain, returned to work" (jen-t'ung fu-kung).[28]

The writer then drew some broader conclusions: the workers had shown their capacity for united action for common interests; the strikes had resulted in the emergence of many new workers' organizations; the workers' conscious defense of their class interests had disproved allegations of planned Communist instigation of these struggles; and the widespread sympathy and support for the strikers, especially from national salvation groups of various circles, showed that the strikes were in fact united-front actions with national support. Thus, despite the oppression and exploitation they suffered at the hands of both foreign and Chinese capitalists, the workers were in fact fighting for national unity and resistance to Japan. The article buttressed this view by pointing again to the modestness of the workers' demands, their readiness to negotiate, and their reluctance to resort to strikes. The problem, therefore, was not that the workers sought to destroy newly developed Chinese enterprise, but rather that the capitalists' intransigence obstructed the development of the national united front. And though the workers had suffered greatly at the hands of the KMT authorities, given the current need "to oppose Japan and save the country we should let bygones be bygones."[29] The workers had shown their sincere attitude by conforming to legal procedures: they petitioned (ch'ing-ch'iu) the appropriate government and union authorities and respected and accepted government mediation (t'iao-chieh). The article pointed out that since the workers' struggle clearly adhered to the goal of national salvation, the KMT authorities should in turn be reasonably responsive to the workers, help them improve their livelihood, and, most importantly, support them in strikes against Japanese enterprises.

The article went on to complain that such help had not been forthcoming. The government had failed to counteract the uncooperative attitude and coercive tactics of the capitalists. Only the most limited worker demands had been granted, and wage increases generally had been refused; the strikers were often subjected to repressive measures, sent back to work, and warned against further strike actions. Under these circumstances, it added, the government slogan of "labor-capital sincere cooperation to achieve joint prosperity" was truly difficult to comprehend.[30] While not advocating a clash between class interests and national liberation, "we resolutely oppose the capitalists' use of the national crisis to sacrifice the interests of the working class."

Declaring that the current workers' struggle was also a rehearsal for full-scale war against Japan, the article pointed to the role played by the big anti-Japanese textile strike in propelling the KMT onto the correct path of resistance. In outlining Communist labor policies for the future, the writer stressed the need to work through the existing legal union structure and to use legal methods of struggle and avoid counterproductive, "strong-arm" tactics. Since the workers' struggle was itself part of the process of constructing a national resistance bastion, unity and cooperation required that the workers' "aspirations" (hsi-wang) not be excessive. It was hoped that the KMT authorities would recognize the importance of the fullest involvement of the worker masses in the development of a powerful resistance effort and how this goal was linked to improvement of the workers' livelihood. Mobilization of the workers was crucial, the article concluded, and it appealed to the Nanking government to take steps to make such mobilization possible. Freedom of action for the workers would not destroy the united front; on the contrary, the united front would be reinforced and better able to confront the coming war.[31]

The Chinese labor movement did undoubtedly play a concrete role in the complex interplay of forces and events that led the Nanking government toward the 1937 united front with the Communists. But the notion that the CCP could and should again develop a strong and politically effective urban labor base which could function, under overall KMT leadership, as an instrument for moving Nanking toward greater democracy and firmer resistance to Japan had contradictory elements and severe limitations, as the Liberation article summarized above illustrated.

Any attempt to mobilize and politicize labor without strongly identifying with and supporting the workers' fundamental economic interests and demands would be self-defeating. Yet these worker demands inevitably led to confrontation with KMT authorities and the Chinese business class—political and economic forces the CCP sought to unite and cooperate with in the resistance struggle. It was also unclear to what extent these "economist" labor strikes and disputes (even those directed at Japanese enterprises) could be interpreted as or raised to the level of national salvation actions. On the other hand, a policy that supported these struggles while simultaneously attempting to place them entirely within the national salvation framework led to an ambivalent stance. Though the CCP endorsed labor demands, it at the same time advised workers to seek satisfaction primarily through legal channels and arbitration, with appeals to mutual goodwill and the shared objectives of the liberation struggle. This put the CCP in the impossible position of vying for labor's support through defense of its interests and simultaneously urging conciliation and compromise in a situation where political and economic power remained in the hands of those reluctant to grant significant concessions (as the spring 1937 silk-mill strikes amply demonstrated) and who could, as the Communists acknowledged, exploit a conciliatory united-front position to deny the legitimate aspirations of the hard-pressed workers.[32]

Moreover, given the KMT's penchant for viewing worker struggles and rank-and-file activities as tending to enhance leftist and Communist influence, it was even less likely that labor would be given the freedom of action, the organizational opportunities, and the satisfaction of their basic interests so necessary for full and effective mobilization in the anti-Japanese struggle. The fact is that the labor movement in the Nationalist-controlled areas remained under generally close KMT organizational control during the wartime period. The China Association of Labor (CAL), set up by the government in 1935 under the jurisdiction of the Ministry of Social Affairs, became the formal representative and spokesman for all labor groups in the country during the war years. In the early united-front period, the CAL invited only one Communist representative to join its Executive Committee of thirty-one, on behalf of the unions in the Shen-Kan-Ning Border Region.[33] Though the laboring population of Shanghai assisted in many ways in the determined and heroic three-month defense of the city against Japanese attack in 1937, the workers were neither armed nor organized into military units by the distrustful KMT authorities.[34]

The struggle for Shanghai served to accentuate (as did Communist efforts the following year to mount a defense of Wuhan) the Comintern-Internationalist focus on the role such major centers of industry and the proletariat were expected to play in the developing resistance war. A Comintern report on the Shanghai struggle characterized the city as "China's nerve center" and as the long-established heart of the labor and national liberation movement. The early (1920s) labor, Communist, and national liberation movements "had acquired a mass character only when the Shanghai proletariat, Shanghai intellectuals, Shanghai handicraftsmen, coolies and apprentices joined them," the report declared. "Shanghai has played and continues to play the same leading role in the struggle of the Chinese people against the Japanese plunderers."[35]

But the Communist assertions in 1937 that the working class was the primary vanguard force in the liberation struggle were clearly unrealistic, not only because of the nature of KMT control, but also because the major industrial cities were among the most exposed and vulnerable targets of Japanese attack.[36] All were to fall into Japanese hands by October 1938, little more than a year after the outbreak of war.

Following his return from Moscow in late 1937,[37] Wang Ming became head of the party's United Front Work Department and of the CCP's Yangtze Bureau and served as the key Communist representative at the temporary national capital at Hankow until the city fell to the Japanese in Ocober 1938.[38] In these capacities, Wang wielded considerable influence in the party's military and political affairs in the Yangtze area. The Yangtze Bureau's hand was keenly felt in the New Fourth Army, organized by the Communists (under authorization of the National government) in December 1937 to wage mobile war against the Japanese on the periphery of the great cities of the lower Yangtze valley.[39] In line with the strong united-front orientation of the Yangtze Bureau, the New Fourth Army in this early wartime period carefully operated within the parameters of united-front policy and coordinated its activities with those of Nationalist elements in the area.[40] The New Fourth Army did not implement the CCP's rent and interest reduction policies, nor did it attempt to establish Communist base areas.[41] The united-front outlook of the New Fourth Army at this time had a decidedly urban and labor orientation. Thus, Yeh T'ing, commander of the New

Fourth Army until his capture in the KMT's January 1941 attack on the army's headquarter detachments (the South Anhui Incident), stated in a 1938 Hankow interview that industrial workers from Shanghai comprised more than half of the nearly one thousand students enrolled in the army's Military and Political Academy—the source of the army's future officers and political cadres.[42] A Hankow-based Communist dispatch from this period declared that the New Fourth Army was "said to be slowly converging upon the Shanghai area in three columns," and that this army had "now become the symbol of resistance against the Japanese in the Shanghai-Nanking area," just as the Eighth Route Army had in the northwest.[43]

Under Wang Ming and his close political ally, Po Ku (Ch'in Pang-hsien), the Yangtze Bureau sought in 1938 to build a strong Communist political base in the Hankow area and to mobilize the masses for the city's defense—moves largely thwarted by the KMT.[44] In a June 1938 article written jointly with Chou En-lai and Po Ku, Wang Ming asserted both the feasibility and importance of defending Wuhan (the Hankow-Wuchang-Hanyang tri-city complex) by using the Republicans' two-year ongoing defense of Madrid in the Spanish Civil War as a model.[45] Outlining a program of mass mobi-lizational and economic measures, the article declared that the Wuhan workers and the Chinese army could successfully defend the city in the manner of their "Spanish brothers."[46] Po Ku, in a July 1938 interview with Edgar Snow, emphasized the importance of worker recruitment, both for the New Fourth Army and for the expansion of the party's ranks in Hankow. He stated that among new party recruits in Hankow, forty percent or more were factory or other industrial workers.[47] He stressed the need to attract workers to the New Fourth Army areas. "This is one of the most important tasks before us," he added. "We must have trained workers in our districts."[48] Snow further reported that "on this point Po Ku con-ceded that a preponderance of students, petty-bourgeois in back-ground, among new Communist party recruits, made it difficult to maintain the labor point of view and interests."[49]

From late 1938 onward, following the loss of Hankow and the shift of the National government's wartime capital to Chungking, the influence of the Wang Ming group steadily eroded, the final eclipse of their power coming in the wake of the New Fourth Army (South Anhui) Incident of January 1941.[50] Wang's waning power had become apparent earlier, in an address he delivered at the May 1940 opening of the Mao Tse-tung Young Cadre School in Yenan. Wang's effusive praise of Mao as party leader and creative theoretician and revolutionary, and as the architect of the guerrilla war strategy and correct united-front policies, seems in the nature of a self-criticism of Wang's own wartime line.[51] In any event, the South Anhui Incident proved a stunning military and political blow to the Internationalist faction, fatally undermining both its united-front political stance and its military base in the New Fourth Army. An administrative reorganization of the CCP following the important Sixth Plenum of the Central Committee in November 1938 had already restricted Wang Ming's authority to a new South China Bureau responsible only for dwindling party interests in the KMT areas.[52] Following the New Fourth Army Incident, which resulted in the killing or capture of the New Fourth's leadership elements, the army was reorganized under a new Central China Bureau headed by Liu Shao-ch'i, who was to emerge as Mao's principal political lieutenant and spokesman.[53] Under Liu's direction, and in a new climate of greatly escalated KMT-CCP friction, the New Fourth (now operating north of the Yangtze) followed a much more activist strategy, promoted peasant mobilization through rent and interest reduction campaigns, and began establishing local Communist administrations.[54]

The views of the Wang Ming faction found expression during the 1938-40 period largely through the pages of the party's *New China Daily* [*Hsin-hua jih-pao*], which was inaugurated in December 1937 in Hankow and moved on to Chungking after Hankow's evacuation. During those two years, the newspaper served in good part as the organ of the Wang Ming-Po Ku party forces in Hankow and Chungking.[55]

Wang Ming's continuing labor orientation was strongly underlined in a lengthy May Day article he wrote for *New China Daily* in
1938.[56] In it he outlined the party's three major tasks for bringing
about the working class's vanguard role in the resistance war. The
first of these was to mobilize labor for a more active part in the war
effort. Wang stressed the important role workers had played in the
political, economic, and military aspects of the anti-Japanese movement since 1931, and particularly in the resistance war since July
1937. He urged unemployed workers and staff personnel to join the
armed forces in large numbers, especially the modernized branches
(tanks, motorized units, artillery, air force), where their production
experience and skills could be effectively transferred to the mastery
of necessary military techniques. Wang was clearly referring here
to the Nationalist forces, not the Communist-led guerrilla units.
Stressing also the support role of labor in production and transport
work, he declared that through all the above means the proletariat
could prove itself the most capable, courageous, and conscious
vanguard force in the resistance cause.

The second major task was to work on improving the workers'
living standards. Wang complained that, despite the fact that labor's
work load and hours had increased during the war, there had been no
improvement in wages and worker treatment. Only when the situation had reached the breaking point, he added, had labor raised
demands in this respect. He castigated the capitalists for using the
war as an excuse to avoid improving workers' livelihood and argued
that only when adequately fed, clothed, and rested could labor's
productive energies come into fuller and more efficient play. While
agreeing that substantial advances would have to await the war's
end, Wang insisted that some amelioration was vital if labor was to
be fully enlisted in the resistance effort. On this issue, as has
already been noted, Wang Ming reflected the dilemmas and weaknesses of his own labor-based united-front strategy.

In order to achieve these twin objectives of labor mobilization
and welfare, Wang emphasized the overriding importance of the

third party task: building a powerful and broadly based national labor organization. On this score, he sharply countered the view that the Chinese proletariat had only a limited strength of one or two million. There were not only some three million industrial workers, he asserted, but also nine or ten million handicraft workers, ten to fifteen million agricultural laborers, and one million staff personnel, all of whom, as wage earners, were qualified to join the projected labor federation. He called for an end to the former division between the KMT yellow unions and the Communist red unions and issued a summons to organize an All-China General Labor Union (*Chung-hua ch'üan-kuo tsung chih-kung hui*) on the basis of national unions for each industry or enterprise.[57]

That Wang sought to build a powerful Communist political base through a revitalized and broadened labor movement (which would serve as the party's primary leverage within the KMT-led united front) was evident. He apparently continued to press for this line of urban labor mobilization at the November 1938 Sixth Plenum; this view was opposed by Mao, who consolidated his political leadership at the expense of Wang Ming at that plenum.[58] Wang's proposals notwithstanding, only the KMT-controlled CAL (with some Communist input) was able to function in wartime Nationalist China, and it was not until August 1948, a full decade later, in an entirely different context and circumstances, that such a new national labor federation was formed under Communist auspices on the basis of the liberated areas' labor unions. Not surprisingly, the labor movement of the major cities (still then in KMT hands) played only a peripheral role in these developments.

The Party Center's urban policy line in post-1938 China—a line which evidently still continued to some extent to be influenced by the views of the Wang Ming group—was outlined in 1939 in a CCP Central Committee May Day directive on the labor movement.[59] While reiterating the theme that the Chinese working class had always been and was still the vanguard of the national liberation movement (as was evidenced by the workers' wartime sacrifices, burdens, and contributions), it conceded that the workers' role in the resistance war had not attained expected levels. Repressive policies, capitalist intransigence in many areas, and lack of worker unity, which stemmed in good part from inadequate party work among labor, were to blame for this unhappy circumstance. To organize the workers and fully develop their strength was one of the most important prerequisites for victory. The directive reaffirmed the party's united-front approach toward all anti-Japanese parties and workers' groups. It offered "friendly assistance" to all unions under anti-Japanese leadership, and stressed the importance of improving workers' political, economic, and cultural status in order to enlist their fullest participation in the war and national construction effort.

In regard to enemy-occupied cities, the directive rather vaguely called on the party to use "all methods and means" to strengthen its work among industrial workers and to prepare for the final expulsion of the Japanese from China. As for any other cities which might soon fall to the Japanese, the party should mobilize the workers to join the rural guerrilla war and prepare a small nucleus of party members to carry on work among the masses.

The directive further called on party organizations to establish factory branches in the Communist base areas, expand worker membership, absorb into the party politically conscious workers who had left their Japanese-occupied or threatened factories and come to the countryside, and educate and develop worker cadres for appropriate party work. Unions should be organized wherever possible and should form close relations with the peasants and all anti-Japanese organizations.[60] Thus, while continuing to affirm the party's urban labor role, the growing shift in emphasis to the base areas' labor movement was evident.

During the two-year period from the fall of Canton and Hankow in October 1938 to the formal Japanese recognition of Wang Ching-wei's puppet Nanking government on 30 November 1940—a period during which the Communists were particularly anxious about the possibility of an overall peace settlement between the KMT and Japan—the CCP also addressed strong anticapitulation, anti-collaboration appeals to the workers in the occupied areas (where some ninety percent of China's former industrial capacity was now located) and to those in Nationalist China. Meanwhile, in occupied Shanghai, moves to organize labor were made by the Japanese (who were interested in promoting labor actions against remaining non-Japanese foreign enterprises) and the Wang Ching-wei group (who were primarily seeking their own political consolidation). Various workers' organizations were formed and these merged in June 1939 into a General Labor Union, under whose jurisdiction union organizational activities proceeded. This body was superseded by the Labor Movement Adjustment Committee in December 1940, which was established under the Wang Ching-wei regime's Ministry of Social Affairs to oversee and direct the labor unions set up in the various industries in the Shanghai area.[61] As was true of the KMT in the decade before the war, the Wang Ching-wei group, in building an organized labor base under its political control, found it necessary to make some economic concessions to labor in the process. If wage increases were secured through the actions of this labor movement, a report on the Shanghai labor scene observed, "the workers would then be bound in gratitude to the group which organized the struggle," thereby strengthening the latter's political hold over the labor community.[62] A Communist report from Chungking at the end of 1939 asserted, however, that the workers in Japanese-controlled factories in occupied Shanghai had not submitted to the enemy but were secretly organized in small groups which carried on activities and contributed funds for the resistance war.[63] And reports from the New Fourth Army, operating in the vicinity of the occupied cities of the lower Yangtze Valley (the most important of which was Shanghai) in the early war years, told of links and support from "secret cells" of workers and intellectuals in those cities.[64]

In July 1939 on the second anniversary of the war, Liu Shao-ch'i (who continued to be a leading labor spokesman for the

Women factory workers in Wu Ch'i Chen, north Shensi, in
1936. (Edgar Snow Collection, courtesy of Lois Wheeler
Snow.)

Internationalist faction leader, Po Ku and Wang Ming, in the 1930s. (Edgar Snow Collection, courtesy of Lois Wheeler Snow.)

Liu Shao-ch'i in the 1930s. *(China Pictorial,* Peking.)

Chou En-lai and his wife, Teng Ying-ch'ao, with Edgar Snow in Wuhan, 1938. (Edgar Snow Collection, courtesy of Lois Wheeler Snow.)

The "Chu-Mao" CCP leaders: Chu Teh (left) and Mao Tse-tung, in
north Shensi, 1936. (Military Museum, Peking.)

Border Region labor head, Teng Fa, in north Shensi, 1936. (Edgar Snow Collection, courtesy of Lois Wheeler Snow.)

Labor leader, Liu Ch'ün-hsien, in north Shensi, 1937. (Courtesy of Helen Foster Snow.)

PLA troops entering Shanghai, 25 May 1949. (Museum of Revolutionary History, Peking.)

party in these years) addressed an open letter to Chinese workers on the "serious crisis" in the anti-Japanese war.[65] Liu stressed the essential role of worker leadership in the mounting of an effective opposition against moves toward a compromise peace and a concomitant new anti-Communist upsurge throughout China. Here again, particularly in the context of the deteriorating united front, the appeal to the workers to unite, organize, and actively carry out these tasks brought endorsement and encouragement for defense of labor interests against capitalist exploiters, though linked with a call for labor-capital unity against pro-Japanese elements.

Compromise and capitulation to Japan, Liu stated, would impose even greater sacrifice and hardship on the workers, and for a far longer time than would continued resistance. He exhorted the working class to stand fast and to "make efforts many times greater than before." He called on the workers to oppose all capitulationist ideas and activities, to develop their independent role and become ideologically and organizationally stronger, and to rally the masses for more determined resistance. The working class, he added, "must enlarge its vision," shoulder its historic responsibilities, and "overcome the narrow guild thinking carried forward from the old society."[66]

In taking on these vital tasks, Liu continued, "the working class must also protect their own rightful interests for survival" and resist selfish capitalists who "disregard the crisis of the state and the people and the hunger of the working class. We must oppose capitalists and exploiters in their oppression of the working class and their class exploitation," he declared. Liu called for proper safeguarding of labor's working conditions (hours, wages, etc.) and rights; only thus "can [we] unite the broad masses of workers." However, he also noted that "workers should never refuse to unite with capitalists and employers in efforts to oppose Japanese imperialism and traitors and capitulationists."[67] Concluding on the theme that "only the working class can entirely integrate its own class liberation with the national liberation," Liu argued that only by making still greater efforts and taking on heavier responsibilities in the liberation struggle could labor "protect its own interests, elevate them to a higher degree and create more facilities for its own further liberation."[68]

Liu's appeal clearly exhibited the ambivalences in the CCP's labor-capital stance for KMT and Occupied China at this critical juncture of the war. This was again manifested in a major 1940 May Day labor policy statement by Teng Fa, which also focused on the presumed threat of a KMT accommodation with Japan.[69] Teng Fa, a prominent party figure, was a Cantonese of proletarian background who had been active in the Communist-led labor movement of the mid-1920s and who served as the party's internal security chief during the 1930s. He emerged as a leader in trade union work in the Border Region from 1940 until his death in a plane crash in the spring of 1946.[70] Teng's article, while continuing to encourage greater worker activism in the Nationalist and occupied areas of China, now veered more toward the conciliatory approach to labor-capital problems. Declaring that "the danger of compromise or even surrender has become more acute than ever," Teng listed the measures necessary to achieve the "fighting mobilization" (chan-tou tung-yüan) of labor in the current crisis. His discussion served again, however, to underline the continuing problems for the party in attempting to enlist labor as a powerful ally in the non-Communist areas.

For the KMT rear area, Teng Fa emphasized the paramount principles of unity and resistance and advocated a conciliatory approach to the problem of improving the workers' livelihood, evidently seeking to skirt some of the class conflict implications of earlier policy positions. Noting that wages had remained stationary or had even been reduced in the face of a constantly rising cost of living, Teng called for negotiation and mediation between labor and capital along the lines of the 1938 labor protection laws and regulations of the Nationalist government. He argued that a modest increase in wages would result in an equivalent increase in the workers' productivity for the war effort, which would be in keeping with the wartime principle that "those with money give money, those with strength give strength" *(yu ch'ien ch'u ch'ien, yu li ch'u li)*. Teng asserted that this would not only avert sharp conflict between labor and capital, but would also improve the workers' livelihood and strengthen their anti-Japanese and production enthusiasm. In fact, the slogan cited by Teng had been used effectively by the Communists in rural areas under their control to exact heavy war contributions from the gentry while simultaneously promoting rural economic and social reform, thus stimulating peasant mobilization.[71] But the ineffectiveness of such appeals to labor and capital in the KMT-controlled areas was evident. The difficulties of such a stance were underscored by Teng Fa's warning regarding the use of "left" slogans by anti-Communist and collaborationist elements who were plotting both to "agitate" the workers into actions leading to disunity and to undermine the war effort. He cited here a rice-looting incident (or riot) in Chengtu as a "tricky plot" to make the Communists look bad.

In turning briefly to the Japanese-occupied areas, Teng directed his attention specifically to the union organizations created by the Japanese and Wang Ching-wei's government. "Under no circumstances should we accept the bribery of the Japanese and traitors, and we should pledge not to participate in the traitor-organized unions," he declared, calling for a struggle against the "minority" of "worker scoundrels" *(kung-tsei)* and their "renegade behavior" and against the plot to lead the workers "on to the anti-Communist surrender path."

In his emerging role as labor leader in the Communist areas, Teng called on workers to join the anti-Japanese armies and guerrila forces in the enemy rear. He exhorted the party to "do its best" to expand its influence among the working class, to absorb advanced worker elements, and to transform the latter into the "backbone" *(ku-kan)* of the party.

As Teng Fa's policy statement indicated, the party's strategy was still to promote a greater Communist influence and a higher degree of anti-Japanese activism among organized labor in the KMT areas by pressing for modest concessions by capital—and to do so within a conciliatory framework of KMT authority and official labor regulations. The goal apparently was to enlist labor to pressure the KMT for unity and resistance while avoiding, particularly at this serious juncture of the war, any further exacerbation of KMT-CCP relations.

A parallel May Day policy pronouncement in 1940 by Po Ku, which appeared in the now Chungking-based *New China Daily*,[72] touched on themes and concerns similar to those in Teng Fa's article, but with an expectedly stronger emphasis on urban labor interests and on organization and mobilization measures. The two years since Wang Ming's 1938 May Day statement had brought serious disappointments to, and put new pressures on, the labor-based united-front point of view. Not only had KMT-CCP relations deteriorated and the major cities been lost, but the Nationalist-based Communist Party organization had been unable to promote a mass labor movement or to advance worker welfare effectively in the face of wartime inflation and the repressive policies of the Nationalist government. The tone and context of Po Ku's article, and of accompanying ones in the *New China Daily*, clearly revealed the impact of these growing antagonisms and frustrations, which were manifested in a more militant prolabor stance that appeared to move in the opposite direction from Teng Fa's position on labor-capital conflict by encouraging more vigorous struggles by labor in defense of its interests.

Po Ku also focused on the traitorous role of the Wang Ching-wei elements and stressed the danger to the resistance cause from forces plotting peace maneuvers and mounting an anti-Communist campaign. Po Ku exhorted the workers (the "most powerful force" in the resistance struggle) to oppose such moves, to work diligently and involve themselves to the fullest in the war effort. As usual in these statements, he dwelt on the correlation between improvement of workers' conditions and the degree of their commitment and sacrifice for the national cause. Describing at length the increasing hardships of labor in both KMT and Occupied China, he noted sympathetically that workers' struggles had broken out in many areas. In offering a general endorsement of such worker efforts to improve their desperate situation, he particularly emphasized the importance of encouraging and assisting labor economic struggles in the occupied areas. The latter struggles, he stated, should be considered part of the anti-Japanese resistance effort and one of the means for thwarting the aggressors. By promoting and aiding such economic actions, they could be directly linked to the liberation war and thereby raised to the level of an anti-Japanese political struggle. (Here, one might note, was the classic Communist concept of labor mobilization strategy. Labor could be organized and its "class consciousness" raised through anticapitalist struggle in defense of its economic interests. With the organizational strength and consciousness thus achieved, the workers, guided by their political vanguard the Communist Party, would advance to higher levels of political struggle transcending "narrow" and short-term economic objectives. Finally, through such growing militancy and politicization labor would ultimately fulfill its Marxist-proclaimed mission as the class destined to bring about the socialist revolution.) In advocating the defense of labor's interests in the KMT areas, he declared that the "authorities" should not stand by and watch the workers suffer while employers profited from the war. But in keeping with a continued united-front position, the workers were again cautioned to keep the overall resistance cause in mind, to abjure violent struggle tactics, and to utilize peaceful and legal means to push their demands. They were to be especially careful of the divisive tactics and plots of traitors and the Japanese enemy.

Po Ku returned to the need for strong labor unions—"organizations that protect the workers' interests"—if labor were to realize its role as a "decisive force" in the war and simultaneously better its welfare. Harking back to the heyday of left-wing labor strength in China (the 1925-27 period), Po Ku referred to the "various historical causes" that had resulted in the (presumably left-wing) labor movement being at its weakest at the time of Japan's aggression, a circumstance which seriously impeded labor's ability to play its full part in the war effort. He declared it "most regrettable" that there had been little progress in organizing labor in the KMT areas during the three years of the war; the workers were still unorganized and the labor movement weak and fragmented.

The situation was intolerable, Po Ku declared, adding that the time had come to stop neglecting union work. He reiterated Wang Ming's 1938 call to build a united organization encompassing all wage earners, one which would protect the workers' daily interests and advance their welfare with the immediate goal of developing lower-level union bodies in all factories and localities in both Occupied and KMT China.

Thus, in the face of growing tensions and problems, Po Ku's primary emphasis was on the plight of the workers and on the importance of the party's identifying with and supporting labor economic struggles in both Nationalist and Occupied China, though for the KMT areas this approach was still circumscribed by the exigencies of the KMT-led national cause. The building of effective local grass-roots unions through which to defend and advance worker interests was especially underscored, in lieu of the now dim prospects for building a Communist-led mass national labor federation in the KMT areas. The more militant prolabor stance and the focus on actively developing worker struggles in Japanese-occupied centers was in marked contrast to the new policy lines beginning to emerge in 1940-41 in the Yenan Party Center under Mao. The latter policies, as shall be shown below, all but dispensed with any notion of the primacy of labor mobilization through economic struggles in either KMT or occupied territories, turning instead toward more forceful peasant mobilization policies in the Communist base areas and toward a new, CCP-led, multiclass, united-front posture for the non-Communist areas in which urban class struggle and labor mobilization became increasingly muted themes.

In reinforcing the points made by Po Ku, an accompanying article in the *New China Daily* dealt specifically with the deteriorating labor conditions in the KMT areas, now declared to be worse than in prewar times.[73] The writer attacked factory management for these worsening conditions, which included not only wage problems but growing job insecurity and longer working hours. The singling out of such violations of workers' rights as not allowing them to participate in the national salvation mass movement and in May Day observances served to underscore the problems of building a left-led mass labor movement in wartime KMT China.

Another *New China Daily* article, which focused on the significance of promoting the workers' struggles in the Japanese-occupied central cities, was evidently intended as a response to the Maoist concentration on CCP-led armed struggle to build rural base areas.[74] In support of his argument, the writer noted that the occupied cities were the nation's major industrial areas and proletarian core. He specifically criticized "some people" who neglected labor movement work in these cities on the grounds that recovery of the urban centers rested with military forces. In the view of such people, the writer continued, the loss of major cities had led to a dispersal of the working class, a belief which resulted in an underestimation of labor's strength. This was a great mistake, he contended, and it was equally misguided to disregard the role the labor movement and workers' armed uprisings could play in coordination with a military counteroffensive. Again, the model was the Communist-led labor movement of the mid-1920s, with the writer extolling the part played by the Shanghai workers in conjunction with the Northern Expedition in 1927.

A "disparaging attitude" (*ch'ing-shih-ti t'ai-tu*) toward the working class forces in the occupied major cities must be overcome, the article declared. While counseling caution in adopting the appropriate forms of struggle and organization and avoidance of unnecessary risks under the repressive conditions of the occupation, the emphasis was on *active* organizational and struggle measures, even if limited in scope and focused on immediate problems and day-to-day issues. The writer recommended that the principles and measures outlined in the article be applied in modified form to union work in the KMT areas as well. The article concluded with a quotation from Lenin to the effect that in a revolutionary period the fighting strength of the proletariat could be multiplied a hundred-fold.

But the difficulties and impracticalities of wartime Communist mobilization of urban labor (as well as the continuing pressures within the party in favor of such policies) were again manifested in a September 1940 inner-party directive. Voicing the recurrent theme of developing party work in the occupied big cities, which were described as "the heartland of the proletariat," it acknowledged that the CCP had yet to be effective in eliminating the "phenomenon" of party separation from these big cities and from "the broad worker masses."[75] Communist commander P'eng Te-huai, writing in the Comintern journal in 1939, had previously pointed up the sharp disparity between the weaknesses in CCP urban labor work and the effective role of the peasants in the Communists' north China resistance struggle. "Unfortunately," he noted, in an obvious understatement, "it has to be stated that the political mass work among the industrial workers is not as well organized as the work among the peasants," a problem he ascribed to the loss of the major centers and railways to the Japanese.[76]

The renewed attempt to build a CCP political base on a mass urban labor movement had obviously collapsed under the weight of Japanese occupation, KMT repressiveness, and the growing effectiveness of the Maoist strategy of an independently mounted, rural base-area armed struggle which integrated anti-Japanese resistance with revolutionary perspectives. Significantly, it was within the framework of this latter strategy that the most important wartime contributions of industrial workers to the Communist cause were made. A sizable number of urban workers, miners, and rail-waymen from the occupied areas left their enterprises to join the Communist-led rural resistance struggle. They operated in guerrilla detachments in the vicinity of Japanese-controlled rail lines and mines in north China and elsewhere, entered regular service with the Eighth Route or New Fourth Armies, and participated in production work in the Border Region and other base areas. Agnes Smedley has documented her visit in November 1937 to partisan forces working with the Eighth Route Army in eastern Shansi, units organized from among some hundreds of miners and railwaymen from Hopei and Shansi whose jobs had evaporated with the Japanese invasion.[77] The next year, Israel Epstein reported on the Communist base areas in Shansi and Hopei (part of the new Chin-Ch'a-Chi Border Region), describing the key role of the few industrial workers there (most of them coming from the conquered cities of north China) in running arsenals and in handling communications and demolition work for the guerrilla forces. He, too, stressed the fighting role of miner and railwaymen partisan units in that area.[78]

Teng Fa summed up these worker contributions in a 1946 article published in the Philippines, where he had stopped en route to China after attending the inaugural congress of the World Federation of Trade Unions (WFTU) in Paris in the fall of 1945 as the representative of the liberated areas' trade unions.[79] Teng Fa, operating then in an international trade union setting in his capacity as the leader of the liberated areas' labor movement and at a time of renewed CCP attention to urban labor in the wake of the Japanese surrender, presumably made the strongest possible case for the workers' role in the Communists' wartime struggle.

Teng wrote that in the course of the eight-year resistance war, forty-six worker-guerrilla detachments (numbering up to one thousand men each) had been formed. These "extremely battle-hardened" units had retained their "working class character" and "form the main core of the 8th Route and New 4th armies."[80] In addition to these detachments, which resumed production work whenever the military situation eased, many other workers had permanently enrolled in the two Communist armies. Teng reported that a total of 24,700 railway workers and miners had joined the Eighth Route Army at the beginning of the war. At the same time, in the lower Yangtze Shanghai-Nanking industrial belt, another four thousand workers had formed their own regiment under the New Fourth Army, while farther south in Kiangsu, workers made up a majority of volunteers and effectives.[81] "From these figures," Teng concluded, "it can be seen that the enthusiasm of the Trade Union workers for enrollment in the army is the great inexhaustive [sic] reserve of the Liberation Army." It is interesting that this entire section of Teng's article, which clearly overstated the significance of the labor role, was deleted when the article was reprinted (in translation from the English-language Philippine version) in the CCP's official *Liberation Daily* after Teng's death in April 1946.[82]

By 1940 the Communist effort was overwhelmingly concentrated on an increasingly independent, protracted, rural resistance strategy, linked to a full Maoist exposition of a multiclass, new-democratic theoretical framework. These developments, precursors to the *cheng-feng* movement initiated in 1941-42, brought major shifts in the balance of power within the party and led to more decisive moves away from the remainders of an urban labor standpoint within the party leadership and to changes not only in the CCP approach to labor and capital in the non-Communist areas, but, as will be detailed below, in labor policy in the Border Region and other Communist base areas as well.

Maoist Multiclass Strategies

Before turning to the main theater of Communist labor policy and developments during the war years—the rural base areas, and particularly the Shen-Kan-Ning Border Region—it is important to sketch at least briefly those strategic conceptions enunciated by

Mao after 1937 which directly challenged the remaining urban-labor orientations within the party leadership and which guided the party's labor policies after 1940.

In his then secret concluding speech to the important Sixth Plenum of the CCP Central Committee in November 1938, Mao carefully distinguished between the strategy of revolution in capitalist countries and in "semi-colonial, semi-feudal" China.[83] For the former, he stressed the importance of urban-oriented, legal struggle: utilizing parliaments, organizing and educating the workers, and conducting strikes. Ultimately, when conditions ripened for insurrection, "the first step will be to seize the cities, and then advance into the countryside, and not the other way around," a strategy which he said had been successful in the Russian Revolution.[84]

But in China, lacking democracy and oppressed by imperialism, Mao went on, "we have no parliament to make use of and have no legal right to organize the workers to strike. Basically the task of the Communist Party here is not to go through a long period of legal struggle before launching insurrection and war, and not to seize the big cities first and then occupy the countryside, but the reverse."[85] In China, "war is the main form of struggle and the army is the main form of organization." The present plenary session, he added, "has clearly defined the direction for our efforts by deciding that the Party's main fields of work are in the battle zones and the enemy's rear."[86] Even in remote rear areas and the Japanese-occupied cities, Mao continued, "Party organizational work and mass work are co-ordinated with the war, and should and must exclusively serve the needs of the front."[87] The contrast with the views expressed in the 1940 *New China Daily* articles cited above is plain.

The political formula expounded by Mao during 1939-40, that of a "proletarian [CCP-led] revolutionary united front" no longer required or implied a break with the bourgeoisie as a class but instead led to an increasingly careful separation of the "national" from the "big" bourgeoisie.[88] The former, viewed as basically anti-imperialist and anti-feudal, could participate in this united front, but, as a politically and economically "flabby" and vacillating force, they were declared incapable of playing a leadership role and were to be dealt with on a "unity-struggle" basis, with the struggle aspect taking on a peaceful and increasingly modulated tone. The big bourgeoisie, on the other hand, were defined as those elements who either had close ties to imperialist interests in China ("comprador-capitalists") or were affiliated with the KMT state economic apparatus and its leading officials ("bureaucrat-capitalists"); this group was identified as "anti-Communist die hards." "With regard to the alignment of the various classes within the country," Mao stated in December 1940, "our basic policy is to develop the progressive forces, win over the middle forces, and isolate the anti-Communist die-hard forces."[89] As antagonism mounted between the CCP and the KMT in the later war years, and later flared into full-scale civil war, the unity approach clearly prevailed with respect to the national capitalists, while the "hard-core" comprador-bureaucratic interests, together with feudal (landlord) and imperialist forces, were directly linked to the KMT as targets of the Communist-led "new-democratic revolution." This new-democratic revolution, Mao stated in December 1939, represented an extended transitional stage directed against imperialism and feudalism that "clears the way for [a restricted] capitalism on the one hand and creates the prerequisites for socialism on the other." The prototype for this new democracy was "the anti-Japanese political power established in the base areas."[90] The goal was a "new type" of republic "under the joint dictatorship of several revolutionary classes,"[91] a concept which ultimately took official form in 1949 as "the people's democratic dictatorship"—a CCP-led, four-class bloc of workers, peasants, petty bourgeoisie, and national capitalists.[92]

In keeping with this strategic perspective, Mao emphasized the long-term importance of the rural base areas in the overall revolutionary struggle. "Since China's key cities have long been occupied by the imperialists and their reactionary Chinese allies," he wrote, "it is imperative for the revolutionary ranks to turn the backward villages into advanced, consolidated base areas, into great military, political, economic and cultural bastions of the revolution." Thus, "victory in the Chinese revolution can be won first in the rural areas" through a protracted struggle consisting primarily of "peasant guerrilla warfare led by the Chinese Communist Party."[93]

Mao added, of course, that the stress on the rural base areas should not mean the abandonment of work in the cities, which were the enemy's main bases and which remained the final objective of the revolution. Yet he again cautioned the party against being "impetuous and adventurist in its propaganda and organizational work in the urban and rural areas which have been occupied by the enemy and dominated by the forces of reaction and darkness for a long time"; rather, the party "must have well-selected cadres working underground, [and] must accumulate its strength and bide its time there."[94]

The class outlook involved in the Maoist political and strategic tenets outlined above led him ultimately to a collaborative labor-capital line, summed up in the CCP formula of "mutual benefits for labor and capital" (lao-tzu liang-li). But this differed fundamentally from the inevitably ambivalent, conciliatory line of the Wang Ming group in the early war years, which aimed to promote Communist mobilization of labor in support and reinforcement of KMT-CCP anti-Japanese unity. This latter position, which viewed labor as the party's key urban, and, indeed, national constituency, at the same time tended to associate the bourgeoisie with the KMT. It thus sought to strengthen unity with the KMT in a concerted war effort, while simultaneously attempting to build a labor political and organizational base in the KMT areas. Though the Wang Ming group continued to regard the labor-capital relationship in essentially adversary terms, this was couched in generally muted and often ambivalent forms in the interests of KMT-CCP amity. The resulting contradictions and difficulties are clearly evident in the various labor policy pronouncements from the 1937-40 period cited above.

In contrast to this line, Mao put increasing emphasis on CCP "independence and initiative" within the overall national united front and on isolating "the anti-Communist die-hards" in the KMT.[95] Using this formula the Communists were able to dissociate the "patriotic and middle-of-the-road" national capitalists and middle-class elements from the KMT government; a policy of building a new "united-front-from-below" to supplement and ultimately replace the deteriorating "united-front-from-above" was pursued. This policy was firmly rooted in the Maoist new-democratic thesis, in which the CCP was affirmed to be the direct leader and representative of a broader multiclass bloc in both rural and urban areas. The CCP thus took on both a labor *and* a capital constituency, with the reconciliation of these interests of great importance to the further development of Communist power. A conciliatory policy toward the national capitalists and the encouragement of capitalist enterprise were thus not pursued primarily as a means of avoiding friction with overall KMT leadership and authority, but rather as a means to consolidating the broadest possible CCP political base in order to confront the KMT—a tactic which became more apparent in the full unfolding of this strategy in the post-1945 civil war period.

Since the mutual benefits policy called for concessions by both labor and capital, it could in fact be implemented only in the rural areas where the Communists exercised military and political authority and could enforce these principles. Yet even in these areas, though Mao had spoken in class collaborative terms as early as 1936, party tendencies to stress worker interests underwent basic change only in the 1940-41 period, as will be described in the next chapter. But in the areas under KMT control (and in occupied areas), the CCP largely contented itself with projecting these policies not as immediate tasks to be carried out under existing conditions, but as the affirmed position of the Communists, to be implemented when a new political order had been established. The credibility of this position depended not only on the Communists' track record in the areas they controlled, but also on the avoidance of a militant anticapitalist appeal to labor in areas not yet under Communist rule. To attempt to build a powerful labor vanguard in the non-Communist urban areas would inevitably have called for much more unequivocal support of labor interests and a consequent exacerbation of the labor-capital conflict. The Maoist strategy for building a Communist military-political rural power base eventually obviated the need for such an urban labor strategy, which was also probably unworkable and even counterproductive, from the standpoint of the CCP effort to construct the broadest possible urban united front.

Thus, by 1941 the May Day labor policy statement by Teng Fa[96] placed primary and major emphasis on the labor movement in the Communist rural base areas and included, as well, specific criticisms of earlier "leftist" labor policies there.[97] As for the KMT areas, Teng stressed particularly the absence of democratic freedoms. While issuing the usual entreaty for workers to support the national war effort, he called on them to struggle for democratic government, an increasingly dominant theme in a broadly based Communist appeal directed against KMT moves to the right and in response to the open antagonism between the Communists and the Kuomintang in the wake of the New Fourth Army Incident in January 1941. As for labor policy in the KMT zones, Teng called on all local party organizations to "explain to the worker masses and all social circles" the party's policies on the protection of worker interests. Affirming the CCP's "sincere advocacy" of improving livelihood in accordance with national salvation policy, he voiced the party's disagreement with "the sharp class struggle method" (chien-jui chieh-chi tou-cheng fang-shih) of strikes, though he added that the CCP certainly opposed the use of the war situation to increase exploitation of workers. He then summed up party policy: "We advocate joint compromise between labor and capital based on mutual respect for each other's interests." This was a more direct Communist identification with the interests of both sides, combined with a clearcut disavowal of class struggle tactics, and was placed in the context of a broadened and more independent Communist political stance in response to the deepening rift between the CCP and the KMT.

Teng exhorted the workers in the Japanese-occupied areas to gather their strength under the slogan, "Do not forget the nation" (pu wang tsu-kuo), and advised that all actions be based on the accumulation and preservation of strength, with attention given to firming up party factory branches, nurturing industrial worker cadres, and reinforcing party links to the worker masses. All opportunities should be utilized broadly to advance united front work "with all levels and classes," he concluded.

It was thus a signal fact that, as the Mao-led party moved toward a more independent and anti-KMT position, its labor-capital line for the non-Communist areas became *less* militant rather than more so. The principal focus was on the rural base areas, with a "lie low" policy in the occupied cities and a broadly based campaign for democracy in the Nationalist areas aimed against KMT authoritarianism and anti-Communism and with the CCP emerging overall as the nationalist leader of a developing multiclass coalition. It was primarily in this context that the CCP's perception of and policies toward urban labor continued to be shaped until the closing months of the war. It is noteworthy, for example, that by 1943, after the full defeat of the Wang Ming forces and policies, the May Day pronouncement in the CCP's *New China Daily* in Chungking was much more low-keyed and less prominently displayed than had been the case in the 1938-40 years.[98] While it noted the continuing problems of worker livelihood and organization, the stress was on the need for continued sacrifice and on increased production as the means for benefiting "the anti-Japanese war, the factory, and the workers themselves"—themes very much in keeping with the labor line in the Yenan Border Region at the time.[99]

As has been indicated, labor policies in the Communist base areas also underwent changes in the years after 1940, in line with Mao's more strongly asserted, rural-centered populist tenets and strategies. But in turning now to labor developments in the base areas, and primarily in the Shen-Kan-Ning Border Region, it is necessary first to examine the early wartime years, which, as with CCP urban labor policy in that period, seemed to be in a transitional stage from the class line of the Kiangsi years to the later fully articulated Maoist position.

CHAPTER VI

Labor Organization and Early Wartime Labor-Industry
Patterns in the Border Region and North China Base Areas

The Shen-Kan-Ning Border Region on the eve of war in 1936–37 was a semiarid, economically backward, poverty-stricken rural area of some 3,800 square miles, with a total population of some 1.5 million.[1] The standard of living in this area before the Communists' arrival was extremely low even by general Chinese standards of the time, "an extraordinarily poor area within China."[2] It was particularly deficient in anything resembling modern industry and, as Edgar Snow described this "medieval world" of north Shensi in 1936, "For hundreds of miles around there is only semi-pastoral country, the people live in cave houses exactly as did their ancestors millenniums ago . . . and the horse, the ass and the camel are the last thing in communications." Candles are a luxury and "electricity is unknown," he added.[3] Snow reported that he found clothing, uniform, shoe, paper, woolen and cotton spinning, and rug factories and coal mines; these industries had sprung up, at least in part, as a result of some machinery and tools carried with them by the Communist forces on the Long March to Shensi, supplemented by raw materials and equipment captured in military forays. Salt refining plants and oil wells producing a variety of petroleum products and by-products were the largest Communist state enterprises.[4]

Snow described a visit to the "industrial center" of Wu Ch'i Chen, which, on a key trade route into Kansu, had the largest concentration of factory workers in the soviet districts and was the site of the Communists' main arsenal. The latter establishment, built

167

into a mountainside, had more than one hundred workers making small arms and explosives ("crude work" used mainly to supply Red partisans rather than the regular Communist forces) and a few farm tools. Most of the machinists in the arsenal had worked in major cities throughout China before joining the soviets. Aside from the workers in the arsenal and the uniform factory, young women from the surrounding areas made up most of the work force in the various small enterprises in Wu Ch'i Chen. "Labour appears to get preferential financial treatment over everybody else in the Soviet districts," Snow noted, with factory workers receiving $10 to $15 monthly (soviet currency), plus room and board furnished by the state. There was an eight-hour workday and a six-day workweek, free medical attention, workmen's compensation, paid maternity leaves, social insurance, and government contributions to workers' education and recreation.[5]

From these primitive beginnings, industry in the Border Region after 1937 underwent significant, if still very modest, development, principally under the aegis of the border government itself. Mao stated in mid-1944 that industrial development in the border area did not "really begin" until 1939, at which time the region had only 700 "industrial workers" (ch'an-yeh kung-jen), a figure which increased to 4,000 in 1942 and to 12,000 in 1944.[6] According to data cited by Hsü Yung-ying in his 1945 study of the Border Region, there were about 15,000 workers in "manufacturing, mining and old-line handicrafts" in 1943, some 1 percent of the area's population.[7] It was further reported in 1944 that seventy-seven state-owned "big factories" had been established in the border area as the "backbone" of industry there.[8] These industries included textiles and bedding, paper, chemicals, tools, glass, ceramics, pig iron, soap, and matches, among others. There was also the fuel-oil industry, in which self-sufficiency for the limited needs of the border area had been achieved. Seventy-eight percent of "modern" industry was reported to be state-owned, with another 20 percent in cooperatives and only 2 percent privately owned.[9] However, the contribution of small-scale private and household enterprise, in what were described as the fastest-growing textile and paper industries, was very substantial indeed, in line with the post-1941 drive to achieve self-sufficiency and mobilize the fullest grass-roots production effort in all fields.[10] The annual production of cotton cloth in 1943 through such private and household units was reported as double that of the state-owned textile factories (in contrast to the figures for 1940, when the state share had almost equalled that of private and household production), while privately-run paper-making enterprises in 1943 employed up to two-thirds as many workers as the state paper factories.[11] Cooperative enterprises also expanded significantly in the post-1941 period, while the number of workers employed in state enterprises actually declined. After reaching a peak of 7,000 in 1941, the number of these state employees decreased to just under 4,000 in 1942 and rose again to 6,300 in 1943. Members of regular cooperatives, on the other hand, increased from 80,000 in 1939 to 200,000 in 1943.[12]

There did in fact appear to be a stronger emphasis in the early wartime period on building a state-owned, centralized industrial establishment in the Border Region as a firmer proletarian-socialist economic and political base of Communist power. The Maoist move away from these policies by 1942 was associated with a greater recognition of and responsiveness to the growing economic burden on the peasants in the Border Region and evidently led to a curtailment of excessive state industrial investment. Thus, a Japanese scholar investigating these aspects of the Yenan period has noted: "The Party wanted badly to build up industry, and could show in Marxist terms that this was in the real interests of the people. But when there was popular protest against the forced savings this would require, the program was dropped."[13] Schran, in his recent study of the Border Region economy, states that most state-operated enterprises were formed during the 1940-41 period; the great bulk of state capital investment was made at that time, peaking sharply in 1940. Schran comments that, subsequently, "the emphasis tended to shift from state enterprises to cooperative home handicrafts."[14]

The state-industrial trend during this time was emphasized by a *New China Daily* correspondent, who, in a report on his talks with labor-union representatives in Yenan in the spring of 1940, noted approvingly that the construction of factories in the Border Region was going on daily: industry was being developed and the workers were playing their vanguard role in the mass movement and in production.[15]

Border Region Labor Organization

In a May 1945 memorandum on the Communist areas submitted to the founding conference of the United Nations in San Francisco, CCP delegate Tung Pi-wu put total union membership in the Border Region at 60,000.[16] It is interesting that a much earlier Communist report, in 1940, had already given a total of 55,694 for the Border Region General Labor Union as of 1940, with 63 percent in agriculture, 22 percent in handicrafts, and 15 percent in industry.[17] Tung Pi-wu gave a figure of 364,000 for the important and much more populous Chin-Ch'a-Chi base; a total of 665,640 for all the north China liberated areas (exclusive of the Border Region); and 200,000 for the central China bases. The grand total for all nineteen Communist base areas, as of February 1945, was 925,640. Tung broke this overall total down as follows: agricultural workers, 55 percent; handicraft workers, 25 percent; industrial workers, 15 percent; and others (presumably shop employees, transport and stevedore workers, etc.), 5 percent.[18] Teng Fa, in giving the same total of 60,000 for the Border Region General Labor Union in February 1946, stated that 20 percent (12,000) of them were (industrial) workers, the same figure reported by Mao in 1944.[19] The percentage of workers (and their families) in the total population of the Border Region was given as 3.9 percent in 1944 (plus 5.1 percent hired [agricultural] laborers). Worker representatives in the Border Region's basic-level people's councils were at this same proportion—as was true of all other class groupings in the population at that time, in keeping with the CCP's wartime united-front policy.[20]

A general labor union had been established in the Border Region even before the war;[21] a more formal organizational structure for the Shen-Kan-Ning Border Region General Labor Union [Shen-Kan-Ning pien-ch'ü tsung kung-hui] emerged from an April 1938 worker representatives' conference in Yenan, with further regulations adopted and perhaps some reorganization and expansion occurring in 1940. It is this last date which is cited in a 1943 Communist account as the one for the formation of the General Labor Union, but this clearly is misleading.[22]

Significant details on the organizational structure, membership, policies, and overall orientation of the labor movement in the Border Region during the initial wartime years are contained in policy documents and organizational regulations adopted by the 1938 worker representatives' conference[23] and in a 1939 Communist source on the organization, composition, and work of the General Labor Union.[24] The orientation during this period toward estabishing close links with a nationwide labor movement was evident in the emphasis on the participation of worker delegates from various cities in KMT China in the 1938 congress; such participation exemplified the "good contacts" of the Border Region labor organization with unions throughout the country.[25] In its organizational regulations, the Border Region union was given the right to unite with unions at all levels throughout the country, to participate in a national labor organization, and to strengthen labor's role in the war.[26] The workers were further exhorted, "under the leadership of a national united workers' organization," to unite with organized labor throughout the world in resisting Japan and supporting the international workers' struggle for peace and democracy.[27]

The General Labor Union's proclaimed goals were to unite the workers, staff persons, and agricultural laborers (hired peasants) of the Border Region, to support labor's interests, and to strive for both national and working-class liberation.[28] The union's program called for raising worker enthusiasm, skills, and efficiency, taking part in economic construction, and activating workers to participate in government and in the war effort. The union was also charged with improving the political and cultural levels of the workers as well as their incomes. Other tasks included guiding agricultural workers, assisting in the development of the agricultural economy, raising the peasants' national consciousness and war enthusiasm.[29]

The union was to represent the workers in contract negotiations, in government labor regulations reform, and in protecting workers' interests in the work place. In labor-capital disputes (*lao-tzu cheng-i*), the union was to adopt "appropriate methods" to reach reasonable solutions so that all strength could be concentrated on the war; the union was specifically called upon to play a mediating (*t'iao-chieh*) role in such disputes.[30]

Other union responsibilities and tasks included the organization of cooperatives and cultural, educational, and recreational facilities for workers and the promotion of workers' militia and war-support units (such as communications and transportation brigades). The union could levy dues (not to exceed 2 percent of wages) on its members and could also obligate employers to help defray overall union expenses. Workers were free to join or withdraw from unions without prejudice, but they were also subject to expulsion on cause. The government could disband any union organization deemed destructive to national unity and anti-Japanese resistance—a stipulation possibly related to "disruptive" Trotskyist influences the unions were urged to combat.[31]

Encompassed by the General Labor Union umbrella were component unions of industrial workers, clerks and handicraft workers, agricultural hired labor, coolie and transport workers, staff employees, and others. In line with the stated Communist principle of democratic centralism, and on the basis of occupation and enterprise, unions were linked hierarchically from the basic village level up through the district, county, and city levels; the pyramid culminated in the all-inclusive Shen-Kan-Ning Border Region General Labor Union. Worker representatives' congresses were declared the ultimate authority at all levels, from *hsiang* (village) congresses meeting at three-month intervals to the biennial Border Region congress.[32] In 1943 the General Labor Union was organized into four regional unions, with 30 *hsien* (county), 196 *ch'ü* (district) and 1,223 *hsiang* (village) branches, and to four special unions for agricultural laborers.[33]

Labor Patterns and Policies

According to a 1939 Border Region report, 90 to 95 percent of the workers in the region were union members—a total of over 48,000 at that time,[34] a figure which increased to over 55,000 in 1940, only a few thousand less than the total for 1945. Of the 1939 total, 2,800 (some 6 percent) were listed as "industrial workers":[35] printers, coal miners, petroleum workers, and arsenal workers.[36] The report stated that all such workers in the region had joined labor unions. Workers in communications and transport (road workers, motor mechanics, postmen, etc.) comprised another 3 percent of union membership. Agricultural laborers (forestry, pastoral, and farm workers) made up over 60 percent.[37]

It was further reported that of the 220 elected officials for Yenan County (presumably an area of greater worker concentration), 48 were workers. Some 70 percent of union members were in self-defense units, some of which had been selected by the unions to go to the front.[38] The report reiterated the unions' role in promoting the peaceful settlement of labor-capital disputes and stressed also the need to improve workers' livelihood in order to stimulate war enthusiasm; it noted that wages had risen by 40-100 percent (though the base period was unclear). In discussing wage arrangements, the account stated that higher wages (to agricultural workers) were paid during the busy harvest season and that disparities in the cost of living in different areas of the Border Region were taken into account in setting wages, as were differences in skill and seasonal variations in food prices.[39] It was observed that improvement in the standard of living called not merely for wage increases per se, but for a rise in real income as well, a point much less emphasized in the later Yenan years.

The report affirmed that land and other assets acquired by farmhands during the "revolutionary period" (pre-1937) were firmly guaranteed.[40] The hired-hand category thus encompassed those who now owned some land and livestock, yet who also continued to hire out their labor. The document also extolled such worker fringe benefits as free medical care, paid maternity leaves, job protection, education, etc. It was also pointed out that the unions' involvement in the anti-opium campaign had reputedly reduced the number of opium smokers in the Yenan unions from over one hundred to only ten (described as mostly "old workers").[41] Literacy was another cause that benefited from union support. The annual monetary wage scales cited (apparently as of 1938) varied considerably: 8-12 yuan for apprentices; 20-30 yuan for agricultural laborers; 50-100 yuan for various worker categories; and 40-80 yuan for clerical and other office workers, with a "special class" (presumably technical or administrative staff) receiving up to 130-40 yuan.[42] The eight-hour workday and six-day workweek still remained the general principle at that time, a principle incorporated into the February 1939 Shen-Kan-Ning Resistance War Administrative Program.[43]

Basic subsistence requirements (food, clothing, shelter) were met by the employing enterprises (in addition to monetary wages). It is difficult to estimate accurately the wage-supply ratio in these early Yenan years. Some wage scales for this period given in later accounts appear to include the cost of the supplied items, costs of which were then deducted from cash wages by the enterprises at special, low, fixed prices to protect workers from the impact of the inflationary price trend in the Border Region after 1937.[44] The inflation (which brought a sevenfold price increase by the end of 1940 and a runaway upward spiral in 1942 and 1943),[45] as well as the replacement of National Government currency (fa-pi) by Border Region currency (pien-pi) in 1941, compounds the difficulty of making accurate assessments. Yet it would seem that, particularly for the limited number of state factory workers and staff personnel, wage scales and benefits up to and probably through 1940 continued to show marked preferential status and treatment.[46] For example, in 1937 and 1938 the Border Region government paid (in addition to subsistence items) a top-money salary of five yuan monthly to heads of regional departments and only half that amount to district magistrates, considerably less than the upper wage scales for state factory workers.[47] At the same time, of course, the notion of special status, whether of workers or others, must be viewed from the perspective of the simple and unadorned life-style of the wartime Border Region.

Internationalist-oriented Communist reports on labor conditions in the Border Region in the 1938-40 period tended to underscore the preferential status noted above. An early 1938 report on the state printing workers in Yenan, for example, pointed to the "abundant" (feng-fu) wages of the more than one hundred workers employed, all of whom, it was emphasized, had incomes at least double those of the highest government officials and Party Central Committee members.[48] An April 1939 report in the Comintern press on the Border Region labor unions also focused on the benefits achieved by the unions.[49] It reported a 96-yuan minimum annual wage for "industrial workers," with a maximum of 336 yuan. It noted the general adoption of the eight-hour workday, and six-day workweek in government factories, with some plants, especially arsenals and munitions factories, adhering to six-and four-hour shifts for youth and child workers, respectively. The report stressed that factories were required to pay double wages for work on rest days. Factory wages were fixed by a Wages Committee composed of worker representatives, with wages varying according to skill. Decisions of the Wages Committee, the report claimed, could be annulled by the workers. Agricultural workers, the article noted, were no longer oppressed and mistreated, and "know how to fight for their rights."[50] In similar vein, a New China Daily account in the spring of 1940 put particular emphasis on the fact that Border

Region workers' benefits surpassed those of all government personnel and that their wages were double those of prewar times.[51] And in relation to the region's peasant population, Nym Wales had observed in 1937 that state-enterprise workers' wages were "much higher than the average income of the local people."[52]

Thus, while Border Region labor-management policy (public and private) now stressed conciliation in place of class struggle, there was at the same time a marked emphasis in the early Yenan years on building as substantial a trade unionist, industrial core as possible. The economic interests and overall status of this sector were specially favored. These policies and attitudes were clearly reflected in the person of Liu Ch'ün-hsien, a dynamic twenty-nine-year-old (in 1937) woman who was a leader in labor and industry in the Border Region at that time. Described by Nym Wales as "a solid, healthy, apple-cheeked working-class woman" and "a natural leader," she had been a teenaged textile factory worker in Wuhsi, near Shanghai, and she became a leader in the Communist-led labor movement there during the 1925-27 high tide of the first CCP-KMT united front.[53] She narrowly escaped with her life in the suppression of the left-wing labor movement in April 1927, and was subsequently (October 1927) sent by the party to Moscow for study.[54] While in Moscow she attended Sun Yat-sen University and met and married Po Ku. The two returned to China as members of the famed "Twenty-eight Bolsheviks" who dominated party affairs during the 1931-34 period.[55] Liu Ch'ün-hsien worked in the underground red labor movement in Shanghai until 1933, at which time she, together with the remaining party leaders in Shanghai, removed to the Kiangsi soviet area. Following the Long March to the northwest, she was elected by a Shensi workers' congress in January 1936 to be director of national mines and factories,[56] and she served concurrently as head of the organization department of the labor union headquarters.[57]

In a 1937 interview with Nym Wales in Yenan, Liu Ch'ün-hsien pointed up the favored wage and benefits situation of the unionized factory workers and stressed the vital and effective role of the labor unions in the Border Region.[58] "We train [selected] workers to take leadership of the peasant movement," she noted, adding that "every factory produces not only goods but revolutionaries trained as leaders for the movement."[59] She commented on the role of workers' propaganda teams in mobilizing the peasants and in helping to organize poor-peasant leagues (presumably in the pre-united front period), and she noted that "workers are sent to the village to collect the peasants for the Red Army, and it was expanded greatly by this work."[60] She dealt rather patronizingly with the worker-peasant relationship, and in pointing to the cooperative and helpful attitude of the workers toward the peasants, she observed, "In general the cultural level of the peasants is very low so the factory workers help to raise this."[61] Nym Wales, in describing a visit she made with Liu Ch'ün-hsien to a state factory in Yenan staffed by women workers, commented that "the factory girls all wore Red Army uniforms and red-starred caps, had bobbed hair, and considered themselves leading a 'proletarian revolution.'"[62]

In a 1938 article on the Border Region workers published in the May Day issue of *New China Daily*, Liu Ch'ün-hsien continued to stress many of the themes cited above.[63] She spelled out the very considerable political, economic, and cultural benefits the workers had gained through their "past struggles," and she underscored the vital and effective role of the unions in the region.[64] Noting the increase achieved in production and the advancement of workers' skills, she linked these to the fact that the workers now had no worries about their livelihood, welfare, and working conditions. In discussing union collective contract agreements between labor and capital, she stressed the role of the government and the unions in revising contract items with which workers were dissatisfied, and that employers were penalized for breaches of contracts. In this regard, she commented on the need to "reform" those unions which paid inadequate attention to improving workers' livelihood and one-sidedly supported the capitalists. She called, finally, for further mobilization of the workers in fulfilling their wartime role.

Liu Ch'ün-hsien evidently ceased to play any significant role in labor-industrial affairs in Yenan after about 1940, and her name did not appear on the fifty-three-member ACFL Executive Committee (nor among the alternates) named at the 1948 Sixth National Labor Congress in Harbin.[65] Helen Snow [Nym Wales] was told, during a 1972 visit to China, that Liu had died "long ago."[66] Apparently in the course of the post-1940 reorganization of the labor movement in the Border Region, Kao Ch'ang-chiu, a Shensi native and veteran northwest guerrilla fighter under Kao Kang, became head of the Border Region General Labor Union and Minister of Construction in the region government.[67] And as already noted, Teng Fa emerged in the later Yenan years as overall head of the labor movement in the liberated areas.

The greater prominence enjoyed by the proletariat in the early resistance period was also evident in a January 1940 report in the Yenan party journal from the Chin-Ch'a-Chi border area on the role of workers in that major north China anti-Japanese base.[68] Chin-Ch'a-Chi, of course, was an active war zone, in contrast to the largely rear-area character of the Border Region. The writer put total union membership there at more than 57,000: 45 percent handicraft workers, 43 percent hired farmhands, and 12 percent industrial workers. The account stressed the rapidity and effectiveness with which the base-area labor movement had been built and declared that the workers stood in the "foremost front line" of the resistance struggle, heroically fulfilling the "vanguard fighting tasks of the vanguard [working] class." The report emphasized the vital role of worker guerrilla units in destroying enemy communications, uncovering and rounding up spies and traitors, carrying out intelligence work, and serving as transport and first-aid teams. Workers also played a "backbone role" (ku-kan tso-yung) in the regular Communist armed forces; 1,680 border-area workers had joined these forces up to May 1939. Workers also took an active part in all government campaigns and were fulfilling and exceeding quotas on the production front. Everywhere, the article declared, in every unit and movement, model workers were playing a vanguard role and were "the most heroic and dedicated soldiers in the national liberation cause."[69]

Jobs had also been provided for many unemployed workers in newly established munitions, soap, paper, and uniform factories, the Chin-Ch'a-Chi report went on. It made the usual assertions of wage increases and benefits and of a reduction in work hours in the area to nine or even eight hours a day. In its discussion of the frictions encountered in the initial phases of the Chin-Ch'a-Chi labor movement, the report zeroed in on the problems of overcoming capitalist intransigence (private enterprise had a much more important place here than in the Shen-Kan-Ning Border Region) and of convincing the capitalists that their common interest dictated avoiding conflict and resisting the Japanese enemy. The capitalists now "understand why they should improve worker livelihood"—to minimize labor-capital clashes and jointly carry on the resistance war. Factory owners have thus "voluntarily" raised wages and reduced hours, with "misunderstandings" handled by government-union mediation and patience on both (labor and capital) sides.[70]

The article also recounted the cultural and educational advances made among the workers and their progress in preparing for leadership work. The Chin-Ch'a-Chi General Labor Union had trained and recommended large numbers of its members as county- and district-level cadres, and there was strong worker participation and representation in the electoral process at all levels.

The above account appeared to be an effort to retain a modified class-line outlook within the context of overall resistance-war unity. And while the emphasis was on persuasive techniques and the peaceful resolution of labor-capital conflicts, the burden for such resolution was put primarily on the capitalists' willingness to improve wages and working conditions. As shall be taken up in the next chapter, these orientations in Chin-Ch'a-Chi also underwent change in the later wartime years.

It was evident that in the economically backward rural environment of north Shensi after 1936, the proletariat played an even more marginal role than had been the case in the Kiangsi soviet base in the early 1930s. Communist labor policy had also undergone a change from the earlier class-struggle line (which had already been somewhat modified in Kiangsi by 1933) to a more conciliatory labor-capital approach. Yet, as has been detailed above, even under these new economic and political circumstances, there continued to be in the earlier Yenan years a discernable tendency to accentuate the role of the Border Region's small industrial labor force; to nurture and develop a state-sponsored industrial-proletarian nucleus; and to build unions committed to maintaining and reinforcing a comparatively privileged status for the worker as the vanguard element through whom "proletarian consciousness" could best be sustained in the peasant hinterland of northwest China. In a major statement in 1948 on Communist labor and tax policies, Ch'en Po-ta (who emerged in the Yenan period as a leading Maoist ideological spokesman)[71] pointed to "mistakes" on the question of wages "in certain old liberated areas in the past," probably a reference to early wartime labor policies in the Border Region and other base areas. Wages at that time, he stated, had been set "excessively high" in proportion to the production levels and the general standard of living in the base areas. State-run factories even required heavy governmental subsidies in order to operate under these policies, a procedure supported by "certain comrades" as "being in the interests of the workers." In addition to its detrimental economic effect, Ch'en added, these wage policies encouraged the "vulgar" spirit of "economism" among workers and the feeling of being a specially privileged group, which resulted in the estrangement of the workers from other laboring elements, particularly the peasantry.[72]

At the same time, it is important to emphasize those elements of continuity in policy that linked the final Kiangsi phase, the early Yenan years as a further transitional stage, and the subsequent cheng-feng period. In the crisis situation of 1933-34 in Kiangsi, new economic construction and labor policies had begun to come to the fore but had been hedged about and undercut by class-line imperatives and escalated rural class-war considerations. The experiences of that period, however, as well as the increasingly prominent role of Mao after 1935, the united-front moves away from class-war policies, and the continuing impact of an economically backward rural environment, all played their part in the further development and implementation of revised class and developmental policies in the early resistance-war period. These included broader-based rural mobilization, labor-capital conciliation, and greater encouragement of private enterprise, handicrafts, and the cooperative movement.[73] Yet it was also evident that the full development of these policies continued to be impeded by the still significant influence of those party leaders and forces which initially attempted to subordinate a rural-base strategy to their principal objective of recreating a central Communist role in the urban centers primarily through a revitalized mass urban-labor movement. From this latter reference point, and as an adjunct to this strategy, they sought also to promote a proletarian core in the Border Region and other base areas as well.

But from the latter part of 1940 on, the Border Region and the other Communist base areas entered a new economic and military crisis period. The Mao party forces responded by moving toward a firmer political consolidation (with final defeat of the Internationalist faction) and more clearcut and independent military-political strategies, in which the central importance of the base areas and of mass-line policies loomed ever larger. With this came further changes in economic and class policies, including a reassessment of labor policy and of the status (in both an economic and political sense) of the modest state industrial establishment in the Border Region. These developments are the subject of the next chapter.

CHAPTER VII

The Labor Policies of Post-1940 "Yenan Communism"

The Border Region, as well as the Communist base areas generally, experienced a serious crisis during the years 1940-42. With the deepening of KMT-CCP hostility, the KMT severely tightened its economic noose around the Border Region and cut off all subsidies to the government there after 1940. Meanwhile, intense Japanese pressure against the Communist bases in northern China (in the form of the infamous "three-all" strategy)[1] incurred heavy losses in overall Communist military strength and a reduction in territorial holdings.[2] The CCP under Mao's leadership responded with a series of policies and approaches which affirmed and reflected a more clear-cut and total commitment to a self-reliant, nationalist-populist, rural base strategy. Mao's policies sought the fullest utilization of local productive energies and resources based on the broadest possible mobilization of the peasant masses in every sphere—economic, military, political, and cultural, a policy summed up in the concept of the "mass line." It was this unequivocal commitment to the rural peasant base as the foundation of Communist military, political, and economic power that marked the blossoming of the Maoist "Yenan" pattern, a pattern which had been given an overall ideological framework in the new-democratic principles propounded by Mao by the beginning of 1940.[3]

Under conditions of material scarcities and severe financial difficulties, the inflationary trend in the Border Region was out of control by the end of 1941. At the same time, the public grain tax increased from under 4 percent of total grain production in 1939 to a peak of some 13 percent in 1941 and the tax base was simultaneously broadened to include all but the very poorest peasant families.[4] A December 1940 inner-party directive composed by Mao, which summarized a series of new policy guidelines issued by the Central Committee in that period, stated that "except for the very poor who should be exempt, all people with an income shall pay taxes to the state, which means that the burden shall be carried by more than 80 percent of the population, including the workers and peasants, and not placed entirely on the landlords and the capitalists."[5] Though these new tax levies were comparatively heavy, they were structured progressively based on peasant income levels and the burden fell more heavily on those more able to pay.[6] Over the 1942-44 period, the public grain tax ranged near the 10 percent mark, with 21 percent of peasant households exempt from taxation.[7]

By 1941-42, the party's response to this crisis situation was based on sustaining and reinforcing the party's broad peasant constituency, which now more than ever had to provide the principal sustenance for the Communists' wartime struggle.[8] In brief, this response included: sharp cutbacks in government and military administrative expenses and personnel; the shifting of cadres, cultural workers, intellectuals, and students to basic village-level work; emphasis on maximizing food production and cutting back the tax burden, particularly with respect to the poorer peasantry; the promotion of self-sufficient spinning, weaving, and food-growing activities by individual households, government organs, public institutions, and military units; encouragement of handicraft production and cooperative and private enterprise; steps to raise labor productivity in state-operated industries; and more egalitarian arrangements for government personnel and workers whose compensation was now to be more completely based upon the subsistence supply system. The new approach also called for peasant-oriented cultural and educational policies and for increased peasant political mobilization via heightened campaigns to reduce rents and interest, and greater encouragement of capitalist productive forces in agriculture (the richer peasantry), industry, and commerce. The new orientations and work style embodied by these policies were promoted through the *cheng-feng* movement of Maoist consolidation in the 1942-44 period.[9] But it is specifically the impact of these years of crisis and change on labor-related policies that shall be considered here.

In his major report on economic and financial policy to a senior cadres conference in Yenan in December 1942, Mao stated that supporting economic development did not mean "reckless or ill-founded expansion. Some comrades who disregard the specific conditions here and now are setting up an empty clamour for development; for example, they are demanding the establishment of heavy industry and putting forward plans for huge salt and armament industries, all of which are unrealistic and unacceptable."[10] Turning specifically to previous industrial policy in the Border Region, he noted that in the first stage of the region's economic development, from 1938 through 1940, government-sponsored industrial construction had been emphasized. Since then, in the second stage, there had been a more broadly based movement for self-sufficient industrial development involving government, public institutions, schools, and the army, and which had brought about more handicraft enterprises and cooperatives and had set a mass weaving campaign into motion. (The industries set up by public organizations and schools in 1942, Mao observed, were all small-scale handicraft factories.) In the third stage that was now beginning, Mao declared that agriculture would come first, with industry, handicrafts, transport and animal husbandry second, and commerce third; all of these sectors were to function on a decentralized, self-reliant basis under the principle of "centralized leadership and decentralized operation."[11]

Mao added that during 1942 a policy of "consolidating the existing public-owned factories and developing handicraft industry in the villages" had been promulgated and had already achieved results.[12] In looking ahead, Mao stressed the need to overcome the bureaucratization of the factories and to strive for complete self-sufficiency in cloth production by 1944.[13] Thus, in the early Yenan years through 1940 and probably into 1941, industry financed and operated by the government (albeit on a modest scale) predominated in development efforts, and the labor force and administrative personnel linked to this sector received relatively favored treatment in the overall Border Region economy. Within this pattern, earlier attempts (beginning in 1939) to increase cloth production had moved in the direction of setting up comparatively large state-private factories, which called for substantial outlays of capital and an increase in full-time workers.[14] But by the end of 1942, the number of government factories had been reduced from a high of 97 to 62 (with a total of just under 4,000 employees) and such consolidation apparently resulted in increased efficiency.[15] Thus, as industrial development underwent a new period of expansion after 1942, it was comprised of a much more heterogeneous mix of government, institutional, private, cooperative, and household enterprise—most particularly in the all-important textiles field, where household (cottage) production grew to be the largest category and where capitalist production for 1943 stood at some 60 percent of the state sector, compared to 45 percent in 1941 and 30 percent in 1940.[16]

This new emphasis on cottage textile production also brought large numbers of peasant women into spinning and weaving work. It was reported in 1945, for example, that in five districts of the Border Region there were 33,457 women thus engaged.[17] The liberating impact of these household and cooperative production activities on the formerly housebound peasant women in the Communist base areas has been described as follows:

> It was common for women to group together to spin, reel and wind yarn, and set up warps. Even when the task did not actually require more than one pair of hands, they tended to work together, sharing heating and lighting expenses. So much contact with others must have had a profound effect on people who had always led rather enclosed and solitary lives. As they worked in groups and arranged for each other's children they learned to organize themselves and their time. So

much was the textile industry the concern of women, that at the village level, it was frequently managed by the Women's Association.[18]

It is interesting that, in accordance with the policies outlined above, Mao told John Service in 1945 that "the Kuomintang has no contact with the agrarian masses of the population. . . . Unwilling to solve the agrarian problem it turns towards the principle of rigidly planned, State directed and controlled industrial development." The CCP, on the other hand, "is the party of the Chinese peasant. . . . The Communist Party will be the means of bringing democracy and sound industrialization to China."[19]

A United States War Department intelligence report of July 1945 noted the "great effort" the Communists had made in developing handicraft industries and stated that numerous such industries then existed throughout the Communist areas. These were producing "cotton, woolen and linen cloth, blankets, stockings, towels, cigarettes, matches, soap, paper, dyes, chinaware, chemicals, machine tools, etc." The report noted that although the Communist areas were still not entirely self-sufficient in the production of such light consumer goods, "their position has greatly improved."[20]

New Directions in Labor Policy

In his inner-party directive of December 1940, Mao stated that "capitalists should be encouraged to come into our anti-Japanese base areas and start enterprises here if they so desire. Private enterprise should be encouraged and state enterprise regarded as only one sector of the economy. The purpose in all this is to achieve self-sufficiency."[21] Turning to labor, Mao, while conceding the need to improve the livelihood of workers if war enthusiasm was to be sustained, emphasized that "we must strictly guard against being ultra-Leftist; there must not be excessive increases in wages or excessive reductions in working hours." Under present conditions, Mao added, the eight-hour workday could not be universally introduced in China, "and a ten-hour working day should still be permitted in certain branches of production." Once a contract between labor and capital is concluded,

> the workers must observe labour discipline and the capitalists must be allowed to make some profit. Otherwise factories will close down, which will neither help the war nor benefit the workers. Particularly in the rural areas, the living standards and wages of the workers should not be raised too high, or it will give rise to complaints from the peasants, create unemployment among the workers and result in a decline in production.[22]

In his May Day labor policy statement of 1941, Teng Fa, the party's emerging labor head, elaborated further on this approach, with specific reference to the Central Committee directive on labor policy which had provided the basis for Mao's comments.[23] All local party organizations in the base area should study this directive, Teng stated, and "effectively correct 'leftist' policies in union work." Such policies disregarded prevailing living standards, work customs, and wartime conditions in the base areas and overemphasized improvement in workers' livelihood by demanding excessively high wages, "unsuitable" working hours, and other unrealistic benefits. Teng averred that such mistaken policies would affect the reciprocal relationship between labor and capital (lao-tzu hu-hsiang kuan-hsi) and the solidarity of the united front. (It was clear that at this juncture in China's political situation Teng was referring, not to the KMT-CCP relationship, but to the CCP-led united front in the base areas.) The workers should thus avoid taking a short-sighted, narrow "guildist" (hang-hui chu-i che) view of their interests. While promoting and protecting workers' interests and their political, economic, and cultural status, the trade unions must not disregard the interests of the capitalists and the protection of their enterprises. Labor policy should accord with the needs of the Communist war effort and of new democracy and should promote the general economic development and well-being of the base areas in the context of wartime conditions.[24] It was in this spirit, Teng concluded, that the unions must examine all their work.

The labor policies of the post-1940 period thus developed as an integral part of the effort to lower government costs, maximize production, reduce the load on the hard-pressed rural economy, and encourage self-support programs and a dispersed, self-reliant, and mixed industrial economy—all linked to simplified structures and a less dominating and economically burdensome role for the "state socialist sector" in the overall economy of the Border Region. Though reminiscent, in some respects, of the 1933 critiques of "ultraleftist" labor policies in Kiangsi, the *cheng-feng* labor line made a fundamental move away from the earlier effort to maintain and reinforce proletarian leadership (in both the agricultural and nonagricultural sectors) and to retain a favored economic status for workers. Policies toward labor were now to be fashioned as component elements in what had become a priority *political* as well as economic and military, commitment to a broad peasant base and in which capitalist forces (agricultural and industrial-commercial) were given respected and protected status. Starting with the premise of guaranteeing a basic subsistence to workers in the face of economic crisis and accelerating inflation, the new labor policies resulted in a decided shift toward wages paid in basic necessities, which had a more egalitarian character than payment in cash, and to the narrowing (though not the elimination) of the gap between minimum and maximum levels of compensation.[25] There was a particular emphasis on raising the quantity and quality of production while reducing its costs. This effort was marked by extended working hours, tighter labor discipline, and the use of exemplary labor models. And finally, there was a more pronounced emphasis on the general interest and on the specific theme of taking into account the interests of both employers (state and private) and workers.

After a move to raise Border Region monetary wages in industry in May 1941 in an attempt to keep up with inflation, the wage
system itself underwent revision in September 1941.[26] Under the
new system, enterprises were obligated each month to supply their
workers with 45 *chin* (60 pounds) of millet, 1 *chin* (catty) each of
meat and salt, and fixed rations of cooking oil, charcoal fuel, and
cash to purchase vegetables. In addition, the factory annually
supplied one set each of underclothes, cotton clothing, and winter
outerwear. These supplies were augmented by money wages varying
from 15 to 50 yuan for workers in light industry to from 25 to 75
yuan for those in heavy industry, though this money wage was becoming less and less meaningful as prices rose to over forty times
the 1937 level by December 1941. Subsistence supplies were also
provided for dependents—for young children and for a nonemployed
wife who had a number of such young children at home.[27]

In May 1942, in response to worsening inflation, the monetary
portion of wages was linked to the current price of a fixed amount
of millet, from a minimum monetary equivalent of 32 pounds to a
maximum of 72 pounds. A detailed 1944 summation of these wage
developments which appeared in the *Liberation Daily* stressed the
point that, since 1941, wages had been able to keep pace with inflation without loss (or gain) to the workers in real wage terms. It
acknowledged that defects remained and held out the prospect for
working out what it called an even more "rational wage system" (*ho-
li-ti kung-tzu chih-tu*).[28] In this relatively egalitarian subsistence
wage system (basically similar to the allowance for the army), wage
differentials were now essentially limited to the supplemental
monetary equivalent of from 32 to 72 pounds of millet per family,
since the monetary wage (in contrast to supplies) went only to the
wage earner.[29] Gunther Stein, also in 1944, reported a somewhat
broader spread in this monetary supplement, from the equivalent of
10 to 20 pounds of millet to "about 100 pounds." His minimum,
however, was for apprentices, while the maximum was reserved for
"highly skilled workers and heads of departments."[30]

In the collective contract regulations for government-operated factories adopted in November 1940, the principle of the eight-hour workday had been reaffirmed, but supplemental provisions stated that the General Labor Union, in response to the wishes of its member unions, had agreed to an increase in the limit to nine hours and to a revision in overtime arrangements as well.[31] With the further new directions in labor policy outlined at the end of 1940, the ten-hour workday became (with certain exceptions) the standard during the following year and was incorporated in labor policies drawn up at a 1941 joint conference of union and government representatives and announced by Border Region chairman Lin Po-ch'ü (or Lin Tsu-han) in May 1941.[32] On May Day of that year, a new Administrative Program for the Shen-Kan-Ning Border Region had been approved by the CCP Political Bureau, which formally adopted the ten-hour workday, stressed labor-capital mediation and improving labor discipline and productivity, and called for "appropriate" (shih-tang— the operative modifier generally used from this period on) improvement in workers' livelihood.[33] A 1943 report on the General Labor Union (which put the new approaches in their most positive light) summed up the goals and parameters of the new policy: to "safeguard and, where necessary, improve the workers' standard of living [a shift from the former emphasis on labor benefits]; to increase production and strengthen the war of resistance"; to place a floor and ceiling on wages, avoiding "over-exploitation" of the workers while at the same time not depriving employers "of all profit"; to reaffirm the eight-hour workday as "an ideal for the future," though "in the war situation a ten-hour day is permissible"; to encourage workers "to respect their contracts and to observe labor discipline so that production can be maintained"; to recognize that wages of industrial and agricultural workers cannot be exactly equal; and to strengthen labor organizations and education to enable them to play their key role in the "anti-Japanese democratic political structure."[34] The General Labor Union "supports the newly-proclaimed labour policy of the Government" and had issued a call for "thorough discussion" of its provisions by all union locals. It praised the workers of the Eighth Route Army Printing Plant not only for being the first "to suggest changing to the ten-hour day, but [for having] volunteered to do an extra hour of unpaid work in addition to the ten hours, until victory is attained." These workers had also issued a proclamation calling on all other workers in the Border Region to follow their example.[35] A January 1944 report by Lin Po-ch'ü declared that 1943 production in government factories had increased by 100 to 400 percent over 1942 and that the cost of production had been reduced by 20 to 30 percent.[36]

At the same time, it is important to emphasize that the livelihood of wage earners in the Border Region had undoubtedly been substantially improved in comparison with the primitive, poverty-stricken, and backward conditions of northern Shensi before the arrival of the Communists, not to speak of the new sense of personal security and status which was a hallmark of the Communists' relationship with the masses in the wartime base areas.[37] But it nevertheless seemed clear that, with the new focus on a broadened grassroots developmental policy, on the encouragement of private enterprise, and on greater austerity in the "urban" sector, the major improvements in industrial wage levels, working conditions, and benefits were principally a product of the early Yenan years (1936-40); the years from 1940 to 1945 saw a levelling off of, and even some cutbacks in, these improvements.[38] Yet even more importantly, the income differentials between industrial workers and the majority of the peasants had considerably narrowed, if not vanished entirely, in the post-1940 years.[39] In November 1941 Lin Po-ch'ü reported that middle peasants had become the most important force in the villages of the region (in the five *hsiang* in the Yenan district, he stated, rich and middle peasants then comprised 60 percent of the peasant population, and of this 60 percent, 49.4 percent were middle peasants) and that these middle peasants were better off than the rich peasants had been in the past.[40] With their incomes rising, peasants were apparently less inclined to leave the land and become workers.[41]

The new labor guidelines, with their move away from the more traditional wages-hours-benefits trade-unionist emphasis, apparently led to attitudes among workers and cadres which minimized and denigrated the role of the unions, though in fact the latter were now expected to play an even more important role in developing the workers' political consciousness, discipline, and productive contribution to the war effort. A December 1941 *Liberation Daily* article specifically pointed to such tendencies on the part of cadres and workers in state-operated enterprises.[42] The workers had become uninterested in union activites, and a "liquidationist" trend had even developed among some union cadres regarding the union's role in representing workers. With this went the tendency (most noticeable among factory management cadres) to minimize the role of the union, relegating it to such minor activities as supervising food arrangements for the factory workers and leaving management in complete charge otherwise. The article declared that this trend had seriously affected both union work and factory operations. The union's ability to raise labor's political consciousness, cultural level, work enthusiasm and discipline, and production skills was now being questioned. Thus, while the interests of the state factories and their workers might be identical, the report concluded, the factory enterprise itself could not be a substitute for the mass organizational character and tasks of the unions.

The September 1941 initial issue of "Chinese Worker" (a semi-monthly insert in the *Liberation Daily)* took up the newly instituted "money and supplies wage system" *(huo-pi yü wu-p'in kung-tzu chih-tu)* and specifically linked it to the theme of avoiding "excessive emphasis" on improving workers' livelihood (wages and hours).[43] Any improvement had to be in conformity with "correct" labor policy which took into account the protracted and difficult war situation, the overall living conditions and standards of the Border Region population, and the need to reduce costs and increase production. In line with these factors, a basic level of subsistence had been defined (food, clothing, shelter); this was to be supplemented by wages which took into consideration the worker's skill level and work experience (seniority). The article maintained that the aim of this combination wage system was to "stabilize" workers' livelihood and also to maintain work enthusiasm and stimulate labor productivity and skills.

The article went on to recommend that, in explaining this system to their members, the trade unions stress the point that workers in state enterprises were in fact working for themselves and that Border Region workers enjoyed democratic freedoms, participation in government, security from unemployment, and other benefits not available to workers in the KMT or the Japanese-occupied areas. Sustained by these advantages, the workers should concentrate on raising and improving their political and technical levels and should aspire to be people's labor models in developing the Border Region's economy.

The importance, in the interests of increased production and labor discipline and morale, of retaining some degree of economic incentive for labor through wage differentials was reaffirmed at an October 1942 Border Region planning commission meeting on wage policy. As reported in *Liberation Daily*, the commission rejected the principle of egalitarianism *(p'ing-chun chü-i)*, stating that wages beyond a base level should be related to quantity and quality of production and should not be determined solely on the basis of hours worked.[44] In his December 1942 report on economic policy, Mao also endorsed such an incentive piecework system. But again the entire thrust was on its role in raising labor productivity, reducing costs, strengthening labor discipline (and "enthusiasm"), and in differentiating between worker "industriousness and laziness."[45] Mao thus directly linked his support for an incentive approach with the need to implement the ten-hour workday "universally" and with a call to the unions to promote the Chao Chan-k'uei movement in all factories—a movement which strongly emphasized the selfless commitment and sacrifices of this model state-enterprise worker.

The continuing impact of the developing *cheng-feng* movement apparently led to a decidedly greater emphasis on social (ideological) incentives (as opposed to wage differentials) as the prime factor for increasing productivity. Chu Te, commander in chief of the Communist armed forces, stressed this point in a speech to a Factory Representatives' Conference held in Yenan in May 1944.[46] Chu spoke of "two very bad tendencies," the first being "economism" *(ching-chi chu-i)*, which he described as the attitude of those who failed to put public before private interests and those (presumably managerial and union cadres) who ignored the political principle of educating the workers and relied instead on wage incentives alone to encourage production, thus catering to a minority of workers who lacked adequate consciousness and awareness. The second tendency was "egalitarianism," which Chu attributed to those workers who, despite their failure to work conscientiously or give attention to their skill levels, still demanded equal wages. (As an indication of the attitude among such workers, Schran cites the saying, " *'kan pu kan, i chin pan!'*—i.e, whether or not one does something, one gets a pound and a half [of grain]!")[47] In criticizing the egalitarian point of view, Chu used the negative argument that it rewarded the undeserving (unproductive) worker by guaranteeing a base salary, rather than making the more positive point that it failed to provide adequate incentive (through greater compensation) for the more productive workers. This theme was further underscored later in the conference by Teng Fa, who stated that in developing the workers' production enthusiasm, creativity, and technique, "we cannot rely only on wage incentives" but must also rely on the "worker masses' own revolutionary political consciousness."[48]

A May 1942 directive of the CCP Central Committee bearing on the labor movement of the important Southeast Shansi base area also reflected the evolving labor policies of the period.[49] It thus stressed the imperatives of the wartime rural-base setting as obstacles to any policy of higher wages, urged implementation of the ten-hour workday, and emphasized the need for "friendly relations between labor and capital" *(lao-tzu shuang-fang yu-hao kuan-hsi)* in the spirit of anti-Japanese unity and the development of production. It exhorted party and union organizations to explain all these matters to the workers and to raise the latter's "political consciousness" with union activities focused on questions of production and skill development.

The turn away from agricultural labor as the party's favored vanguard rural constituency was an underlying theme of the directive. The party's "proletarian" commitment to hired labor was now similarly being reduced in the interests of stimulating agricultural production, to which the party's stronger incentives to and encouragement of the middle and rich peasant strata bore witness. Thus, in dealing with "agricultural labor-capital relations" *(nung ts'un lao-tzu kuan-hsi)*, the directive observed that agricultural employers *(ku-chu)* preferred not to hire activist union elements, but instead to take on backward hinterland peasants or youth. This was because of the "worker struggle" attitude of the activists (one complaint being that their excessive meetings slowed down production) and also because of the fact that these elements sometimes abused their union authority to bully others and to make unreasonable demands. If left unattended, such problems could lower agricultural production, create bad habits among the workers, bring on unemployment, and isolate the union from the masses (presumably from the majority of the peasantry who were not hired laborers). The only way to improve agricultural laborers' livelihood, increase production, and bring harmony to labor-capital relations was to publicize the slogan of "plant more, plant early, and harvest more to resist Japan." The directive cautioned employers not to take advantage of the corrected labor policy to make excessive work demands on the hired laborers.[50] Compromise in accord with concrete circumstances should be the rule, with the government available as mediator and everything based on the general principle of the "mutual interests of labor and capital" *(lao-tzu shuang-fang-ti li-i)*.

It is also instructive to compare a major pronouncement on labor policy by the Chin-Ch'a-Chi border-area government, dating apparently from 1942 or 1943, with the January 1940 report (discussed in Chapter VI) on the labor movement in that region.[51] While the earlier report continued to show class-line tendencies and to emphasize labor benefits, the latter document took a markedly different tone in accord with the party's new line. The labor policies spelled out in the more recent document were formulated in the context of *cheng-feng* economic and financial policies and so reflected their encouragement of private enterprise and investment, the development of handicraft industry, and the promotion of household enterprise.[52] In the by now familiar phrase, it affirmed the need to improve (industrial and agricultural) labor's livelihood "appropriately" and to guarantee its rights and cultural-educational opportunities in order to promote labor enthusiasm, skills, and productivity. However, if employers (in industry and agriculture) could not make a profit or even suffered losses, the result would be stagnating or declining production and the flight of capital away from beneficial productive uses in the base area. The statement acknowledged the privations suffered by many workers and their families as a result of the wartime inflation, which had outdistanced earlier wage increases. On the other hand, it noted, in some places improvement in living conditions had improperly placed excessive burdens on employers, with negative results on production. A correct resolution of all the above questions was thus a matter of utmost urgency.

The document affirmed that the general principle on which new policies should be based was the unity of all classes, which would enhance production enthusiasm and support for the resistance war struggle. The alternative was enslavement by the Japanese and an end to all class interests. While improvements should continue to be made in labor's situation to mobilize them for the war effort, sharp class struggle was to be avoided and harmonious relations, based on anti-Japanese unity, promoted. Though not neglecting labor's needs, "we must not permit the workers unilaterally to determine conditions" and to compel employers to meet them, the report declared.[53] All sides should abide by government regulations (which in turn should ensure the rights and interests of all classes) and mediation procedures. The unions were cautioned against abrogating to themselves governmental authority or engaging in activities in violation of these laws. Improvements in worker treatment and in wage and hour arrangements must be based on the principle of "suitability to the needs of the war" *(shih-ho chan-cheng-ti hsü-yao)*; it would be impossible under base-area war conditions and prevailing living standards to advance worker livelihood to levels beyond its "former" *(ts'ung-ch'ien*—presumably "preinflationary" or possibly "prewar") status.

In terms of specific wage policies, the document stipulated that dealing with the impact of price inflation on workers' real income must be balanced with equal consideration for the interests of capitalists and agricultural employers. Wages should not be uniform but should be geared to local living standards and to individual skills and productivity; a minimum wage that was adequate for the subsistence needs of the worker and of at least one additional family member was a necessity. It endorsed a half-supplies, half-monetary wage system to counter inflation, with the prospect of moving ultimately all the way to a system based solely on supplies. As to work hours, the document called on state-enterprise workers to emulate the example of Shen-Kan-Ning workers in moving to a ten-hour workday (evidently still not officially mandated at the time). In the handicraft and agricultural sector, where a twelve-hour workday had been the norm, only slight reductions of perhaps half an hour or an hour were to be considered. The use of regular work hours for union and other outside activities and meetings was severely restricted, as were employer obligations for employee medical expenses and disability compensation. Wages of employees joining the armed forces were to terminate as of the day of enlistment, and the employer bore no obligation for severance pay.

The policy statement insisted that labor contracts must be agreed to by both capital and labor. Workers had the right to "withdraw from work" (t'ui-kung—a careful avoidance of the word "strike," pa-kung) only in cases of employer contract violations (though "reasonable" solutions through mediation were emphasized for disputes on both sides). Workers were admonished not to insist on setting their own terms and conditions for hire and were further warned that they could not prevent employers, on expiration of a contract, from laying off workers. The statement went on to say that the problems of the unemployed should be dealt with by finding alternative employment in factories and cooperatives, not through welfare programs. Apprentices, after acquiring some degree of competence, should be given "some wages," and their "excessive exploitation" should be prohibited. The "same work, same pay" slogan, it emphasized, referred not simply to the job, but to the amount of work accomplished. The document noted, significantly, that in areas where "the masses have already been mobilized" (apparently referring to previously unionized areas), class interests were often placed first, leading to comparatively high demands which could not be met under existing conditions. It was necessary to educate the masses to put national before class interests and to take long-term as well as immediate interests into account. Employers had also to be persuaded to concern themselves not only with their own interests, but with the masses' livelihood needs as well. Thus, in line with the exigencies of wartime adversity and the now more explicit multiclass concepts of new democracy, the overall emphasis in the policies and prnciples enunciated was clearly on the theme of mutual benefits and interests, with a very decided move away from any remaining struggle-and-benefits approach to labor mobilization.[54]

The cheng-feng movement itself apparently played an important part in implanting the revised labor-industry policies and in "rectifying" those management, union, and other worker attitudes, practices, and goals which clashed with the new developmental principles and approaches. In its objective of instilling Maoist mass-line policies and values, *cheng-feng* clearly involved a more decisive turn away from an "urban" Communist concept of economic development and its corollary of preferential status and treatment for a state industrial constituency of management and union bureaucrats and factory staffs and workers.

In his May Day statement of 1942, Teng Fa referred to a Central Committee *cheng-feng* directive of the same date addressed to party members in the labor movement.[55] The directive called for a study of the changes occurring in the labor-capital relationship and in the character of the labor movement during the resistance war and for a review of the management system of state factories and options for improving production techniques. A fifty-day Factories Conference held in the spring of 1943 appeared to be one major outcome of this rectification campaign.[56] In a concluding speech to the conference, Teng Fa spoke of the now-exposed (through the rectification movement) role of "counter-revolutionary" elements in the state factories and of the problems of bureaucratism and dogmatism in party and union work in industry.[57] He emphasized the identity of interests between labor and management in the state factories and the fundamental need for mutual cooperation in fulfilling production targets. Those in the factories whose actions adversely affected the goal of increasing output and reducing costs were in effect engaging in "counter-revolutionary behavior."

While endorsing the usual policy of "appropriate improvement" in workers' livelihood in line with increasing levels of production—"the more the workers produce, the better their livelihood will be"—Teng at the same time cautioned against a policy of relying solely on wage incentives, declaring that "we must educate the workers in the new labor attitude" (*hsin lao-tung t'ai-tu*), a theme first sounded for state-enterprise workers by Liu Shao-ch'i in the final months of the Kiangsi Soviet. The production front was as vital as the battlefront, and the wealth produced by labor supported the revolution and thus the interests of the working class itself. But these concepts, in

Teng's view, had not yet been firmly grasped by management, party, and union functionaries in the factories.

Despite the fact that the *cheng-feng* process of self-criticism, investigation, and study had already achieved some positive results, Teng complained that the great majority of factory party and union organizations had continued on the wrong track. Some even took an "adversary position" *(tui-li ti-wei)* toward management, with the unions often adopting a strongly economist approach and using against their own factories the old economic struggle tactics they had applied against the capitalists in the past. These leaders uncritically passed along to management the demands of backward workers—a reflection both of the influence of "guildism" among the workers and of "the kind of brains of some of our comrades!" as Teng caustically remarked.

Teng pointed also to the prevalence of bureaucratism in union work, which, he said, had led to union separation from the worker masses and resulted in a "cold attitude" among many workers toward the unions. Party organizations in the factories had initially done little to correct this phenomenom and had been lax in genuinely implementing the rectification movement. Only later, under correct leadership, Teng commented, did a real awakening take place, with "Bolshevik power" emerging to take up the struggle.[58] Finally, Teng told the conference that workers' education had followed an academic "education for education's sake" approach, rather than being oriented toward the concrete goals of raising political consciousness, fostering labor enthusiasm, and promoting the fulfillment of production tasks.

Teng attributed these various shortcomings to a number of factors. First, there was the dominance of "destructive elements" *(p'o-huai fen-tzu)* in many union and party branches and the lack of a mass-line approach by management. The second factor was the inadequacies of party and union cadres who took into the state factories "antiquated thinking on the role of unions" *(ch'en-chiu ssu-hsiang-ti kung-hui tso-yung)*, and "everywhere exhibited their economist thinking." The last factor cited was management's failure to recognize the important role that party and union organizations could play in promoting production and the mobilization of the workers. Management mistakenly relied on the stimulus of higher wages (whose efficacy Teng minimized), which only encouraged the growth of economism among the workers.

Teng called for a thoroughgoing struggle against corruption and waste. The unions were exhorted to instill among the workers a love and concern for the factories, under the slogan "treat the factory as you would your own family." He further stressed the significance of the Chao Chan-k'uei (model-worker) movement and of collective competitions; the former was of particular value in instilling the "self-sacrificing spirit of the working class." The unions should assist management in enforcing labor discipline, struggle against "lazy elements" (lan-to fen-tzu), nurture the positive workers, and, ultimately, absorb the latter into the party. At the same time, he encouraged a greater attention to problems arising in the course of the workers' daily lives. The party and unions were also called upon to correct management's tendency to rely on wage incentives alone to increase worker efficiency. Teng Fa projected a dual approach to this critical problem, in which the appeal to the worker would be based on an appropriate blend of political education and "reasonable wages" (ho-li-ti kung-tzu). It was now necessary to reexamine labor practices and revise "impractical regulations" in line with these principles.

Teng's report was clearly a severe attack on those who had been the dominant elements in state-factory management and on union and party functionaries in the industrial sector. Its themes were underscored in another major address to the conference by Chang Wen-t'ien, who had shifted his support to Mao's side on the eve of the Long March in late 1934.[59] Chang spoke of the exposure of the "plots" of "secret agents" as well as of the role of the conference in correcting "our own mistakes."[60] In discussing the cheng-feng movement in the factories, Chang also attacked "counter-revolutionaries" who had wielded influence in industry. He added that since in the past "we [the Maoist forces?] did not emphasize factory work," this sector had become the "stronghold" of these elements. He declared that a worker's responsibilities and duties in the state factories were analogous to those of a soldier in the Eighth Route Army. Bad elements had to be opposed and bureaucrats fought in order to transform thoroughly the work of the factories; the central tasks were production and education and the training of a superior corps of cadres.

Significantly, Lin Po-ch'ü reported in January 1944 that the "government factories, too, showed great progress after the Factories Conference and the movement for purging non-Marxist [i.e., non-Maoist] ideology in factories."[61] He noted that, as a result, every factory had greatly exceeded its planned production targets for 1943; quality was much improved and production costs had been reduced in comparison with the previous year.[62]

Cheng-feng also brought widely promoted emulation campaigns publicizing model individuals in various fields. The most important model worker campaign, the "learn from Chao Chan-k'uei" movement launched in the fall of 1942, highlighted the basic themes subsequently spelled out by Teng Fa at the 1943 Factories Conference. It was thus directly linked to the rectification of worker attitudes and to the inculcation of labor's duties and responsibilities. *Liberation Daily's* May Day editorial of 1943, for example, was wholly concerned with the promotion of the Chao Chan-k'uei movement[63] (the General Labor Union was accorded responsibility for leading the movement in each factory); a follow-up article by Teng Fa appeared a few days later.[64] The unfolding of the movement was linked to the 1943 Factories Conference, which had resulted in the "responsible comrades" in each factory gaining an initial understanding of the movement. This model worker campaign was directly linked to the task of increasing production and reducing costs, which in turn called for clearing out all "destructive elements" from the factories, and opposing waste and the "coveting" of public funds (presumably referring to excessive worker demands).

All factories were called upon to mobilize their workers to follow the example of Chao Chan-k'uei as the path to becoming more progressive and revolutionary.[65]

The Chao Chan-k'uei movement had been officially initiated in September 1942 in a *Liberation Daily* editorial.[66] Chao, then in his mid-forties, had come from a poverty-stricken background and worked as a blacksmith's apprentice as a teen-age boy, then as a construction worker, and later in a railway repair shop in the north-west. Together with other railroad workers, he had fled from the Japanese occupation to Sian in 1938.[67] From Sian he went to Yenan and studied there at the Anti-Japanese University (*K'ang-ta*) and the Workers' School. The editorial noted that Chao's studies had brought him to understand the identity of his personal interests with those of the Communist Party and the revolution and to realize the necessity of regarding the state factories as revolutionary assets. Transferred to the production line in 1939, Chao performed "plain, ordinary work" as a furnace man in the agricultural tools factory. He worked at this laborious job without slacking, arriving earlier and leaving later than the others. "He is completely different from the slackers who only seek high wages, demand special preferential treatment, and work erratically and half-heartedly." Chao took on extra tasks relating to the general welfare of both the factory and the workers. Doing the most and the best work, he neither boasted nor sought personal credit, but viewed his work as part of a collective effort and labored in a self-sacrificing spirit to increase production for the war and the revolution. He never discussed his personal gains or losses, he disciplined himself in service to the people, and his attitude, the article stated, "is just the reverse of those who only pursue their immediate personal interests, seek increased wages whether the factory can afford it or not, and even go so far as to oppose the factory by wasting materials, adopting slowdown strikes, and sabotaging production."

Chao himself had waged a successful struggle against "idlers" in his work department who had used such tactics. He had proposed many ideas for improving production and the workers' lives and had fostered a friendly spirit of unity in the entire factory. Though himself a veteran skilled worker, "he doesn't have the bad habits of the average veteran worker." He shared his skills with others and was particularly solicitous of the apprentices. In carrying out production tasks, protecting revolutionary property, and promoting the general welfare, the article concluded, Chao was a model for all workers in the Border Region's state factories. He had consistently displayed "exactly the new attitude towards labor which state factory workers in the new-democratic areas ought to have," and the hope was expressed that his example would inspire thousands like him in the Border Region.[68]

In October 1942 the General Labor Union called on all factory workers to study the spirit and labor attitude of Chao and to make the *Liberation Daily* editorial about him one of the documents in the factory rectification movement. This movement, the union declared, had profound ideological importance in educating workers, reforming union work, and igniting a vast movement to overcome the difficulties facing the Border Region.[69] A December report, however, complained that many factories had either not yet launched a Chao Chan-k'uei movement or had initiated the movement in a superficial way, viewing Chao as just an ordinary worker rather than as a key example of the kind of worker the revolution needed.[70] Based on the Chao model, the General Labor Union had set out the requisites for model-worker status: (1) to love the factory and strictly adhere to discipline; (2) to work with enthusiasm and consistency; (3) to be the best in achieving quality and quantity of production; (4) to care for tools and avoid waste; (5) to work hard now for later enjoyment; (6) to study diligently and help others; and (7) to practice self-discipline, serve the people, and unite with the masses. The report reiterated the pivotal role of the movement in reforming labor attitudes and opposing economist ideas and described it as "the central task" of all factory trade unions.[71] The sustained character of the Chao Chan-k'uei movement was indicated in Tung Pi-wu's specific references to it in his May 1945 memorandum to the United Nations on the liberated areas. "This movement," he stated, "has raised the morale of the workers, who have become more conscious of the fact that they are working for national emancipation and the welfare of the common people."[72]

The protracted nature and the content of the Chao Chan-k'uei movement itself pointed up the difficulties, in terms of worker productivity and motivation, of implementing a "new labor attitude" based primarily on the concept of selfless service and on comparatively uniform and less advantaged wage policies. The sharp critiques of economist approaches and attitudes of managers and workers, and the fact that wage differentials based on productivity and skills did retain a place, however limited, in Border Region wage scales, attested to these difficulties as well. The concerns and problems these issues created were strikingly expressed by Teng Fa in his May 1943 article on the Chao Chan-k'uei movement.[73]

Teng first of all noted that the movement was not restricted to the Border Region but was developing also in the various north China base areas, in some cases using homegrown labor heroes as models. The primary focus, however, was on the problems faced in attempting to mobilize the mass of state factory workers in the Chao Chan-k'uei movement. Teng concluded that only a minority of the workers were at that time participants in the movement. He felt constrained to add that this minority was "by no means isolated," since they were backed by the Party, the new-democratic regime, and the union. He spoke also of the "comparatively complex" character and the varied levels of political consciousness of the labor forces in the factories. He advised a policy of persuasion to absorb nonparticipants into the movement, thus avoiding friction and the danger that "we might even isolate ourselves."

The most interesting section of Teng's article is his frank discussion of the difficulties of mounting a movement based on an altruistic public-spirited appeal to the workers. This was contrasted to a parallel movement then in progress for greater agricultural productivity that was built around a "new rich" peasant model named Wu Man-yu. There was "some logic" to the latter approach, Teng wrote, since the peasant producers were being encouraged to work for themselves, while the state workers were being entreated to produce for the public (state). Therefore, "to carry out the Wu Man-yu movement among the peasantry is easier, this is a fact." But this did not mean that the Chao Chan-k'uei movement was an "impossible task"; as long as the workers understood that to produce for the public was in accord with their basic interests, they would voluntarily cooperate. But this would take "a deeply penetrating" campaign of publicity and education, combined also with adherence to the principle of consideration for both public and private interests. With regard to this latter point, Teng brought up the matter of material incentives and suggested that workers participating in the Chao Chan-k'uei movement be rewarded with a percentage of production above their targets.[74] It was evident that the incentive issue in labor policy formulation remained a thorny one.

At this same time, the peasantry's steadily improving living standard, based on incentive policies and a broad range of income differentials (even with the impact of the progressive tax system on the richer peasants), stood in marked contrast to the labor line—a contrast tellingly revealed in the Wu Man-yu movement. Wu Man-yu, according to Harrison Forman's report on his 1944 visit to the Shen-Kan-Ning base, was "the Border Region's Labor Hero Number One."[75] A destitute refugee whose first wife had died of starvation and who had been forced to sell his three-year-old daughter, Wu received some hillside land in the Communists' land-redistribution program before the war and diligently reclaimed an additional large tract of wasteland; he eventually became the head of a prosperous farm household. The official biography stressed Wu's effective use of party-encouraged labor exchange teams and other cooperative activities as important factors in his success.[76] Described by Forman in 1944 as "sixtyish, strong-bodied, red-faced, with merry eyes and a friendly smile," he could neither read nor write. But with his extraordinary knowledge of farming methods and his ingenuity, he had built up a farm of over sixty-five acres.[77] His immediate family of eleven members was supplemented by four hired laborers (famine refugees from Honan Province), and he had a flock of forty sheep and goats, four oxen, one horse, four beehives, and, in his own words, "I don't know how many chickens."[78]

Wu Man-yu was a symbol of the party's reliance on the individual peasant proprietor and of the encouragement and reassurance given to those peasants able to achieve a new prosperity (including the "new-rich" peasant).[79] In its encouragement of "capitalist forces" in the countryside (the use of hired labor by the more prosperous peasantry), the CCP in this period avoided any overcommitment to agricultural hired labor and stressed the labor-capital harmony theme here as well as in industry. This policy reflected both the overriding interest in raising agricultural output and the political considerations implicit in the party's reliance on the broadest possible peasant base. By rejecting earlier class strategies which had attempted to develop an agricultural labor constituency as the Party's rural vanguard, the CCP was now able to avoid the contradictions and obstacles the former strategy had put in the way of building a broad peasant base. Significantly, the Wu Man-yu movement raised queries in the Party in 1943 as to whether such rich-peasant models did not undercut the party's long-standing commitment to the cause of hired agricultural labor.[80] The response, in an internal party publication, was as follows:

> Unmistakably Wu Man-yu is at present a rich peasant. Wu Man-yu's recent economy is built on the foundation of his own labor and hired labor. The hired portion of labor derives from an exploitative relation. There is no question that the Wu Man-yu-style economic development is of capitalist nature, and what is strange or dreadful about that?[81]

The writer, while denying that the "Wu Man-yu-style" rich-peasant policy undermined the party commitment to hired labor,

went on to state that "in the past not a few comrades have misunderstood the Party's proposal to oppose capitalist thought within
the Party." This had led to the "completely mistaken" idea that
"there is no need to develop capitalism in the society," a notion
contradicted by Mao's "On New Democracy" and the January 1942
Party Central Committee directive on land policy in the base
areas.[82]

The January 1942 Central Committee directive spoke of the
"more progressive" character of capitalist production in China and
noted that the rich peasants were "the capitalists in the rural areas
and [were] an indispensable force in the anti-Japanese war and in
the battle of production." The policy of the CCP "is not to weaken
capitalism and the bourgeoisie, nor to weaken the rich peasant class
and their productive force, but to encourage capitalist production
and ally with the bourgeoisie and encourage production by rich
peasants and ally with the rich peasants, on the condition that
proper improvements are made in the living conditions of the
workers."[83]

Teng Fa, in a speech to the Factories Conference in Yenan in
May 1944 (presumably a follow-up to the 1943 conference), summed
up the results of *cheng-feng* on union and party work in the state
factories.[84] He noted that the formerly strong economist trend in
these organizations had been "basically" overcome as a result of the
rectification campaign (including an "anti-privileged class struggle"
[*fan-tui t'e-ch'üan chieh-chi tou-cheng*]) and the Chao Chan-k'uei
movement.[85] He acknowledged, however, that since the state
factory unions had recognized that it was wrong to create labor-
management confrontations and to "toy" with economism, their
motivation had waned. They had relinquished their independent role,
deferring everything to the factory heads, serving in many cases
merely as the latter's "messengers." These organizations still had
much important work to do in once again defining the unions' key
role in motivating worker performance. Teng also cautioned that
the factory union and party organizations should voice their views on

worker livelihood questions in accord with the overall principle of regard for public and private interests, with the former taking precedence.[86]

The standard Maoist formula of this period equated the party's peasant-landlord line, based on a moderate rent and interest reduction policy (reaffirmed in the January 1942 Central Committee directive on land policy), with its new labor-capital policies. In November 1941, for example, Mao stated that

> in agrarian relations, on the one hand we carry out reduction of rent and interest so that the peasants will have food, and on the other we provide for the payment of the reduced rent and interest so that the landlords, too, can live. In the relations between labour and capital, on the one hand we help the workers so that they have both work and food, and on the other we pursue a policy of developing industry so that the capitalists may obtain some profit.[87]

Yet there were, in fact, important differences between the two sides of this peasant-landlord, worker-capitalist equation. In the very years during which "leftist" labor policies were being modified and "anti-Marxist" elements in the unions and factories were coming under attack, the rent reduction campaign went into high gear as a vigorously promoted "movement" in the various base areas and in those districts of the Border Region where land redistribution had not taken place.[88] The campaign was presumably part of the overall effort to alleviate the lot of the poorer peasantry, which had been forced to carry relatively heavy tax burdens in the crisis period after 1940, and it greatly heightened the pressure against the landlords. It was designed to mobilize and organize the masses of poor and middle peasants through a still-limited struggle movement directed at "feudal" exploitative elements in the countryside, while at the same time carefully shielding capitalist forces, both industrial-commercial and agricultural.

In an October 1943 party directive, Mao wrote that "rent reduction is a mass struggle by the peasants" and that to "bestow rent reduction as a favour instead of arousing the masses to achieve it by their own action is wrong, and the results will not be solid." Mao added that "peasant organizations should be formed or reconstituted in the struggle for rent reduction. . . . Now that the base areas have shrunk in size, it is of more immediate importance than at any time in the past six years for the Party to win the masses there by patient, conscientious and thorough work."[89] Kataoka notes that the rent and interest reduction movement and the new tax policies were designed "to favor the tenants and to squeeze landlording out of existence" at the same time that they encouraged landlords to transform themselves into capitalists. He adds that the CCP's 1942-43 policies indicated that the rural areas under their control "were going through rapid social change which bordered on upheaval," with the entire process "just barely contained behind the facade of rent reduction and progressive tax."[90]

The taxation policies of the later Yenan years (the progressive tax system) are fully in line with the measures described above. Michael Lindsay has observed that "the tax system was an instrument of social policy as well as a means for raising revenue. Its most important feature was a rather sharp discrimination against income from rent, since the landlord had to pay both income tax on his rent and property tax on his land." This discrimination "combined with the effectively enforced 37.5 per cent maximum on rents, gave landlords a strong economic inducement to sell land to their tenants and to put their capital into trade or industry, where it did not incur property tax or, even better, into the forms of industry which were completely tax exempt." In this process of landlords selling out to their tenants, Lindsay continued, the "more competent and energetic farmers could buy land and become prosperous and, at the time, were praised as 'labour heroes' in the Communist press."[91]

The new labor policies and approaches, on the other hand, were clearly designed to eliminate the struggle approach altogether and to reduce the preferential status of the workers in relation to both state and private enterprise. These changes were accompanied by a major economic reorganization which greatly enhanced the role of the rural villages in "industrial" development and also opened the door to a much broader sphere of activity for capitalist enterprise. Seen from a long-term perspective, the peasantry were once more being mobilized for what would ultimately be a full-scale social revolution in the countryside after 1946.[92] In contrast, the new labor guidelines marked a further significant step in the Maoist move away from any primary political commitment to a worker base, and reflected Mao's policy of defusing labor-capital class antagonisms, an approach which was to emerge fully in the "mutual benefits" theme in CCP urban policy in subsequent years.

It is clear that important elements in the CCP leadership from 1936 to 1940-41 operated on the premise that the party's proletarian roots and character could best be sustained in the rural setting of the Border Region by seeking to promote "modern" state industry. The workers and staff and the union and party bureaucracy associated with this sector were accorded a comparatively favored status as "advanced" elements through whom "proletarian consciousness," leadership of the "backward" peasants, and economic modernization could be fostered. At the same time, these party forces reached out for a much larger constituency through an attempted revival of a national labor movement as the party's political mainstay in the KMT-led national resistance front against Japan.

In the meantime, of course, in response to their rural base environment, the party in the early Yenan period led by Mao, pursued policies along the lines of the economic construction measures of the final Kiangsi phase. These were built around broader rural mobilization and economic development policies and encouragement of private enterprise, handicrafts, and cooperatives. Though such policies were now less hamstrung by the overriding class-line considerations that had prevailed in the 1933-34 period in Kiangsi, they were nevertheless still colored and checked by the outlook of the proletarian-minded elements.

The rapid Japanese occupation of the cities, the economic and political impediments to effective Communist mobilization of labor in the KMT areas, and the erosion of the united front all served to frustrate the aspirations for a new, left-led labor upsurge along the lines of the 1925-27 revolutionary years. These very obstacles served at the same time to enhance the Maoist strategy of an essentially independent armed-resistance struggle operating in the rural base areas and helped to consolidate Maoist political and military power. All of these factors (as well as the further deterioration of the party's international ties) led inexorably to the full eclipse of the urban-proletarian line in CCP wartime politics and strategies.

With the economic and military crisis of 1940-42 in the base areas as a catalyst, the Maoist leadership initiated a "mass line" that was reflected in all phases of policy during the 1942-44 years of the rectification movement. This set of policies included a clear shift away from the earlier emphasis on a "modern" industrial-proletarian core in the Border Region toward policies in which the peasants and the villages loomed large. Privileged status for the industrial workers was deemphasized in favor of a stronger focus on decentralized rural development, on reduced state expenditures, and on more egalitarian approaches to the worker-peasant and industry-agriculture relationships. In line with these policies, the party concentrated on greater peasant mobilization, which became linked to a broadened class strategy in which capitalist forces, both agricultural and industrial, received more positive encouragement. Labor-capital "contradictions" became increasingly submerged in the concept of a multiclass coalition led by the CCP which would represent the interests of both labor and capital.

Emerging in microcosmic form in the Border Region and the other base areas, these developmental policies and worker-peasant relationships were to become notable features of the Maoist outlook from the late 1950s on. In 1961-62, for example, in his then unpublished comments on a Soviet text on political economy, Mao remarked: "When we were in the base areas, we enforced a free supply system. People were a little healthier then. They did not quarrel on account of their going after wages."[93] But after liberation "we instituted a wage system and assigned all personnel in order of rank. On the contrary, more troubles arose."[94] Up to the early stages of liberation "people on the whole lived an egalitarian life, they worked hard and fought bravely on the battlefield. They absolutely did not rely on material incentive for encouragement, but on revolutionary spirit."[95] These historical experiences, Mao observed, "are of great significance to us in solving problems of socialist construction."[96] As to the problems of China's huge rural population, Mao advised: "Don't crowd into the cities. Vigorously develop industry in the countryside and turn peasants into workers on the spot." Such a task raised "a very important question of policy. This is that rural living standards must not be lower than in the cities."[97]

Mao's observations on this issue notwithstanding, it is important to remember that even in the rural environment and egalitarian spirit of the resistance-war years, party labor policy was compelled to balance a primarily social incentive approach with at least some attention to differential wage policies based on skills and productivity. Shifting emphasis and controversy in regard to the balance of social and material incentives continued to characterize post-liberation labor policy in China as well.

The approaching end of the war in 1945, and the subsequent renewed attention to and contact with urban centers, brought new complexities to Communist labor policies. The pressures on the CCP in the initial postwar period generated by labor constituencies in newly occupied cities and towns led also to some resurgence of a "left" proletarian line. But this came under sharp criticism and the basic outlines of Maoist labor-capital policy and of the rural-centered revolution were again asserted by the party center during the civil war years that led to final Communist victory in 1949. It is to the policies of these years that we turn next.

CHAPTER VIII

From the Japanese Surrender to Communist Victory:
1945-48 Labor Policies

As the war moved into its final phase during the first half of 1945, the CCP again turned its attention to the cities and to the urban labor movement in anticipation of occupying many towns and cities (particularly in north China) during the final battles against the Japanese as well as in preparation for the inevitable postwar political and/or military contest with the KMT. The Communist position vis-à-vis the KMT in 1945 was, of course, far stronger than it had been at the time of the 1937 united-front agreements; at the same time, the hostility of each side toward the other had been intensifying, the formerly unifying pressures of the Japanese threat no longer operative.[1] Both sides moved to improve their military positions in the wake of the Japanese surrender in August 1945, while efforts to negotiate cease-fire arrangements and to resolve the complex political and military issues separating the two parties were undertaken. This proved to be an intricate, protracted, and ultimately fruitless task, which finally exploded into full-scale civil war by the end of 1946.

As an indication of their intensified military pressure against Japanese-occupied areas during the early months of 1945, the Communists reported more than a hundred towns under their control by May 1945, a number which increased to 175 two weeks after the Japanese surrender and to more than 190 by the end of 1945.[2] Among them was the important city of Kalgan (Changchiak'ou), capital of Chahar Province, which was under Communist control from late August 1945 until its occupation by Nationalist forces in

215

early October 1946. In the spring of 1946, as part of the great postwar expansion of their power in Manchuria, the Communists occupied Harbin, the major north Manchurian city, which remained permanently in their hands and became the scene of the 1948 congress which reconstituted a national labor federation under Communist leadership for the first time since the 1920s.

In response to this developing situation, the CCP took steps early in 1945 to create a unified structure for the labor organizations of the Communist base areas. This was presumably envisaged as both a nucleus and a foundation for future progress toward a new national labor body and, more immediately, as a Communist labor grouping that could parallel the functions of the KMT-sponsored CAL on the national scene and at the same time maintain an affiliation with the latter body.[3] Reporting to the United States State Department from Yenan on this development, John Service observed that this action was "a logical step" toward an open Communist challenge to the National government and toward a possible move to consolidate the various base areas under a single government. Noting that the Communists were then claiming a union membership of 800,000 (including secret organizations among workers in Japanese-held mines and railways in north and central China), Service added that in "setting up their own general labor organization, the Communists prepare for competition with the Kuomintang when it [the KMT] tries to regain control of [the] cities and the occupied areas of Central and North China."[4]

The workers in the urban centers that were coming under Communist control were basically fitted into the Maoist schema of labor-capital collaboration and the labor policies of the later Yenan years. However, as I shall note, party cadres, in organizing this new constituency, also promoted labor's "narrower" class interests. This resulted in some later criticized "leftist" deviations from the overall guidelines of the Party Center. In these economically more advanced centers, it led also to more complex and differentiated wage arrangements than had been the case in the Border Region. On the eve of this new stage, in January 1945, Mao had stressed the continuing problem of those comrades whose handling of various matters, including "the workers', peasants', youth and women's movements, is often incorrect or only partially correct. They approach rural affairs from an urban view-point." Mao added that as a result of the *cheng-feng* movement "our comrades have made much progress," but he cautioned that the above point had still to be kept in mind.[5] Indeed, a key issue in the labor movement after 1945, and more particularly after 1948, would be the degree to and manner in which the "village" vantage point now required modification or transformation as a consequence of the party's new and increasingly important urban environment.

The famous Maoist summing up of party history, adopted by the Seventh Plenum of the Sixth Central Committee in April 1945 on the eve of the party's Seventh National Congress, reaffirmed the continuing new-democratic character of the Chinese revolution as "an anti-imperialist and anti-feudal revolution under the leadership of the proletariat, with the workers and peasants forming the main body and with other broad social strata taking part."[6] It attacked the various "left lines" in party policy from 1927 to the end of the Kiangsi soviet period in 1934, criticizing particularly the "third left line" of the Russian-returned student leadership from 1931 to 1934 which, among other things, "put the struggle against the bourgeoisie on a par with the struggle against imperialism and feudalism . . . and laid particular stress on the struggle against the rich peasant."[7] In censuring the leftists, the resolution stated that the party's urban policy after 1927 should have been of a defensive character, and "until such time as the general situation again made it possible to form democratic governments in the cities, the Chinese revolutionary movement should have made rural work primary and urban work supplementary."[8] Even after the shift of the Party Center to the Kiangsi base area in 1933, the exponents of the left line "continued to direct all the work in the Red Army and the base areas from their erroneous urban viewpoint and caused great damage to the work."[9]

A change in the overall situation was "now imminent," the document noted. Only now, in the final stages of the war and with Communist power immeasurably strengthened, "is it correct to place work in the Japanese-occupied cities on a par with work in the liberated areas," to prepare for coordinated attacks on the cities from within and without, "and then to shift the centre of gravity of our work to these cities." When the occupied cities "are liberated by the people and a unified democratic coalition government is really established and consolidated, the rural base areas will have accomplished their historical task."[10]

These latter stipulations were in fact not to be met until 1949, and it was only at the Second Plenum of the Seventh Central Committee in March 1949 that this shift in the center of gravity was finally proclaimed.[11] It thus quickly became evident in the immediate postwar years that the party's renewed attention to the cities and the fashioning of its urban and labor policies in that period would proceed (despite some early manifestations of a "neo-proletarian" line) under the influence of the Maoist criticism of the various left lines of the past—all the more so since the rural bases in 1946-48 became more than ever the decisive centers of Communist military and political power and the theater of a profound and massive social revolution.

Mao's major report to the Seventh Congress, delivered in late April 1945, underlined the continued rural orientation of the party.[12] He reiterated the need to overcome an urban standpoint in dealing with rural problems, stressed the central role of the agrarian question in Chinese politics, and delivered a paean of praise to the Chinese peasants as the source of industrial workers and of the army, the main market for industry, "the main political force for democracy in China," and "the chief concern of China's cultural movement at the present stage." Mao carefully added that "in saying this, I am of course not ignoring the . . . importance of the rest of the people . . . and in particular am not ignoring the working class, which is politically the most conscious and therefore qualified to lead the whole revolutionary movement. Let there be no mis-understanding."[13] Yet the main thrust of his argument could not itself be misunderstood.

It is interesting that Mao's other references in this report to the role of the working class were couched almost entirely in future terms. Noting briefly that during "the Northern Expedition, the Agrarian Revolutionary War and the War of Resistance against Japan, the working class and Communist Party of China [an ambi-guous pairing, since the leadership role of the CCP was obvious] have worked extremely hard and made an invaluable contribution to the cause of the liberation of the Chinese people," Mao stated that in the recovery of the big cities in the final defeat of Japan, "the Chinese working class will play a very great role. And it can be predicted that after the anti-Japanese war, the effort and contribu-tion of the Chinese working class will be even greater."[14]

In projecting this future role of the workers, Mao completely avoided class-struggle themes, declaring that the

policy of adjusting the interests of labour and capital will be adopted under the new democratic state system. On the one hand, it will protect the interests of the workers, institute an eight- to ten-hour working day according to circumstances, provide suitable unemployment relief and social insurance and safeguard trade union rights; on the other hand it will guarantee legitimate profits to properly managed state, private and cooperative enterprises—so that both the public and the private sectors and both labour and capital will work together to develop industrial production.[15]

A *Liberation Daily* editorial of 7 February 1945 initiated the call for the creation of a "China Liberated Areas' Labor Federation" (*Chung-kuo chieh-fang ch'ü chih-kung lien-ho hui*).[16] By linking this call with the 7 February anniversary of the 1923 massacre of the Communist-led Peking-Hankow railway strikers, the essay under-scored both the new national role projected for the base areas' labor movement and the reactivated effort to restore links with labor in the non-Communist areas. At the same time, it was symbolic of the efforts to enlist labor's assistance in what was seen as a final phase of the war, the phase in which Communist attention would be directed against Japanese-held railway networks. The editorial stressed the military and production role of the workers in the Communists' resistance struggle and noted specifically the guerrilla-war contributions of workers from the Japanese-occupied areas, particularly of north China railwaymen and miners. It called for Communist activity within the urban transport systems in occupied areas and exhorted transport workers to study armed resistance and prepare for the coming liberation.

The editorial portrayed the projected labor federation as a key step in promoting the solidarity of all of China's workers in opposition to the KMT's one-party rule; it was viewed as supportive of the goal of coalition government and as a first step toward a united national labor organization. Labor representatives from non-Communist areas were thus invited to participate in the work of the new organization. In turning to the tasks of the federation within the base areas, the editorial stressed the value of communication among workers from the various areas on ways to stimulate worker commitment and efficiency and emphasized labor-capital unity in the effort to increase production.[17]

A conference of representatives from the base-area unions was held in Yenan in the spring of 1945 and resulted in the formation of a preparatory "Committee of the Trade Unions of the Liberated Areas" with Teng Fa as chairman. The committee was apparently an interim step in the creation of a federation.[18] No further definitive organizational moves seem to have been made in this direction, evidently reflecting the CCP's postwar avoidance of steps toward a politically unified "Liberated China" which might be interpreted as a direct challenge to the Nationalist government at a time when negotiations between the two sides were in progress.[19] With the onset of civil war, further organizational measures had to await the

creation, in mid-1948, of a new national labor federation, proclaimed as a direct successor to the Communist-led ACFL in the
1920s.

As Communist forces moved into many of the towns and
smaller cities of north China and Manchuria after the Japanese
surrender, the CCP naturally gave much attention to organizing the
workers in these newly occupied areas.[20] At the same time, the
Communists were brought into much greater contact with the urban
private business class, now increasingly viewed in the Maoist new-
democratic strategy as an essential component of a CCP-led multiclass constituency. Active Communist organizational work among
urban labor in the new areas and a policy of "appropriately" improving the latter's living standards were therefore coordinated with
strong emphasis on encouraging private enterprise and guaranteeing
profits, on class cooperation based on the mutual benefits formula,
and on higher productivity as the key objective and the principal
road to both increased profits and greater worker benefits. As has
been noted above, the CCP, as the governing authority in this situation, could now implement these policies without being limited to
appeals to the "good will" of the capitalists or the "self-restraint" of
the workers. Similar urban policies (shorn of "leftist deviations"
which occurred in 1945-46) could subsequently be more credibly
promoted by the CCP in its appeal to the KMT-ruled cities during
the final phases of the civil war. The CCP's approach to the urban
business and middle classes during the post-1946 civil war was thus
significantly strengthened by the party's ability to reforge (but now
under its own direct leadership) the four-class bloc of the 1924-27
united-front period under circumstances where the party was no
longer compelled to promote a highly militant urban labor movement
as the principal cutting edge in realizing political hegemony. For
example, a party directive drafted by Mao on the 1946 policy for the
liberated areas stated that

> all areas must launch movements in 1946 for the reduc-
> tion of rent and interest in their newly liberated areas,

movements on a large scale, of a mass character, but
with leadership. As for the workers, wages should be
appropriately raised. Through these movements the
broad masses should be able to emancipate themselves,
organize and become the conscious masters of the
Liberated Areas.[21]

The focus of mass struggle movements continued to be the
peasants in the countryside.[22]

Yet, at the same time, this first experience of extended
Communist control and governance of comparatively large urban
centers apparently reactiviated (and recruited) proletarian-minded
elements within the party. Labor mobilization and organization
linked to worker economic interests and demands again came into
play; labor cadres in some areas during the early postwar period
evidently resorted to anticapitalist struggle techniques and supported "excessive" worker demands. However, as the Communist
record in Kalgan shows, these subsequently denounced "left adventurist" trends were increasingly subordinated to the dominant labor-
capital themes outlined above, themes which were even more
vigorously promoted as the Communist forces prepared for the final
entry into China's great cities in 1948. While movements to "settle
accounts" with "traitors and secret agents" in the factories were
launched among the workers in the newly occupied areas in 1945-46,
the targets were limited to those explicitly accused of pro-Japanese
or pro-KMT "destructive activities."[23] As shall be detailed below,
wage patterns in newly occupied cities did in fact take on a more
complex and production-oriented form than had been the case in the
rural base areas, with much greater emphasis on incentive policies
and wage differentials. This was particularly true in Harbin, for
example, where the growing Soviet Russian influence and model was
evident in such wage policies.[24]

With regard to the rural sector, the move during 1946-47
toward full land revolution also brought a leftist resurgence reminiscent, in some respects, of the rural class line of the Kiangsi

period; this was later to be referred to as a "poor and hired peasant line."[25] This line was marked by what was subsequently to be criticized as a preoccupation with the property demands and interests of the poor peasants and hired hands. This leftist current was characterized by moves toward complete equalization of land ownership (often at the expense of middle-peasant interests), the takeover of landlord and rich-peasant industrial and commercial undertakings, and a failure to differentiate carefully among landlord, rich-peasant, and middle-peasant categories.[26] By the end of 1947 and early 1948, Mao was taking steps to reaffirm a broader rural-class stance and to shield rural capitalist forces. Thus, in January 1948 Mao criticized as "wrong" the slogan which stated that "the poor peasants and farm labourers conquer the country and should rule the country." In the villages, Mao observed, "it is the farm labourers, poor peasants, middle peasants and other working people, united together under the Chinese Communist Party, who conquer the country and should rule the country."[27] Mao also qualified his support at this time of the poor peasants' demand for equal distribution of the land by rejecting the notion of "absolute egalitarianism"; he noted that a "section of the middle peasants must be allowed to keep some land over and above the average obtained by the poor peasants."[28] The target of land reform was

the system of feudal exploitation by the landlord class and by the old-type rich peasants [as distinguished from the "new rich" peasant class spawned in the Communist areas], and there should be no encroachment either upon the national bourgeoisie or upon the industrial and commercial enterprises run by the landlords and rich peasants [with both these latter categories to receive allotments of land and property equal to that given the peasants].[29]

The party acted also to correct errors in class designations, reissuing for this purpose at the end of 1947 the documents on class status

Mao had drafted in October 1933 (which had been a source of contention between Mao and the Internationalists at that time), now
modified to protect more prosperous middle peasants from inclusion
in the rich-peasant group.[30] But it is the policy developments on
the urban labor scene that will be our most immediate concern.

A lead article in *Liberation Daily* in late September 1945
delineated the party's basic labor policy for the urban and mining
areas occupied by the Communists since the Japanese surrender,
areas which, the article specifically noted, contained many
thousands of workers.[31] The suffering and exploitation these
workers had undergone at the hands of the Japanese were emphasized, as were the wartime anti-Japanese guerrilla operations of
north China miners acting in coordination with the Eighth Route
Army. The workers were praised for their cooperation with the
Communist armies in safeguarding industrial and mining properties
during the takeover from Japanese and puppet forces. The article
made much of the new and better life already being enjoyed by these
workers, who had now become "one of the masters of the new democratic regime." As a result, work enthusiasm had reached
"unequalled heights," with many working around the clock and
beyond their physical limits to express their gratitude to and support
of the liberation forces.

In urging maximum efforts, the article enumerated three
crucial tasks. The first item was the organization of unions to
defend the interests of "the workers and the people" and to handle
such immediately pressing needs as relief for destitute workers and
jobs for the unemployed. The unions would help the new administration protect workers' interests and "adjust" (*t'iao-cheng*) labor-
capital relations. The second was the need to raise production and
support the front. The workers' slogan, the paper observed, had
changed from "the slower the better," under the Japanese, to the
current "the faster the better." And the third task for the workers
in the newly liberated areas was to help the new authorities to
eliminate "traitors and secret agents."

It is noteworthy that in its emphasis on the role, organization, and interests of its expanding labor constituency, the party focused its attack on the Japanese occupiers and their collaborators and viewed the workers' liberation in this context. However, even though the immediate postliberation targets of worker struggles were to be limited to the "traitor-secret agent" category, when such struggles were directed at factory owners and businessmen, they often focused on demands for wage increases and other benefits.[32]

An official pronouncement on industrial policy in the liberated areas during the early postsurrender period summed up the policy objectives as the restoration and expansion of production, the reduction of costs, and the realization of a "certain degree" of profit on the part of enterprises.[33] The document advocated low-interest loans and reduction in or exemption from industrial taxes—policies equally applicable to public, private, or joint enterprises. In areas liberated since the end of the war, it noted, private enterprises had been freely restored to their original owners; loans had been advanced, tax rebates given, and arrangements made to ensure a supply of raw materials to help them start up again. Assistance had also been provided for the establishment of new, privately owned consumer industries. The report claimed that as a result of all these measures, production had expanded and profits increased.[34]

In a section on wage policies, the document cautioned that wage and hour arrangements required careful handling since such policies affected not only production and profits, but also workers' attitudes and livelihood. It stated that the liberated areas' regulations called for an eight- to ten-hour workday, depending on the type of work (generally ten hours in light industry), and a maximum of sixty hours a week. Wages were determined by a number of factors: nature of the work, skills, responsibilities, productivity, seniority, and so on, with the minimum not less than what was sufficient for the livelihood of 1 to 1.5 persons. The basic guidelines in setting hours and wages were to be determined by the principles of public-private mutual benefits and labor-capital mutual benefits (*kung-ssu liang-li* and *lao-tzu liang-li*), which remained the key CCP labor-capital policy formulas through the civil war period. These principles guaranteed the workers a "certain level" of livelihood, while ensuring that factory regulations and labor discipline were observed so that profits could be realized.[35]

Citing the example of factories in Kalgan, the document described the "progressive" or graduated wage system in force there under the Communists in 1946. In this system (in which wages were usually paid half in money and half in supplies), output above a certain fixed standard received progressively higher wages. This basic structure was augmented by other systems of incentive awards and bonuses or dividends (all of which had raised labor enthusiasm and increased production by 40 to 100 percent), thus guaranteeing both workers' livelihood and industry's profits.[36] A Communist news agency report from Kalgan in September 1946 stressed the "frank and above-board discussions" taking place between employers and employees "to fix wages, increase efficiency, speed up output and keep down costs." The "common ground" of these discussions was that "employers are to run their factories on a profit basis while the workers must be provided with decent means of living and working conditions and not demand overmuch from the employers."[37] It was evident that, in these more sophisticated and industrialized surroundings (compared with the rural base areas) where private enterprise played a more significant role, there was now an emphasis on more elaborate incentive arrangements than had been the case in the simpler and more austere environment of the wartime rural areas. But the basic labor-capital class guidelines of the later wartime period remained in force, as the following examination of policies and developments in the Kalgan area will illustrate.[38]

In December 1945, *Worker*, Kalgan's labor publication, reported that 153 unions had been established with a total membership of 13,846.[39] Under the unions' leadership, 131 "settle-accounts" struggles had been waged with the participation of nearly 12,000 workers.[40] In detailing the advances made in workers' circumstances, status, and participation in government, the paper noted certain shortcomings in work as well. During the early months when the unions were first being established, "bad elements" had "disrupted" union work in regard to such matters as wages, working hours, labor protection, factory management, and so on. However, with CCP guidance, fuller worker participation, and the preparations for establishing a General Labor Union, these problems were being overcome.[41] Though not explicitly articulated, the implication was that such "bad elements" had raised "disruptive" (unreasonable) demands. This issue surfaced again at the First Workers' Representatives' Congress held in Kalgan at the end of December 1945, at which the Kalgan General Labor Union was formally established.[42] In the keynote speech to the congress, Ma Hui-chih, a representative of the Chin-Ch'a-Chi General Labor Union, explained the CCP's public-private, labor-capital mutual benefits formulas as they applied, respectively, to public and private factories, and he added that there was still a small number of workers who lacked adequate enthusiasm, did not "clearly understand" these principles, and could thus be used by bad elements. In his view, this reflected the still insufficient level of political consciousness among the workers, as well as the fact that there continued to be undesirable elements hiding among the workers that remained to be flushed out.[43]

In this same speech, Ma emphasized that the gains made by Kalgan's workers had been largely due to the Eighth Route Army's eight years of struggle and its liberation of the city. In detailing the crucial role of the Communist armed forces, Ma referred to the "bitter and bloody lesson" of 1927, when the workers had relinquished their weapons to the KMT, and asserted that in the currently very different circumstances the CCP and its armed forces would not repeat this error.

The general character of the settle-accounts struggles (ch'ing-suan tou-cheng) can be discerned from a number of accounts published in the Kalgan labor paper during this period. One report recounted the story of an unscrupulous merchant who had collaborated with the Japanese in distributing grain rations to the workers of a power plant and had, in the process, adulterated the grain.[44] When the Japanese were leaving, he removed equipment from the plant, telling the suspicious but intimidated workers that it had been given to him by the Japanese. With the arrival of the Eighth Route Army, the formation of a union, and the organization of a workers' self-defense corps, the workers decided to settle accounts with the culprit. The latter, however, had by this time fled, and the workers struggled instead against his clerk, forcing him to confess that the equipment had been sold by his boss. Within a week, the proceeds of the sale were recovered by the workers, who turned it over to their plant, requesting that the plant manager use half of it to purchase a truck to transport the workers to and from work and the other half to set up a cooperative for the workers. The account concluded that throughout this struggle the workers had shown their deep attachment for their plant.

Another episode illustrating the role of the workers in protecting their factories told of a KMT agent who had secretly sabotaged factory work and had attempted to recruit workers (promising large rewards) for the KMT army in Peiping (Peking). One of the workers, Pai Hsieh-feng, heard about this, reported it to the factory head, and then led a five-man team from the defense unit to arrest the agent. The factory rewarded Pai with the equivalent of about one month's wages and urged all its workers to emulate him in protecting the factory.[45]

The approach in handling direct worker-employer confrontations was exemplified in the account of a restaurant owner who had complained to his employees that he would be forced to close the restaurant because of increased wages and the bad habits of the employees, who ate only the most expensive food and spent much of their working hours in brothels.[46] He also argued that his workers should not be union members but should be in the merchant-controlled commercial association. The incensed workers decided to "settle" with him at a formal union meeting. At this meeting they explained to him that even though wages had increased there had also been some rise in the cost of living. They denied his other charges, saying that due to the educational influence of the union only very few workers still patronized brothels and, in any case, not during business hours. The boss realized he had insulted the workers and apologized. The union representative at the meeting cautioned the workers against "making a small thing too big" and pointed out the need to be fair to all concerned. The aim, he continued, was to get at the facts, minimize problem areas, reinforce the unity of all sides, and work together to establish a prosperous new Kalgan. In effect, this account focused attention on both the negative habits of the employees and the injustice of the boss's complaints and highlighted as well the basic theme of avoiding an adversary approach in resolving employer-employee problems.

Other major themes in this Kalgan paper during the early months of 1946 dealt with production competitions to support the front, a "recall the past" movement (to make explicit the contrast with the brighter present), and sessions of criticism and self-criticism to overcome shortcomings among workers.[47] The model worker campaign was especially promoted in conjunction with the March 1946 Kalgan city elections. At that time, the city's newly formed General Labor Union listed the key attributes of a model worker candidate for office: a "pure" background (presumably no history of collusion with the Japanese or the KMT), a good record in protecting factory property and in participating in settle-accounts struggles, love for the factory and enthusiasm for production, and the ability "to unite the workers and the factory side."[48] One such model candidate, a veteran factory worker named Hsü Ping-yen, was particularly praised for his exemplary approach in wage discussions: he had insisted on taking a monthly wage somewhat under that originally set (340 rather than 350 catties of grain), since he felt he could no longer work as fast as others.[49]

In general, the qualities of the model workers singled out closely resembled the virtues publicized during the Chao Chan-k'uei movement in the Border Region,[50] though for Kalgan there was an additional stress on underground union work during the Japanese occupation and on exemplary action to protect industrial properties from damage during the August 1945 interregnum prior to the arrival of the Communist forces.[51]

While not among the dominant motifs in the Kalgan labor press during this first Communist occupation, there were nonetheless frequent references to the improved worker benefits and protections gained under the Communists, natural enough in the appeal to this more highly concentrated urban worker constituency. The benefits in question appear to have been largely the product of the early occupation months in 1945. After substantial initial increases, new wage standards for workers in public enterprises were announced in October 1945, to be paid in cash but calculated in terms of the price of millet and adjusted each month to keep pace with inflation.[52] Wages on this scale varied from 100 to 200 catties (133 to 267 pounds) of millet per month for youths, women, and apprentices, and from 300 to 450 catties for skilled workers, with the top of the latter scale reserved for skilled workers in heavy industry.[53] Basic wage rates appear to have been stabilized (in terms of millet) at roughly the same levels until the Communist evacuation of Kalgan in the fall of 1946. Anna Louise Strong reported from Kalgan in mid-1946 (after a year of Communist occupation) that a "rational wage system," based on the price of millet, had been instituted there, with monthly wages ranging from 250 pounds of millet for apprentices to 300 pounds for unskilled workers and all the way up to 900 pounds for a special category of skilled technician or manager. In a soap factory she visited, she was told that most of the workers were skilled and received monthly wages of 500 pounds of millet.[54] Though the wages reported by Strong represented total family income, out of which came clothing and other expenses, it was nevertheless evident that in this urban industrial center the wage spread was greater and the upper wage limits higher than had previously been the case in the rural bases. Wage levels in the private sector in Kalgan were probably considerably lower than those cited above for public enterprises.[55] The party's basic labor-capital line had been affirmed at the December 1945 First Workers' Representatives' Congress in Kalgan: wages should be raised "appropriately," employers allowed to make a profit, and specific wage issues to be settled on the basis of conditions within individual business establishments.[56]

The stabilized wage patterns and firmer handling of worker demands apparently reflected the tougher attitude that was emerging in December 1945, by which time the Communists had completed the creation of a union structure under their leadership in Kalgan. As has been noted, the public-private, labor-capital mutual benefits line was clearly the approved one at the time and "disruptive" worker elements who presumably had made excessive wage-hour and other demands were being criticized. Later, a Chin-Ch'a-Chi representative at the 1948 Harbin labor congress explicitly criticized tendencies in the public-run enterprises in Kalgan during the initial postwar Communist occupation period to set detrimentally high wage levels and to provide relatively high welfare payments to unemployed workers instead of involving them in productive work.[57] These criticisms were in keeping with, and designed to reemphasize, the anti-leftist 1948 labor policy themes. And from the representative's oblique references to "egalitarianism" and "political considerations" in connection with wages, it was apparent that the crux of the wage issue was that the economic well-being and advancement of these state enterprises had to have priority. Wages, therefore, in line with the 1948 theme of "the more work, the more pay," ought to be strictly linked to worker productivity rather than determined by political considerations or principles of equality.[58] These later critiques, however, did not challenge or quarrel with the basic wage principles or the labor-capital class stratégies followed in Kalgan in 1945-46. In fact, the 1948 more work, more pay formula was itself directly linked by the Chin-Ch'a-Chi representative with the progressive wage system which had been implemented in more rudimentary form in Kalgan in that earlier period.[59] And the latter, in turn, had its antecedents in the productivity-linked wage component of the later Yenan years.

The more elaborate and differentiated wage policies emerging by 1948 reflected also the CCP's fast developing responsibility for China's urban economy, an economy in a state of virtual collapse and for which austerity measures and the restoration and development of production took on the highest priority.[60] These wage structures coincided with an anti-"left adventurist" labor policy campaign launched by the party in the first half of 1948. A major feature of this campaign were the "negative examples" from 1945-46 of labor movement cadres in some areas who had one-sidedly emphasized labor benefits and welfare at the expense of increasing production and reducing costs. Such leftist policies had also promoted labor dissension by pitting apprentices and ordinary workers against "exploitative" master craftsmen and skilled workers, a situation clearly damaging to production efficiency.[61] The antileft campaign, which shall be discussed in greater detail below, thus aimed to accentuate and reaffirm the production-centered labor policy line of the party at a time when the CCP faced the prospect of dealing with the rising expectations and demands of a militant but (from the Communist point of view) far from "politically conscious" labor movement in the soon-to-be-occupied major cities.

It is noteworthy that a main center of the left labor line in 1946-47 was the Communist-controlled north Manchurian city of Harbin. Li Li-san, erstwhile urban labor leader of the CCP, had returned from Russian "exile" with the Soviet forces entering Manchuria in August 1945 to become a key figure in both the CCP's Northeast Bureau and the labor movement centered in Harbin.[62] According to later criticisms, labor policies had been excessive, with privately owned factories particularly hard hit by substantial wage hikes and other benefits.[63] By late 1947, however, the Maoist mutual-benefits line, with its exhortations for greater worker austerity and sacrifice, was being strongly promoted in Harbin, though interlaced during 1948 with a complex Soviet-style graduated piece-rate wage and reward system and labor competition movement. The questions raised by the interaction of Maoist labor principles and this highly differentiated base-pay structure, with the latter's inevitably "economist"-oriented reward and emulation wage system, in some respects presaged later wage policy issues in postliberation China. Suzanne Pepper, in her recent study of the post-1945 civil war period, notes that many cadres and party members in Harbin disapproved of the piece-rate wage system from the standpoint of socialist values. She remarks, "Just as excessively high wages tended to produce an 'economic viewpoint' among the workers they feared this [piece-rate] system would have a like effect. They also feared that differences in take-home pay would lead to conflicts and disunity within the labor force."[64]

At the same time, it is well to reiterate that "Maoist" (Yenan) labor policies also included some attention to wage incentives and differentials. The new urban-industrial environment and labor constituencies after 1945 and the imperatives of production more sharply accentuated this aspect of wage policy, as the Kalgan experience demonstrated. By 1948 this had evolved into the much more complex grade-based wage system noted above, a sign of the growing Communist preoccupation with urban-centered industrial production and development. But while these policies gave greater encouragement and rewards to the more skilled and productive workers and technicians, it also sought to hold the line on overall labor benefits. These approaches would ultimately become issues in the resurgence of less urban-centered developmental patterns, inspired by Mao, in the later 1950s and the 1960s. These points will be more fully discussed below.

As for the 1945-46 Kalgan experience, the labor policies and class strategies pursued there essentially followed (despite some early deviations) the labor-capital principles put forth by the Party Center in that period, principles which were vigorously reaffirmed in a 1946 *Liberation Daily* May Day editorial. This May Day pronouncement focused on the theme of labor-capital cooperation. While taking note of the political and economic advances already achieved by labor in the liberated areas, it linked further worker benefits to the continually reiterated production-cost formula.[65] The article called on the trade unions to persist in the policy of labor-capital mutual benefits and interests, cooperation and harmony. Arguing that private capital was essential to the economic construction of the liberated areas, it pointed to the difficulties Chinese national industry had faced through oppression by foreign and domestic monopoly capitalists. To help overcome these difficulties and attain prosperity, mutual concessions by labor and capital were vital and would prove beneficial not only to the two sides, but to the entire nation and people.

The editorial went on to say that the trade unions should "persuade" the private capitalists to raise wages and improve conditions since the resulting benefits to capital from improved labor efficiency and enthusiasm would more than offset any concessions made to the workers. On the other hand, the unions should persuade the workers to restrict their demands on the capitalists and to consider long-term, rather than merely immediate, interests. The two sides should agree on production plans and how to go about reducing waste, rationalizing operations, promoting production competitions, reinforcing labor discipline, and improving technique; both should be geared to the goals of increasing quality and quantity and reducing costs. The editorial warned that the capitalists would otherwise see little opportunity for profits in the Communist areas and would invest elsewhere, which in turn would lead to cutbacks in industry that could only damage labor's cause.

To ensure the support of the masses, the unions were urged to give greater attention to worker welfare matters, such as effectively implementing the labor protection system, encouraging savings, and establishing cooperatives to provide daily necessities inexpensively and as a means of building up labor welfare funds. In pressing for more educational and cultural work to enhance political consciousness and enthusiasm, the editorial called for promotion of the Chao Chan-k'uei movement and underscored the importance of a new labor attitude in the efforts both to develop production and to overcome a "narrow, one-sided economist point of view."[66] As for labor in the KMT areas, the editorial issued a rather general appeal for unity with the workers still under "the oppression of the reactionaries."

Yenan radio subsequently reported that over 800,000 trade unionists throughout the liberated areas of north and central China had participated in May Day meetings and had pledged to speed up economic reconstruction "by cooperating with the capitalists to raise the living standards of the workers and [by] enabling the factory and mine owners to run the factories and mines on a profit basis by speeding up the output, raising the quality of products and keeping down the costs."[67] A June NCNA dispatch, in a report on increased output based on a "fair adjustment of wages by labor and capital," also noted that "cases were reported of workers voluntarily reducing wages when they discovered that they had demanded over-much from the factory." A progressive wage system based on individual output and skills, it added, more fairly took into account the interests of both the workers and the factory owners.[68]

The fresh Communist urban contacts in 1945-46 thus provided a new and more important arena for implementing the Maoist labor-capital collaborative line. These contacts at the same time generated pressures that led to a revival of sorts of labor-oriented forces and policies within the CCP. The more differentiated wage arrangements, a result of production pressures brought to bear on a more complex industrial environment, became the prototype for the new and even more highly stratified wage system formulated in 1948, on the eve of the Communist takeover of the major cities. The latter wage policies would subsequently be viewed critically by Mao as he moved toward policies more in keeping with the "spirit" of Yenan.[69] But the multiclass urban strategy, with its notion of both a labor and a capital constituency, its mutual benefits theme, and its concomitant avoidance of class-struggle mobilization techniques and policies, were clearly the prevailing motifs in the Party Center's labor line in this early postwar period. They were to be even more strongly affirmed as the Chinese civil war moved rapidly to its climax in late 1947 and 1948.

Labor Policies on the Eve of Victory, 1947-48

By the closing months of 1946, a fully unfolded civil war essentially ended the postwar phase of the party's urban-labor policy. Though the Communists retained their hold on some urban centers for the duration of the conflict (the most notable being Harbin), they lost control of many cities and towns (including Kalgan) which were not to be retaken, in most cases, until the People's Liberation Army (PLA) moved to the strategic offensive in 1948.[70] By the close of 1947, as the CCP prepared politically for the impending takeover of the major industrial centers of China— which for the first time since the 1920s would bring the Communists into massive organizational contact with the main elements of the Chinese working class—the potential dangers for the Maoist urban strategy posed by "leftist" tendencies in the Communist labor movement were evident. In this connection, a major party statement on labor policy in February 1948 noted that some big cities, mines, and rail lines had already been liberated by Communist forces and even more soon would be. As a result, the workers' movement in the Communist-controlled areas would soon be raised to an even more important position and the correctness or incorrectness of the labor movement line would consequently have "greater influence than ever before on the development of the revolutionary war and the establishment of new democracy."[71]

It was time also to abandon completely any remaining "rural guerrilla" viewpoint toward the cities and to view them instead as essential and valuable legacies of productive capacity to be safe-guarded for the future. In this regard, a June 1948 directive of the Northeast Bureau of the CCP (whose urban responsibilities were already substantial) pointed to the problem of a continuing rural-guerrilla attitude toward the cities, stemming from when the cities had been the bastions of the enemy. Under these former circumstances, when a city was temporarily occupied by the Communists, its wealth was confiscated, destroyed, or carted away by the Communist troops or the peasantry. Now, however, "we have cities and we should love and protect them," and troops and administrative personnel should receive education on the party's commercial and industrial policies and on the need to safeguard enterprises in the newly occupied cities.[72]

It seemed to be particularly important at this juncture for the Maoist leadership to reaffirm the multiclass strategy, to reassert and reinforce the party's broad rural base and appeal, and to counteract any pressures within the party for a more militantly anticapitalist "class" labor line. Such pressures could obviously undercut the collaborative appeal to urban business and the middle classes, seriously damage the party's united-front political strategy, and undermine its production-centered economic program. At the same time, a more militant urban class line could bring to the fore a strong and indigenous Communist urban labor leadership which could conceivably begin to challenge Maoist supremacy, particularly as urban-centered, postliberation industrialization plans unfolded. It is interesting that an April 1948 critique of "left adventurist" policies in the Central Hopei base-area labor movement attacked "closed-doorism" (kuan-men-chu-i) within the union organization, an attitude which even included suggestions that those cadres who did not come from a worker background be removed.[73]

In restating and amplifying the labor-capital mutual benefits line, party policy pronouncements on the eve of the new urban stage of the civil war (the end of 1947 and the early months of 1948) warned against left deviations from this approach which had occurred in various areas and which have already been alluded to above. It might also be noted that in the fall of 1948 the potential dangers of moving too far to the right, in reaction to the antileft attacks, were also aired. The Party Center had already attacked the party leadership of the Kiangsi period for having taken too strong an anticapitalist line and for having overemphasized the role of the working class—tendencies which continued to affect party policy to some degree until the eve of the *cheng-feng* movement in Yenan.[74] As the CCP now at long last began to shift its attention to the cities as "the center of gravity," the Maoist leadership again focused on and attacked these trends within the party.

In his December 1947 report to the party's Central Committee, Mao set the basic guidelines for the period ahead.[75] He listed the "three major economic policies of the new democratic revolution" as the confiscation and redistribution to the peasants of the land of "the feudal class," the confiscation by the new state of "state monopoly" or "bureaucrat-capital,"[76] and the protection of the industry and commerce of the national bourgeoisie who, Mao stated, were themselves oppressed by bureaucrat-capital.[77] In calling for protection of the small and middle capitalist sectors of the economy, both urban and rural, Mao pointedly referred to the Kiangsi Soviet period and warned against any repetition of the "ultra-left" policies followed by the party during the 1931-34 period. These policies were described as involving "unduly advanced labour conditions, excessive income tax rates, encroachments on the interests of industrialists and merchants during land reform, and the adoption of a goal of the so-called 'workers' welfare.' " Criticizing this last goal as "a short-sighted and one-sided concept," Mao reaffirmed the basic principles of the party's economic policies in a four-point summary which was to be invoked repeatedly throughout the next year: "developing production, promoting economic prosperity, giving consideration to both public and private interests and benefiting both labour and capital."[78]

In a directive of February 1948, Mao again criticized "the narrow-minded policy of 'relief,' which purports to uphold the workers' welfare but in fact damages industry and commerce and impairs the cause of the people's revolution."[79] He called for educating party members in the trade unions and the masses of the workers "to enable them to understand that they should not see merely the immediate and partial interests of the working class while forgetting its broad, long-range interests." And in reiterating the program of mutual benefits, reduced costs, and increased output, he added that the "mistakes committed in many places are due to the failure to grasp all, most or some of the above policies."[80]

In a major statement on Communist labor and tax policies in April 1948, party spokesman Ch'en Po-ta pointed to "mistakes" on the question of wages "in certain old liberated areas in the past." He observed that working conditions and wages had been set "excessively high," without regard for either production levels or the general standard of living in the base areas.[81] These artificially high and unreasonable wage levels were not only detrimental to the development of industry, but also encouraged economism and worker elitism (a privileged-class mentality) and had a negative impact on labor's political consciousness, production efforts, and frugality.[82]

The CCP labor policy statement of February 1948 (issued in the form of an NCNA editorial) strongly underscored the "left adventurist" theme expounded by Mao in December 1947.[83] Addressed primarily to the labor movement in the rapidly expanding liberated areas, and particularly to workers in state-operated enterprises in the northeast (the region of heaviest industrial concentration as well as of left-leaning labor policies), it dealt with labor issues and tactics in the KMT areas as well. While acknowledging the status of the working class as "the most advanced and revolutionary class," it emphasized the concept of a multiclass constituency in which the workers, peasants, small and middle bourgeoisie, and other patriotic elements in the Communist areas were "the masters of the nation and the society."[84] In contrast, both workers and national capitalists in the KMT areas were enslaved and oppressed by the imperialists and the bureaucrat-capitalists and had to struggle for survival and for the overthrow of the Nationalist regime. While granting that the workers should press for improvement in their livelihood from the national capitalists, the statement also enjoined them to unite with the latter in a common struggle against their joint oppressors. In essence, the workers in the KMT areas were being told to wage a primarily *political* struggle in alliance with all "oppressed people" against the KMT. The principal stress was on the theme of unity with the mass of private entrepreneurs—a line increasingly promoted during 1948 as the PLA began to enter the cities of China.

The editorial further remarked that in the liberated areas, since state and cooperative enterprises belonged in essence to the workers themselves, there were neither exploiters nor exploited, nor any "so-called" labor-capitalist conflict. As for private enterprises in the Communist zones, the statement reasoned, in terms analogous to Chang Wen-t'ien's 1933 Kiangsi articles, that workers should tolerate a "certain limited" exploitation since their long-term interests called for encouraging the private enterprises to produce more and develop further in order to advance the overall prosperity and strength of the new society. Under new democracy (in contrast to eventual socialism), private enterprise was an indispensable productive force whose destruction would be detrimental to all, including the workers. The latter should therefore oppose strikes and other destructive acts against private capitalists and cooperate with those capitalists willing to continue production. Such cooperation would guarantee both the workers' "appropriate livelihood" and the capitalists' "appropriate profits."

The editorial pointed to the economic burdens being borne by the peasantry in support of the Communist war effort and exhorted the workers to accept like burdens in fulfilling their responsibility for the development of industry. As an advanced revolutionary class, the workers should "endure bitterness and work harder" (literally, "eat bitterness and work more"—*ch'ih-ti k'u, tso-ti to)* and, in line with Mao's four-point principles of economic policy, emulate model workers such as Chao Chan-k'uei by accepting the ten-hour day and less advanced working conditions.[85]

For state enterprises the editorial advocated the creation of factory management committees *(kung-ch'ang kuan-li wei-yuan-hui)*, chaired by the factory head, which would involve worker representatives in discussions of how to reduce costs and raise production. This method could gradually be introduced into private enterprise; there it would help in the implementation of the labor-capital mutual benefits policy.

The statement acknowledged the continuing presence within the party of a narrowly proletarian standpoint, an outlook which had presumably been revitalized by the CCP's greatly expanded contacts with industrial labor since the close of the anti-Japanese war. Citing Mao's December 1947 criticisms of the "ultra-left" line of the Kiangsi period, it added:

It is necessary to point out that, looking at today's CCP, there are not a few Party members, not a few cadres, not a few trade union work personnel, and even not a few leadership personnel in responsible high positions who do not understand the policy on industry and the line of the staff and workers' movement. They see only the trees and not the forest. They are aware only of one-sided, narrow, and short-sighted so-called "workers' interests" but are totally incapable of seeing a little farther. They have forgotten the Left adventurist industrial policy and staff and workers' line which was carried out in the 1931-34 period and which dealt such great losses both to the laboring people of the proletariat and to the revolutionary government. They have not done any research at all on the industrial policy and the staff and workers' movement policy which the CCP has put forth many times during the 11 years since 1933 [sic: 1937].[86] They obstinately oppose the Party's line. In quite a few places the leading organs have for a long time not even formally discussed the propagated explanations of the line of the Center, even to the point that the work personnel of the workers' movement completely misunderstand the line of the Center.[87]

This situation had now reached "the limit of endurance," the statement concluded, calling for the correction at local party levels of "all left adventurist thought, policies and methods."

By September 1948 (perhaps in response to pressures generated at the August labor congress in Harbin) the CCP felt obliged to couple the attack on left deviation with warnings against veering off in a rightist direction. An editorial statement in September, after first elaborating on previous leftist errors (including the use of rural "anti-feudal struggle" methods against "ordinary" [p'u-t'ung] capitalists), added that such mistakes had already been or were in the process of being corrected wherever they had occurred.[88] But it was now equally important to avoid the rightist deviation of one-sidedly defending capitalist interests. To recognize the capitalists' place in the new-democratic order did not in any way cancel or weaken the paramount role of state enterprises and of "proletarian political leadership," nor should such recognition provide capitalists with the opportunity to oppress workers and peasants. The commentary concluded that in protecting the interests of both labor and capital, constant vigilance would be required to steer a correct course free of both deviations.

It was thus quite clear by this time that with Communist forces poised for the final campaigns of the civil war, which would take them into the major urban strongholds of both private capitalism and organized labor, the "correct path" of labor-capital cooperation would become an increasingly complex and difficult one to follow—particularly under conditions where the party would be facing the pressures and demands of a labor force operating in the heady new atmosphere of liberation.[89] It was also apparent, however, as more detailed examination of the 1947-48 Communist stance toward labor in the KMT-ruled cities will illustrate, that the CCP had ruled out the propagation of a militantly class-conscious urban labor struggle movement, either in preparation for or in conjunction with the occupation of the cities. Such a strategy would have been economically undesirable, militarily unnecessary, politically counterproductive, and largely irrelevant to the Maoist notion of "proletarian" leadership.

In his exposition of the party's labor policy in April 1948, Ch'en Po-ta hailed the positive impact on work efficiency and output of the movement launched in the rapidly growing Communist areas to "establish a new labor attitude."[90] He described these developments as manifestations of the workers' growing political consciousness, not only in the state-operated sector but also in private enterprise, when "labor-capital relations are handled correctly." "To consolidate and continue to raise in every way this political consciousness of the workers will be the most reliable guarantee for constructing the new democratic national economy," he stated. The "liberal bourgeoisie," had responded with great enthusiasm to the economic opportunities now open to them in the liberated areas. Within the trade union movement, once "feudalistic oppression and constrictions" on the workers had been removed, the CCP "firmly opposes the 'leftist' adventurism" of excessive wage increases which would be detrimental to production.[91]

Ch'en also warned against egalitarian wage policies and failing to distinguish between ordinary workers and skilled technicians and staff personnel. "Political liberation" had released the workers' initiative, but this element alone would prove inadequate and must be reinforced by "a correct policy on wages which can constantly stimulate the initiative in production of workers and employees."[92] In outlining such a wage policy, Ch'en essentially built on the CCP's urban labor experiences and policies as they had evolved from 1945 on: once "reasonable and proper adjustments" had been made in the preliberation wage base, a "progressive" wage-and-award or dividend system, geared to quantity, quality, and cost efficiency of individual output, should be introduced. This system was to be implemented through committees involving both management and labor.

Based on the Communists' previous experience, Ch'en continued, this wage-and-award system would have a salutary impact on production enthusiasm, labor discipline, and the further development of skills. Though factory wage outlays would be more than before, the increased income from greater output and efficiency would more than offset these higher labor costs: "The workers obtain increased emoluments because they have put forth increased labor and energy." This system should also lead to the establishment of inspection and arbitration procedures to reward the deserving workers and to mete out "deserved punishment" to those who "go slow, waste materials, and engage in theft and graft."[93]

Turning to the trade union question, Ch'en emphasized that in order to establish a new labor attitude, the unions must encourage worker initiative and hammer out production plans and wage agreements in consultation with management and labor in both the state and private sectors; the trade unions were to function as "political and production schools of new democracy." The unions should also establish cooperatives which could provide the workers with rationed quantities of daily necessities at fixed prices and thereby permit wages, despite the pressures of continuing wartime conditions, to remain stable over a period of time without inflationary loss to the workers.[94] This system of guaranteed supplies at low prices (evidently a modified version of the Yenan wage-supply system) was apparently often linked to cutbacks in actual take-home pay, and it was thus viewed unenthusiastically by workers, according to reports from the northeast.[95]

The proper role of the unions in the state-operated sector was outlined in a June 1948 North Shensi radio report:

> In a recent inspection of a certain public factory in Shansi-Suiyüan, the general opinion of the inspectors was that the union of the factory had made some improvements, such as the guaranteeing of production, the training of new workers, and the maintenance of sanitary conditions. However, in this inspection it was discovered that some members and officers of the union are befuddled about their duty in a public factory. They thought that a strong stand against management is the

best weapon in attaining benefits for the workers. This is the main reason the union cannot have a sound development. The duty of the union in the public factory according to the opinion of the inspectors, is to cooperate with the management. The unions should guarantee the fulfillment of the production plan, increase the quality and quantity of the product, reduce its cost, take good care of the factory, and economize in the use of raw materials so as to support the front. At the same time, if conditions permit and if the demand is logical the union should try to solve the difficulties of the workers' livelihood and to develop activities beneficial to workers so as to assure a good livelihood for the workers and to unify democratically the union and management.[96]

The party's policies on wages and working conditions in the industrial sector of the economy were summed up in a resolution on the tasks of the trade union movement adopted by the Sixth National Labor Congress in Harbin in August 1948.[97] The resolution called for a minimum guaranteed wage for all workers that was to be linked to fluctuations in the cost of living; the wage had to be sufficient for the livelihood of two persons, including the worker. Starting from this wage floor, the resolution outlined a method of compensation built on an overlapping and graduated system of classifications, based on both time and piece-rate scales.[98] Wages were generally to be calculated in terms of the cost of selected essential commodities, with payment a combination of cash and supplies, supplemented by a food rationing system to be gradually extended throughout the country.[99] This "overlapping progressive wage system" (chiao-ch'ia lei-chin kung-tzu chih-tu), the September elaboration of these policies declared, was based on the principle "the more work, the more pay."[100]

Under continuing wartime conditions the workday was set generally at eight to ten hours.[101] Paid maternity leaves and special protection for women and juvenile workers were stipulated, as was the principle of equal pay for equal work. Government regulated safety and sanitary measures and a broad range of medical, old-age, and disability benefits and worker welfare provisions were projected as the responsibility of the individual factories at this stage,[102] though government-sponsored social insurance programs were envisioned for the larger industrial cities.[103] All working conditions, benefits, awards, and penalties were to be incorporated in collective contracts binding both management and labor; disputes were to be settled by negotiation and conciliation, with arbitration reserved as a last resort.

Under the general principles of Mao's four-point policy formula, the resolution summoned the unions to promote labor enthusiasm and discipline (and to continue encouragement of a "correctly guided" model worker movement), to protect labor's basic interests, to raise the latter's cultural, technical, and professional levels, and to develop workers' administrative abilities in both the public and private sectors. The need to train large numbers of administrative and technical cadres for industry was emphasized, a program in which union-established schools would be called upon to play a role.

Ch'en Yün, veteran labor leader and CCP economic expert, was elected chairman of the ACFL at the Harbin congress and delivered an eight-hour speech to the congress which dealt with the themes summed up in the resolution described above.[104] He called for the formation of factory administrative committees composed of equal numbers of management and worker representatives, a procedure applicable to private enterprise as well. In its new leadership role in the state, "the working class must shoulder the responsibility for developing industry . . . and strive to accomplish more than the assigned tasks." Evincing concern over actual or potential tendencies to weight the mutual benefits formula in favor of the capitalists, Ch'en Yün added that workers in private industry "must abide by their agreements, but have the right to demand the implementation of the principle of 'benefits to both labor and capital' and to ensure that the capitalists carry out the law."[105]

It is perhaps ironic that while the CCP continued in this period to reject "narrow and one-sided" worker interests, its developing policy of linking wage scales and benefits with individual labor productivity and factory performance, and its stress on advancement through greater technical and administrative proficiency, helped set the stage for the emergence, under the post-1949 program of accelerated industrialization, of an economically more favored urban force of skilled workers and technical-administrative staff.[106] When viewed against the overall background of CCP labor policies and experiences over the two decades to 1949, one can better understand Mao's subsequent ambivalence toward these developments.

The CCP and Labor in the KMT Areas, 1945-48

While the organizational center of the Chinese labor movement increasingly gravitated to the Communist areas after 1945, the CCP sought concurrently to develop its links to organized labor in the KMT areas. Thus, during the 1945-46 period of KMT-CCP unity negotiations, the Communists moved to revive and reinforce the base-area unions' affiliation with the CAL. The latter body had a membership, according to a KMT source, of 617,720 in October 1945, and represented Chinese labor in the International Labor Organization (ILO).[107] In the early postwar climate of attempted reconciliation, the Nationalist government sanctioned the joint KMT-CCP representation of Chinese labor (by Chu Hsüeh-fan, leader of the CAL, and Teng Fa) at the September 1945 Paris meeting of the WFTU.[108] The trade unions of the liberated areas had submitted an eight-point program to the CAL, which the latter accepted and incorporated into a subsequent twenty-three-point platform of its own.[109]

The CCP continued to emphasize these contacts and to build its influence within the CAL during 1946 as it became evident that many elements in the latter organization, including Chu Hsüeh-fan himself, were increasingly finding themselves in conflict with the

KMT authorities over the latter's anti-Communist policies and suppression of democratic freedoms.[110] This growing independence was further reinforced by the impact of labor unrest and strikes in the newly recovered major urban centers, which stemmed from steep inflation and unemployment. The growing pressure on the KMT from organized labor spawned a cost-of-living index (with 1936 as 100) in April 1946.[111] National government statistics reported a total of 6,465 labor disputes involving 1,886,994 workers during the 1945-48 period; approximately half of the total pertained to Shanghai alone. Protests over the dismissal of workers and demands for wage increases were the two main causes of the disputes.[112]

As a Hong Kong-based British report on 1946 economic developments in China noted, "labour continued to be restive" in the larger coastal cities in the face of rising living costs, despite the cost-of-living index, with "active unionization among industrial workers . . . a marked feature of recent labour developments." This "unrest" was due, the report added, to the suspicion that the index (which stood at 184,573 in February 1946) did not fully reflect actual price increases and also to the fact that wage adjustments based on the index lagged one month behind price changes.[113] On the other hand, the 1936 wage base for the index had itself been adjusted to favor the workers so that base pay for unskilled workers equalled the 1936 scale for skilled workers.[114] The chairman of the British Chamber of Commerce in Shanghai complained in July 1947 that on account of the cost-of-living index "the average worker has materially improved his earnings compared with pre-war years." He added that "we are witnessing an attempt to impose advanced trade unionism on a country which is ill-prepared for it."[115]

An attempt by the government early in 1947 to freeze wages and prices at the January 1947 levels quickly broke down in the face of soaring inflation and labor protests and strikes, and the index system was reinstituted in May 1947—a move opposed by business and industry circles. A May 1948 report by the British Chamber of Commerce in Shanghai thus noted sympathetically the efforts by

Chinese factory owners to have the wage index frozen but added that the authorities had ruled that "the index provided the labourers' cost of living and that any move to freeze this index would lead to serious repercussions from labour."[116]   And A. Doak Barnett reported from Shanghai in October 1948 that "in recent years, labor has used its bargaining power to good advantage. Working conditions have improved considerably by comparison with before the war—at least until the current trend toward economic deterioration."[117] While a detailed analysis of the wage-price-employment situation in the KMT cities in the 1946-48 period is beyond the scope of the present study, it appears that, within the context of generally deteriorating economic conditions affecting virtually all groups and a spiraling inflation in which wages could never catch up with prices, industrial labor in public and private enterprises was one urban group capable of holding off the full impact of these adverse circumstances.[118]

The remarks of a Shanghai labor leader delegate, Ouyang Tsu-jun, support this point. Ouyang described to the 1948 Harbin labor congress the various Shanghai strike movements between 1945 and 1948. Though he emphasized (particularly for the 1947-48 period) labor confrontations with and persecution by the KMT authorities, his comments reveal the degree to which labor had been able to achieve at least its minimum economic demands in these years.[119] The capacity of organized labor in the Nationalist-ruled cities to defend its economic interests was a striking characteristic of the complex urban political equation in this period, particularly in Shanghai. The KMT-area labor movement had in fact emerged as a powerful interest group able to challenge governmental authority at the same time that it operated within the framework of that authority. "In a vague but nevertheless real way," Barnett observed in October 1948, "the influence of unions is also bolstered by the simple fact that tremendous numbers of people are directly or indirectly involved in them. . . . The sheer size of the labor movement makes some people in Shanghai apprehensive about it."[120] The total number in the organized labor movement in Shanghai (in unions affiliated with the officially sponsored Shanghai General Labor Union) was reported to have risen from 260,305 at the end of 1946 to 557,651 in July 1948.[121]

Though underground Communist elements were active in the KMT-area labor movement and played a role in its growing militancy,[122] it was far from being the revolutionary trade union movement the party had sought to recreate in the cities after 1927. Organized labor after the war had clearly built upon a trend already discernible in the 1928-37 decade: an essentially economist labor movement had developed with the ability to assert its day-to-day interests within the political confines of an authoritarian, but by no means all-powerful, regime.[123] Rather than emerging as the CCP's revolutionary vanguard, the postwar urban labor movement had become instead in many respects, a troublesome element for Communist urban policy, one which was initially hard to reconcile with its labor-capital united-front line.[124] "In the cities," Suzanne Pepper has observed,

> the Party apparently had little choice but to tolerate a short period of "excessive" behavior on the part of the workers immediately after liberation. Given the relatively advanced development of the labor movement in China's major cities and the relatively weak state of its own preparedness there, the Party was in no position to enforce at once its policy of safeguarding capitalist production against the demands of the urban proletariat.[125]

Recently published Chinese accounts of Shanghai labor struggles just prior to liberation indicate the relatively small size of the underground CCP forces in the Shanghai labor movement and show why it was necessary for the Communists to work with and through the legal union organizations. An account of the publicized January 1948 sit-in strike at a large Shanghai cotton mill (Shen-hsin No. 9

mill) notes that out of a total of more than 7,000 workers at the plant, there were then fewer than thirty members in the underground CCP factory branch.[126] Another of these sources gives a total of some 8,000 CCP members in Shanghai (about 40 percent workers) at the time of the PLA's entry into the city in late May 1949—presumably a preliberation peak.[127]

The union at the Shen-hsin mill, according to the account of the 1948 sit-in strike cited above, was dominated by two contending organizations, one of them a branch of the KMT-sponsored "workers' welfare association" led by a secret military police agent and the other a "brotherhood society" led by a worker "traitor" or "scab" (kung-tsei). A third gang element was also involved in the union power struggle.[128]

Once the strike had begun on 30 January, Communist representatives were apparently able to assume an active leadership role by taking advantage of the "contradictions" among the contending groups and using them as a "cover." The sit-in itself, which was triggered by the cut-off of the workers' coal and rice rations (or subsidies) since September 1947, broke up on 2 February in a violent clash between the strikers and the military and police. There were many worker casualties and arrests. The ambiguous role the non-Communist union leaders played in this struggle was itself a reflection of the complex relationship between the labor movement and the KMT in this period.[129] While extolling the heroism and the sacrifices of the resisting workers in this brief strike, the key thrust of this Communist account is on the subsequent role of the Shen-hsin workers in protecting their factory and maintaining uninterrupted production during the PLA occupation of Shanghai in late May 1949.[130]

Chu Hsüeh-fan and Liu Ning-yi (who had replaced Teng Fa as head of the preparatory committee of the liberated areas' trade union federation after Teng's death in April 1946) again jointly represented Chinese labor at a WFTU meeting in Moscow in June 1946. Chu's increasingly strong anti-civil war stance, and KMT raids and arrests on CAL offices and staff in Chungking and other cities, led eventually to Chu's flight to Hong Kong in November 1946; the CAL subsequently underwent a government "reorganization" and was ultimately replaced by a KMT-sponsored General Labor Union.[131] Chu established a CAL headquarters-in-exile in Hong Kong,[132] and in the latter half of 1947 he again joined Liu Ning-yi in WFTU sessions in Prague and Paris, after which both went to Harbin in preparation for the August 1948 labor congress. On arriving in Harbin in February 1948, Chu dispatched a telegram to Mao and Chou En-lai pledging full support to the CCP in the anti-KMT struggle.[133]

As the CCP prepared for the return to the cities, it issued numerous appeals, policy statements, and directives addressing labor in the Nationalist areas. These statements delineated basic policy lines and clearly avoided any encouragement of labor struggles directed at the mass of private capitalists. The emphasis was instead on labor's "alliance" with these "national capitalists" against the KMT regime.[134]

In describing the November 1948 Communist occupation of Fushun in southern Manchuria, NCNA reported that workers had secretly set up "protection committees" to guard all mines and factories against KMT sabotage during the battle for the city. "While the battle raged in the city, determined miners stayed at their posts, digging over a thousand tons of coal for the people that very day." When the PLA arrived, "more than 30,000 miners and factory workers poured out, to give *their liberators* a thunderous welcome" (emphasis added).[135] A February 1948 article on the labor movement in KMT China noted that with Communist troops poised on the Yangtze, "a new line of action is emerging," with the trade union movement taking "different forms and expressions."[136] Under this new approach, large numbers of unemployed workers and skilled labor were leaving for Communist territories to participate in reconstruction. "There also seems to be a trend towards the workers adopting a reasonably compromising attitude towards Chinese private industrial enterprisers [sic]; while towards the Nanking government-owned or bureaucrat-capital controlled enterprises, they are fighting for thorough satisfaction of their demands."[137]

But whether the "thorough satisfaction of demands" approach to opposing bureaucratic capital fully conformed to CCP policy was itself open to question.[138] The Sixth National Labor Congress, in its August 1948 resolution on union tasks, called on the labor movement in the KMT areas to "more than ever before increase their connections with the masses, accumulate strength and enlarge their ranks in order to welcome the arrival of the PLA." Labor was directed to aim its struggles at obstructing KMT military transport and arms manufacture and at the same time to protect all publicly and privately owned enterprises, factories, machinery, and materials from destruction. The resolution urged workers to unite with the "oppressed and restricted" national capitalists and stand together with them in opposing imperialism and bureaucrat-capitalism (defined by Mao as the Nationalist state economic structure). On the principle of safeguarding national industrial and commerical enterprises, the workers could then press the capitalists to "appropriately improve" labor's lot and thereby fulfill the policy of mutual benefits to labor and capital.[139]

Another labor congress statement which sought to clarify and explain these policies to the KMT-area labor movement revealed the CCP's anxiety about the struggle-oriented and strongly economist character of the labor unions in the KMT cities.[140] In stressing the theme of "sincerely uniting" with the national capitalists, it called for a shift from struggle to improve livelihood to "political" struggle directed at the KMT "bureaucrat-capitalist" regime. It underlined the "fundamental differences" between bureaucrat-capital and the national capitalists and exhorted the KMT-based labor movement leadership to do its part in developing the capitalists' understanding and support of the new-democratic revolution—the sole road to "a bright future" for the latter. The statement called for the broadest unity of workers, staff, and administrators. While acknowledging the necessities of the struggle for livelihood, it emphasized the importance of knowing when to terminate such struggles and focus instead on the overriding imperatives and ultimate benefits of the final liberation conflict.

A September report on the Harbin labor congress summed up the "four immediate tasks" of workers in the KMT areas as follows:

(1) the consolidation of their own strength and the expansion of their fighting ranks so as to prepare for the arrival of the Liberation Army; (2) cooperation with the national industrialists in their common fight against the bureaucratic capitalists; (3) the dispatch of skilled technicians into the Liberated Areas for their industrial and commercial reconstruction; (4) the protection of all factories and machines from destruction so that they can be taken over intact by the Liberation Army when it took [sic] control.[141]

The role of urban labor as a supportive though relatively passive adjunct to the liberation armies was clearly projected.

Historical accounts and recollections published in Shanghai in 1979 on the thirtieth anniversary of the city's liberation by PLA forces also strongly underline the 1948–49 themes of factory protection and cooperation with the national capitalists.[142] These reports, authored for the most part by participants in those events, stress the role of the CCP and the Shanghai workers in those final days of KMT rule in maintaining operation of the power, water, communications, and transport utilities, as well as major industrial enterprises. They focus on the campaign to thwart the KMT in its efforts to remove materials to Taiwan and to pressure privately owned enterprises to do likewise. The underground Communist apparatus is represented as concentrating its efforts not only on protecting KMT-controlled enterprises from dismantlement, but also on persuading private capitalists and managers to remain in Shanghai and to cooperate with their workers in continuing production.

Thus, in an account of the Shanghai workers' "protect-the-factory struggle," the writer recalls his role as a member of the underground CCP Shanghai Party Committee.[143] As part of this movement, the author notes, the party worked to persuade national capitalists not to dismantle their factories and leave with the KMT. He cites numerous instances of success among such factory owners and managers who agreed "to remain and welcome liberation." The theme stressed, again, is the great effort by the Shanghai party to win over the capitalists, to promote their cooperation with the workers in protecting facilities and maintaining operations. As a result, the writer declares, when the PLA took over Shanghai on 27 May 1949, the key utilities were never disrupted and the majority of factories did not halt production "even for a minute."[144] This, he adds, was the "victorious achievement" of the Shanghai party and won high praise from Mao. And the PLA, on entering Shanghai did not rely on locally organized workers' militia to police the city, but instead detailed its own forces to do this job.[145] A popular drama, widely presented in China in the 1960s, concerns the role of the rural PLA during this early takeover period in Shanghai as the guardian of "proletarian standpoint" against the temptations and corruptions of the metropolis. One of the characters, a PLA soldier named Chao, complains of being called a "dark-skinned peasant" in Shanghai and declares, "If it weren't for dark faces like mine there wouldn't be any liberation."[146]

The Communists also avoided any commitment to satisfy labor demands in the immediate aftermath of urban takeovers. Mao himself, in April 1948, on the occasion of the Communist capture of the city of Loyang, directed:

> On entering the city, do not lightly advance slogans of raising wages and reducing working hours. In wartime it is good enough if production can continue and existing working hours and original wage levels can be maintained. Whether or not suitable reductions in working hours and increases in wages are to be made later will depend on economic conditions, that is, on whether the enterprises thrive.[147]

Mao also cautioned against haste in organizing "the people of the city to struggle for democratic reforms and improvements in livelihood." These matters should await the stabilization of municipal administration, the return of public calm, and the completion of "careful surveys," on the basis of which "appropriate measures" would be worked out. He also called for "a clear line of demarcation in defining bureaucrat capital"; the new government was instructed to take over and operate only those enterprises "which are definitely verified as having been run by the Kuomintang's central, provincial, county or municipal governments, that is, enterprises operated wholly by official bodies." The workers and technicians in these enterprises should be organized to participate in management, Mao added. If the KMT personnel had fled, a management committee of representatives elected by the workers and technicians should be set up, pending appointment by the new government of "managers and directors who will manage it together with the workers." Enterprises run by "notorious big bureaucrats of the Kuomintang" were to be dealt with along similar lines, but no other businesses were to be confiscated, even if run by "small bureaucrats." Encroachment on the enterprises of the national capitalists was strictly prohibited.[148]

*Reestablishment of a National Labor Federation
under CCP Leadership*

The CCP-organized labor congress which met in Harbin from 1 August (the PLA anniversary date) to 22 August 1948 was initially planned as the first "All-Liberated Areas Trade Union Congress," in line with the 25 March 1948 call by Liu Ning-yi to establish an All-Liberated Areas Trade Union Federation.[149] But given the situation in mid-1948, such a projected federation was already obviously of national scope. Given the mammoth expansion of the Communist areas by that time, a June 1948 Communist report on the projected congress observed, "Such a federation . . . will essentially be an overture to an All-China T. U. Federation."[150] The congress, originally scheduled for June, was postponed until August and was at that time transformed into the Sixth National Labor Congress; the Fifth Congress had met clandestinely in Shanghai in November 1929. The fact that the congress did not await the occupation of China's major industrial centers and the full involvement of their urban labor forces underscored the crucial role of the liberated areas' labor movement in the creation of a new national federation. It is noteworthy that a Seventh Congress was not convened until May 1953, four years after the Communists took Shanghai.

The CCP-sponsored labor congress was attended by 518 delegates who reportedly represented some 2.85 million organized industrial workers, including some in underground "democratic unions" in the KMT areas.[151] The decision to transform the meetings into the Sixth National Labor Congress and to establish a national organization again known as the ACFL (literally, "China National General Labor Union" [*Chung-hua ch'üan-kuo tsung kung-hui*]) was reportedly made on 31 July. It was based on a joint proposal by "the trade unions of the liberated areas, the delegates of the various underground democratic unions from areas still occupied by Chiang Kai-shek, and by the Chinese Association of Labor."[152]

The constitution unanimously adopted by the Harbin congress called for democratic centralism as the organizational principle of the ACFL.[153] Biennial congresses were to be convened by the ACFL Executive Committee, though these could be postponed or held earlier under special circumstances or at the request of member unions representing at least one-third of the ACFL membership. Electoral procedures for and representation at these congresses were also to be determined by the Executive Committee. The declared aims of the ACFL were to unite the workers of the entire country, to protect their interests, and to fight for the liberation of the working class and the Chinese people "in alliance with all the oppressed people of the whole country."

The ACFL was to be comprised essentially of its affiliated union bodies and organized along either industrial or craft lines. Membership in these unions, open (on a voluntary basis) to all those classified as manual and nonmanual workers, totaled 1,448,200 in 1948, increasing to 2,373,900 in 1949.[154] The national congress was empowered to determine and amend the constitution, to formulate the policies of the trade union movement, and to examine the reports of the Executive Committee and elect the latter body. The Executive Committee was described as "the sovereign authority" of the ACFL between national congresses. The fifty-three member Sixth Executive Committee elected at the Harbin congress included five CAL figures; another five were among the twenty alternate members.[155] The overwhelming CCP predominance in the federations' leadership perhaps reflected the scarcity of politically reliable indigenous non-Communist labor leaders in the former KMT areas.[156]

The chairman and vice-chairman of the ACFL were to be elected by the Executive Committee and together with others elected by this committee were to form the Standing Committee.[157] A general secretary, appointed by the Standing Committee, was to take charge of routine administrative work under the direction of the ACFL chairman and vice-chairman. The constitution provided for the establishment of a secretariat, seven departments (organization, education and culture, production, welfare, youth, women, and international relations), a private-enterprise committee to supervise trade union work in that sector, and a committee to direct work in the labor movement in the remaining KMT areas. The production department was to oversee union participation in factory management and to study problems of wages, production plans, technical experience, and other matters related to production.[158] The welfare department was to be in charge of the labor insurance program, to examine the labor contracts and welfare work of its affiliated unions, and to assist the government in inspecting factory hygiene and safety conditions.

Given the principle of democratic centralism and the subsequent five-year delay in convening another national congress, the paramount role of the ACFL Standing Committee was evident.[159]

Its members and the ACFL top leadership were named by the newly elected Sixth Executive Committee at its first session (held after the close of the Harbin congress). Ch'en Yün was elected chairman of the ACFL, with Li Li-san, Liu Ning-yi, and Chu Hsüeh-fan as vice-chairmen.[160] Liu Shao-ch'i was named honorary chairman in 1949.[161] In February 1949 the labor federation moved its headquarters from Harbin to newly liberated Peking. In November 1949 the CAL (which had become an affiliated labor organization under the ACFL) convened a congress in Peking at which the organization was officially disbanded; its members were urged to join one of the various unions under the ACFL. Chu Hsüeh-fan reported to the congress that the "historical tasks" of the CAL had been accomplished with the victory of the liberation war.[162]

The prestigious status and impressive labor leadership backgrounds of the CCP figures placed in the top posts of the labor federation attested to the great importance the party attached to the labor movement at this juncture. The CCP now stood poised on the threshold of nationwide victory. Liu Shao-ch'i, the symbolic head of the ACFL, was then second only to Mao in the Communist hierarchy and had himself played a major role in the Communist-led labor movement from the early 1920s to the Yenan period. Ch'en Yün, a Politburo member and the party's leading economic expert during the Yenan period, had been a printing worker and a leading Communist labor organizer during the mid-1920s in Shanghai and later took a conspicuous part in the Kiangsi Soviet labor movement.[163] Li Li-san had originally gained prominence as a youthful labor organizer during the May 30th Movement in 1925, and though he had later suffered disgrace as the architect of the Li Li-san line in 1930, his subsequent fifteen years in the Soviet Union and his return to Manchuria in 1945 with the Soviet armies had restored his status within the CCP leadership; he had been elected to the Seventh Central Committee in 1945 and took an active role in the CCP Northeast Bureau's affairs during the civil war years. Liu Ning-yi had begun his revolutionary career as a young student activist in the May 30th Movement and later worked as a miner and labor organizer in the Kailan mines; he had endured many years of imprisonment for his labor activities. He was apparently active in underground work in Shanghai during the early war years and later rose to prominence in the Border Region labor movement, ultimately succeeding Teng Fa as head of the liberated areas' unions in 1946.[164] It should be noted, as the backgrounds of the top CCP echelon in the ACFL indicate, that no major Communist labor leader emerged directly out of the post-1935 urban labor movement; only Liu Ning-yi was reported to have worked for a time in underground labor activities in Shanghai after 1937.[165] Biographical sketches of twenty-one members of the ACFL Executive Committee published by the Communists in 1948 gave essentially the same picture.[166]

With Ch'en Yün preoccupied with economic matters, Li Li-san emerged in the initial years of the labor federation as the major spokesman and executive director of its affairs. Li served concurrently as Minister of Labor in the Peking government. Liu Ning-yi continued his previous activist role in international liaison work and travel. Well after Li Li-san's political eclipse and the end of his leadership role in the labor movement by 1953-54, Liu Ning-yi was to serve as chairman of the labor federation from 1958 until its dissolution at the height of the Cultural Revolution in 1967-68.[167]

Li Li-san, earlier identified with an urban labor Communist strategy and in 1948 once again in the foreground of CCP labor affairs, reflected in his outlook the new importance of the urban labor constituency in Chinese Communism. In his opening address to the Harbin labor congress, Li dwelt on the revolutionary role of the labor movement of the 1920s and spoke of the working class as "clearly" having been the vanguard and leader of the entire national liberation struggle since that time.[168] He stressed "the heroic, stubborn struggles" of the workers under the KMT before 1937, particularly the anti-Japanese strike movement after 1931. The underground activities of the workers in the Japanese-occupied cities after 1937 and the subsequent strike struggles in Shanghai and other major cities in KMT China in the years since the Japanese surrender were also extolled. Li emphasized labor's wartime "leading class" role in the base areas, adding that the successes won in the liberation struggle had to be credited to "the several decades of bloody struggle by the Chinese revolutionary working class and peasants," though he also paid special tribute to the key role of the PLA (composed of workers, peasants and other laboring people, he noted).[169] While there were undoubtedly rhetorical flourishes in Li's speech, there was clearly an intent to build up the historical revolutionary leadership role of the Chinese working class in preparation and expectation of its enhanced new status and influence.

As has been shown above, the CCP took steps on a number of fronts to ready itself for the approaching period of urban-centered national power. It acted to nip "left-adventurist" trends in the Communist-led labor movement, to reemphasize the obligation of workers in state enterprises to the goals of increased production and reduced costs, and to clarify and reiterate the labor-capital mutual benefits theme in the private economic sector. As for the still unoccupied major industrial centers, the party carefully restricted its struggle to KMT-linked bureaucrat-capital and continued to discourage broader anticapitalist sentiments. The CCP projected a relatively passive and supportive role for urban labor, that of maintaining production and protecting industrial properties; the actual task of liberation was to be left to the PLA forces. In fact, the large and relatively militant urban labor movement that emerged in KMT China in the years after the Japanese surrender, presented something of a problem to the Communists in their initial consolidation of power in 1949-50. At the same time, the party, in preparing for the new urban-industrial phase, formulated a relatively elaborate, graded wage system based on incentives, linked to individual worker output and skills, and geared to the development of a modern, urban industrial economy. In this transition to the new vistas of post-1949 "socialist construction," the CCP also at long last acted to create a national labor organization which initiated a new era in the party's relations with the urban working class. It was apparent that the mix of labor policies and developments in the 1947–48 transition from the rural revolutionary phase to the urban-focused construction stage ahead already contained ingredients for the later "struggle between two lines" (Maoist and "revisionist") in Chinese labor and industrial policies.

CONCLUSION

It is evident that the proletariat in China, both urban and rural, played a distinctly secondary role in the post-1927, Communist-led phase of the Chinese revolution. But much more significantly, Communist efforts under various versions of the proletarian (or class) line to place labor in the vanguard position proved not only impractical, but essentially counterproductive as well. This line, with its labor class-struggle tactics, its urban orientation, and its promotion of a favored political and economic status for labor, seriously hindered the fashioning of an effective strategy on both the urban *and* rural fronts and was at odds with the overall interests and successful advance of the 1928-48 revolutionary movement. It raises the question of whether a "class-conscious" labor movement could indeed become the revolutionary leading force in a poor agrarian society such as China, where peasant interests predominated and where private and generally small-scale industry and commerce filled a necessary and still "progressive" function. Not only had the revolution to be based on small peasant proprietors (and on those aspiring to be such), but it also required that both rural and urban capitalist forces be encouraged and protected. In these circumstances, a leading role for the comparatively small proletariat proved politically divisive, economically disruptive, and strategically unworkable. Even in the high tide of the Communist-led urban labor movement of the mid-1920s, Jean Chesneaux notes, it "failed to arrive at a correct solution of the contradictions arising from the alliance with the bourgeoisie, and in particular of the contradictions between the alliance with the bourgeoisie and the alliance with the

peasants."[1] As has been shown in this study, as long as the proletariat was looked upon as the cutting edge of the revolution
(whether on the urban or rural front), such "contradictions" could not
in fact be resolved.

After the Chinese Communist crisis in 1927, the effort to
rebuild a revolutionary urban labor movement collapsed in the face
of ruthless KMT repression and a corresponding political caution
among workers. The reality was that of a developing organized
labor movement, largely outside of Communist control and focused
essentially on day-to-day economic issues. Despite KMT domination
and restrictions, it was possible for this labor movement to act,
albeit with limited success, to redress grievances. Labor's growing
role became a notable feature of the post-1945 civil war years in the
KMT-ruled cities, especially in Shanghai. Ironically, this increasingly strong and assertive labor movement came to be something of
an embarrassment to the CCP, which was intent on liberating the
cities from without and on promoting a broad urban united front
based on labor-capital harmony and muted labor militancy. As for
the Communist-governed base areas in the two-decade period after
1927, any "over-assertion" of labor interests and demands, agricultural or nonagricultural, proved detrimental to the construction of
the broadest possible peasant base of support and to the pressing
economic construction needs of those areas.

Final Communist victory and entry into the major cities in
1949 ushered in a new and vastly more complex stage in the CCP's
relations with the working class, a stage already foreshadowed in the
more sophisticated and differentiated wage incentive policies taking
shape in Communist-controlled urban areas by 1948. By the early
1950s, the impact and importance of a much larger urban-labor
constituency and a more specialized corps of labor-union cadres,
operating in the context of Soviet-patterned industrialization, added
further new dimensions and intricacies to labor policy and to the
role of labor in socialist construction.[2]

Yet the legacies of the base-area years, particularly of the
cheng-feng period, continued to be felt long after the Communist

victory. The continuing post-1949 role of the national capitalists, the concept of mutual benefits and of a "new labor attitude," the distrust of a supercentralized state economic apparatus, the growing controversies over wage incentive policies, and the emphasis on the continued revolutionization, transformation, and development of the countryside all are examples of the impact of the revolutionary experiences and class strategies of the rural base years on post-1949 policies.

During the First Five-Year Plan period (1953-57), wage policies based increasingly on material incentives culminated in the comprehensive wage reform of 1956, which provided significant wage increases for industrial workers based on skill and productivity.[3] It was at this same time, however, that Mao obliquely questioned such wage policies in his famous "Ten Great Relationships" report, which already signaled his break, in the Great Leap Forward of 1958, from Soviet-style developmental and incentive policies. While acknowledging that it would be "wrong" not to adjust wages according to productivity, Mao stressed the fact that families now generally had two or more employed members: "If their wages are added up, their standard of living will be good," despite comparatively low wage levels. Mao added that it was necessary to bring into play not only the initiative and enthusiasm of the individual worker (presumably through wage increases), but also that of the factory as a whole.[4]

The early 1960s, in the wake of the disastrous collapse of Mao's Great Leap Forward, saw the return of policies which placed greater emphasis on material incentives; larger wage differentials and bonuses based on skill and performance became the order of the day.[5] As was noted in Chapter VII, Mao again countered this trend, emphasizing the great importance of equalizing rural and urban living standards; he recalled the more egalitarian life-style of the wartime base areas, when people did not "quarrel on account of their going after wages."[6] In this context, Mao criticized wage incentive policies for technically advanced workers, stressing that the primary incentive for developing such skills should be "for the sake of socialist construction, industrialization, service to the people, and collective interests. We should not, above all, regard it as for the sake of high wages."[7]

The Cultural Revolution of the later 1960s, which forced the disbandment of the Trade Union Federation, brought "rebel" (Maoist) attacks on that organization for its "revisionist" wage policies.[8] And in the political and policy controversies of Mao's final years, "Gang of Four" spokesman Yao Wen-yuan in 1975 again attacked material incentive wage patterns and "unlimited" differential spreads as fostering the creation of a privileged labor aristocracy, a view which had overtones of the "anti-privileged class" movement of the *cheng-feng* years.[9] But at the same time, it is well to remember that even in the rural setting and egalitarian style of the anti-Japanese wartime bases, the Party found it necessary, despite a primarily social incentive approach, to include some differentials based on skill and performance. Yao's 1975 article itself reflected the continuing conflicts and uncertainties over these issues, manifest in the wage policies of the early 1970s, which highlighted the complications, difficulties, and contradictions involved in working out a "rational" wage and incentive policy.[10]

Ironically, the radical efforts from the Cultural Revolution on to foster "rebel" worker groups and movements against the former managerial-union bureaucracy largely backfired into a new form of economically and politically disruptive labor "class struggle," including work stoppages. These worker groups saw themselves in rebellion against managerial authority, "irrational" rules and regulations, and the more orthodox concepts of labor discipline and productivity. The widespread disruptions, it is now asserted by the post-Mao leadership, created conditions of virtual anarchy in China's industrial economy in the decade after 1966.[11]

In the post-Mao era, the balance has once again veered in the direction of more pronounced stress on material rewards geared to individual work performance. This is, in turn, linked to the "four modernizations" program with its inevitably less populist focus on rapid technological, scientific, and industrial advancement. In line with these developments, the Trade Union Federation (ACFTU), now fully reconstituted, held its Ninth National Congress in October 1978, after a lapse of over two decades since the Eighth Congress in 1957. Labor federation head Ni Chih-fu reported to the Executive Committee of the ACFTU in October 1981 that trade union organizations at all levels have been "gradually rectified" of Gang-of-Four leadership influences.[12]

Yet policy uncertainties and ambivalences have remained as China seeks to construct an effective economic modernization program. By 1979 and 1980 there was already pressure for retrenchment ("readjustment") from overambitious industrialization goals, with talk of capital shortages and of large budgetary deficits in which the labor wage increases and bonuses since 1977 were said to have played a part.[13] There was again a strong accent on agriculture as the foundation of the economy, on light industry, and on greater returns to the peasantry through higher state grain prices and reduced taxes.[14] These policies, however, are now being promoted in the context of much expanded individual peasant incentives and freer market arrangements.[15] Early 1981 press commentaries, in criticizing the "adventurous advance" economic construction policies of 1978, stressed the importance of taking into account China's poor and largely agrarian character. "Especially given the large population of our country, its weak foundation, its 800 million peasants, its low technical and management levels, and the realities of poverty and backwardness, our national economy cannot possibly produce any miracle within a short period of time," one such article noted.[16]

Attention was again focused in 1980 on the question of achieving a proper balance between "material rewards and moral encouragement" in labor policy.[17] The prevailing motif, however, has increasingly been on "the more work, the more pay" theme reminiscent of wage policies affirmed in 1948. Egalitarian wage concepts are now condemned as "eating out of the same big pot." Industrious workers should be rewarded and the indolent penalized, or even fired.[18] Labor discipline has become a central issue with the promulgation in 1982 of new State Council regulations on rewards and penalties for workers and staff members. It was acknowledged that the "pernicious influence of anarchism," a holdover from Cultural Revolution days, had not yet been eradicated and that "modern socialized mass production calls for strict discipline."[19] All this would help to "heal the wounds caused by the 10 years [1966-76] of turmoil."[20]

In pushing the current wage and reward policy geared to labor productivity and discipline, it is now officially reported that total wage increases for the 1978-81 years considerably surpassed the total growth in agricultural and industrial output value for that period. Under the newly-proclaimed principle of "first, feed the people and second, build the country," consideration should be given, it is affirmed, to both national construction and improved livelihood "rather than stressing one at the expense of the other."[21]

Issues of class strategies and contradictions thus continue to manifest themselves in the complexities and problems of China's modernization drive. The current watchword is balanced development within the means and resources available, and in which the roles of agriculture and light (consumer) industry will be highlighted. It is probably safe to say that as the revolutionary base-area experience and model recede further into the past, the encircling impact of China's vast and still poor countryside, and of its well-organized, politicized, and massive peasantry, will continue to influence the role and status of labor, of the worker-peasant relationship generally, and of the form and content of the "dictatorship of the proletariat" in the People's Republic of China.

ABBREVIATIONS FOR SOURCES

CCRM	Center for Chinese Research Materials
CF	*Chieh-fang* [Liberation]
CFJP	*Chieh-fang jih-pao* [Liberation daily]
CQ	*China Quarterly*
CSH	*Chinese Studies in History*
CWLS	*Collected Works of Liu Shao-ch'i: Before 1944*
FBIS	*Foreign Broadcast Information Service*
FEER	*Far Eastern Economic Review*
HHJP	*Hsin-hua jih-pao* [New China daily]
HSCH	*Hung-se chung-hua* [Red China]
Inprecorr	*International Press Correspondence*
KJP	*Kung-jen pao* [Worker]
SCKJ	*Su-ch'ü kung-jen* [Soviet worker]
SW	*Selected Works of Mao Tse-tung*
TC	*Tou-cheng* [Struggle]
USIS	United States Information Service
WMHC	*Wang Ming hsüan-chi* [Selected works of Wang Ming]

NOTES

Introduction

1. "Resolution on Certain Questions in the History of Our Party" (adopted on 20 April 1945 by the enlarged Seventh Plenum of the CCP Central Committee), in SW 3:197-200.

2. O. B. Borisov and B. T. Koloskov, *Soviet-Chinese Relations, 1945-1970*, p. 113. This volume is an edited translation of the 1971 Russian edition published in Moscow. According to Vladimir Petrov, editor of the Indiana edition, the authors' names are "pseudonyms for two high-ranking [Soviet] specialists in Chinese affairs" (p. xiii). See also Peter Vladimirov, *The Vladimirov Diaries*, pp. 496-97. This diary of the Tass correspondent and Comintern liaison agent in Yenan was published in Moscow in 1974, twenty years after Vladimirov's death. The 1975 Doubleday edition has been edited from an English translation supplied by the official Novosti Press Agency Publishing House in Moscow.

3. Nym Wales, *The Chinese Labor Movement*, pp. 164-65.

4. Jean Chesneaux, *The Chinese Labor Movement, 1919-1927*, p. 293.

5. See S. Bernard Thomas, *"Proletarian Hegemony" in the Chinese Revolution and the Canton Commune of 1927*, pp. 19-28.

6. Central Notice no. 50, "On the Labor Movement" (Party Central, 25 May 1928), originally published in *Chung-yang cheng-chih t'ung-hsün* [Central political correspondence], northern ed., no. 30 (3 July 1928), in Hyobom Pak, ed. and trans., *Documents of the Chinese Communist Party, 1927-1930*, p. 427.

7. Wales, *Chinese Labor Movement*, p. 165, citing figures supplied by Liu Shao-ch'i, who played a leading role in the red labor movement in the early 1930s.

8. Chou En-lai, "Report to the Third Plenum" (24 September 1930); excerpt in Conrad Brandt et al., *A Documentary History of Chinese Communism*, p. 206.

9. "Tasks of the Revolutionary Trade Union Movement of China" (resolution of the eighth session of the RILU Central Council), *Inprecorr* 12, no. 10 (3 March 1932):190.

10. See Liu Shao-ch'i, "The Trade Union Movement in Soviet Areas during the Past Two Years" (31 January 1934; a report to the Second National Soviet Congress), in CWLS, pp. 3-10; and Mao Tse-tung, "Report to the Second National Soviet Congress" (22 January 1934), in Victor Yakhontoff, *The Chinese Soviets*, pp. 262-66.

11. This thesis is strongly argued by Ilpyong Kim in *The Politics of Chinese Communism*; see especially pp. 201-4.

12. See Tetsuya Kataoka, *Resistance and Revolution in China*, p. 47, for a statement of this thesis of the "two distinct strategies of revolution": the Wang Ming urban and the Mao rural lines.

13. "Resolution on the Land Question" (Sixth CCP Congress, Moscow, 1928), CSH 4, nos. 2-3 (Winter-Spring 1971):98.

Notes to Chapter I

1. "Resolution on the Chinese Question" (25 February 1928), *Inprecorr* 8, no. 16 (15 March 1928):321.

2. Ibid.

3. Yüeh Sheng, *Sun Yat-sen University in Moscow and the Chinese Revolution*, p. 185; O. B. Borisov and B. T. Koloskov, *Soviet-Chinese Relations, 1945-1970*, p. 113. Of 57,957 party members reported by the CCP's Fifth Congress in April 1927, 53.8 percent were listed as workers. Nym Wales, *The Chinese Labor Movement*, p. 60.

4. Nikolai Bukharin, "The Chinese Revolution and the Tasks of the Chinese Communists," pt. 2, CSH 4, no. 1 (Fall 1970):18.

5. Bukharin, "Chinese Revolution," pt. 1," CSH 3, no. 4 (Summer 1970):288.

6. "Political Resolution of the Sixth CCP Congress" (September 1928), in Conrad Brandt et al., *A Documentary History of Chinese Communism*, p. 143.

7. Bukharin, "Chinese Revolution," pt. 2, p. 19.

8. *Inprecorr* 8, no. 50 (16 April 1928):894. A recent Soviet analysis of the Sixth CCP Congress notes that "on the question of the relationship of the labor movement and peasant action, Ch'ü Ch'iu-pai occupied a position that was identical to the viewpoint of the Comintern, which believed that 'without the support and leadership of an industrial center, the revolution cannot be victorious by the peasant movement alone.' " L. P. Deliusin, "The Sixth Congress of the Chinese Communist Party and Its Agrarian-Peasant Program," CSH 8, no. 3 (Spring 1975):71.

9. Bukharin, a rightist leader in the factional infighting in the Soviet party and the Comintern, exhibited in his report a clear populist appreciation of the peasant masses ("an immense class," "our main allies . . . [and] brothers," "an extraordinarily great revolutionary force") and the antilandlord, agrarian revolution generally, an attitude presumably reflected in the decisions of the CCP Congress. See "Chinese Revolution," pt. 1, p. 285. Bukharin's relatively propeasant orientation was manifested in his losing post-Sixth Congress struggle with Stalin over the latter's "super-industrialization" policies, which Bukharin declared were based on "the military-feudal exploitation of the peasantry." Stephen Cohen, *Bukharin and the Bolshevik Revolution*, p. 306.

10. See Sheng, *Sun Yat-sen University*, pp. 184-204; and Richard Thornton, *The Comintern and the Chinese Communists, 1928-1931*, pp. 38-59.

11. Thornton, *Comintern and the Chinese Communists*, p. 41. The resolutions on China of the subsequent Sixth Comintern Congress were based on those of the Sixth CCP Congress. Benjamin Schwartz, *Chinese Communism and the Rise of Mao*, p. 227, n. 24.

12. See ch. III, pp. 77-78, for further description and definition of the various rural class categories in China in the 1930s.

13. "Resolution on the Peasant Movement" (September 1928), in Brandt, *Documentary History*, p. 159.

14. Ibid., p. 164.

15. Ibid.

16. Thornton, *Comintern and the Chinese Communists*, p. 26; and Cohen, *Bukharin and the Bolshevik Revolution*, p. 294. By mid-1929, after Stalin's break with Bukharin, the Stalin-directed Comintern took a more unequivocally hostile stand on the rich peasant question. Thornton, pp. 26-27; Cohen, p. 329.

17. Cited in Deliusin, "Sixth Congress and Its Agrarian-Peasant Program," p. 83. Ch'ü added that the rich peasant was also often a semilandlord. It was in these two roles that the rich peasants were struggled against during the soviet period.

18. Ibid.

19. Brandt, *Documentary History*, p. 157.

20. Ibid.

21. "Resolution on the Land Question" (Sixth CCP Congress, Moscow, 1928), CSH 4, nos. 2-3 (Winter-Spring 1971):91.

22. Ibid., p. 92.

23. Ibid., p. 93.

24. Deliusin, "Sixth Congress and Its Agrarian-Peasant Program," p. 90.

25. Ibid.

26. Hsiao Tso-liang, *The Land Revolution in China, 1930-1934*, p. 9. A. M. Grigor'ev, "An Important Landmark in the History of the Chinese Communist Party," CSH 8, no. 3 (Spring 1975):32.

27. "Resolution on the Land Question," p. 99.

28. Ibid., p. 98.

29. Ibid., p. 99.

30. "Resolution on the Trade Union Movement in China" (Sixth CCP Congress, Moscow, 1928), CSH 4, no. 1 (Fall 1970):53.

31. Ibid.

32. Ibid., p. 54. In addition to the above, the resolution listed annual vacations, minimum wages, no child labor under age fourteen, a six-hour day for youth workers, equal wages and special benefits and protections for women workers.

33. Ibid., p. 57.

34. Ibid., p. 58.

35. Ibid., p. 60.

36. Ibid., p. 63.

37. "Outline of the Resolution on the Question of Organization" (Sixth CCP Congress, Moscow 1928), CSH 4, no. 1 (Fall 1970):35, 39.

38. Ibid., p. 29.

39. Industrial workers included textile, railway, mine, tobacco, and metal workers, seamen, and municipal government and postal workers. "Resolution on the Trade Union Movement," p. 60.

40. Jane Degras, ed., *The Communist International, 1919-1943: Documents* 3:31-36; Hsiao, *Land Revolution in China*, pp. 36, 39-40.

41. Degras, *Communist International* 3:34-35.

42. A. M. Grigor'ev, "The Comintern and the Revolutionary Movement in China under the Slogan of the Soviets, 1928-1930," in L. P. Deliusin et al., eds., *Komintern i Vostok*, p. 327. In correcting "the false line of 'union with the kulaks' " circulating in the CCP leadership, Grigor'ev writes, the ECCI under pressure from Stalin excessively sharpened the anti-rich peasant struggle. This "opened up a path pinching the middle peasant who had resorted to hiring labor and who was trying to develop his farm.".

43. See Hsiao, *Land Revolution in China*, pp. 37-39, for a summation of 1930-31 documents on the rich peasant problem issued by various CCP organs in the central soviet area.

44. See, for example, Ch'en Shao-yü's (Wang Ming's) comments in *Red Flag*, 17 May 1930, translated in Harold Isaacs, *The Tragedy of the Chinese Revolution*, p. 343; and Ch'en Shao-yü, "Again, on the Question of Opposing the Rich Peasants," *Red Flag*, 26 March 1930, in Hyobom Pak, ed. and trans., *Documents of the Chinese Communist Party, 1927-1930*, pp. 553-57. See also Lynda Schaefer Bell, "Agricultural Laborers and Rural Revolution," in Philip Huang et al., *Chinese Communists and Rural Society, 1927-1934*, pp. 34-38, for a discussion of the 1930 *Red Flag* articles on this theme by Wang Ming and others.

45. "Resolution on the Chinese Question" (ECCI, 23 July 1930), in Pak, *Documents of the CCP*, pp. 567-80; and Thornton, *Comintern and the Chinese Communists*, p. 168.

46. "Resolution on the Chinese Question," in Pak, *Documents of the CCP*, p. 570.

47. Ibid., p. 571.

48. Ibid., p. 572.

49. Ibid., p. 580.

50. See excerpts from an ECCI "Letter to the Central Committee of the CCP" (16 November 1930), in Degras, *Communist International* 3:140.

51. "Statement of the Enlarged Fourth Plenum of the Central Committee of the CCP to All Party Comrades" (15 January 1931), in Pak, *Documents of the CCP*, pp. 602-3.

52. "ECCI Resolution on the Tasks of the CCP" (26 August 1931), excerpts in Degras, *Communist International* 3:172.

53. Grigor'ev, "An Important Landmark," p. 34.

54. Wang Ming, for example, carefully argued this point in his influential 1931-32 anti-Li Li-san treatise, *The Two Lines*. See S. Bernard Thomas, *"Proletarian Hegemony" in the Chinese Revolution and the Canton Commune of 1927*, p. 86.

55. This thesis is forcefully presented by Thornton in *Comintern and the Chinese Communists* and by Grigor'ev in "An Important Landmark" and "Comintern and the Revolutionary Movement."

56. Soviet scholar L. P. Deliusin, for example, acknowledges that the "author" of the Sixth CCP Congress's resolution on the land (agrarian) question "exaggerated the role and the significance of capitalist and proletarian elements" in the Chinese countryside. He is also critical of the congress's "sharply hostile attitude" toward the national bourgeoisie. "Sixth Congress and Its Agrarian Peasant Program," pp. 94, 110.

57. C. Martin Wilbur, "The Influence of the Past: How the Early Years Helped to Shape the Future of the Chinese Communist Party," CQ 36 (October-December 1968):41.

58. Borisov and Koloskov, *Soviet-Chinese Relations*, p. 115.

Chapter II

1. Thomas Hammond, *Lenin on Trade Unions and Revolution, 1893-1917*, p. 16.

2. Ibid., pp. 24, 74.

3. These yellow unions generally had a pre-1927 revolutionary history and, though remaining mass organizations, were taken over by the Kuomintang and led by corrupt professional union leaders with ties to the secret societies. Edward Hammond, *Organized Labor in Shanghai, 1927-1937*, p. 8. See also Walter Gourlay, " 'Yellow' Unionism in Shanghai," *Harvard Papers on China* 7 (February 1973):103-35.

4. Augusta Wagner, *Labor Legislation in China*, pp. 8-10. Much of my brief summary of labor conditions and employment in China is based on this careful and informative study (pp. 1-23). Additional comparative data from other studies are cited below. Jean Chesneaux, in *The Chinese Labor Movement, 1919-1927*, pp. 24-47, gives a detailed description of the size and distribution of the Chinese working class, by region and industry, in the early 1920s. His findings represent approximations based on estimates and data of varying reliability and completeness.

5. Albert Feuerwerker, *The Chinese Economy, 1912-1949*, p. 10.

6. Ibid.

7. Lowe Chuan-hua, *Labor Conditions in China*, p. 94.

8. See also Kang Chao, "The Growth of a Modern Cotton Textile Industry," in Dwight Perkins, ed., *China's Modern Economy in Historical Perspective;* and Feuerwerker, *Chinese Economy*, p. 23.

9. See Feuerwerker, *Chinese Economy*, p. 19, for 1933 data on 2,435 Chinese-owned factories, which indicate that women and children comprised almost 60 percent of the 493,257 workers employed.

10. Ibid.

11. See Carl Riskin, "Surplus and Stagnation in Modern China," in Perkins, *China's Modern Economy*, table, 1, p. 71, for 1933 comparative wage figures for a broad spectrum of occupations.

12. Labor contractors took an average of 10 percent of workers' wages. In Shanghai, such contractors were frequently gang members engaged in racketeering and other criminal activities. "Five Years of Kuomintang Reaction," *China Forum* (Shanghai) 1, nos. 11-13, special ed. (May 1932):11.

13. Eleanor Hinder, *Life and Labour in Shanghai*, pp. 44-45.

14. R. H. Tawney, *Land and Labour in China*, p. 149.

15. Ta Chen, "Labour," in *China Year Book, 1933*, ed. H. G. W. Woodhead, p. 360.

16. Ibid., pp. 359-60; and Chuan-hua Lowe, *Facing Labor Issues in China*, pp. 21-22. See also Lynda Shaffer, *Mao and the Workers*, pp. 79-85, for a detailed description of the key role of labor contractors at the famous P'inghsiang coal mines at Anyuan in the 1920s.

17. Ellsworth Carlson, *The Kaiping Mines, 1877-1912*, pp. 137-39.

18. Leonard Ting, "The Coal Industry in China," pt. 1, *Nankai Social and Economic Quarterly* (Tientsin) 10, no. 1 (April 1937):59.

19. Carlson, *Kaiping Mines*, pp. 48-49; 174, n. 174.

20. The Kailan miners' association had been described as one of the "pillars of the Red trade union movement" by Communist sources in 1929. See Nym Wales, *The Chinese Labor Movement*, p. 178. The major 1934 strike involving perhaps thirty thousand miners in the Tangshan area was pointed up by the CCP for its "political coloring" as well as its economic significance. See *Economic Conditions in China*, pp. 9-10.

21. Ma Ch'ao-chün, *History of the Labor Movement in China*, pp. 160-65; Ma Ch'ao-chün et al., eds., *Chung-kuo lao-kung yün-tung shih* 3:776-79, 807-14. Note that these are respectively the English translation and Chinese original of the Ma book.

22. Wagner, *Labor Legislation*, pp. 234-35; Israel Epstein, *Notes on Labor Problems in Nationalist China*, pp. 57-61.

23. Wagner, *Labor Legislation*, p. 238.

24. Ibid., p. 239.

25. Lowe, *Facing Labor Issues*, p. 73. The law was apparently ambiguous on the possibility, for certain specified purposes, of establishing a labor federation for a single trade or industry. See also Wagner, *Labor Legislation*, p. 241. As Hammond notes, such "federations" would in effect be national unions, not federations of different unions. *Organized Labor*, p. 69.

26. Ma, *Lao-kung shih* 3:921-22, 947, 985.

27. Ma, *History of the Labor Movement*, p. 162.

28. Ma, *Lao-kung shih* 3:1203-4; Wagner, *Labor Legislation*, pp. 238-39; Hammond, *Organized Labor*, pp. 82-83.

29. Wagner, *Labor Legislation*, p. 230; Ma, *Lao-kung shih* 3:944-46, 1030.

30. Wagner, *Labor Legislation*, pp. 103-4.

31. Lowe, *Facing Labor Issues*, p. 91.

32. Wagner, *Labor Legislation*, p. 142.

33. Ma, *History of the Labor Movement*, p. 168.

34. Lowe, *Labor Conditions in China*, p. 98.

35. Among such examples of genuinely active and functioning trade unions, Wagner lists the Machinists' Union, the Postal Workers' Union, the Railway Workers' Union, the Commercial Press Union, and the British American Tobacco Company Workers' Union (*Labor Legislation*, p. 246). Four of the above were among the group known as the "Big Seven," which dominated the Shanghai labor scene. Hammond, *Organized Labor*, p. 58. The leader of the Postal Workers' Union, Chu Hsüeh-fan, became chairman of the Shanghai General Labor Union, which emerged in the early 1930s, and he was later to play a prominent role in the wartime and postwar labor movement as head of the CAL.

36. Wagner, *Labor Legislation*, p. 246.

37. Lowe, *Facing Labor Issues*, p. 73.

38. Wagner, *Labor Legislation*, p. 232. The Shanghai Bureau of Social Affairs study of these disputes showed, according to Wagner, "a distinct decline in the later years in the number of cases where the decision was completely favorable to the workers and an increase in those not favorable to them." The study attributed this to economic depression in the later years and to the increasing power of employers' associations. In his study of the strike data for 1932, however, Ta Chen concludes that "the workers have usually obtained satisfactory results," with their demands either fully or partially accepted in 50 percent of the strikes for which the results were known." See "Labour," in *China Year Book*, *1933*, p. 372.

39. Feuerwerker (*Chinese Economy*, p. 13) states that "from 1931 through 1935, the Chinese economy experienced considerable difficulty," particularly in modern industry in Shanghai and other urban centers. John K. Chang, however, concludes from his quantitative analysis of pre-1949 Chinese industrial development that there was a steady growth of the modern industrial sector from the early 1920s through 1936. See *Industrial Development in Pre-Communist China*, pp. 60–62. In the 1977 revised version of his monograph cited above, Feuerwerker takes Chang's figures as superseding all previous output estimates. He notes, however, that Chang's industrial output index includes Chinese and foreign-owned firms and covers Manchuria as well as China proper: "Some upward bias is introduced for the depression years by combining China proper and Manchuria in that Shanghai industry was more severely affected than was industrial enterprise in Manchuria" (*Economic Trends in the Republic of China, 1912-1949*, p. 25). Contemporary analyses for those years strongly emphasize the factor of business depression and the consequent prevalence of wage and employment issues. See Wagner, *Labor Legislation*, p. 232; *Chinese Year Book, 1935-1936*, pp. 900-18.

40. *China Year Book, 1935*, p. 352. The Japanese attack on Shanghai in January 1932 further worsened labor's plight, with great numbers thrown out of work by the general destruction and the suspension of operations by Chinese- and Japanese-owned mills. *China Forum* 1, no. 5 (25 March 1932):1.

41. Wales, *Chinese Labor Movement*, p. 167; *Chinese Year Book, 1935-1936*, pp. 913, 927.

42. See Ma, *Lao-kung shih* 3:1185-87, on the 1934 call by Chiang Kai-shek to end union strikes during the national "emergency."

43. See Hammond, *Organized Labor*, pp. 86-134, 171-212, for detailed accounts of these Shanghai labor struggles. For contemporary accounts of the 1933 British-American Tobacco Company labor struggles, see *China Forum* 2, no. 6 (29 May 1933):13-14; 2, no. 10 (18 September 1933):12-13; 2, no. 12 (22 October 1933):11; 3, no. 2 (30 November 1933):13. These accounts, in this strongly anti-KMT, anti-yellow union periodical, stress the role of both the BAT union and the KMT authorities in defusing the strikers' militancy and "selling out" the workers.

44. Hammond, *Organized Labor*, p. 127.

45. Ibid., pp. 128-34. The 1930-31 strikes of the workers and union of the French Electric Company in the French Concession in Shanghai also brought partial, and restraining, KMT

support in a struggle which again took on a strong antiimperialist tone. Ibid., pp. 193–204.

46. Ibid., p. 127. *China Forum*, reflecting the CCP's stance at the time, gave a sharply negative view of the role of the BAT union. See n. 43 above.

47. Hammond, *Organized Labor*, pp. 159–70.

48. Writing on the Chinese labor movement in 1939, Liu Shao-ch'i (who worked in the white-area red labor underground in the early 1930s) observed that the KMT "carried out extensive reorganisation work on trade unions"; he added that the Communists had been wrong to "oppose themselves to the yellow unions and refuse to join them." He noted further that the Nanking government's labor legislation included provisions favorable to the workers and that "although the KMT was reactionary at that time, it still cared more or less for the workers' interests." See "A Concise History of Workers' Movement in China" (May 1939), in CWLS, p. 136.

49. Wales, *Chinese Labor Movement*, p. 165.

50. Ibid., p. 60.

51. Ibid., p. 56.

52. Teng Chung-hsia, "Report to the Tenth Plenum, E.C.C.I.," *Inprecorr* 9, no. 57 (9 October 1929):1232. Teng stated that "we have as yet no exact statistics" on the numerical strength of the red unions.

53. Ho Kan-chih, *A History of the Modern Chinese Revolution*, pp. 177–78.

54. Wales, *Chinese Labor Movement*, p. 61.

55. James Harrison, *The Long March to Power*, p. 161.

56. Conrad Brandt et al., *A Documentary History of Chinese Communism*, p. 206.

57. Harrison, *Long March to Power*, pp. 161–62.

58. Wan Min [Wang Ming] and Kang Sin [K'ang Sheng], *Revolutionary China Today*, p. 48.

59. Wales, *Chinese Labor Movement*, p. 71; *Short History of Chinese Labor Movement, Current Background*, no. 108, p. 25 (published serially in *Ta-kung-pao* [Shanghai], November 1950-February 1951).

60. Warren Kuo, *Analytical History of the Chinese Communist Party* 2:119.

61. Wan and Kang [Wang and K'ang], *Revolutionary China Today*, p. 12.

62. Donald Klein and Anne Clark, *Biographic Dictionary of Chinese Communism, 1921-1965* 1:619.

63. *Trade Unions in People's China*, pp. 10–11.

64. Yüeh Sheng, *Sun Yat-sen University in Moscow and the Chinese Revolution*, p. 250.

65. For example, K'ang Sheng's report to the ECCI Thirteenth Plenum in December 1933, "The Development of the Revolutionary Movement in Non-Soviet China and the Work of the Communist Party," in *Revolutionary China Today*, pp. 72–96.

66. Wales, *Chinese Labor Movement*, p. 178.

67. "I-chiu san-i nien chih-kung yün-tung-ti tsung-chieh" [Summary of the 1931 staff-workers' movement], *Hung-ch'i chou-pao* [Red flag weekly] (Shanghai) (March 1932):30. The report listed 1,148 members, a total based on reports from various localities.

68. Ibid., pp. 25–32.

69. "Resolution on Certain Questions in the History of Our Party" (adopted 20 April 1945 by Enlarged Seventh Plenum of the CCP Central Committee), in SW 3:200.

70. O. B. Borisov and B. T. Koloskov, *Soviet-Chinese Relations, 1945-1970*, p. 113.

71. Ibid.

72. Hammond, *Organized Labor*, p. 204.

73. Ibid. Hsü was imprisoned in 1931 as an accused Communist.

74. Sheng, *Sun Yat-sen University*, pp. 235-51.

75. *Inprecorr* 9, no. 57 (9 October 1929):1230-33.

76. Ibid., p. 1232.

77. Ibid.

78. "Resolûtion of the E.C.C.I. on Communist Work in the Trade Unions of China," *Inprecorr* 9, no. 52 (20 September 1929):1126-27.

79. Ibid., p. 1126.

80. Ibid., p. 1127.

81. Ibid.

82. Pantus, "The V. Congress of the All-China Federation of Labor," *Inprecorr* 9, no. 70 (20 December 1929):1483-84.

83. Ibid., p. 1484.

84. Jane Degras, ed., *The Communist International, 1919-1943: Documents* 3:87; and A. M. Grigor'ev, "The Comintern and the Revolutionary Movement in China Under the Slogan of the Soviets, 1928-1930," in L. P. Deliusin et al., eds., *Komintern i Vostok*, p. 328.

85. See CSH 3, no. 3 (Spring 1970):242. The full text of this new translation of the original text can be found on pp. 224-50.

86. Kuo, *Analytical History* 2:255-76; see also Hsiao Tso-liang, *Power Relations within the Chinese Communist Movement, 1930-1934* 1:125-46.

87. Grigor'ev, "Comintern and the Revolutionary Movement," pp. 330-35.

88. "Ho Meng-hsiung i-chien-shu" [Statement of the views of Ho Meng-hsiung], 8 September 1930; released by the Central Secretariat on 6 January 1931. Chinese text in Hsiao, *Power Relations* 2:112-19; English summary in Hsiao, *Power Relations* 1:50-53.

89. Hsiao, *Power Relations* 2:114.

90. Ibid., pp. 115-16.

91. Cited in Grigor'ev, "Comintern and the Revolutionary Movement," p. 343.

92. S. Bernard Thomas, *"Proletarian Hegemony" in the Chinese Revolution and the Canton Commune of 1927*. Wang Ming, in the 1932 Moscow edition of his *Two Lines*, argued that criticism of the "adventurist" Red Army occupation of Changsha during the 1930 Li Li-san period should not obscure the continuing importance of taking major cities under conditions of strengthened red military and political power. See p. 72, n. 102.

93. Pavel Mif subsequently wrote that the Fourth Plenum had "exposed" the Li Li-san line and "repelled the attempt of the Right opportunists to impose a defeatist program of retreat upon the Party." See his *Heroic China*, p. 69.

94. Hsiao, *Power Relations* 1:131.

95. "Enigma of the Five Martyrs," in Tsi-an Hsia, *The Gate of Darkness*, pp. 164-65.

96. Hsiao, *Power Relations* 1:131.

97. After his release from prison, Lo reportedly maintained ties to Trotskyite circles in China. Klein and Clark, *Biographic Dictionary* 1:637.

98. Kuo, *Analytical History* 2:215-33.

99. Klein and Clark, *Biographic Dictionary* 1:322.

100. Ibid., p. 323.

101. Ibid., p. 619.

102. Sheng, *Sun Yat-sen University*, p. 250; and Otto Braun, *Chinesische Aufzeichnungen (1932-1939)*, p. 39. Braun, the famous Li Te, Comintern military adviser to the Chinese

Communists during the fifth KMT encirclement campaign of 1933-34, arrived in Shanghai in 1932 and went to the central soviet area in the fall of 1933. He notes the departure from Shanghai for Kiangsi in the spring of 1933 of Party Center leaders Po Ku and Lo Fu, and also of Ch'en Yün, who he states had been responsible for trade union work.

103. Hsiao, *Power Relations* 1:142-43 (summary of an anti-rightist party document of 5 February 1931).

104. Kuo, *Analytical History* 2:313.

105. Sheng, *Sun Yat-sen University*, p. 245. Wang Ming briefly replaced Hsiang as secretary general but soon left for Moscow (evidently afraid to remain in Shanghai, according to Sheng) to become CCP representative to the Comintern. Wang did not return to China until late 1937 (pp. 246-47).

106. Kuo, *Analytical History* 2:313; Harrison, *Long March to Power*, p. 220.

107. Kuo, *Analytical History* 2:320.

108. Nym Wales and Kim San, *Song of Ariran*, pp. 265-66.

109. Ibid., p. 286.

110. "Chih-kung yün-tung-ti tsung-chieh."

111. Ibid., 31-33.

112. Hsüeh K'ang, "Chi-hui chu-i-ti chih-kung yün-tung tsung-chieh" [Summing up the opportunist labor movement] (4 June 1932), Ch'en Ch'eng Collection, reel 12.

113. Ibid.

114. "Wei chih-kung yün-tung chih t'ung-chih-ti i feng hsin" [A Letter for labor movement comrades] (25 March 1932), Yushodo Collection, reel 11.

115. Ibid. This seventeen-page document is illegible in many places. Enough can be read, however, to provide the basis for the summary given above.

116. See, for example, "Appeal of the All-China Trade Union Federation [the ACFL]" (Shanghai, 28 April 1932), *Inprecorr* 12, no. 20 (5 May 1932):395. This was directed against the Japanese attack on Shanghai.

117. Hsiao, *Power Relations* 1:187-88.

118. Up to sixty thousand workers reportedly had participated in this largely unsuccessful strike against thirty-four Japanese cotton mills. "Japanese Mill Struggle Comes to an End: Solidarity, Spirit Shown," *China Forum* 1, no. 14 (21 May 1932):4. This pro-Communist source strongly emphasized that the strike "was not only against the miserable conditions of slavery in the mills but against the Japanese invaders of Chinese soil" (ibid.).

119. P[avel] Mif, "New Developments in the Revolutionary Crisis in China," *Communist International* 10, no. 9 (15 May 1933):302, 304.

120. Cited in Lee Min, "Review of the Underground Communist Press in KMT China," *Communist International* 11, no. 18 (20 September 1934):617.

121. "Tasks of the Revolutionary Trade Union Movement of China," *Inprecorr* 12, no. 10 (3 March 1932):189-93.

122. Ibid., p. 190.

123. Ibid., p. 191.

124. Ibid., p. 192.

125. Ibid., p. 193.

126. Kang Sin [K'ang Sheng], "The Development of the Revolutionary Movement in Non-Soviet China and the Work of the Communist Party," in Wan and Kang [Wang and K'ang], *Revolutionary China Today*, pp. 86-87. In a November 1933 article, K'ang Sheng had claimed a Shanghai party membership of four thousand (80 percent of them workers) and

a total of eight thousand for Kiangsu Province. Kon Sin [K'ang Sheng], "The Growth of the Communist Party in Kuomintang China," *Communist International* 10, no. 21 (1 November 1933):767.

127. K'ang, "Revolutionary Movement in Non-Soviet China," p. 85.

128. "Labor," in *Chinese Year Book, 1935-1936*, p. 913.

129. Ibid. See also nn. 39, 40, 41, above.

130. Wang Ming, "The Revolutionary Movement in the Colonial and Semi-Colonial Countries and the Tactics of the Communist Parties," *Communist International* 12, no. 18 (20 September 1935):1325-26. Referring to CCP tactics during the 1932 defense of Shanghai against the Japanese, Wang stated that because "of the erroneous position of some of our party leaders who considered the slogan of 'the union of workers, peasants, soldiers, merchants, and intellectuals' to be impermissible, a really wide anti-Japanese people's front was not established" (ibid.).

131. K'ang, "Revolutionary Movement in Non-Soviet China," p. 87.

132. Wang Ming, "Revolution, War and Intervention in China and the Tasks of the Communist Party," in Wan and Kang [Wang and K'ang], *Revolutionary China Today*, p. 52.

133. "Wu-chung ch'üan-hui kuan-yu pai-se ch'ü-yu chung ching-chi tou-cheng yü kung-hui kung-tso-ti chueh-i" [Resolution of the Fifth Plenum of the Central Committee on economic struggle and union work in the white areas], TC, no. 50 (11 March 1934):1-2.

134. A Communist account of such successes in the strike struggle during 1933 claimed a red leadership role in major strikes of printing, tobacco, and textile workers in Shanghai. It also asserted that in north China from January to June 1933, "the Party and the Red trade unions participated in the conduct of 27 strikes and struggles of the industrial workers and led 17 struggles absolutely independently." Eighteen of the twenty-seven actions, it added, ended in "partial or complete victory for the workers." Lin Ming, "Some Experiences of the Communist Party of China in Organizing and Leading Strike Struggles," *Communist International* 11, no. 9 (May 1934):335.

135. "Wu-chung ch'üan-hui," p. 3.

136. Ibid., p. 1.

137. Klein and Clark, *Biographic Dictionary* 1:150.

138. "Hung wu-i ch'ien-yen-ti ch'üan-kuo wu-ch'an chieh-chi wei-ta-ti tou-cheng" [The great struggles of the national proletariat on the eve of Red May First], TC, no. 57 (28 April 1934):9-11.

139. "New Upsurge of the Strike Movement of the Working Class in Kuomintang China," *Communist International* 11, no. 13 (5 July 1934):446-47.

140. Ibid., p. 447.

141. Hammond, *Organized Labor*, p. 239.

142. Wang, "Revolutionary Movement in the Colonial and Semi-Colonial Countries," p. 1328.

Chapter III

1. See, for example, the ECCI "Resolution on the Chinese Question" (23 July 1930), in Hyobom Pak, ed. and trans., *Documents of the Chinese Communist Party, 1927-1930*, p. 569; and the ECCI "Letter to the Central Committee of the CCP" (16 November 1930), in Jane Degras, ed., *The Communist International* 3:140.

2. "Resolution of the Enlarged Fourth Plenum of the Central Committee of the CCP," in Conrad Brandt et al., *A Documentary History of Chinese Communism*, p. 210.

3. V. Kuchumov, "The Struggle for the Bolshevisation of the Communist Party of China," *Communist International* 8, no. 6 (15 March 1931):163. As the third task, Kuchumov

called for the "further unleashing" of "partial economic struggles" of the proletariat in the big industrial centers, "further revolutionising" of such struggles, and linking them with the struggle to defend the soviet areas and establish a soviet regime. Kuchumov was a Comintern official directly concerned with Chinese affairs.

4. Ch'en Shao-yü, "Again, on the Question of Opposing the Rich Peasants," *Red Flag*, 26 March 1930, in Pak, *Documents of the CCP*, pp. 553-57.

5. Quoted in Harold Isaacs, *The Tragedy of the Chinese Revolution*, p. 343, from "Why Not Organize Agricultural Laborers' Unions?," *Red Flag*, 17 May 1930.

6. Ibid.

7. "Resolution on the Chinese Question," in Pak, *Documents of the CCP*, p. 570.

8. Hsiao Tso-Liang, *The Land Revolution in China, 1930-1934*, pp. 41, 56.

9. Hsiao Tso-Liang, *Power Relations within the Chinese Communist Movement, 1930-1934* 1:150.

10. Ibid., pp. 150-52. The General Front Committee, Mao's party stronghold in the Red Army, was abolished by the CBSA in its first circular notice, 15 January 1931 (ibid.). See also Ilpyong Kim, *The Politics of Chinese Communism*, pp. 67, 90-91. Kim, though seeing a "careful balance" of power in the composition of the CBSA, also notes the strong representation in it of a group of younger leaders, "all of whom were either members of the returned-student group or sympathetic to their policy position" (p. 67). A further leadership reorganization, probably after the November 1931 First Soviet Congress, seemingly strengthened the returned-student role (p. 91).

11. "How to Analyze the Classes" (adopted by the Eight-County Conference on the Land Investigation Drive [Movement], 17-21 June 1933, and approved by the central government of the Chinese Soviet Republic, 10 October 1933), in Hsiao, *Land Revolution in China*, doc. 96, pp. 254-57.

12. "Decisions Concerning Some Problems Arising from the Agrarian Struggle" (adopted by Council of People's Commissars [Ministers] of the Chinese Soviet Republic, 10 October 1933), in ibid., doc. 101, p. 262.

13. Trygvie Lötveit, *Chinese Communism 1931-1934*, pp. 147-51.

14. "How to Analyze the Classes," pp. 256-57.

15. Hsiao, *Land Revolution in China*, pp. 27-30; Lötveit, *Chinese Communism 1931-1934*, table 12, pp. 148-49. Mao's figures are rounded off and total 99 percent rather than 100 percent. His percentages are based on families, not individuals, and thus tend to underestimate the landlord and rich-peasant proportion of the population, where family size would probably be greater. Mao further noted that if absentee landlords had been included, the landlord percentage would have risen to 2 or 3 percent of the population. Lötveit, *Chinese Communism, 1931-1934*, p. 149.

16. In reissuing in 1941 his rural surveys of the 1928-30 period, Mao observed that his investigations had been ridiculed as "narrow empiricism." He used the occasion of the reissuance of these surveys to criticize the escalated class-struggle policies followed in the central soviet area from 1931 on. "Preface and Postscript to *Rural Surveys*" (March and April 1941), in SW 3:13-14.

17. Dwight Perkins, *Agricultural Development in China, 1368-1968*, pp. 87-89 and table V.1, p. 91. See also J. Lossing Buck, *Land Utilization in China*, table 22, p. 196.

18. Sidney Gamble, *Ting Hsien*, p. 211.

19. Angus McDonald, for example, in investigating pre-Communist rural society in Hunan, has emphasized the variety of tenancy relationships there, running the gamut from rich to poor. "Reflections on Divided Elites, Social Cleavages, and Rural Revolution in Hunan."

20. R. H. Tawney, *Land and Labour in China*, pp. 33-34. According to the Nanking government's National Land Commission study of twenty-three counties in Hopei and eighteen counties in Shantung, "agricultural workers" comprised 4.41 percent of the total in Hopei and 2.26 percent in Shantung. Ramon Myers, *The Chinese Farm Economy*, table A-6, p. 303. Gamble's *Ting Hsien* study shows hired labor as 1.2 percent of the families in that county (table 63, p. 224).

21. Tawney, *Land and Labour in China*, p. 34. A 1951 survey of areas of Kiangsi Province not yet affected by land reform reported that agricultural laborers made up only 3.7 percent of the rural population. Lynda Schaefer Bell, "Agricultural Laborers and Rural Revolution," in Philip Huang et al., *Chinese Communists and Rural Society, 1927-1934*, pp. 29-56.

22. Sun Hsiao-tsun, "The Problem of Farm Management in Contemporary China," pt. 3, *Quarterly Review of the Sun Yat-sen Institute* (Nanking) 3, no. 2 (Summer 1936); included in *Agrarian China*, p. 71.

23. Bell, "Agricultural Laborers," pp. 42-43.

24. Gamble, *Ting Hsien*, table 92, p. 312.

25. Tawney, *Land and Labour in China*, p. 114.

26. Victor Yakhontoff, *The Chinese Soviets*, p. 148. The number of "industrial workers" (presumably employed in factories conforming to factory law definitions) for Kiangsi Province as a whole in this period was estimated to be only 8,995, with 6,882 concentrated in the provincial capital of Nanch'ang. Kim, *Politics of Chinese Communism*, p. 27.

27. CBSA Notice no. 3, "Su-wei-ai yü kung-hui-ti kuan-hsi wen-t'i" [Problems (or questions) of soviet-union relations] (21 January 1931), Ch'en Ch'eng Collection, reel 12.

28. Hsiao, *Power Relations* 1:109-11.

29. CBSA, "Su-wei-ai yü kung-hui," p. 1.

30. CBSA Notice no. 17, "Kung-hui yün-tung yü kung-tso lu-hsien" [Union movement and work line] (1 March 1931), Ch'en Ch'eng Collection, reel 11.

31. Lötveit, *Chinese Communism 1931-1934*, p. 150. According to a 1934 report by Liu Shao-ch'i, this exemption apparently applied also to other types of workers in the rural areas who were given land in the Communists' redistribution program. See "The Trade Union Movement in Soviet Areas during the Past Two Years," in CWLS, p. 5.

32. Hsiao, *Land Revolution in China*, pp. 40-43.

33. "Provisional Regulations for the Hired-Farmhand Union" (February 1931), in ibid., doc. 27, pp. 170-71.

34. Ibid., p. 173.

35. "Regulations for the Poor-Peasant Association [Corps]," in Hsiao, *Land Revolution in China*, doc. 28, p. 175. Since this association *(hui)* is usually referred to as the Poor Peasant Corps, in line with its later designation as *t'uan* ("corps"), I have used the latter term.

36. Ibid., p. 176.

37. Ibid., p. 177.

38. "Organic Law of the Poor-Peasant Association and Its Tasks" (n.d., but probably 1931), in Hsiao, *Land Revolution in China*, pp. 182-83.

39. Ibid., p. 184.

40. Ibid.

41. Hsiao, *Land Revolution in China*, doc. 66, pp. 212-13; Kim, *Politics of Chinese Communism*, pp. 16-17.

42. See Hsiao, *Land Revolution in China*, p. 91, for a summation of "General Principles of Organization and Function of the Poor-Peasant Corps" (15 July 1933).

43. Southwest Kiangsi Special Area Committee Notice no. 29, "Ku-kung-hui-ti kung-tso went'i" [Problems of hired hands' union work] (31 March 1931), Ch'en Ch'eng Collection, reel 12.

44. Hsiao, *Power Relations* 1:164.

45. "Su-ch'ü kung-hui yün-tung chüeh-i-an" [Resolution on the soviet-area union movement] (adopted by the First Party Congress of the Soviet Areas, November 1931, and published by the CBSA), Ch'en Ch'eng Collection, reel 12. My summary above is without further footnote citation to this lengthy eighteen-page document.

46. *Räte China* [Soviets in China], p. 89. This important collection of reports and documents was first published in Russian and German in 1933. My citations are to the introductory essay by J. Johanson and O. Taube, "The Soviet Movement in China," pp. 9-136. Though this volume reappeared in a 1934 edition, when CCP and Comintern labor and economic policies for the soviet areas had already undergone some important modifications, its strongly asserted anticapitalist-struggle line still conformed to the overall pre-1935 international Communist stance.

47. "Constitution of the Chinese Soviet Republic" (7 November 1931), in Brandt, *Documentary History*, p. 220.

48. See, for example, Liu Shao-ch'i's, "Trade Union Movement," p. 8. The method of election outlined for the November 1931 First Soviet Congress had given workers and agricultural laborers a ten-to-one advantage over other enfranchised elements in the population in electing representatives to the congress. Bell, "Agricultural Laborers," p. 47. At *hsiang*-level ("township") elections, each village was designated an electoral unit, with all "factory" (presumably nonagricultural) workers in the *hsiang* collectively designated as one electoral unit. Thus, in one such *hsiang* in Hsingkuo County, according to a 1933 report by Mao, there were five such units: four village and one factory workers' electoral units. Kim, *Politics of Chinese Communism*, pp. 176-77.

49. "Constitution of the Chinese Soviet Republic," p. 221.

50. See Hsiao, *Power Relations* 1:180-82, for a summary comparing the two texts.

51. For the English text of the labor law, see Yakhontoff, *Chinese Soviets*, pp. 224-35. The Chinese text is in Hsiao, *Power Relations* 2:440-43; and in *Su-wei-ai Chung-kuo* [Soviet China], pp. 117-42. The law was promulgated by the Central Executive Committee of the Soviet Republic on 20 December 1931, to take effect on 1 January 1932.

52. "Kuan-yü ching-chi cheng-ts'e chüeh-i-an" [Resolution on economic policy], in *Su-wei-ai Chung-kuo*, p. 148.

53. Ibid., p. 150.

54. "Lao-tung fa pao-kao" [Report on the labor law] (November 1931), issued by Executive Bureau of the Soviet Areas' ACFL, Ch'en Ch'eng Collection, reel 12.

55. Ibid., p. 3. Wang Ming subsequently complained that these agricultural labor categories benefited twice over, from the labor law itself and from the supplementary regulations referred to by Hsiang. This placed a particularly heavy burden on the middle peasants who were their primary employers. See Wang Ming, "Chung-kuo su-wei-ai cheng-ch'üan-ti ching-chi cheng-ts'e" [Economic policies of the Chinese soviet government], in *WMHC* 3:33.

56. "Lao-tung fa pao-kao," p. 6.

57. Ibid., p. 11.

58. See Wang Chien-min, *Chung-kuo Kung-ch'an-tang shih-kao* [Draft history of the Chinese Communist Party] 2:408-9, which includes a chart comparing provisions of the 1930 draft, the 1931 labor law, and the October 1933 revision of the labor law. The 1933

revisions will be discussed in ch. IV. The forty-yuan minimum wage stipulation apparently appeared in the political program adopted by the 1930 conference rather than in the text of the labor law itself. Hsiao, *Power Relations* 1:20.

59. Wang, *Chung-kuo Kung-ch'an-tang* 2:408-9. This was particularly true in its social insurance provisions, in employer contributions to union expenses, and in a greater union role in implementing collective agreements and production supervision.

60. "Chung-kung chung-yang kuan-yü su-ch'ü ch'ih-se kung-hui-ti jen-wu ho mu-ch'ien-ti kung-tso chüeh-i" [CC-CCP resolution on soviet-area red unions' tasks and current work] (21 December 1931, issued by CBSA on 20 February 1932), Ch'en Ch'eng Collection, reel 12.

61. The A-B League was the KMT-led anti-Communist (anti-Bolshevik) organization in Kiangsi which the CCP leadership in 1931 (both Mao and the Bolshevik group) often equated with remaining Li Li-sanist influences in soviet party and labor organs.

62. "Chung-kung chung-yang chüeh-i," p. 2.

63. The criticism regarding alien class elements was repeated in the party labor bureau's report for 1931 (see n. 64, below) and strongly reiterated in a late 1932 letter to the soviet-area unions from the Shanghai-based ACFL center. Pointing to the continuing presence of such alien class elements, the letter described the soviet unions as "anti-proletarian in character, representing more the interests of the landlords, rich peasants, and employers." "Letter to the Labor Unions in the Soviet Districts on the Question of Labor Union Membership from the Standing Committee of the ACFL," *Red Flag*, 15 November 1932; cited in Isaacs, *Tragedy of the Chinese Revolution*, p. 347.

64. "I-chiu san-i nien chih-kung yün-tung-ti tsung-chieh" [Summary of the 1931 staff-workers' movement]. As noted in ch. II, while this report subsequently came under some fire for its "opportunist" stance, this allegation probably applied more to its pessimistic depiction of the urban labor scene than to its rather standard (in party documents of the time) assessment of the soviet labor movement.

65. "Tasks of the Revolutionary Trade Union Movement," *Inprecorr* 12, no. 10 (3 March 1932):192.

66. Ibid., p. 193.

67. "The Revolutionary Crisis in China and the Tasks of the Chinese Communists," *Communist International* 8, no. 20 (1 December 1931):660.

68. Johanson and Taube, "Soviet Movement in China," p. 117.

69. Wang Chien-min, in *Chung-kuo Kung-ch'an-tang* 2:411, reproduces the report on the congress from the CCP's *Hung-ch'i chou-pao* [Red flag weekly], no. 50 (10 September 1932).

70. Ibid.

71. "Chin-nien-ti 'erh-ch'i' chi-nien yü Chung-kuo kung-jen chieh-chi-ti chung-hsin jen-wu" [This year's "February 7" anniversary and the central tasks of the Chinese working class], HSCH, no. 8 (3 February 1932), supplement, p. 2, Ch'en Ch'eng Collection, reel 16. Chou also addressed the labor congress as the representative of the CBSA. Wang, *Chung-kuo Kung-ch'an-tang* 2:411.

72. "Kiangsi sheng su-ch'ü kung-jen tou-cheng kang-ling" [Kiangsi soviet-area workers' struggle program] (adopted by the Executive Committee, Union Federation of Kiangsi, 25 March 1932), Ch'en Ch'eng Collection, reel 12.

73. Wan Min [Wang Ming], "Revolution, War and Intervention in China and the Tasks of the Communist Party" (December 1933), in Wan Min [Wang Ming] and Kang Sin [K'ang Sheng], *Revolutionary China Today*, p. 49.

74. In September 1933 Wang Ming also criticized this particular provision of the labor law, remarking that under current conditions in the soviet area this requirement was, "to say the least," difficult to implement. See "Chung-kuo ching-chi cheng-ts'e," in WMHC 3:3-4.

75. In stating that rich peasants could hire labor only through the farmhands' union, the "Struggle Program" indicated that this class continued to have such labor-hiring capabilities.

76. "Tasks of the Revolutionary Trade Union Movement," p. 193.

77. Ibid., pp. 192-93.

78. Kuo-chi ku-nung wei-yüan-hui mi-shu-ch'ü [Secretariat of the international farm-laborer committee], "Kuan-yü Chung-kuo ku-nung kung-hui-ti chüeh-i-an" [Resolution regarding the Chinese farm-laborer union], Yushodo Collection, reel 11. This document is listed under the heading "CC, CCP Documents, 1932-1933."

79. Ibid.

80. "Nung-ts'un lao-tung tsan-hsing fa-ling" [Provisional regulations on rural labor], cited in Wang, Chung-kuo Kung-ch'an-tang 2:409.

81. Ibid.

82. Ibid.

83. "Chi-chung huo-li fan-tui yu-ch'ing chi-hui chu-i" [Concentrate firepower against right opportunism], SCKJ, no. 3 (11 June 1932), Ch'en Ch'eng Collection, reel 1. While only scattered and incomplete issues of this journal are available for 1932, 1933, and 1934, they are valuable as a reasonably representative reflection of the outlook of the soviet ACFL leadership. SCKJ was published by the executive bureau of the ACFL for the soviet areas.

84. "Chung-kuo nung-yeh kung-jen ti-i-tz'u tai-piao ta-hui-ti i-i chi jen-wu" [Significance and tasks of the First Chinese Agricultural Workers' Congress], HSCH, no. 66 (2 April 1933):1 (Ch'en Ch'eng Collection, reel 16).

85. Ibid.

86. "Hui-ch'ang shih ch'ih-se tsung kung-hui ti-i-tz'u tai-piao ta-hui chüeh-i-an" [Resolution of the first congress of the Huich'ang Red General Labor Union] (10 December 1931), Ch'en Ch'eng Collection, reel 12.

87. "Chi-chung huo-li."

88. Ibid.

89. Po T'ai, "Ning-tu su-wei-ai kung-tso chih i-pan" [Overview of the work of the Ningtu soviet], HSCH, no. 18 (21 April 1932), p. 6 (Ch'en Ch'eng Collection, reel 16).

90. Ibid.

91. The following summary of Wang's views is based on the Chinese text of the postscript, "Kuan-yü Chung-kuo ko-ming yün-tung fa-chan pu p'ing-heng wen-t'i" [The question of the uneven development of the Chinese revolution], in Hsiao, Power Relations 2:559-63. Hsiao gives a brief summary of this section in vol. 1, pp. 204-5.

92. In line with the emphasis placed upon (and probable overstatement of) the growing proletarianization of the Red Army, a Comintern source gave a percentage comparison of the changing social composition of officer graduates from the Red Army infantry schools from the first graduating class (presumably before 1931) to the sixth graduating class (probably toward the end of the Kiangsi period). In the first class, workers made up 7.5 percent, coolies 50 percent, poor peasants 0.4 percent, middle peasants 19 percent, and "others" 23.1 percent. In the sixth class, workers comprised 24.4 percent, coolies 56.4 percent, poor peasants 7.2 percent, middle peasants 4.5 percent, and others 7.5 percent. Li Huan, "The Workers' and Peasants' Red Army as It Is," in China at Bay, pp. 37-38. The writer also reported that the overall social composition of the Red Army units of the central soviet area in April 1934 was 30 percent workers, 68 percent peasants, 1 percent clerks, and 1 percent others. The above data are stated to be from the "Organizational and Statistical Sector of the Political Board of the Red Army of China" (ibid.).

Chapter IV

1. Ilpyong Kim, *The Politics of Chinese Communism*, pp. 94-95.

2. "Chi-nien 'erh-ch'i' yü wo-men-ti chung-hsin jen-wu" [Our central tasks in commemorating "February 7"], HSCH, no. 50 (7 February 1933):1.

3. Ibid.

4. Teng Ying-ch'ao, "Shih-chi wei kung-ku yü chia-ch'iang wu-ch'an chieh-chi ling-tao-ch'üan erh tou-cheng-ti chien-t'ao" [Review of the struggle for the real strengthening and reinforcing of proletarian hegemony], TC, no. 1 (4 February 1933):13-14.

5. Donald Klein and Anne Clark, *Biographic Dictionary of Chinese Communism, 1921-1965* 2:839-40.

6. Teng, "Shih-chi wei kung-ku," p. 13.

7. Hsiao Tso-liang, *Power Relations within the Chinese Communist Movement, 1930-1934* 1:214-15, 230-31.

8. Teng, "Shih-chi wei kung-ku," p. 13.

9. Hsiao, *Power Relations* 1:214.

10. Teng, "Shih-chi wei kung-ku," p. 14.

11. Evidence of stresses and strains between the unions and the soviet government at local administrative levels was apparent in measures by the central soviet government's Ministry of Labor to disband social insurance offices set up by the unions. It was stated that the unions had not handled this well, with insurance monies in some cases simply being transferred to higher-level union organizations instead of being used for the workers' welfare. Such social insurance matters were now to be handled by the soviet government labor bureaus. "Chung-yang lao-tung jen-min wei-yüan-pu ming-ling" [Central Government People's Commissariat (Ministry) of Labor order], 30 December 1932, order nn. 2, HSCH, no. 47 (14 January 1933):6.

12. Teng, "Shih-chi wei kung-ku," p. 14.

13. Ibid., p. 15.

14. See nn. 40 and 41 below.

15. "Chung-kuo nung-yeh kung-jen ti-i-tz'u tai-piao ta-hui" [First congress of Chinese agricultural workers], HSCH, no. 66 (2 April 1933):1; "Hsiang ch'üan-kuo shou-i, tien-yüan kung-jen ti-i-tz'u tai-piao ta-hui chih hung wu-i-ti wu-ch'an chieh-chi ching-li" [Red May Day proletarian salute to the first national congress of handicraft workers and shop employees], HSCH, no. 74 (29 April 1933):1.

16. Ibid.

17. "Hsiang ch'üan-kuo shou-i," p. 1; and "Chung-kuo tien-yüan, shou-i kung-hui chü-hsing ch'ou-pei hui chüeh-i" [Resolutions of the preparatory meeting of the Chinese shop employees' and handicraft workers' union], HSCH, no. 57 (3 March 1933):4.

18. "Wei wu-i chieh cheng-shou tang-yüan yün-tung, kao su-ch'ü min-chung shu" [Letter to soviet-area masses on the May Day party member enlistment movement], HSCH, no. 70 (17 April 1933):1.

19. J. Johanson and O. Taube, "The Soviet Movement in China," in *Räte China*, pp. 83-84.

20. Wang Chien-min, *Chung-kuo Kung-ch'an-tang shih-kao* 2:410. Teng Ying-ch'ao had commented in her February TC article (see n. 4 above) that some local soviet government personnel proclaimed such "anti-worker nonsense" as "workers are reactionary," and "distribute no land to workers" (p. 14).

21. A new People's Commission for National Economy was formally organized by the central soviet government at the end of April 1933 for the express purpose of developing the economy to counter the enemy blockade. Kim, *Politics of Chinese Communism*, pp.

94-95. Two major economic construction conferences were held in the central soviet area under soviet government auspices in August 1933. Hsiao, *Power Relations* 1:221-22.

22. Lo Fu [Chang Wen-t'ien], "Wu-i chieh yü lao-tung fa chih-hsing-ti chien-yüeh" [May Day and a review of the implementation of the labor law], TC, no. 10 (1 May 1933):7-12.

23. Ibid., p. 8. To buttress his position, Chang cited also relevant points in the resolution of the International Farm Laborers' Committee, discussed in ch. III of this study.

24. Ibid., p. 10.

25. Ibid., p. 12.

26. Lo Fu, "Su-wei-ai cheng-ch'üan hsia-ti chieh-chi tou-cheng" [Class struggle under soviet political power], pt. 1, TC, no. 14 (5 June 1933):6-13; pt. 2, no. 15 (15 June 1933):9-14. Issues no. 10 (1 May 1933) and no. 14 (5 June 1933) are among those missing in the Ch'en Ch'eng Collection microfilm run of this journal, and I am indebted to the Hoover Library for making copies of the Lo Fu articles from those issues available to me.

27. Ibid., pt. 1, p. 7.

28. Ibid., pt. 1, p. 12.

29. Wang Ming, "Chung-kuo su-wei-ai cheng-ch'üan-ti ching-chi cheng-ts'e" [Economic policies of the Chinese soviet government] in WMHC 3:23-45.

30. P[avel] Mif, "New Developments in the Revolutionary Crisis in China," *Communist International* 10, no. 9 (15 May 1933):302-10.

31. Trygvie Lötveit, *Chinese Communism 1931-1934*, p. 186.

32. Wang, "Chung-kuo ching-chi cheng-ts'e," in WMHC 3:25-28.

33. Mif, "Revolutionary Crisis in China," p. 309.

34. These measures included expansion of cultivated area; encouragement of household gardens; organizing mutual-aid associations; soil, fertilizer, and irrigation improvements on the agricultural front; restoration and development of local private and cooperative industry and commerce (including an end to "intemperate" confiscatory and liquidationist policies toward private merchants); shoring up soviet paper currency (rejecting here the union demands for worker wage payments in silver); encouraging soviet bank savings and loans; and more flexible business and customs tax policies to stimulate production and help counter the KMT blockade. Wang, "Chung-kuo ching-chi cheng-ts'e," in WMHC 3:35-43.

35. Alfred Meyer, *Leninism*, pp. 114-15. Many of the big and middle merchants had in fact fled the soviet areas.

36. Mif, "Revolutionary Crisis in China," p. 310.

37. "Chung-hua su-wei-ai kung-ho-kuo lao-tung fa" [Labor law of the Chinese Soviet Republic] (15 October 1933). Text in Hsiao, *Power Relations* 2:747-56. My discussion of this law is based both on this text and on the detailed comparison of the document with the 1931 law in Wang, *Chung-kuo Kung-ch'an-tang* 2:408.

38. "Wei-fan lao-tung fa-ling ch'eng-fa t'iao-li" [Regulations for punishment of labor law violators] (15 October 1933), in *Su-wei-ai fa-tien* [Soviet law code] 2:70-74, Ch'en Ch'eng Collection, reel 16.

39. Ibid., article 9, 2:73-74.

40. "T'ing-chou shih kung-hui chin-hsing kai-ting chi-t'i ho-t'ung yün-tung" [T'ing-chou city unions progress in the movement to revise collective contracts], HSCH, no. 55 (22 February 1933):4.

41. Ch'en Yün, "Tsen-yang ting-li lao-tung ho-t'ung" [How to conclude a labor contract], TC, no. 18 (15 July 1933):9-13.

42. Ibid., pp. 12-13.

43. Wang, *Chung-kuo Kung-ch'an-tang* 2:410, recounts (perhaps exaggeratedly in this strongly anti-CCP source) examples of such worker backlash in this final period of the soviet republic.

44. Lo Fu, "Huo-li hsiang-che yu-ch'ing chi-hui chu-i" [Direct fire at right opportunism], TC, no. 17 (5 July 1933):3.

45. Ch'en Yün, "K'o-fu kung-hui kung-tso-ti lo-hou" [Overcome the backwardness of union work], TC, no. 23 (22 August 1933):8-13.

46. Ibid., p. 9.

47. Ibid., p. 10.

48. Ibid., p. 11.

49. An economic construction resolution of the January 1934 Second National Soviet Congress thus accused capitalist elements of attempts to disrupt and destroy the soviet economy through lockouts, work stoppages, undermining confidence in the soviet currency, engaging in speculation, and deliberately raising prices. See "Kuan-yü su-wei-ai ching-chi chien-she-ti chüeh-i" [Resolution on soviet economic construction], HSCH, no. 105 (16 February 1934):2.

50. Ch'i T'ien, "T'ing-chou shih ching-kuo-yeh kung-jen kai-ting ho-t'ung ching-kuo ch'ing hsing" [T'ing-chou fruit trade workers contract revision experiences], SCKJ, no. 5 (25 December 1933):8.

51. Liu Shao-ch'i, "Lun kuo-chia kung-ch'ang-ti kuan-li" [On the management of state factories], TC, no. 53 (31 March 1934):5. Printing plants, the mint, and mining were other state enterprises.

52. Nym Wales, *Inside Red China*, p. 198.

53. Liu Shao-ch'i, "Lun kuo-chia kung-ch'ang-ti kuan-li," pp. 5-10; and "Yung hsin-ti t'ai-tu tui-tai hsin-ti lao-tung" [A new attitude for new labor], TC, no. 54 (7 April 1934):6-8.

54. "Ch'üan-tsung chih-hsing chü kuan-yü Su-ch'ü kung-hui 'wu-i' lao-tung chieh kung-tso-ti chüeh-ting" [ACFL executive bureau decision on soviet-area unions' May Day work], SCKJ, no. 11 (25 March 1934):1.

55. "Su-wei-ai kuo-chia ch'i-yeh kung-jen kung-hui ti-i-tz'u tai-piao ta-hui chüeh-i" [Resolution of the First Representatives' Congress of Soviet State Enterprise Workers' Union], SCKJ, no. 24 (20 July 1934):5-6. In advancing Liu Shao-ch'i's themes of a maximum production effort and a disciplined adherence to factory rules, the congress continued formally to affirm the eight-hour workday, urging the workers "not to waste a minute" of it.

56. Ibid., p. 6.

57. "The Trade Union Movement in Soviet Areas during the Past Two Years," in CWLS, pp. 3-10.

58. Ibid., pp. 4, 7.

59. Ibid., p. 8.

60. Ibid., p. 4.

61. In his report to this congress, Mao gave a total of 110,000 union members for the central soviet area alone. See his *Red China*, p. 20.

62. "Trade Union Movement," p. 8.

63. Ibid., p. 10.

64. According to Otto Braun (Li Te), the Comintern adviser in the central soviet area, Mao did not participate in the Fifth Plenum, claiming illness. Braun quotes party leader Po Ku as remarking sarcastically that Mao was suffering once again from a "diplomatic illness." See Otto Braun, *Chinesische Aufzeichnungen (1932-1939)*, p. 70.

65. "Wu chung ch'üan-hui kei erh-tz'u ch'üan su ta-hui tang-t'uan-ti chih-ling" [Fifth Plenum, Central Committee directive to the party group in the Second National Soviet Congress], TC, no. 47 (16 February 1934):16-20. The soviet government journal, HSCH, in a special issue on the soviet congress, also emphasized intensified class struggle, including "ruthless suppression" of rich peasants and capitalists and their "reactionary plots." "Ying-chieh Chung-kuo su-wei-ai sheng-li-ti ta ko-ming" [Greet the Chinese soviet victorious great revolution], HSCH, special issue no. 1 (22 January 1934):1.

66. Ibid.

67. Mao, Red China, pp. 17-21.

68. Mao Tse-tung, "Our Economic Policy" (23 January 1934), in SW 2:141-45; Mao Tse-tung, "Pay Attention to Economic Work" (20 August 1933), in SW 1:129-36.

69. "Kuan-yü su-wei-ai ching-chi," p. 2.

70. Ibid. See also n. 49 above. In Chinese Communism 1931-1934, Lötveit points to several instances of businessmen being executed, beginning in early 1934, for the crime of currency speculation (p. 186).

71. " 'Wu-i' lao-tung chieh piao-yü" [May Day labor holiday slogans], SCKJ, no. 12 (5 April 1934):3-4.

72. General Political Department of the Red Army, comp., "Kung-ku Hung-chün chung wu-ch'an chieh-chi ling-tao wen-t'i pao-kao ta-kang" [Outline report on the question of strengthening proletarian leadership in the Red Army], 4 January 1934, Ch'en Ch'eng Collection, reel 8; and "Lao-tung fa yü kung-jen yün-tung" [The labor law and the workers' movement], Hung-chün tu-pen [Red Army reader] (March 1934) 2:14-17, published by the General Political Department of the Red Army, Ch'en Ch'eng Collection, reel 8.

73. Warren Kuo, Analytical History of the Chinese Communist Party 2:602.

74. "Instruction No. 11 of the Council of People's Commissars of the Provisional Central Government of the Chinese Soviet Republic—Launching an Extensive and Intensive Land Investigation Drive" (1 June 1933), in Hsiao Tso-liang, The Land Revolution in China, 1930-1934, doc. 60, pp. 198-202.

75. Mao Tse-tung, "The Land Investigation Drive is the Central Task of Great Magnitude in Vast Areas," in ibid., doc. 62, pp. 202-5. Originally published in HSCH, no. 86 (17 June 1933).

76. "Only the Soviets Can Save China," Communist International 11, no. 11 (5 June 1934):373.

77. "Conclusions Reached by the Conference of Responsible Soviet Authorities of Eight Counties on and above the District Level on the Land Investigation Drive," in Hsiao, Land Revolution in China, doc. 69, p. 227. Originally published in HSCH, no. 89 (29 July 1933).

78. Lötveit, Chinese Communism in China, p. 160.

79. Ibid., p. 162.

80. Lo [Chang], "Su-wei-ai cheng-ch'üan," pt. 2, TC, no. 15 (15 June 1933):9-14. Chang's two-part article was dated 26 May, just when the Land Investigation Movement was first being launched.

81. Ibid., pp. 9-10

82. Ibid., p. 12.

83. Ibid.

84. According to Wang Ming, writing in September 1933, under the land tax in the soviet area, rich peasants were taxed at a 15 percent rate, middle peasants at 5 percent, and poor peasants at 3 percent or even exempt (probably in the case of former agricultural laborers). "Chung-kuo ching-chi cheng-ts'e," in WMHC 3:42.

85. Lötveit, Chinese Communism 1931-1934, p. 17.

86. Lo Fu, "Lun nung-ts'un chung-ti chieh-chi tou-cheng" [On the class struggle in the countryside], TC, no. 20 (5 August 1933):16; and TC, no. 21 (12 August 1933):15.

87. Ibid., TC, no. 20 (5 August 1933):16.

88. Ibid., TC, no. 21 (12 August 1933):15.

89. Mao Tse-tung, "Preliminary Conclusions Drawn from the Land Investigation Drive," in Hsiao, Land Revolution in China, doc. 84, pp. 236-54. Originally published in TC, no. 24 (29 August 1933).

90. Ibid., p. 254.

91. "How to Analyze Classes" (10 October 1933), in Hsiao, Land Revolution in China, doc. 96, pp. 254-57; Lötveit, Chinese Communism 1931-1934, p. 173.

92. "Decisions Concerning Some Problems Arising from the Agrarian Struggle," in Hsiao, Land Revolution in China, doc. 101, pp. 257-82. Adopted by the Council of People's Commissars on 10 October 1933.

93. Lötveit, Chinese Communism 1931-1934, p. 173.

94. "Decisions Concerning the Agrarian Struggle," p. 262.

95. Ibid., p. 269.

96. Ibid., p. 271.

97. Ibid., pp. 279, 281.

98. Mao, "Preliminary Conclusions," pp. 244-45.

99. Lötveit, Chinese Communism 1931-1934, pp. 177-78.

100. Ibid., p. 178.

101. Kuo, Analytical History 2:563.

102. Ibid., 2:564.

103. "On the Question of Reopening the Land Investigation Drive—Instruction, Serial Character Chung, No. 1, of the Council of People's Commissars, March 15, 1934," in Hsiao, Land Revolution in China, doc. 106, p. 282. Originally published in HSCH, no. 164 (20 March 1934).

104. Ibid., p. 283.

105. Ibid., p. 284.

106. Chang Wen-t'ien, "Kuan-yü k'ai-chan Ch'a-t'ien yün-tung chung i-ko wen-t'i-ti ta-fu Chang chu-hsi chi Wang t'ung-chih-ti hsin" [Reply to a question concerning the development of the Land Investigation Movement—a letter from Chairman Chang to Comrade Wang], HSCH, no. 14 (29 March 1934):3; translated and cited by Lötveit, Chinese Communism 1931-1934, p. 180.

107. Patricia Griffin, The Chinese Communist Treatment of Counter-revolutionaries, 1924-1949, pp. 47-58.

108. Chang Wen-t'ien, "Oppose Petty Bourgeois Ultraleftism" (24 June 1934), TC, no. 67, (10 July 1934):2-6, summarized in Hsiao, Land Revolution in China, p. 122; "Should We Stand Firm in Suppressing the Counterrevolutionaries or Get Mad and Confused in Face of Them?" (25 June 1934), HSCH, no. 208 (28 June 1934):1-2, in Hsiao, Land Revolution in China, doc. 117, pp. 285-90.

109. "Should We Stand Firm?," p. 286.

110. Ibid., p. 290.

111. Chang "played a useful role" at Tsunyi, Mao commented in 1966. "A Talk at the General Report Conference" (24 October 1966), in Jerome Ch'en, ed., Mao, pp. 95-96.

112. Harold Isaacs, The Tragedy of the Chinese Revolution, p. 343.

113. Jerome Ch'en has noted that while the Internationalist faction was defeated at Tsunyi, "it still commanded considerable strength in the Party and the backing of the International itself." See "Resolutions of the Tsunyi Conference," trans. Jerome Ch'en, CQ, no. 40 (October–December 1969):20.

Chapter V

1. See Lyman Van Slyke, *Enemies and Friends: The United Front in Chinese Communist History*, pp. 48–91.

2. Mark Selden, *The Yenan Way in Revolutionary China*, p. 97.

3. Ibid., p. 99.

4. For an Internationalist espousal of these policies, see Wan Min [Wang Ming], "For a Change in All Spheres of Our Work," *Inprecorr* 16, no. 8 (6 February 1936):223–24.

5. Ibid., p. 223, and Gregor Benton, "The 'Second Wang Ming Line' (1935-38)," CQ, no. 61 (March 1975):66.

6. Van Slyke, *Enemies and Friends*, p. 90.

7. "Reply of the Chinese Soviets to Program of the National Salvation Union," *China Today* 3, no. 4 (January 1937):42.

8. Ibid., p. 43.

9. Edgar Snow, "Interviews with Mao Tse-tung, Communist Leader" (July 1936), in Mao Tse-tung et al., *China: The March Toward Unity*, p. 49.

10. According to Selden, of the twenty-five districts in north Shensi where the Communists were active in the spring of 1937, "land revolution was completed in a central area of fifteen districts and partially effected in ten more" *(Yenan Way*, p. 124).

11. Henry Schwarz, *Liu Shao-ch'i and "People's War,"* pp. 16–17.

12. Liu Shao-ch'i, "Various Questions Concerning Fundamental Policies in Anti-Japanese Guerrilla Warfare" (16 October 1937), in CWLS, p. 41.

13. See Donald Gillin, *Warlord: Yen Hsi-shan in Shansi Province, 1911-1949*, pp. 265–69, for a discussion of these Communist policies in Shansi in 1937–38.

14. See, for example, Wan Min [Wang Ming], "Fifteen Years of Struggle for the Independence and Freedom of the Chinese People," *Inprecorr* 16, no. 44 (26 September 1936):1209–14. A 1969 Soviet study characterizes Wang's September 1936 article as reflecting "the most important recommendations of the Comintern." K. V. Kukushkin, "The Comintern and the United National Anti-Japanese Front in China (1935-1943)," in L. P. Deliusin et al., eds., *Komintern i Vostok*, p. 362, n. 22. For an example of Wang's unqualified united-front stance in the early stages of the resistance war, see his statement to the December 1937 CCP Political Bureau Conference in Yenan, shortly after his arrival there from Moscow. Ch'en Shao-yü [Wang Ming], "Current Situation and Tasks in the War of Resistance," in Warren Kuo, *Analytical History of the Chinese Communist Party* 3:360–64.

15. *China Year Book, 1935*, H. W. G. Woodhead, ed., pp. 352–53; wages in many places were reduced by 10 percent or more in 1935. Chuan-hua Lowe, "Labour Conditions," in *Chinese Year Book, 1937*, p. 759. See also Ma Ch'ao-chün et al., eds., *Chung-kuo lao-kung yün-tung shih* [History of the Chinese labor movement] 3:1247–48, for 1935 statistics on labor layoffs and business closures in the Shanghai textile industry.

16. Lowe, "Labour Conditions," pp. 759, 767 (tables 5 and 6).

17. *China Year Book, 1938*, H. G. W. Woodhead, ed., pp. 326–27; *China Year Book, 1939*, H. G. W. Woodhead, ed., pp. 492–93. My approximation of the number of workers involved is based upon the statistics given in the 1938 and 1939 year books and also by Israel Epstein (see n. 19 below).

18. Lowe Chuan-hua, *Labor Conditions in China*, p. 112.

19. Israel Epstein, *Notes on Labor Problems in Nationalist China*, pp. iv, 237-45. Communist commentaries on the 1936-37 strike movement strongly emphasized the latter's national salvation significance.

20. Edward Hammond, *Organized Labor in Shanghai, 1927-1937*, pp. 236-37.

21. Wang Ming, *China Can Win!*, p. 40; appeared originally in *Communist International* 14, no. 10 (October 1937):719-36, under the title "The New Stage of Japanese Aggression and the New Period of the Struggle of the Chinese People."

22. Ibid., p. 45. It is significant that as late as July 1940 Wang Ming republished in Yenan the 1932 Moscow edition of his major treatise, *The Two Lines*, under the title *Struggle for the More Complete Bolshevization of the Chinese Communist Party*, a work which strongly reflected Wang's urban and proletarian viewpoints. See Hsiao Tso-Liang, *Power Relations within the Chinese Communist Movement, 1930-1934* 1:202-7.

23. Kukushkin, "Comintern and Anti-Japanese Front," p. 357.

24. Ibid., p. 374.

25. Chen Lin, *China's Fight for National Liberation*, p. 23.

26. *Chieh-fang* (CF), the official organ of the Central Committee of the CCP, was published approximately every ten days from April 1937 to June 1941. It was superseded by the daily newspaper, *Chieh-fang jih-pao* (CFJP), published in Yenan from 16 May 1941 to 5 February 1947. The May Day editorial referred to is "Wu-i kan-yen" [May Day sentiments], CF, 1 May 1937, pp. 1-2.

27. Ch'i Hua, "Kung-jen tou-cheng-ti hsien chieh-tuan" [The current stage of the workers' struggle], CF, 9 May 1937, pp. 19-22. The author of this article was reputed to be in charge of labor work under the party's Central Committee in the late 1940s. See James Harrison, *The Long March to Power*, p. 397.

28. Ch'i, "Kung-jen tou-cheng," p. 19. The compromise wage increase settlement worked out by the Shanghai government Bureau of Social Affairs [BSA] was evidently then successfully appealed by the silk companies. Though some of the workers resumed the strike, they were all ultimately forced under BSA pressure to return to work. See Hammond, *Organized Labor*, p. 238.

29. Ch'i, "Kung-jen tou-cheng," p. 20. "Pu chi kuo-ch'ü ch'ou-hen" is, literally, "Don't reckon up past hatreds."

30. Ibid., p. 21.

31. Ibid., p. 22.

32. The weaknesses of this Communist stance in the early war period are revealed in Epstein's account of a 1938 May Day parade and mass meeting held in the important industrial center of Hankow (Wuhan), serving then as a wartime capital of the Nationalist government prior to its fall to the Japanese later that year. Sponsored by the KMT Mass Movement Committee, the meeting was addressed by KMT officials, by the head of the government-sponsored China Association of Labor (CAL), and by Wang Ming, the CCP's representative in Hankow. Epstein, in Hankow at that time, observes somewhat wryly that "Wang Ming appealed only for support of the government and the war effort, for patriotic activity and increased production" (*Notes on Labor Problems*, p. 83).

33. Ibid., pp. 82-83, and "The Chinese Labor Movement," *Amerasia* 8, no. 10 (12 May 1944):155.

34. Epstein, *Notes on Labor Problems*, p. 79.

35. "Shanghai—China's Nerve Centre," *Inprecorr* 17, no. 36 (28 August 1937):815.

36. Party leader Po Ku (Ch'in Pang-hsien) acknowledged to Edgar Snow in July 1938 that CCP work in Shanghai had been "extremely weak" both before and after the outbreak of the war. Edgar Snow, *Random Notes on Red China, 1936-1945*, p. 23.

37. An account of the effusive welcome given Wang by the Yenan party leadership on the arrival of his plane is given in Lu P'ing, comp., *Sheng-huo tsai Yenan* [Life in Yenan], pp. 57-66.

38. Donald Klein and Anne Clark, *Biographic Dictionary of Chinese Communism, 1921-1965* 1:131.

39. William Whitson, *The Chinese High Command*, pp. 210-11.

40. Ibid., pp. 212-13.

41. Israel Epstein, *The People's War*, pp. 262-63; and Jerome Ch'en, *Mao and the Chinese Revolution*, p. 250.

42. Epstein, *People's War*, p. 275.

43. Wang Teh, "Shanghai is Still Fighting," *World News and Views* 18, no. 54 (12 November 1938):1242.

44. Klein and Clark, *Biographic Dictionary* 1:131-32; and Benton, " 'Second Wang Ming Line,' " pp. 88-89.

45. Wang Ming, "Wo-men tui-yü pao-wei Wuhan yü ti-san ch'i k'ang-chan wen-t'i-ti i-chien" [Our views regarding the question of the defense of Wuhan and the third stage of the resistance war], in WMHC 5:160-83. Originally published in HHJP (Hankow ed.), 15 June 1938.

46. Ibid., p. 160.

47. Snow, *Random Notes*, p. 23.

48. Ibid.

49. Ibid.

50. Richard Thornton, *China, the Struggle for Power, 1917-1972*, p. 124.

51. Wang Ming, "Hsüeh-hsi Mao Tse-tung" [Learn from Mao Tse-tung], in WMHC 5:319-24. There seems, however, to have been some ambiguity in Wang's stance at that time. (Were there pejorative implications in one of his characterizations of Mao in this address as a "yu-ming-ti nung-min kung-tso ta-wang," "famous peasant work king" [p. 323]?) In July 1940, as I have noted, he republished in Yenan his influential 1932 class-line treatise, *The Two Lines*.

52. Whitson, *Chinese High Command*, pp. 212-13.

53. Ibid., pp. 219-21.

54. Ibid., pp. 220-21.

55. Thornton, *China, the Struggle for Power*, p. 124.

56. Ch'en Shao-yü [Wang Ming], "Chin-nien-ti Wu-i chieh yü Chung-kuo kung-jen" [This year's May Day holiday and the Chinese workers], in WMHC 5:138-46. Originally published in HHJP (Hankow ed.), 1 May 1938.

57. Ibid.

58. Otto Braun, *Chinesische Aufzeichnungen (1932-1939)*, p. 325, cited in Benton, " 'Second Wang Ming Line,' " pp. 89-90, n. 43.

59. "Chung-kung chung-yang kuan-yü k'ai-chan chih-kung yün-tung yü Wu-i kung-tso ti chüeh-ting" [CC, CCP decision on promoting the staff-workers' (labor) movement and May Day work], CF, 1 May 1939, p. 6.

60. Ibid.

61. Eleanor Hinder, *Life and Labour in Shanghai*, pp. 73-74.

62. Ibid., p. 74. Hinder remarks, "It is interesting to note that the new Nanking authorities [the Wang Ching-wei regime] pursued a course not unlike that of the Kuomintang Government a decade earlier."

63. Wang Teh, "Chinese Workers Fight for Their Country's Freedom," *World News and Views* 19, no. 57 (9 December 1939):1138-39.

64. Israel Epstein, *The Unfinished Revolution in China*, p. 139.

65. "A Letter to Chinese Workers on the 2nd Anniversary of the War of Resistance" (July 1939), in CWLS, pp. 145-50. Translated from the text appearing in CF, 20 July 1939.

66. Ibid., p. 148.

67. Ibid., p. 149.

68. Ibid. The translation here is awkward, but the meaning seems clear.

69. Teng Fa, "Ying-chieh wei-ta-ti 'Wu-i' kuo-chi lao-tung chieh" [Welcome the great May Day international holiday], CF, no. 105 (30 April 1940):2-4.

70. Klein and Clark, *Biographic Dictionary* 2:818.

71. Gillin, for example, notes the Communists' adoption of this slogan (which he renders as "those having wealth must contribute money; those with muscle, their strength") in furthering the activities of the Eighth Route Army in Shansi after the Japanese attack in 1937. Taxes on the peasants, he writes, were reduced drastically or abolished, while necessary supplies and funds were requisitioned from the gentry. See *Warlord*, p. 267.

72. Po Ku, "Chin-nien Wu-i ho Chung-kuo kung-jen" [This year's May Day and the Chinese workers], HHJP (Chungking ed.), 1 May 1940, p. 1.

73. Hsü T'iao-hsin, "Ta hou-fang kung-jen tui-yü k'ang-chan-ti kung-hsien chi ch'i sheng-huo" [Regarding the Resistance War contributions of the workers in the great rear (KMT) areas and their livelihood], HHJP (Chungking ed.), 1 May 1940, p. 4.

74. Wu K'o-chien, "Lun ti-hou chung-hsin ch'eng-shih kung-jen yün-tung-ti kung tso" [On the work of the workers' movement in the central cities of the enemy rear], HHJP (Chungking ed.), 1 May 1940, p. 4. Wu was active in Shanghai and East China government affairs after 1949 and in labor-related administrative work there in the early 1950s. *Who's Who in Communist China* 2:725.

75. "Directive on the Work in Major Cities Behind the Enemy Line" (issued by the Secretariat of the CCP Central Committee in early September 1940), in Kuo, *Analytical History* 4:206-9.

76. Pen Deh-Hwai [P'eng Te-huai], "Political Mass Work and the Mass Organizations in North China," *Communist International* 16, no. 6 (June 1939):496.

77. Agnes Smedley, *China Fights Back*, pp. 156-57. A CCP wartime account described the role played by the miners of the famous Kailan mines near Tangshan in Hopei. In the spring of 1938, sixty thousand miners went on strike against the Japanese for higher wages, and during the month-long strike the miners kept in contact with Communist guerrillas operating in the vicinity. Some five thousand of the miners spontaneously formed guerrilla detachments which cooperated with local peasant guerrilla forces. And when the strike ended, two thousand miners left their work and remained with the guerrillas. See Stuart Gelder, ed., *The Chinese Communists*, p. 247.

78. Epstein, *People's War*, pp. 244-45. Epstein, whose reportorial work in this early wartime period centered on the Hankow region and on the activities of the New Fourth Army, tended strongly to emphasize the significance of the worker component of the resistance struggle. See n. 84 below.

79. Teng Fa, "Trade Unions in Liberated Areas," *New China Review* (Manila) 1, no. 10 (1 February 1946). I am indebted to the library of the University of the Philippines for making this article available to me.

80. Ibid.

81. Po Ku told Edgar Snow in an interview in Hankow in July 1938 that the CCP had recruited two hundred workers from Shanghai for the New Fourth Army up to that time, and that more would soon be mobilized. Snow, *Random Notes*, p. 23. Nym Wales (Helen

Snow) has cited examples known to her personally of young women workers formerly employed in Japanese-run Shanghai factories who joined the New Fourth Army guerrilla forces in the vicinity of Shanghai in the pre-1941 period. See *The Chinese Labor Movement*, pp. 86-88.

82. Teng Fa, "Chieh-fang ch'ü chih-kung hui" [Trade unions in the liberated areas], CFJP, 2 May 1946, p. 4.

83. "Problems of War and Strategy" (6 November 1938), in SW 2:219-35. There is apparently no contemporary text of this speech available, but the points I shall cite are clearly in accordance with the development of Mao's ideas in this period, as reflected in his further writings during 1939 and 1940. As already noted, the Sixth Plenum marked a major early step in Maoist ideological and political consolidation within the CCP, including the initial formulation of the concept of a "Sinified" Marxism. See Raymond Wylie, *The Emergence of Maoism*, pp. 88-99.

84. "Problems of War and Strategy," p. 220.

85. Ibid.

86. Ibid., p. 222.

87. Ibid., p. 223.

88. For an initial exposition of these ideas by Mao, see "Introducing *The Communist*" (4 October 1939), in SW 2:285-96. They were more fully elaborated over the next few months in two other major essays, "The Chinese Revolution and the Chinese Communist Party" (December 1939), in SW 2:305-34; and "On New Democracy" (January 1940), in SW 2:339-84. Only the second part of "The Chinese Revolution and the CCP" is entirely attributed to Mao; however, this is the only section I shall cite. The cited portions of the SW texts have been checked against earlier editions of these latter two essays.

89. "On Policy" (25 December 1940), in SW 2:442.

90. "Chinese Revolution and the CCP," p. 327.

91. "On New Democracy," p. 350.

92. "On People's Democratic Dictatorship" (30 June 1949), in SW 4:417.

93. "Chinese Revolution and the CCP," pp. 316-17.

94. Ibid., p. 318.

95. "On Policy," p. 442.

96. "Chung-kuo kung-jen chieh-chi tang-ch'ien-ti jen-wu" [Current tasks of the Chinese working class], CF, 20 April 1941, pp. 2-3.

97. These labor policy developments in the base areas will be discussed in ch. VII of this study.

98. "Lao-tung chan-hsien shang-ti wei-li" [The great strength of the labor front], HHJP (Chungking ed.), 1 May 1943, p. 2.

99. It avoided any class struggle exhortations and mildly expressed its "belief" that if there were effective implementation of the (KMT) government's labor protection and welfare provisions, this would solve "a fair amount of the problem." Ibid.

Chapter VI

1. See Peter Schran, *Guerrilla Economy*, for detailed data and estimates of the Border Region's area and population from 1936 to the early 1940s.

2. Ibid., pp. 40-41.

3. Edgar Snow, *Red Star Over China*, p. 243.

4. Ibid., p. 245.

5. Snow observed that the food supplied was simple and the housing primitive and that cash wages could purchase only the limited available necessities (ibid., p. 251). Liu Ch'ün-hsien, the young woman labor head in Yenan at that time, told Nym Wales in June 1937 that wages for women workers in the state factories ranged from 3 to 15 yuan per month, plus the various fringe benefits noted by Edgar Snow above (see Nym Wales, *My Yenan Notebooks*, p. 95). Wages in this period were reportedly determined by union wage committees in the factories.

6. "Mao Tse-tung t'ung-chih hao-chao fa-chan kung-yeh, ta-tao Jih k'ou" [Comrade Mao Tse-tung's call to develop industry and overthrow the Japanese bandits], CFJP, 26 May 1944 (a talk by Mao on 22 May at a banquet given in conjunction with a workers'-factory managers' representatives' conference held in Yenan at that time). Liu Ch'ün-hsien told Nym Wales in 1937 that there were seven hundred men and six hundred women workers in the Border Region state factories (*Yenan Notebooks*, p. 96). A 1939 Communist source gave a figure of twenty-eight thousand unionized "industrial workers" in the Border Region at that time, which also is at odds with Mao's figures cited above. These earlier sources may have overstated the industrial worker component of the labor force by using a looser definition of this category. Mao, on the other hand, may have minimized the earlier totals in order to accentuate more sharply the gains made during the 1940s. The total of twelve thousand given for 1944 presumably included those employed in private and cooperative enterprises, which underwent important expansion after 1942. The fact that the General Labor Union apparently increased its total membership by less than five thousand from 1940 to 1945 also indicates that the varying numbers cited for industrial workers to some degree reflected differing definitions of worker categories.

7. Hsü Yung-ying, *A Survey of Shensi-Kansu-Ninghsia Border Region*, pt. 2, p. 108.

8. "Pien-chü kung-yeh hsün-su fa-chan" [Border area industry rapidly expands], CFJP, 28 April 1944.

9. Ibid.

10. Gunther Stein, *The Challenge of Red China*, pp. 171–73.

11. CFJP, 28 April 1944; and Hsü, *Survey of Shen-Kan-Ning*, pt. 2, p. 94. The Chinese Industrial Cooperatives (CIC) movement played a substantial role in the development of cooperative textile enterprises in the Border Region after 1939. A CFJP report of 12 November 1941 noted that there were then twenty-one CIC spinning and weaving cooperatives (as compared with twenty-two state-owned and thirty privately owned enterprises), and that they at that time accounted for some 7 percent of the total cloth production of the Border Region. Cited in Nym Wales, "Notes on the Beginnings of the Industrial Cooperatives in China," p. 61.

12. Schran, *Guerrilla Economy*, p. 71, table 4.1.

13. Yuji Muramatsu, "Revolution and Chinese Tradition in Yenan Communism," p. 24.

14. Schran, *Guerrilla Economy*, pp. 75, 148, 150 (table 6.8). Schran attributes the 1940-41 period of expansion to the renewed KMT blockade at that time. After this initial phase of "blind expansion," state enterprises underwent consolidation in 1942, and more "conscious" growth thereafter (p. 75). The later increased emphasis on the cooperative and private sector reflected also changes in developmental strategy.

15. Hsia Chiang, "Chin-pu chung-ti Shen-Kan-Ning pien-ch'ü kung-jen" [Shen-Kan-Ning border region workers progressing], HHJP (Chungking ed.), 1 May 1940.

16. Tung Pi-wu, "Memorandum on China's Liberated Areas," San Francisco, 18 May 1945, p. 26.

17. "The Labour Movement and General Labour Union of the Shen-Kan-Ning Border Region," in Stuart Gelder, ed., *The Chinese Communists*, p. 221.

18. Tung, "Memorandum," pp. 25-26. Teng Fa gave a total of 300,000 for the Chin-Ch'a-Chi area and an overall total of 900,000. "Trade Unions in Liberated Areas," *New China Review* (Manila) 1, no. 10 (1 February 1946).

19. Teng, "Trade Unions in Liberated Areas."

20. Israel Epstein, *The Unfinished Revolution in China*, p. 247.

21. Tung, "Memorandum," p. 25.

22. "Labour Movement and General Labour Union," p. 221. Nym Wales, *The Chinese Labor Movement*, p. 91, apparently using a similar 1943 source, also cites the 1940 date.

23. "Shen-Kan-Ning pien-ch'ü tsung kung-hui chang-ch'eng" [Regulations of the Shen-Kan-Ning Border Region General Labor Union] (April 1938); "Shen-Kan-Ning pien-ch'ü tsung kung-hui k'ang-chan ch'i-chien kung-tso kang-ling" [Wartime work outline of the Shen-Kan-Ning General Labor Union] (April 1938); "Shen-Kan-Ning pien-ch'ü k'ang-chan ch'i-chien kung-hui tsu-chih t'iao-li" [Wartime labor union organizational regulations of the Shen-Kan-Ning border region], draft, n.d., but also clearly stemming from this same period. All are in *K'ang-Jih ken chu-ti cheng-ts'e t'iao-li hui-chi* [Compendium of policies and regulations of the anti-Japanese base areas].

24. "Shen-Kan-Ning pien-ch'ü-ti ch'ün-chung t'uan-t'i" [Mass organizations of the Shen-Kan-Ning border region], in Ch'i Li, ed., *Shen-Kan-Ning pien-ch'ü shih-lu* [Historical account of the Shen-Kan-Ning border region], pp. 83-97.

25. Ibid., pp. 93-94.

26. "K'ang-chan kung-hui t'iao-li," ch. 6, art. 19; and "Regulations of the General Labor Union," ch. 1. As noted above, one Communist representative of the Border Region unions was appointed to the executive committee of the KMT-sponsored CAL in 1938.

27. "K'ang-chan kung-tso kang-ling," art. 14.

28. "Tsung kung-hui chang-ch'eng," ch. 1.

29. "K'ang-chan kung-tso kang-ling," arts. 3-12.

30. "Tsung kung-hui chang-ch'eng," ch. 1; "K'ang-chan kung-tso kang-ling," art 8; and "K'ang-chan kung-hui t'iao-li," ch. 3.

31. "K'ang-chan kung-tso kang-ling," art. 13.

32. "Tsung kung-hui chang-ch'eng," chs. 2 and 3; and "K'ang-chan kung-hui t'iao-li," ch. 1.

33. "Labour Movement and General Labour Union," p. 221.

34. Ch'i, *Shen-Kan-Ning*, p. 84.

35. See n. 6 above.

36. This was apparently a broader definition of the industrial worker category than that used by Mao in 1944 when he cited the figure of 700 for 1939. See n. 6 above.

37. Ch'i, *Shen-Kan-Ning*, p. 84

38. Ibid., pp. 89-91.

39. Ibid., pp. 91-92.

40. In discussing the work of union cadres, the report stressed the need for more knowledge and experience in dealing with agricultural labor—by far the most numerous category of union membership (ibid., p. 94).

41. Ibid.

42. Ibid., pp. 91-92.

43. Adopted by the First Session of the First Assembly of the Border Region, meeting in January-February 1939. *Shen-Kan-Ning pien-ch'ü ts'an-i hui wen-hsien hui-chi* [Compendium of Shen-Kan-Ning border region assembly documents], pp. 39-41.

44. "Pien-ch'ü kung-ying kung-ch'ang li-nien lai kung-tzu chi kung-jen sheng-huo kai-k'ang" [Wages in border region public-run factories in previous years and the workers' general livelihood situation], CFJP, 8 May 1944.

45. Schran, *Guerrilla Economy*, p. 184, table 7.3. The price of millet, the staple grain of the Border Region, increased much less steeply than did the general price index. Thus, while the index for all commodities stood at 717 in December 1940 (with 1937 as 100), the index for millet was 304. In December 1943 the overall index was 344,000, and that for millet was 90,500.

46. Schran concludes that the incomes of workers in the state-operated industrial enterprises in 1938 were twice as high as the incomes of most craftsmen and common store employees at that time (*Guerrilla Economy*, p. 243). Labor contract regulations for government-operated factories in November 1940 set a 16-40 yuan monthly wage scale (with the addendum that those with "special skills" would be differently evaluated). It was specifically noted that these wages included the cost of food and clothing, presumably deducted from wages at fixed low prices. "Shen-Kan-Ning pien-ch'ü chan-shih kung-ch'ang chi-t'i ho-t'ung" [Regulations for collective factory contracts for the Shen-Kan-Ning border region], in *Cheng-ts'e t'iao-li hui-chi*, ch. 3. Given the factory-subsidized, low price scale for daily necessities, these wages appeared to continue to favor the industrial workers, despite the overall price inflation.

47. Mark Selden, *The Yenan Way in Revolutionary China*, p. 154. Five dollars, in 1937 Yenan prices, had a purchasing power of ninety pounds of millet.

48. "Yin-shua kung-jen-men-ti sheng-huo" [Printing workers' life], in Lu P'ing, comp., *Sheng-huo tsai Yenan* [Life in Yenan], p. 135. Noting the absence of low wages and long working hours, this account detailed the many benefits and the cultural-educational advantages provided for the workers by the factory union and party committees. The report closed with a detailed description of the 7 November 1937 Yenan celebration of the twentieth anniversary of the October Revolution, for which the workers had a two-day holiday.

49. Wang Teh, "The Workers' Unions of the Border Region," *World News and Views* 19, no. 23 (22 April 1939):461-63.

50. Ibid., p. 463.

51. Hsia, "Chin-pu chung-ti Shen-Kan-Ning," HHJP (Chungking ed.), 1 May 1940. Initial pressures were developing at this time in Yenan to cut back on such sacrosanct worker privileges as the eight-hour workday, and the writer thus also noted that some workers had "voluntarily requested" an increase of one hour in the working day and a reduction in the number of holidays, in line with the drive for increased production and self-sufficiency in the region.

52. Nym Wales, *Inside Red China*, p. 198.

53. Helen Snow [Nym Wales], *The Chinese Communists*, pp. 229-30.

54. These details are from Liu's personal story as told to Nym Wales. Ibid., pp. 231-49.

55. Howard Boorman, ed., *Biographical Dictionary of Republican China* 1:386. Liu and Po Ku were subsequently divorced, probably after 1937.

56. Helen Snow, *Chinese Communists*, p. 249.

57. Wales, *Inside Red China*, p. 197.

58. Wales, *Yenan Notebooks*, pp. 95-100. The interview took place on 5 June 1937.

59. Ibid., p. 97.

60. Ibid.

61. Ibid.

62. Wales, *Inside Red China*, p. 197.

63. "Pien-ch'ü kung-jen-ti chi-nien wu-i lao-tung chieh" [Border Region workers May 1 labor holiday commemoration], HHJP (Hankow ed.), 1 May 1938.

64. These included the usual stress on the eight-hour, six-day system, paid revolutionary holidays, and a month's vacation with pay.

65. Li Kuang, ed., Ti-liu tz'u ch'üan-kuo lao-tung ta-hui [The sixth national labor congress], pp. 41-42. Of the twenty-one members for whom biographical details were given, five were women (pp. 53-63).

66. Private communication with Helen Snow, 3 April 1976.

67. Li, Ti-liu ta-hui, p. 61. After 1945 he headed the Communist labor movement in the northeast under Kao Kang and was elected to the ACFL executive committee in 1948.

68. "Tsai tou-cheng chung-ti Chin-Ch'a-Chi pien-ch'ü kung-jen" [Workers of the Chin-Ch'a-Chi border region in the midst of struggle], CF, no. 97 (30 January 1940):24-26.

69. Ibid., p. 25.

70. Ibid., p. 26.

71. See Raymond Wylie, The Emergence of Maoism, on Ch'en Po-ta's key role in helping to formulate and propagate Maoist ideology during the 1935-45 decade.

72. "Labor Policy and Tax Policy for Developing Industry," pt. 1, NCNA, North Shensi Radio, 26 April 1948, in Foreign Broadcast Information Service (FBIS), 27 April 1948, p. PPP4, with minor changes based on the Chinese text in Ch'en Po-ta et al., Kuan-yü kung-shang-yeh-ti cheng-ts'e [On industrial and commercial policy], pp. 16-17.

73. See Schran, Guerrilla Economy, pp. 56-65, for an exposition of this concept of continuity.

Chapter VII

1. These were: "Kill all, burn all, destroy all." See Chalmers Johnson, Peasant Nationalism and Communist Power, pp. 55-56; and Mark Selden, The Yenan Way in Revolutionary China, pp. 179-80.

2. Selden, Yenan Way, p. 179.

3. Selden's Yenan Way includes a detailed and informative discussion of these policies as they took form and were implemented during the 1941-43 period (see especially pp. 208-76).

4. Ibid., pp. 180-82; and Peter Schran, Guerrilla Economy, pp. 186-89.

5. "On Policy," in SW 2:446. In a December 1942 report, Mao noted that particularly in 1940 and 1941 the Border Region had been "in dire straits," with a "very acute scarcity of clothing, cooking oil, paper and vegetables, of footwear for our soldiers and of winter bedding for our civilian personnel." See "Economic and Financial Problems in the Anti-Japanese War," in SW 3:112. Only the brief introductory chapter of this important report to a senior cadres' conference in Yenan is included in SW. The full report was published under the title Ching-chi wen-t'i yü ts'ai-cheng wen-t'i in Hong Kong in 1949. This Chinese edition is used to refer to sections of the report not included in SW. (A complete English translation by Andrew Watson has been published under the title Mao Zedong and the Political Economy of the Border Region).

6. Schran, Guerrilla Economy, p. 187.

7. Ibid., table 7.4, pp. 186, 189.

8. In his December 1942 report, Mao, while defending the need for increasing taxes during the crisis years, added that it would be a mistake to adopt a policy of " 'draining the pond to catch the fish', that is, making endless demands on the people, disregarding their hardships and considering the needs only of the government and the army." Mao noted that the Border Region was able to avoid this by moving to develop production on the part of

the army, government and other organizations, and schools. "The greater our self-supporting economic activities, the more we shall be able to lighten the people's tax burdens." See "Economic and Financial Problems," in SW 3:114. It should be emphasized, however, that Maoist policy, oriented toward a broadly based rural constituency including the richer peasantry and capitalist elements, did not move entirely to exempt the poor peasants and workers from taxation.

9. See Boyd Compton, Mao's China, for an insightful essay on the cheng-feng movement and for a translation of ideological documents used as study materials in the movement. See also Selden, Yenan Way, pp. 188-206, for a more recent analytical discussion of the movement.

10. "Economic and Financial Problems," in SW 3:113.

11. Mao, Ching-chi wen-t'i, pp. 101-3.

12. Ibid., p. 108.

13. Ibid., pp. 114-15. In calling for reductions in factory staffs, Mao criticized the practice of administering the small factories of the Border Region in the manner of large factories.

14. Delia Davin, "Women in the Liberated Areas," in Marilyn Young, ed., Women in China, p. 78.

15. Selden, Yenan Way, p. 257.

16. Schran, Guerrilla Economy, table 6.6, p. 146; and Selden, Yenan Way, pp. 256-57.

17. Tung Pi-wu, "Memorandum on China's Liberated Areas," p. 28.

18. Davin, "Women in the Liberated Areas," p. 79. She also notes that "other supplementary occupations in which women began to play an important part included the production of vegetable oil, cured leather, and paper. Even more important were the sewing workshops which served the army" (p. 80).

19. Cited in Lyman Van Slyke, ed., The Chinese Communist Movement, p. 219.

20. Ibid., p. 150.

21. "On Policy," in SW 2:447.

22. Ibid., pp. 445-46. Though this directive was only published later, Mao's comments on labor policy correspond entirely with contemporaneous statements. A Central Committee directive on labor policy was apparently issued on 13 December 1940 and was so referred to by Teng Fa in a 1941 May Day article. Teng's discussion of labor policy based on this (unavailable) document was fully consistent with the points made by Mao in the SW directive.

23. "Current Tasks of the Chinese Working Class" (13 December 1940), CF, 30 April 1941.

24. The linkage of labor policy with new-democratic principles is new at this point but becomes fairly standard thereafter.

25. Gunther Stein, in his account of his 1944 trip to the Border Region, observed that "the near standardization of hours and wages restricts the professional functions of the trade unions to the protection of their members in minor regards, like the inspection of their food and living quarters, the supervision of safety devices, and the prevention of individual injustices" (The Challenge of Red China, p. 179).

26. "Wages of Public-run Factories in the Border Region," CFJP, 8 May 1944.

27. Ibid. All the above data on wage policies are from this article.

28. Ibid. Some adjustments may have been made as a result of a Workers'-Factory Managers' Conference held in May 1944. At any rate, shortly thereafter, in the summer of 1944, Stein reported workers' rations to be somewhat higher than stated in the data above: 3.3 pounds of meat instead of 1.3, a few ounces more of cooking oil, and an annual allowance of three pairs of cloth shoes, two towels, and twelve cakes of soap (Challenge of Red China, p. 178).

29. As a measure of comparison, it may be noted that a five-dollar supplemental monthly wage in 1937-38 (which represented the low end of worker monetary wage scales at that time) had a purchasing power of eighty to ninety pounds of millet (ninety pounds in 1937; somewhat less by 1938). See Selden, *Yenan Way*, p. 154. One should also keep in mind the change in the standard working day from eight to ten hours and the cutbacks in earlier special holiday and vacation benefits.

30. Stein, *Challenge of Red China*, p. 179.

31. "Shen-Kan-Ning pien-ch'ü chan-shih kung-ch'ang chi-t'i ho-t'ung chan-hsing chun-tse" [Temporary wartime standard regulations for collective contracts for the Shen-Kan-Ning Border Region], (issued by Border Region General Labor Union, 1 November 1940), in *K'ang-Jih ken chu-ti cheng-ts'e t'iao-li hui-chi: Shen-Kan-Ning chih-pu*, ch. 7. It also provided that in overtime work, seven hours would be equivalent to a full working day, rather than the six hours that had previously been the equivalent.

32. *Allied Labor News* dispatch from Chungking (8 July 1943), cited in Nym Wales, *The Chinese Labor Movement*, p. 95.

33. "Shen-Kan-Ning pien-ch'ü shih-cheng kang-ling" [Shen-Kan-Ning border region administrative program] (1 May 1941), in *Shen-Kan-Ning pien-ch'ü ts'an-i hui wen-hsien hui-chi* [Compendium of Shen-Kan-Ning border region assembly documents], art. 12, p. 105.

34. "Labour Movement and General Labour Union of the Shen-Kan-Ning Border Region," in Stuart Gelder, ed., *The Chinese Communists*, p. 225.

35. Ibid.

36. "Annual Report of the Shensi-Kansu-Ninghsia Border Region Government for the Year 1943" (6 January 1944), in ibid., p. 113.

37. Tung Pi-wu stated in 1945: "Real income of the workers has increased by 50 to 100 per cent compared to the pre-war level. The public-owned factories pay expenses equal to three per cent of the wages for the promotion of workers' benefits. The factories have their clubs, nurseries, night school, school for workers' children, wall-papers and free medical treatment" ("Memorandum," p. 29.)

38. Schran, *Guerrilla Economy*, in citing a 1943 millet equivalent of 1,200 kilograms (some 2,650 pounds) for a factory workers' average annual wage (table 8.2, p. 208), remarks that "factory workers received relatively high incomes at that time" (p. 209). However, a number of qualifying considerations should be kept in mind. First, Schran himself describes "the extreme degree of income equalization" that had taken place in the public (state) sector (p. 242). Second, the supplementary monetary wage incomes I have cited for 1937-38 were nearly equivalent to the total millet wage figure cited by Schran for 1943. Third, the *purchasing value* of millet in relation to the prices of other basic commodities had declined quite sharply from 1937-38 to 1943. In the Yenan area, for example, the price index for a list of such commodities (cloth, cotton fiber, pork, salt, and millet) in June 1943 showed a rate of increase, compared to 1937, sixfold that for millet alone (table 7.3, p. 184). Finally, peasant income levels were on the rise in 1943; the income in grain in that year for the (now) middle-peasant majority (and even more so for the upper-middle and rich peasants) probably at least equalled that of factory workers.• (My estimate, using a standard of four to five family members is based on Schran, table 8.11, pp. 240-41, which gives per capita grain income for various peasant classes in 1943 before and after taxes. I have used the after-tax figures.)

39. See n. 38 above.

40. "Pien-ch'ü cheng-fu kung-tso-ti pao-kao" [Report on Border Region Government work], (delivered to Second Border Region Assembly, 8 November 1941), in *Pien-ch'u wen-hsien hui-chi*, p. 94; cited also in Tetsuya Kataoka, *Resistance and Revolution in China*, pp. 256-58.

41. *Pien-ch'ü wen-hsien hui-chi*, p. 94.

42. Hsi Wen, "Tsai kung-ying kung-ch'ang kung-hui kung-tso chung-ti liang chung p'ien-hsiang" [Two tendencies in union work in the public factories], in "Chinese Worker," CFJP, supp. no. 6, 3 December 1941.

43. Hsi Wen, "Kuan-yü pien-ch'ü kung-tzu wen-t'i" [On the question of border region wages], in "Chinese Worker," CFJP, supp. no. 1, 24 September 1941.

44. "T'i-kao sheng-ch'an je-ch'un kung-tzu pu ying p'ing-chün" [To raise production enthusiasm, wages should not be equalized], CFJP, 20 October 1942.

45. Mao, Ching-chi wen-t'i, pp. 114-15.

46. "Chu tsung-ssu-ling hao-chao kai-ching chi-shu t'i-kao chih-liang" [Commander in chief Chu's call: improve technique and raise quality and quantity], 10 May 1944 talk to plenary session of Factory Representatives' Conference, CFJP, 13 May 1944.

47. Schran, Guerrilla Economy, p. 90.

48. "T'i-kao chih-liang yen-chiu chi-shu" [Raise quality and quantity and study technique], CFJP, 24 May 1944.

49. "Chung-yang tui Chin tung-nan k'ang-Jih ken chü-ti chih-kung yün-tung-ti chih-shih" [Central Committee directive to the staff-workers' movement of the Southeast Shansi anti-Japanese base area], CFJP, 1 May 1942. Forwarded by the North China Bureau of the CCP to Southeast Shansi Party Committee.

50. A March 1941 article had discussed the improved status of agricultural laborers in the Southeast Shansi base as compared with prewar (pre-Communist) conditions. It stressed not merely the rather modest material improvement but the greatly enhanced personal status of the laborers in relation to their employers. "Chan-hou ku-kung sheng-huo-ti pien-hua" [Transformation in the livelihood of hired labor since the outbreak of the war], in "Chinese Worker," CFJP, supp. no. 13, 27 March 1941.

51. Chin-Ch'a-Chi Border Area Government, comp., "K'ang-Jih min-chu cheng-ch'üan chi-ch'i ko-chung chi-pen cheng-ts'e" [Fundamental policies of anti-Japanese democratic government] (n.p., n.d., but probably the 1942-43 period), Yushodo Collection, reel 15. My citations are from secs. 5 and 7, on economic and financial policies and on labor policy, respectively (pp. 25-36, 49-56).

52. Ibid., sec. 5, p. 36.

53. Ibid., sec. 7, p. 52.

54. Ibid., p. 56. It is also noteworthy that in dealing with Communist work in the Japanese-occupied areas (in the Chin-Ch'a-Chi region), the emphasis again was on overall interests and on harmonizing class relations in joint unity against the enemy, with the struggle there to be focused on "hard core big traitors." Ibid., sec. 8, (Policies for Occupation Area Work). Page numberings for this section begin with 56 but repeat that number to the end of the section.

55. "Chan-tou-ti wu-i chi-nien" [The fighting May 1 anniversary], CFJP, 1 May 1942.

56. "Pien-ch'ü kung-ch'ang hui-i pi-mu" [Border Region Factories Conference closes], CFJP, 1 May 1943. A subheading declared, "Public industry thoroughly rectified."

57. "Lun kung-ying kung-ch'ang tang yü chih-kung-hui kung-tso" [On the work of the party and trade unions in public factories], CFJP, 1 May 1943.

58. During cheng-feng, the "Bolshevik" label, which had been the banner of the Wang Ming faction of the CCP, was itself taken over by the Maoist leadership and used against the Wang Ming group and others who were now described as "dogmatists," "Mensheviks," etc. Liu Shao-ch'i expounded this ideological strategy in a 1 July 1943 party anniversary article, "Liquidate the Menshevist Ideology Within the Party," in CWLS, pp. 437-47.

59. See Dieter Heinzig, "The Otto Braun Memoirs and Mao's Rise to Power," CQ 46 (April-June 1971):285.

60. "Kuan-yü kung-ying kung-ch'ang-ti chi-ko wen-t'i" [Some questions regarding public factories], CFJP, 1 May 1943.

61. "Annual Report of the Shensi-Kansu-Ninghsia Border Region Government for the Year 1943," in Gelder, *Chinese Communists*, p. 113.

62. Production had been increased from 20 to 30 percent (ibid.). Lin also reported the positive impact on production of "encouraging labour heroes" and of the implementation of the antibureaucratic policy that " 'responsible members should work with their own hands' " (ibid., pp. 116, 126).

63. "Chi-nien 'wu-i', chia-chin sheng-ch'an: Chao Chan-k'uei yün-tung p'u-p'ien chan-k'ai" [To commemorate May Day, to intensify production: widely unfold the Chao Chan-k'uei movement], CFJP, 1 May 1943.

64. "Tsai kung-ying kung-ch'ang chung ju-ho k'ai-chan Chao Chan-k'uei yün-tung" [How to unfold the Chao Chan-k'uei movement in the public factories], CFJP, 7 May 1943.

65. "Chi-nien 'wu-i,' " CFJP, 1 May 1943.

66. "Hsiang mo-fan kung-jen Chao Chan-k'uei hsüeh-hsi" [Learn from model worker Chao Chan-k'uei], CFJP, 11 September 1942.

67. Ibid.; and Li Kuang, ed., *Ti-liu tz'u ch'üan-kuo lao-tung ta-hui* [The sixth national labor congress], pp. 56-57. A 26 September mass celebration and awards rally for Chao Chan-k'uei was lengthily described in "Nung-chü kung-ch'ang chiang-li mo-fan kung-jen Chao Chan-k'uei" [Agricultural tools factory rewards model worker Chao Chan-k'uei], CFJP, 29 September 1942.

68. "Hsiang mo-fan kung-jen."

69. "Tsung kung-hui hao-chao k'ai-chan Chao Chan-k'uei yün-tung chia-ch'iang chiao-yü t'i-kao sheng-ch'an" [General Labor Union call to unfold the Chao Chan-k'uei movement, intensify education, and raise production], CFJP, 12 October 1942.

70. "Chi-hsü k'ai-chan Chao Chan-k'uei yün-tung" [Continuously unfold (or promote) the Chao Chan-k'uei Movement], CFJP, 22 December 1942.

71. The article added, in the standard formula, that the unions should give close attention to day-to-day problems of the workers and, "in consultation with the factory," try to improve livelihood (ibid.). Another model worker publicized in 1944 was said to have emerged from the Chao Chan-k'uei movement and essentially identical qualities were attributed to him. He, too, was pictured as one who had had to struggle against "destructive elements" in the factories and who had developed a completely selfless, collective work spirit, to the degree that he even voluntarily reduced his millet wage ration and contributed it to support the army and help refugees coming into the Border Region. "Mo-fan kung-jen Li Chi-hua" [Model worker Li Chi-hua], CFJP, 17 May 1944.

72. Tung, "Memorandum," p. 26.

73. See n. 64 above.

74. Ibid.

75. Harrison Forman, *Report from Red China*, p. 63. Wu Man-yu was also the subject of numerous articles in the Yenan press, for example, "Fa-chan Wu Man-yu yün-tung" [Develop the Wu Man-yu movement], CFJP, 11 January 1943.

76. Forman, *Report from Red China*, pp. 62-63.

77. Ibid., pp. 63-64.

78. Ibid., p. 64.

79. In a group of twenty-four villages in the Taihang district of the Chin-Ch'a-Chi base, rich-peasant households, which declined to a low of 1.78 percent of the total in 1941, expanded again to 7.88 percent by 1942. A good number of the latter were "new rich peasants" who had risen in status from middle or poor peasants. Kataoka, *Resistance and*

Revolution in China, pp. 255–56. In the five *hsiang* in Yenan County, rich peasants made up 10.6 percent of the total in late 1941 (p. 258); see also n. 40 above.

80. Ibid., pp. 258–59.

81. Ibid.

82. Ibid.

83. "Decision of the Central Committee on Land Policy in the Anti-Japanese Base Areas" (28 January 1942), in Conrad Brandt et al., *A Documentary History of Chinese Communism*, p. 278. The directive added, however, that since part of rich-peasant income constituted "feudal exploitation," rent and interest payable to rich peasants should be reduced (pp. 278–79).

84. "Kuan-yü kung-ying kung-ch'ang tang ho chih-kung hui kung-tso" [On party and union work in public factories], 24 May 1944, speech to Factories Conference, in Shen-Kan-Ning Border Region Government, *Wei kung-yeh p'in ti ch'üan-mien tzu-chi erh fen-tou* [Struggle for complete industrial self-sufficiency], pp. 32–39.

85. Ibid., p. 32.

86. Ibid., p. 39. Teng expressed the concept of public interest primacy in the term *hsien-kung, hou-ssu* (literally, "first public, later private"). That there were morale problems among cadres working in the state industrial sector was evidenced in Liu Shao-ch'i's report to this same 1944 conference. Liu sought to counter the attitude among such cadres that their work had little prestige or career opportunities compared with the work of those assigned to military duties. He stressed the ultimately bright future for those who became experienced and expert in industrial work, declaring that they would not forever be operating in a rustic environment living in caves but would be returning to the cities to play a leading role in industrializing the new China. "Liu Shao-ch'i t'ung-chih tsai kung-ch'ang tai-p'iao ta-hui shang-ti chiang-hua" [Comrade Liu Shao-ch'i's speech to the factories conference], 20 May 1944, in *Wei kung-yeh p'in*, pp. 1–6.

87. "Speech at the Assembly of Representatives of the Shensi-Kansu-Ninghsia Border Region" (21 November 1941), in SW 3:32. This section of the SW version of this speech is essentially identical to the original Chinese text published in CFJP, 22 November 1941.

88. See Selden, *Yenan Way*, pp. 232–37.

89. "Spread the Campaigns to Reduce Rent, Increase Production and 'Support the Government and Cherish the People' in the Base Areas" (1 October 1943), in SW 3:131–32. For a contemporary article with an identical thrust, see "Fa-chan ch'ün-chung chien-tsu yün-tung" [Develop the mass rent reduction movement], CFJP, 15 November 1943.

90. Kataoka, *Resistance and Revolution in China*, pp. 249–50.

91. Michael Lindsay, "The Taxation System of the Shansi-Chahar-Hopei Border Region, 1938–1945," CQ 42 (April–June 1970):10–11. He also cites a report on the 1944 tax rate in a representative area of the Chin-Ch'a-Chi region: "The highest rate on landlords was 52 per cent. of income, on rich peasants 18 per cent., on middle peasants 10 per cent. and on poor peasants 4 to 5 per cent." (p. 9).

92. The key role of the rent reduction movement in mobilizing the peasant masses on the eve of civil war in 1946 was indicated in major editorials and articles in the Yenan press at that time. The 1946 New Year's editorial, for example, called for the implementation of a large-scale rent reduction movement in the newly liberated areas in order to raise the peasants' political consciousness. "Hsin-nien hsien-tz'u" [A New Year's statement], CFJP, 1 January 1946.

93. "Reading Notes on the Soviet Union's 'Political Economics' (Economy) (1961–1962)," in *Miscellany of Mao Tse-tung Thought (1949–1968)* 2:247–313. This is the second volume of a translation by the Joint Publications Research Service of materials from two Chinese-language volumes entitled *Mao Tse-tung Ssu-hsiang Wan-sui* [Long live Mao Tse-tung thought], apparently published in China in 1967 and 1969 for internal use, but later made available through Taiwan sources.

94. Ibid., p. 282.

95. Ibid.

96. Ibid., p. 283.

97. Ibid., p. 313. Mao also criticized giving undue weight to the welfare mission of the trade unions and voiced his skepticism, on both economic and ideological grounds, of the policy of using high-wage incentives for technically advanced skilled workers (pp. 274, 283).

Chapter VIII

1. As of the spring of 1945, the Communists claimed control of regions inhabited by 95.5 million people, organized into nineteen large liberated areas. James Harrison, *The Long March to Power*, pp. 371-72.

2. Ibid., p. 372.

3. Thus, Teng Fa, as chairman of the newly established Preparatory Committee of the Liberated Areas' Trade Union Federation, and Chu Hsüeh-fan, as head of the CAL, jointly represented the Chinese labor movement at the inaugural congress of the World Federation of Trade Unions (WFTU) and at the 27th International Labor Congress, both held in Paris in the fall of 1945. Donald Klein and Anne Clark, *Biographic Dictionary of Chinese Communism, 1921-1965* 2:818-19.

4. Communication no. 18 to the U.S. State Department from John S. Service in Yenan, 18 March 1945, in *The Amerasia Papers: A Clue to the Catastrophe of China* 2:1423-25. Service added that "significantly, the Communists make no specific claims in this figure [of 800,000] of labor organizations in such cities as Hankow and Shanghai," though he noted that "their leaders" had spoken repeatedly of extensive underground organizations in these centers (pp. 1424-25).

5. "We Must Learn to Do Economic Work" (10 January 1945), speech to labor heroes and model workers of Shen-Kan-Ning Border Region, in SW 3:240. An inferior translation of the essentially identical original text appears in Mao Tse-tung, *Our Tasks in 1945*, pp. 41-49.

6. "Resolution on Certain Questions in Party History," in SW 3:194.

7. Ibid., p. 196.

8. Ibid., pp. 198-99.

9. Ibid., p. 200.

10 Ibid., p. 201.

11. See Conrad Brandt et al., *A Documentary History of Chinese Communism*, pp. 443-45; and Mao's report to the Second Plenum (5 March 1949), in SW 4:361-75.

12. "On Coalition Government" (24 April 1945), in SW 4:255-320.

13. Ibid., p. 300.

14. Ibid., pp. 303-4.

15. Ibid.

16. "Wei tu-li yü min-chu erh chan: chun-pei ch'eng-li Chung-kuo chieh-fang ch'ü chih-kung lien-ho-hui" [To fight for independence and democracy: prepare to establish a China liberated areas' labor federation], CFJP, 7 February 1945, p. 1.

17. Ibid.

18. Tung Pi-wu, "Memorandum on China's Liberated Areas," San Francisco, 18 May 1945, p. 26.

19. A July 1946 Yenan report of an anti-civil war telegram sent to a WFTU meeting in Moscow referred only to "the preparatory committee of the Chinese Liberated Area

Trade Union Federation." Yenan radio, 11 July 1946; United States Information Service (USIS), Shanghai, *Yenan Broadcasts*, 12 July 1946.

20. By 1947 the Communists reported that they had organized some 1.5 million workers in northern China. Harrison, *Long March to Power*, p. 403. The February 1945 figure for the same area was 665,000 organized workers. Tung, "Memorandum," p. 26.

21. "Policy for Work in the Liberated Areas for 1946" (15 December 1945), in SW 4:76.

22. In a talk on the labor–capital relationship to a north China cadres' meeting in May 1949, Liu Shao-ch'i reportedly declared that they had cautioned cadres in Tientsin against using the slogan *kung-jen fan-shen* (lit., "turning over," meaning "revolutionizing the workers") as a paraphrase of the Communists' rural revolutionary slogan *nung-min fan-shen* ("turning over" the peasantry). See Liu Shao-ch'i, *Liu Shao-ch'i wu-ko ts'ai-liao* [Five statements by Liu Shao-ch'i], p. 27.

23. See, for example, the summary of a "Directive on Arming the Masses" (issued by the Jehol Provincial Committee of the CCP in December 1945), in "Build Stable Base Areas in the Northeast," in SW 4:85, n. 2.

24. In line with Soviet practice, the Communists in Harbin instituted a seven-grade wage system in state enterprises, differentiated on the basis of skill and experience, and a separate (and much higher) fifteen-grade scale for technicians and staff members. Suzanne Pepper, *Civil War in China*, p. 358.

25. For a graphic account of this leftist agrarian line, see William Hinton, *Fanshen*.

26. See Pepper, *Civil War*, pp. 229-330, for a detailed analysis of 1946-48 CCP land-reform policies.

27. "On Some Important Problems of the Party's Present Policy" (18 January 1948), in SW 4:182.

28. "Speech at a Conference of Cadres in the Shansi-Suiyüan Liberated Area" (1 April 1948), in SW 4:235. Pepper discusses in detail the question of land equalization and its impact on middle-peasant interests, as well as some remaining ambivalences on this score during the early months of 1948 in areas where land reform was still under way. See *Civil War*, pp. 316-30. "The most serious efforts to conciliate middle peasants," Pepper concludes, "were reserved for areas where land reform had already been thoroughly implemented" (p. 330). But, despite the evident impact of revolutionary pressures from the poorer peasantry, a broadened rural class base was a notable objective of Maoist policy in this period.

29. "Speech at a Conference of Cadres," p. 236.

30. Chao Kuo-chün, *Agrarian Policy of the Chinese Communist Party, 1921-1959*, pp. 79-80. A middle peasant could now receive up to 25 percent of his gross income from rent, loans, and the use of hired labor before being classified as a rich peasant.

31. "Hsin chieh-fang ch'ü kung-jen-ti ying-yung tou-cheng" [Heroic struggles of the workers in the newly liberated areas], CFJP, 25 September 1945, p. 1.

32. Pepper, *Civil War*, p. 336, with reference to early postliberation struggle movement in Kalgan.

33. *Chieh-fang ch'ü kung-yeh chien-she* [Liberated areas' industrial construction], pp. 6-7.

34. Ibid., pp. 6-10. See Anna Strong, *The Chinese Conquer China*, pp. 139-43, for descriptive details on the implementation of these policies in Kalgan in 1945-46, based on her interviews with official spokesmen there at that time.

35. *Chieh-fang ch'ü kung-yeh chieh-she*, pp. 10-11.

36. Ibid., pp. 11-12.

37. NCNA, Yenan, 28 August 1946, reporting from Kalgan (USIS, *Yenan Broadcasts*, 29 August 1946). In reference to the "progressive wage system" adopted in Kalgan, the report stated: "The employers and employees fix the standard output and wage for each

person. . . . Output in excess of this standard is paid for with progressive increases in wages."

38. These details are based on a particularly valuable source located at the Harvard-Yenching library: a six-month run, published at five-day intervals, of the *Kung-jen pao* (KJP) (Chang-chia-k'ou) [The worker (Kalgan)] from November 1945 to April 1946.

39. KJP, 15 December 1945.

40. A subsequent report noted that these "big and small" settle-accounts struggles had netted about 12 million yuan (KJP, 25 December 1945).

41. Thus, an earlier report (KJP, 25 November 1945) on new labor rules formulated by the workers of a cloisonné factory in the neighboring center of Hsüen-hua (also under CCP control) listed the following items to be adhered to by the workers: no self-initiated rest time without adequate reason; no leaving a work post without reporting first to the section production head; no gambling; promptness in reporting for work (latecomers to be subjected to criticism by the other workers); promotion and development of work responsibility and an enthusiastic work attitude.

42. Reports on this congress, which opened on 20 December 1945, were carried in KJP, 25 and 30 December 1945.

43. "Pien-ch'ü tsung kung-hui Ma Hui-chih t'ung-chih tsai Chang-shih kung-jen shou-tz'u tai-piao ta-hui k'ai-mu tien-li shang-ti chiang-hua chih-yao" [Summary of the talk by Comrade Ma Hui-chih of the (Chin-Ch'a-Chi) Border Region General Labor Union at the opening ceremonies of the First Workers' Representatives' Congress in Kalgan], KJP, 25 December 1945.

44. KJP, 30 November 1945.

45. KJP, 5 December 1945.

46. KJP, 30 January 1946.

47. KJP, 20 December 1945; 10 January, 20 and 25 February, 1946. The "recall the past movement" *(hui-i yün-tung)* focused on the workers' change in status from the virtual slavery of the past to the new "master" role of the present. Reports of "wage discussions" detailed the experiences of workers who, in the course of accepting wage increases, openly criticized their own shortcomings and pledged to do better work.

48. KJP, 25 March 1946.

49. KJP, 30 March 1946.

50. In particular, "Hsiang Ch'eng Kuei-hsiang hsüeh-hsi" [Learn from Ch'eng Kuei-hsiang], KJP, 5 December 1945.

51. KJP, 15 April 1946.

52. Pepper, *Civil War*, p. 337.

53. Ibid.

54. Strong, *Chinese Conquer China*, pp. 145–46.

55. Pepper cites a June 1946 NCNA report showing wage rates in a privately owned Kalgan tea factory ranging only from 120 to 160 catties of millet per month. *Civil War*, p. 339.

56. Ibid.; and KJP, 25 December 1945 (see n. 43 above).

57. Li Kuang, ed., *Ti-liu tz'u ch'üan-kuo lao-tung ta-hui* [The sixth national labor congress], p. 19.

58. A May 1948 North China Liberated Area Conference on Industry and Commerce thus emphasized the seriousness of such defects in the wage system of public-run enterprises in north China. See Pepper, *Civil War*, p. 353.

59. Li, *Ti-liu ta-hui*, p. 19.

60. For a description of these policies, as implemented in Harbin in 1948, see Pepper, *Civil War*, pp. 354-58. These policies were based on similar piece-rate principles as the progressive wage system earlier instituted in Kalgan, though now with much more elaborate grade classifications and greater wage differentials, with a 6 or 7 to 1 base-pay ratio from the first worker pay grade to the top technician grade, plus progressive wage increases of from 10 to 100 percent of base pay for exceeding their production norm by 5 to 70 or more percent. (These figures are taken from specific examples of Harbin enterprises cited by Pepper.)

61. Ch'en Pao-yü, head of the General Labor Union of the Central Hopei base area, in April 1948 voiced the above criticisms of the "left adventurist" policies pursued by the labor movement in that area since the Japanese surrender. Referring to three workers' representatives' conferences held in the Central Hopei base during 1945-46, Ch'en criticized their "one-sided" emphasis on worker benefits and their relatively little attention to the question of developing production. When the union cadres went into the factories, he stated, they talked only of wage and livelihood questions and seldom of production problems. "Chien-t'ao chih-kung yün-tung chung-ti tso-ch'ing mao-hsien chu-i" [Critically examine left adventurism within the labor movement] (summary of a report by Ch'en Pao-yü to the Central Hopei area first industrial conference, 28 April 1948), in Ch'en Po-ta et al., *Kuan-yü kung-shang-yeh-ti cheng-ts'e* [On industrial and commercial policy], pp. 46-47.

62. Klein and Clark, *Biographic Dictionary* 1:517.

63. Pepper, *Civil War*, pp. 352-54.

64. Ibid., p. 355.

65. "Chieh-fang ch'ü chih-kung yün-tung-ti jen wu" [Tasks of the liberated areas' trade union movement], CFJP, 30 April 1946.

66. Ibid.

67. Yenan radio, 3 May 1946 (USIS, *Yenan Broadcasts* 4 May 1946). Chu Te, addressing a May Day gathering of two thousand trade unionists in Yenan, focused on a similar labor-capital cooperation theme. CFJP, 2 May 1946.

68. NCNA, Yenan, 10 May 1946, in *NCNA Bulletin* (Peiping), 14 May 1946, p. 3.

69. See ch. VII, pp. 213-14, for references to these later Mao views.

70. According to a July 1948 CCP source, the Communists suffered a net loss of forty-five cities from mid-1946 to mid-1947. Cited in Kenneth Lieberthal, "Mao Versus Liu? Policy Towards Industry and Commerce: 1946-1949," CQ, no. 47 (July-September 1971):496-97, n. 15.

71. "Chien-ch'ih chih-kung yün-tung cheng-ch'üeh lu-hsien, fan-tui 'tso'-ch'ing mao-hsien-chu-i" [Firmly follow the correct line of the labor movement, oppose 'left' adventurism], NCNA, 7 February 1948, in Ch'en, *Kuan-yü kung-shang-yeh-ti cheng-ts'e*, p. 22.

72. "Chung-kung tung-pei chung-yang chü kuan-yü pao-hu hsin shou-fu ch'eng-shih-ti chih-shih" [Directive of the CCP Northeast Central Bureau on protecting newly recovered cities] (10 June 1948), in *Kuan-yü ch'eng-shih cheng-ts'e-ti chi-ko wen-hsien* [Several documents on city policy], pp. 4-10.

73. "Chien-t'ao chih-kung yün-tung," p. 46. See also n. 61 above.

74. See "Resolution on Questions in Party History," pp. 177-225.

75. "The Present Situation and Our Tasks" (25 December 1947), in SW 4:157-76.

76. Mao defined bureaucrat-capital *(kuan-li tzu-ch'an)* as monopoly capital closely tied to imperialism and to the KMT state apparatus and leadership, whom he accused of piling up fortunes valued at ten to twenty billion dollars (U.S.) and of monopolizing the "economic lifelines of the whole country" (ibid., p. 167). Much of China's limited industry and modern transport, communications, and finance were in fact under state control,

particularly after the reversion of Japanese-owned assets in 1945. Thus, "confiscation" was essentially a question of shifting to new forms of state ownership and control under the new government.

77. "Present Situation and Our Tasks," p. 167.

78. Ibid., pp. 168-69.

79. "On the Policy Concerning Industry and Commerce" (27 February 1948), in SW 4:203.

80. Ibid., pp. 203-4.

81. "Labor Policy and Tax Policy for Developing Industry," pt. 1, FBIS, 27 April 1948, p. PPP4.

82. Ch'en Po-ta's criticisms closely resembled those that Teng Fa directed at union and party work in the Border Region factories in his speech to the 1943 Factories Conference in Yenan.

83. "Chien-ch'ih chih-kung yün-tung," pp. 22-26.

84. Ibid., p. 23.

85. Ibid., p. 25.

86. The illogical 1933 date is evidently a textual error.

87. I have used here the translation of this portion of the NCNA editorial given in Lieberthal, "Mao Versus Liu?," p. 502; the corresponding Chinese text is in "Chien-ch'ih chih-kung yün-tung," p. 26. The term "staff and workers" (chih-kung) has elsewhere been translated as "labor."

88. "Cheng-ch'üeh chih-hsing lao-tzu liang-li fang-chen" [Correctly carry out the labor-capital mutual benefits policy], NCNA commentary, 21 September 1948, in Kuan-yü ch'eng-shih cheng-ts'e, pp. 34-36.

89. For a first-hand account of the problems faced by the Communists along these lines during the initial postliberation period in Shanghai, see Lynn and Amos Landman, Profile of Red China, pp. 43-47. After the arrival of the Communists, they write, "labor set out to pluck the fruits of its new and lofty position. . . . The Shanghai Labor Bureau reported that it had handled 1,684 'disputes' in June, July, and August [1949], but acknowledged that many never came to its attention" (pp. 43-44).

90. "Labor Policy and Tax Policy," pt. 1, p. PPP1.

'91. Ibid., pp. PPP2-3. A "North China Liberated Areas Conference on Industry and Commerce," meeting in Shihchiachuang, Hopei, in May-June 1948, took a similar line in implementation of Mao's four-point economic principles. See Lieberthal, "Mao Versus Liu?," pp. 501-2, for a summary of the decisions of this conference.

92. "Labor Policy and Tax Policy," pt. 1, pp. PPP2-3.

93. "Labor Policy and Tax Policy," pt. 2, FBIS, 28 April 1948, pp. CCC1-4.

94. "Labor Policy and Tax Policy," pt. 3, FBIS, 29 April 1948, pp. PPP1-2.

95. Pepper, Civil War, p. 359.

96. North Shensi radio, 3 June 1948 (FBIS, 4 June 1948, p. CCC1).

97. "On Trade Union Movement in China," China Digest 5, no. 5 (28 December 1948):11-13. I have used this somewhat abridged and summarized translation of the resolution, supplemented by references where necessary to the complete Chinese text, "Kuan-yü Chung-kuo chih-kung yün-tung tang-ch'ien jen-wu-ti chüeh-i" [Resolution on the current tasks of the Chinese labor movement], in Kuan-yü ch'eng-shih cheng-ts'e, pp. 18-33.

98. A supplemental explanatory statement issued in September 1948 by the Executive Committee of the newly reconstituted ACFL delineated three basic worker classifications, exclusive of staff personnel: ordinary workers, skilled workers, and technicians, with differing (though overlapping) minimum and maximum wage levels for each category.

Each was in turn further divided into numerous grade levels, totalling as many as thirteen in larger enterprises; correspondingly complex classifications and grades for administrative and technical personnel were also in force. Grade and wage levels were linked to seniority, skills, responsibilities, and productive effort. In cited examples, the maximum wage level for technicians was approximately double that for unskilled (ordinary) workers. See "Kuan-yü chih-kung yün-tung tang-ch'ien jen-wu chüeh-i-an-chung chi-ko wen-t'i-ti shuo-ming" [Explanation of several questions in the draft resolution on the current tasks of the labor movement], in Mao Tse-tung et al., *Hsin min-chu chu-i kung-shang cheng-ts'e* [New democratic industrial and commercial policies], pp. 99-104.

99. In state-run enterprises in newly liberated areas, the September statement called for interim retention of the already existing staff and worker wage patterns (though it also noted the need to correct situations where some higher-level staff personnel enjoyed "bureaucratic" privileges). Ibid., pp. 104-5.

100. Ibid., p. 103.

101. The September statement stipulated that under special circumstances the work day could be extended to a maximum of twelve hours, though it also noted that in cases of unusually severe working conditions, the number of hours could be reduced. It deplored the excessive number of holidays and called for a work year of over three hundred days, but added that some consideration should be shown for customary practices in this regard. Ibid., pp. 99-100, 108-9.

102. One welfare arrangement proposed in the September ACFL explanation was for the factory to contribute a sum equal to 2.5 percent of its payroll to a staff-worker welfare fund, to which employees would contribute 0.5 percent of their wages. It would then be used for contingencies not covered in the collective contract, such as maternity assistance, family sickness or death, natural calamities, aid to unusually large families, etc. Ibid., p. 107.

103. A "Temporary [Provisional?] Wartime Workers' Insurance Bill," proposed by a representative of the Northeast [Manchurian] Industrial Department, was approved "in principle" by the Sixth National Labor Congress and also by a northeast workers' representatives' conference held on 16 August 1948. This bill required that the enterprise contribute 3 percent of the worker's salary, the worker 5 percent, and the government 10 percent to an insurance fund which would cover medical expenses of the workers and provide "old-age security" for those employees over sixty who had worked for more than twenty-five years. North Shensi radio, 10 September 1948, (FBIS, 13 September 1948, p. CCC6).

104. A summary of Ch'en Yün's report was carried by North Shensi radio, NCNA, 9 August 1948, (FBIS, 10 August 1948, pp. CCC1-3).

105. Ibid., p. CCC2.

106. For example, Joyce K. Kallgren has noted the key role played by union-administered social welfare programs after 1949 in placing industrial workers and the trade union bureaucracy in a specially favored position. See "Social Welfare and China's Industrial Workers," in A. Doak Barnett, ed., *Chinese Communist Politics in Action*, pp. 540-73.

107. Chungking radio report on "Chinese Labor Organization," FBIS, 20 October 1945, p. G1. See also "The Chinese Association of Labor," *Amerasia* 11, no. 3 (March 1947):80-81, which states, presumably for a somewhat later period, that the CAL had "a paper membership of 1,266,514. By June 1948 the total membership of labor unions registered with the National government's Ministry of Social Affairs was officially reported to be 5,003,598. *China Handbook*, 1950, p. 432.

108. "Chinese Association of Labor," p. 81.

109. Chu Hsüeh-fan, "Are the Workers in China Divided?," *China Weekly Review* 105, no. 2 (8 March 1947):37. The texts of both the eight-point and twenty-three-point programs are provided with this article (pp. 38-39). The CCP's program called for establishment of a peaceful, united, and democratic new China; punishment of all corrupt officials and

traitors; confiscation of all enemy property; dissolution of all "puppet labor unions"; guarantees of fundamental rights, including political and union organizational rights for workers; prohibition of long hours of factory work; the principle of equal pay for equal work and abolition of the apprentice system of compensation; free education for workers and improvement in workers' skills in order to develop industry.

110. Paul Harper, "Political Role of Trade Unions in Communist China," pp. 174–75. Harper stresses the role of Yi Li-jung, appointed secretary-general of the CAL in 1943, who had been an active Communist labor organizer in the 1920s and who used his leadership position to strengthen the pro-CCP forces within the association. For a brief Communist account of Yi Li-jung's role in the CAL in the 1943–46 period, see Li, *Ti-liu ta-hui*, pp. 59–60.

111. "Development of Labor Unions in China," FEER 3, no. 19 (17 September 1947):384.

112. *China Handbook, 1950*, p. 434.

113. John Stenhouse and A. Bland Calder, "Review of the Economy of China: One Year of Peace," FEER 2, no. 6 (5 February 1947):75.

114. Pepper, *Civil War*, p. 101.

115. John Keswick, "Review of the Economy of China," FEER 3, no. 9 (9 July 1947):147–48.

116. "The Situation in China," FEER 4, no. 19 (12 May 1948):456.

117. A. Doak Barnett, *China on the Eve of Communist Takeover*, p. 79.

118. See Julian R. Friedman, "Labor in Nationalist China, 1945–48," supplement to Israel Epstein's *Notes on Labor Problems in Nationalist China*, pp. 119–23.

119. Euyang [Ouyang] Tsu-jen, "Shanghai Workers—A Sketch of Their Struggle since V-J Day to Summer, 1948," *China Digest* 4, no. 12 (19 October 1948):5–8.

120. *China on the Eve of Takeover*, pp. 78–79. Barnett also notes that "generally speaking, labor unions have been in fairly good bargaining position in Shanghai. Vis-à-vis management, unions of skilled laborers have been in an excellent position because of the scarcity of skilled workers in China, and some of the other unions have been able to fall back on government support in dealing with their employers" (ibid.).

121. Ma Ch'ao-chün et al., eds., *Chung-kuo lao-kung yün-tung shih* [History of the Chinese labor movement] 4:1792.

122. See Pepper, *Civil War*, pp. 112–18, for some individual examples of Communist underground activity in the postwar labor movement. These details are based largely on articles published in the Communist press in Shanghai in mid-1951, at a time when, particularly in Shanghai, the vanguard role of the working class was being strongly promoted and the revolutionary contributions and character of the pre-1949 labor movement extolled and highlighted. See, for example, the 1951 pamphlet published under the auspices of the newly organized Shanghai Federation of Labor, *San-shih nien lai-ti Shanghai kung yün* [Shanghai labor movement in the past thirty years]. Pepper herself concludes that the Communist role "was more a symptom than a cause" of the militant Shanghai labor movement of the late 1940s (p. 118).

123. Pepper states, "While the pattern of government control varied from union to union and was less successful overall in Shanghai than elsewhere, the trend toward independent union activity, open criticism of the Government's labor policy, disregard of its decrees, and leadership support for the demands of the rank and file was general" (*Civil War*, p. 107).

124. See ibid., pp. 398–401.

125. Ibid., pp. 400–01.

126. Shang Yi-jen, "Shen-hsin chiu ch'ang erh-erh tou-cheng chi-yao" [Summary of the February 2 struggle of the Shen-hsin no. 9 factory], in *Wen-shih tzu-liao hsüan-chi* [Selected historical materials] 3, no. 25, pp. 13–25.

127. Chang Ch'i, "Hui-i Shanghai kung-jen-ti hu-ch'ang tou-cheng" [Recalling the Shanghai workers' protect-factory struggle], in *Wen-shih tzu-liao hsüan-chi* 2, no. 24, p. 85.

128. Shang, "Shen-hsin erh-erh tou-cheng," pp. 15-16.

129. Thus, the head of the "brotherhood association," Wang Chung-liang, though serving as one of the strike leaders, is pictured as urging the workers to "cooperate" with rather than resist the police forces sent to occupy the mill on February 2. Ibid., pp. 18-20. The factory management ultimately did restore the workers' coal and rice allotments.

130. Ibid., p. 25.

131. *China Weekly Review* 105, no. 2 (8 March 1947):38. Also Ma, *Lao-kung shih* 4:1678-74, for March 1947 CAL pronouncement disclaiming Chu's role in representing Chinese workers. In April 1948 the KMT formed a new National Federation of Labor, or General Labor Union. This federation was formed in Nanking at a meeting attended by 117 delegates reported to represent twenty provincial, ten municipal, and six regional trade unions. *China Handbook, 1950*, p. 432.

132. Chang Li-ping, "China's Labour Representative Chu Hsüeh-fan," *China Digest* 1, no. 2 (14 January 1947):11.

133. "KMT Labour Leader in Communist Area," *China Digest* 3, no. 9 (23 March 1948):14.

134. See, for example, the CCP Central Committee's 1948 May Day slogans, NCNA, North Shensi radio, 30 April 1948 (FBIS, 3 May 1948, p. PPP9).

135. North Shensi radio, 23 November 1948 (FBIS, 24 November 1948, p. CCC2).

136. Chih Ming, "Labour's Fight Against Kuomintang Suppression," *China Digest* 3, no. 7 (24 February 1948):4.

137. Ibid.

138. Li Li-san, in November 1949, described the immediate postliberation wage policy in state enterprises (the former bureaucrat-capitalist sector) as follows: "In the newly liberated cities at present, the method of fundamentally maintaining 'former position, former pay' is adopted temporarily in order to guarantee the systematic and complete taking over of State and public enterprise." Li Li-san, *Report on the Trade Union Movement in China*, p. 15; speech delivered to Trade Union Conference of Asian and Australasian Countries, Peking, November 1949. Li summed up the wage principles in state enterprises as " 'pay according to work done', and 'more work, more pay' " (ibid.).

139. *Kuan-yü ch'eng-shih cheng-ts'e*, pp. 21-22; and *China Digest* 5, no. 5 (28 December 1948):11. See n. 97 above for full citation of Chinese text and of *China Digest* abridged version. In the latter's summary of this section of the resolution, this last sentence states only, "Then workers should demand that their living standard be raised."

140. Ch'en Chih, "Mu-ch'ien Chiang-kuan ch'ü chih-kung yün-tung-ti jen-wu" [Current tasks of the labor movement in the Chiang-ruled areas], in Li, *Ti-liu ta-hui*, pp. 67-74.

141. Hua Shan, "All China Federation of Labour," *China Digest* 4, no. 10 (21 September 1948):7.

142. *Wen-shih tzu-liao hsüan-chi*, vols. 2-4, has a number of articles, mostly recollections by participants, on the workers' struggle to protect their factories and maintain operations in such key areas as electric power, gas, water, telephone, and shipping, as well as in textiles, machinery, and others. See nn. 126 and 127 above.

143. Chang, "Hui-i hu-ch'ang tou-cheng," pp. 80-90.

144. Ibid., p. 94.

145. Lynn T. White, III, "Shanghai's Polity in Cultural Revolution," in John Lewis, ed., *The City in Communist China*, p. 327.

146. Shen Hsi-meng et al., *On Guard Beneath the Neon Lights*, p. 36.

147. "Telegram to the Headquarters of the Loyang Front After the Recapture of the City" (8 April 1948), in SW 4:248.

148. Ibid., pp. 247-48.

149. L. W. Yang, "Trades Union Congress in Liberated China," *China Digest* 4, no. 4 (29 June 1948):3.

150. Ibid.

151. NCNA, North Shensi radio, 7 August 1948 (FBIS, 9 August 1948, p. CCC1).

152. Ibid., p. CCC2.

153. This principle was defined in Article 8 of the constitution: "Namely: the minority must submit to the majority; lower organizations submit to higher organizations; affiliated trade unions submit to the decisions and directions of the ACFL." For English text, see Epstein, *Notes on Labor Problems*, app. B, p. 142.

154. *Trade Unions in People's China*, p. 23.

155. Harper, "Political Role of Trade Unions," p. 175. The ultimate size of the Executive Committee was set at fifty-nine full and twenty-two alternate members, with eight of these positions left vacant pending liberation of the remaining cities. See Li, *Ti-liu ta-hui*, pp. 40-41.

156. See Harper, "Political Role of Trade Unions," p. 166. Apparently, a considerable number of skilled textile workers from Shanghai accompanied their employers when many of the latter relocated in the Hong Kong territories during the economic crises and uncertainties of 1948-49 (correspondence with Professor Graham Johnson, University of British Columbia, Vancouver). Mao himself in 1969 reportedly referred to the problem of pre-liberation KMT influence among the workers. See "Mao Tse-tung's Speech to the First Plenum of the CCP's Ninth Central Committee" (28 April 1969), *Issues and Studies* (Taipei) 6, no. 6 (March 1970):95.

157. In fact, three vice-chairmen were subsequently elected.

158. According to a 1949 report, separate departments of production and of wages were set up. *China Digest* 6, no. 5 (14 June 1949):18.

159. The ACFL did, however, convene a national conference on trade union work in July 1949 in Peking. *Trade Unions in People's China*, p. 13.

160. NCNA, Harbin, 14 October 1948 (FBIS, 15 October 1948, p. CCC3). The Standing Committee numbered fourteen full and six alternate members.

161. *China Digest* 6, no. 5 (14 June 1949):18.

162. NCNA, *Daily News Release* (Peking), no. 190 (8 November 1949):34. The CAL cadres were to be "encouraged to participate in suitable work in trade union organs; in both study and work, they must be treated on a par with the original trade union cadres." ACFL "Notice on Ending the Chinese Association of Labor," cited in Harper, "Political Role of Trade Unions," p. 177.

163. Klein and Clark, *Biographic Dictionary* 1:149-51.

164. Ibid., pp. 604-6.

165. Li, *Ti-liu ta-hui*, p. 55. In this biographical sketch, Liu Ning-yi's post-1937 Shanghai activities merited only a phrase. Yi Li-jung's CAL-affiliated career may be viewed as a possible exception to the point made above.

166. Ibid., pp. 53-63. Those few (five) among the seventeen Communist members included who came directly out of the urban labor movement were all relatively young (twenties and thirties) worker activists whose labor activities spanned only the most recent years.

167. *Who's Who in Communist China* 1:453.

168. Li, *Ti-liu ta-hui*, p. 12.

169. Ibid.

Conclusion

1. *The Chinese Labor Movement, 1919-1927*, p. 409. Chesneaux states that out of the labor struggles of the 1919-27 years came "the hard core" of seasoned "working class militants and intellectuals . . . [who] provided the peasants with the leadership that they needed and that they would have been unable to supply themselves" (p. 410). It was a number of such leaders, however, and the entire concept of worker "leadership" of the peasants which provided a strong basis for the class line after 1927.

2. See Paul Harper, "Political Role of Trade Unions in Communist China," pp. 150-55, for a discussion of the more professionally oriented character and attitudes of the post-1949 trade union bureaucracy.

3. Barry Richman, *Industrial Society in Communist China*, p. 314.

4. "On the Ten Great Relationships" (25 April 1956), in Stuart Schram, ed., *Mao Tse-tung Unrehearsed, Talks and Letters: 1956-71*, p. 69.

5. Richman, *Industrial Society*, p. 316. These trends culminated in a new wage reform in 1963.

6. "Reading Notes on the Soviet Union's 'Political Economics' [Economy] (1961-1962)," in *Miscellany of Mao Tse-tung Thought (1949-1968)* 2:282. See also ch. VII, nn. 93 and 97.

7. Ibid., pp. 282-83. In a newly published volume of Ch'en Yün's economic policy writings and reports from the mid-1950s through the early 1960s, the editors show him to have been (presumably in contrast to Mao) a strong advocate of greater individual rural incentive policies in the post-Great Leap crisis years. Nicholas Lardy and Kenneth Lieberthal, eds., *Ch'en Yün's Strategy for China's Development: A Non-Maoist Alternative*, p. xxxi.

8. "The Struggle Between the Two Lines in China's Trade Union Movement," by proletarian revolutionaries in the All-China Federation of Trade Unions (ACFTU), *Peking Review* 11, no. 26 (28 June 1968):18.

9. "On the Social Basis of the Lin Piao Anti-Party Clique," *Peking Review* 18, no. 10 (7 March 1975):5-10.

10. See Christopher Howe, "Labour Organization and Incentives in Industry Before and After the Cultural Revolution," in Stuart Schram, ed., *Authority, Participation and Cultural Change in China*, pp. 233-56.

11. Teng Hsiao-p'ing, speech to Ninth National Trade Union Congress, 11 October 1978 (FBIS, 12 October 1978, p. E7). Teng, of course, blamed all such developments on "Lin Piao and the Gang of Four."

12. Ni Zhifu [Ni Chih-fu], "Work Report Delivered at Third Enlarged Session of the Ninth Executive Committee of the All-China Federation of Trade Unions," *Gongren ribao* [*Kung-jen jih-pao*], 13 October 1981 (FBIS, 4 November 1981, p. K8).

13. From a report by Vice-Premier Li Hsien-nien to an April 1979 central work conference, as carried in *Ming Pao* (Hong Kong), 14 June 1979, p. 4 (FBIS, 9 June 1979, pp. L11-12); also Wang Bingqian [Wang Ping-ch'ien], "Report on Financial Work," report by the Minister of Finance to the Third Session of the Fifth National People's Congress, 30 August 1980, *Beijing Review* 23, no. 39 (29 September 1980):12.

14. From Premier Hua Kuo-feng's report to the Second Session of the Fifth National People's Congress, as transmitted by Xinhua (NCNA), 20 June 1979 (FBIS, 21 June 1979, p. L5); and from Vice-Premier Yu Ch'iu-li's report of 21 June to the congress on measures to strengthen agriculture (FBIS, 22 June 1979, p. L5). Vice-Premier Teng Hsiao-p'ing, China's key policy maker, reemphasized in an April 1981 interview with a visiting Japanese parliamentary delegation, that "Comrade Mao Zedong set forth the policy of putting stress on agriculture, light industry and heavy industry, in that order." *Mainichi Shimbun* (Tokyo), 15 April 1981 (FBIS, 16 April 1981, Annex, p. 2).

15. See "Some Questions Concerning the Current Rural Economic Policies" (excerpts from CCP Central Committee Document no. 1, for 1983), Xinhua, Beijing, 10 April 1983 (FBIS, 13 April 1983, pp. K1-K13).

16. Shih Shih-yin, "An Elementary Discussion of Planning that 'Puts the Cart Before the Horse,' " *Guangming ribao* [*Kuang-ming jih-pao*], 17 January 1981 (FBIS, 28 January 1981, pp. L14-15). See also "Restore and Develop Yan'an [Yenan] Spirit," *Renmin ribao* [*Jen-min jih-pao*], 9 January 1981 (FBIS, 12 January 1981, pp. L9-10).

17. See "Certain Questions on Arousing Workers' Enthusiasm," *Gongren ribao*, 22 May 1980 (FBIS, 25 June 1980, pp. L4-13); and "Where Does Labour Enthusiasm Come From?," *Beijing Review* 23, no. 19 (12 May 1980):16-23.

18. "It is Imperative to Reform the System of the Iron Rice Bowl and Everybody Eating Out of the Same Big Pot," *Gongren ribao*, 13 January 1983 (FBIS, 17 January 1983, pp. K10-12).

19. "Both Rewards and Penalties Are Essential," *Renmin ribao*, editorial, 3 May 1982 (FBIS, 7 May 1982, p. K17).

20. Xinhua, 22 May 1982, carried the text of and commentary on the eight rules of conduct (FBIS, 3 May 1982, pp. K7-8).

21. Finance Minister Wang Bingqian's [Wang Ping-ch'ien] report on the state budget, as transmitted by Xinhua, 14 December 1982 (FBIS, 14 December 1982, p. K45).

BIBLIOGRAPHY

Chinese Language Sources

CBSA Notice, no. 17. "Kung-hui yün-tung yü kung-tso lu-hsien" [Union movement and work line], 1 March 1931. Ch'en Ch'eng Collection, reel 11.

CBSA Notice, no. 3. "Su-wei-ai yü kung-hui-ti kuan-hsi wen-t'i" [Problems (or questions) of soviet-union relations], 21 January 1931. Ch'en Ch'eng Collection, reel 12.

Chan Ming K. *Historiography of the Chinese Labor Movement, 1895-1949: A Critical Survey and Bibliography of Selected Chinese Source Materials at the Hoover Institution.* Hoover Press Bibliographical Series, no. 60. Stanford: Hoover Institution Press, 1981.

Ch'en Ch'eng Collection. Twenty-one-reel Hoover Institution microfilm of this major collection of CCP source materials of the Kiangsi soviet period. This collection, now located in Taiwan, was gathered by Nationalist General Ch'en Ch'eng during the KMT's anti-Communist campaigns in the early 1930s. Individual items from the collection are listed alphabetically in the bibliography.

Ch'en Po-ta et al. *Kuan-yü kung-shang-yeh-ti cheng-ts'e* [On industrial and commercial policy]. Hong Kong: Hsin min-chu ch'u-pan she, 1949.

Ch'i Li, ed. *Shen-Kan-Ning pien-ch'ü shih-lu* [Historical account of the Shen-Kan-Ning border region]. N.p.: Chieh-fang she, 1939. Reprint. Washington, D.C.: CCRM, 1970.

Chieh-fang [Liberation]. Yenan, April 1937–June 1941. Hoover Institution, Stanford. Microfilm.

Chieh-fang ch'ü kung-yeh chien-she [Liberated areas' industrial construction]. N.p.: Chien-she ch'u-pan she, 1946. Reprint. Washington, D.C.: CCRM, n.d.

Chieh-fang jih-pao [Liberation daily]. Yenan, May 1941-February 1947. Hoover Institution, Stanford. Microfilm.

Chin-Ch'a-Chi Border Area Government, comp. "K'ang-Jih min-chu cheng-ch'üan chi-ch'i ko-chung chi-pen cheng-ts'e" [Fundamental policies of the anti-Japanese democratic government], probably 1942-43. Yushodo Collection, reel 15.

"Chung-kung chung-yang kuan-yü su-ch'ü ch'ih-se kung-hui-ti jen-wu ho mu-ch'ien-ti kung-tso chüeh-i" [Central Committee, CCP resolution on soviet-area red unions' tasks and current work], 21 December 1931. Ch'en Ch'eng Collection, reel 12.

Chung-kuo kung-jen [Chinese worker], nos. 1-13. Biweekly supplement to CFJP. Yenan, September 1941-March 1942. Hoover Institution, Stanford. Microfilm.

First Party Congress of the Soviet Areas. "Su-ch'ü kung-hui yün-tung chüeh-i-an" [Resolution on the soviet-area union movement], November 1931. Ch'en Ch'eng Collection, reel 12.

General Political Department of the Red Army, comp. "Kung-ku Hung-chün chung wu-ch'an chieh-chi ling-tao wen-t'i pao-kao ta-kang" [Outline report on the question of strengthening proletarian leadership in the Red Army], 4 January 1934. Ch'en Ch'eng Collection, reel 8.

General Political Department of the Red Army. "Lao-tung fa yü kung-jen yün-tung" [The labor law and the workers' movement], March 1934. Ch'en Ch'eng Collection, reel 8.

Hsiang Ying. "Lao-tung fa pao-kao" [Report on the labor law], November 1931. Ch'en Ch'eng Collection, reel 12.

Hsiao Tso-liang, *Power Relations within the Chinese Communist Movement, 1930-1934.* Vol. 2. *The Chinese Documents.* Seattle: University of Washington Press, 1967.

Hsin-hua jih-pao. [New China daily]. Hankow and Chungking, 1938-46. Hoover Institution, Stanford. Microfilm.

Hsüeh K'ang. "Chi-hui chu-i-ti chih-kung yün-tung tsung-chieh" [Summing up on the opportunist labor movement], 4 June 1932. Ch'en Ch'eng Collection, reel 12.

"Hui-ch'ang shih ch'ih-se tsung kung-hui ti-i-tz'u tai-piao ta-hui chüeh-i-an" [Resolution of the first congress of the Huich'ang Red General Labor Union], 10 December 1931. Ch'en Ch'eng Collection, reel 12.

Hung-se Chung-hua [Red China]. Juichin, Kiangsi, December 1931-October 1934. Ch'en Ch'eng Collection, reels 16 and 17.

"I-chiu san-i nien chih-kung yün-tung-ti tsung-chieh" [Summary of the 1931 staff-workers' movement]. *Hung-ch'i chou-pao* [Red flag weekly] (Shanghai) 11 (March 1932). Hoover Institution, Stanford. Microfilm.

K'ang-Jih ken chu-ti cheng-ts'e t'iao-li hui-chi: Shen-Kan-Ning chih-pu [Compendium of policies and regulations of the anti-Japanese base areas: Shen-Kan-Ning area]. Yenan: Shen-Kan-Ning pien-ch'ü cheng-fu, 1942. Hoover Institution, Stanford. Microfilm.

"Kiangsi sheng su-ch'ü kung-jen tou-cheng kang-ling" [Kiangsi soviet-area workers' struggle program]. Union Federation of Kiangsi, 25 March 1932. Ch'en Ch'eng Collection, reel 12.

Kuan-yü ch'eng-shih cheng-ts'e-ti chi-ko wen-hsien [Several documents on city policy]. Hantan, Hopei: Hua-pei hsin-hua shu-tien, 1949. Reprint. Washington, D.C.: CCRM, n.d.

Kung-jen pao (Chang-chia-k'ou) [The worker] (Kalgan), November 1945-April 1946. Harvard-Yenching Library, Harvard University, Cambridge.

Kuo-chi ku-nung wei-yüan-hui mi-shu-ch'ü [Secretariat of the international farm-laborer committee]. "Kuan-yü Chung-kuo ku-nung kung-hui-ti chüeh-i-an" [Resolution regarding the Chinese farm-laborer union], 1932 or 1933. Yushodo Collection, reel 11.

Li Kuang, ed. *Ti-liu tz'u ch'üan-kuo lao-tung ta-hui* [The sixth national labor congress]. Hong Kong: Kung-jen wen-hua she, 1948.

Liu Shao-ch'i, *Liu Shao-ch'i wu-ko ts'ai-liao* [Five statements by Liu Shao-ch'i]. New York: East Asian Institute, Columbia University, n.d. Reproduced from Red Guard sources.

Lu P'ing, comp. *Sheng-huo tsai Yenan* [Life in Yenan]. Sian: n.p., 1938. Hoover Institution, Stanford. Microfilm.

Ma Ch'ao-chün et al., eds. *Chung-kuo lao-kung yün-tung shih* [History of the Chinese labor movement]. 2d ed. 5 vols. Taipei: Lao-kung fu-li, 1966.

Mao Tse-tung. *Ching-chi wen-t'i yü ts'ai-cheng wen-t'i* [Economic and financial problems]. Hong Kong: Hsin min-chu ch'u-pan she, 1949.

Mao Tse-tung et al. *Hsin min-chu chu-i kung-shang cheng-ts'e* [New democratic industrial and commercial policies]. Hong Kong: Hsin min-chu ch'u-pan she, 1949.

San-shih nien lai-ti Shanghai kung yün [Shanghai labor movement in the past thirty years]. Edited by Shanghai Tsung Kung-hui, Wen Chiao Pu [Shanghai Federation of Labor, Department of Culture and Education]. Shanghai: Lao-tung ch'u-pan she, 1951.

Shen-Kan-Ning Border Region Government. *Wei kung-yeh p'in ti ch'üan-mien tzu-chi erh fen-tou* [Struggle for complete industrial self-sufficiency]. Yenan: Shen-Kan-Ning pien-ch'ü cheng-fu pan-kung t'ing, 1944. Reprint. Washington, D.C.: CCRM, n.d.

Shen-Kan-Ning pien-ch'ü ts'an-i hui wen-hsien hui-chi [Compendium of Shen-Kan-Ning border region assembly documents]. Peking: K'o-hsueh ch'u-pan she, 1958.

Southwest Kiangsi Special Area Committee Notice, no. 29. "Ku-kung-hui-ti kung-tso wen-t'i" [Problems of hired hands' union work], 31 March 1931. Ch'en Ch'eng Collection, reel 12.

Su-ch'ü kung-jen [Soviet worker]. Juichin, Kiangsi, scattered issues, 1932-34. Ch'en Ch'eng Collection, reel 1.

Su-wei-ai Chung-kuo [Soviet China]. Moscow: USSR Foreign Workers Publishing House, 1933.

Tou-cheng [Struggle]. Juichin, Kiangsi, February 1933-September 1934. Ch'en Ch'eng Collection, reel 18. The Hoover Institution also supplied issues missing from the collection.

Wang Chien-min. *Chung-kuo Kung-ch'an-tang shih-kao* [Draft history of the Chinese Communist Party]. 3 vols. Taipei: Privately printed, 1965.

Wang Ming. *Wang Ming hsüan-chi* [Selected works of Wang Ming]. 5 vols. Tokyo: Chi Ku Shu Yuan, 1971-75.

"Wei chih-kung yün-tung chih t'ung-chih-ti i feng hsin" [A letter for labor movement comrades], 25 March 1932. Yushodo Collection, reel 11.

"Wei-fan lao-tung fa-ling ch'eng-fa t'iao-li" [Regulations for punishment of labor law violators]. Juichin, Kiangsi, 15 October 1933. Ch'en Ch'eng Collection, reel 16.

Wen-shih tzu liao hsüan-chi [Selected historical materials]. Compiled by the Shanghai Municipal Committee, Chinese People's Political Consultative Conference. Vol. 2, no. 24; vol. 3, no. 25; vol. 4, no. 26. Shanghai: Jen-min ch'u-pan she, 1979.

Yushodo Collection. (*Materials on the Communist Party of China.* Tokyo: Yushodo Film Publications.) Twenty-reel microfilm from the Bureau of Investigation Collection, Ministry of Justice, Taiwan. The collection is comprised mainly of materials from the Yenan period, 1937-45, but also includes key Communist documents from 1932-33. Individual items from the collection are listed alphabetically in the bibliography. This collection is also part of the holdings at the Asia Library at The University of Michigan.

Western Language Sources

Agrarian China: Selected Source Materials from Chinese Authors. Chicago: University of Chicago Press, 1938. Compiled and translated by the research staff of the Institute of Pacific Relations.

The Amerasia Papers: A Clue to the Catastrophe of China. 2 vols. Washington, D.C.: Government Printing Office, 1970. Prepared by the Committee on the Judiciary, United States Senate.

Barnett, A. Doak. *China on the Eve of the Communist Takeover.* New York: Praeger, 1963.

Barnett, A. Doak, ed. *Chinese Communist Politics in Action.* Seattle: University of Washington Press, 1969.

Benton, Gregor. "The 'Second Wang Ming Line' (1935-38)." *China Quarterly* 61 (March 1975): 61-94.

Boorman, Howard L., ed. *Biographical Dictionary of Republican China.* 4 vols. New York: Columbia University Press, 1967-71.

Borisov, O. B., and B. T. Koloskov. *Soviet-Chinese Relations, 1945-1970.* Bloomington: Indiana University Press, 1975.

Brandt, Conrad, Benjamin Schwartz, and John K. Fairbank. *A Documentary History of Chinese Communism.* Cambridge: Harvard University Press, 1952.

Braun, Otto. *Chinesische Aufzeichnungen (1932-1939)* [Chinese records (1932-39)]. Berlin: Dietz Verlag, 1973.

Braun, Otto. *A Comintern Agent in China.* Translated from German by Jeanne Moore. Stanford: Stanford University Press, 1982.

Brugger, William. *Democracy and Organization in the Chinese Industrial Enterprise, 1948-1953*. Cambridge: Cambridge University Press, 1976.

Buck, J. Lossing. *Land Utilization in China*. Chicago: University of Chicago Press, 1937.

Bukharin, Nikolai. "The Chinese Revolution and the Tasks of the Chinese Communists." Translated from Russian by Douglas Merwin. Report to the Sixth CCP Congress, Moscow, 1928. Parts 1, 2. *Chinese Studies in History* 3, 4, nos. 4, 1 (Summer, Fall, 1970):261-324, 4-28.

Carlson, Ellsworth C. *The Kaiping Mines, 1877-1912*. 2d ed. Harvard East Asian Monographs, no. 3. Cambridge: Harvard University Press, 1971.

Chang, John K. *Industrial Development in Pre-Communist China*. Chicago: Aldine, 1969.

Chao Kuo-chün. *Agrarian Policy of the Chinese Communist Party, 1921-1959*. New Delhi: Asia Publishing House, 1960.

Ch'en, Jerome. *Mao and the Chinese Revolution*. New York: Oxford University Press, 1967.

Ch'en, Jerome. "Resolutions of the Tsunyi Conference." *China Quarterly* 40 (October-December 1969):1-38.

Ch'en, Jerome, ed. *Mao*. Englewood Cliffs, N.J.: Prentice-Hall, 1969.

Chen Lin, *China's Fight for National Liberation*. New York: Workers Library, 1938.

Chesneaux, Jean. *The Chinese Labor Movement, 1919-1927*. Translated by H. M. Wright. Stanford: Stanford University Press, 1968.

China at Bay. London: Modern Books, 1936. Special supplement to *Communist International*.

China Digest (Hong Kong) (1947-50).

China Forum. Shanghai, 13 January 1932 (vol. 1, no. 1) to 13 January 1934 (vol. 3, no. 4). Edited and published by Harold R. Isaacs. Forty issues published over the two-year period. Reprinted by CCRM, Washington, D.C., 1976.

China Handbook, 1950. New York: Rockport Press, 1950.

China Weekly Review (Shanghai) (1946-49).

China Year Book, 1933. Edited by H. G. W. Woodhead. Shanghai: North China Daily News and Herald, 1933.

China Year Book, 1935. Edited by H. G. W. Woodhead. Shanghai: North China Daily News and Herald, 1935.

China Year Book, 1938. Edited by H. G. W. Woodhead. Shanghai: North China Daily News and Herald, 1938.

China Year Book, 1939. Edited by H. G. W. Woodhead. Shanghai: North China Daily News and Herald, 1939.

"The Chinese Association of Labor." *Amerasia* 11, no. 3 (March 1947):80-81.

"The Chinese Labor Movement." *Amerasia* 8, no. 10 (12 May 1944):152-56.

Chinese Year Book, 1935-36. Edited by Kwei [Kuei] Chungshu. Shanghai: Commercial Press, 1936.

Chinese Year Book, 1937. Prepared by Council of International Affairs, Nanking. Shanghai: Commercial Press, 1937.

Ch'ü Ch'iu-pai. "The Past and Future of the Chinese Communist Party." Translated by Man Kwok-Chuen. *Chinese Studies in History* 5, no. 1 (Fall 1971):4-72. Report to the Sixth CCP Congress, Moscow, 1928.

Cohen, Stephen F. *Bukharin and the Bolshevik Revolution: A Political Biography, 1888-1938*. New York: Alfred A. Knopf, 1973.

Committee on the Judiciary, United States Senate. *The Amerasia Papers: A Clue to the Catastrophe of China*. 2 vols. Washington, D.C.: Government Printing Office, 1970.

Compton, Boyd. *Mao's China: Party Reform Documents, 1942-44.* Seattle: University of Washington Press, 1952.

Degras, Jane, ed. *The Communist International, 1919-1943: Documents.* 3 vols. London: Oxford University Press, 1956-65.

Deliusin, L. P. "The Sixth Congress of the Chinese Communist Party and its Agrarian-Peasant Program." Translated from Russian by Arlo Schultz. *Chinese Studies in History* 8, no. 3 (Spring 1975):45-114.

Deliusin, L. P., M. A. Persits, A. B. Reznikov, R. A. Ul'ianovsky, eds. *Komintern i Vostok* [The Comintern and the East]. Moscow: Eastern Literature Office, 1969.

Economic Conditions in China, January 1934-March 1935. Shanghai and Peiping: Chinese Workers' Correspondence, n.d.

Epstein, Israel. *Notes on Labor Problems in Nationalist China.* New York: Institute of Pacific Relations, 1949.

Epstein, Israel. *The People's War.* London: Victor Gollancz, 1939.

Epstein, Israel. *The Unfinished Revolution in China.* Boston: Little, Brown, 1947.

Far Eastern Economic Review (Hong Kong) (1946-48).

Feuerwerker, Albert. *The Chinese Economy, 1912-1949.* Michigan Papers in Chinese Studies, no. 1. Ann Arbor: Center for Chinese Studies, The University of Michigan, 1968.

Feuerwerker, Albert. *Economic Trends in the Republic of China, 1912-1949.* Michigan Papers in Chinese Studies, no. 31. Ann Arbor: Center for Chinese Studies, The University of Michigan, 1977.

Forman, Harrison. *Report from Red China.* New York: Henry Holt, 1945.

Gamble, Sidney D. *Ting Hsien: A North China Rural Community.* New York: Institute of Pacific Relations, 1954.

Gelder, Stuart, ed. *The Chinese Communists.* London: Victor Gollancz, 1946.

Gillin, Donald G. *Warlord: Yen Hsi-shan in Shansi Province, 1911-1949.* Princeton: Princeton University Press, 1967.

Gourlay, Walter. " 'Yellow' Unionism in Shanghai: A Study of Kuomintang Technique in Labor Control, 1927-37." *Harvard Papers on China* 7 (February 1953):103-35.

Griffin, Patricia E. *The Chinese Communist Treatment of Counter-revolutionaries, 1924-1949.* Princeton: Princeton University Press, 1976.

Grigor'ev, A. M. "An Important Landmark in the History of the Chinese Communist Party." Translated from Russian by Arlo Schultz. *Chinese Studies in History* 8, no. 3 (Spring 1975):18-44.

Hammond, Edward Roy, III. *Organized Labor in Shanghai, 1927-1937.* Ann Arbor: University Microfilms International, 1978.

Hammond, Thomas Taylor. *Lenin on Trade Unions and Revolution, 1893-1917.* New York: Columbia University Press, 1957.

Harper, Paul. "Political Role of Trade Unions in Communist China." Ph.D. diss., Cornell University, 1968.

Harrison, James Pinckney. *The Long March to Power: A History of the Chinese Communist Party, 1921-72.* New York: Praeger, 1972.

Heinzig, Dieter. "The Otto Braun Memoirs and Mao's Rise to Power." *China Quarterly* 46 (April-June 1971):274-88.

Hinder, Eleanor M. *Life and Labour in Shanghai.* New York: Institute of Pacific Relations, 1944.

Hinton, William. *Fanshen: A Documentary of Revolution in a Chinese Village.* New York: Vintage Books, 1966.

Ho Kan-chih. *A History of the Modern Chinese Revolution.* Peking: Foreign Languages Press, 1959.

Hoffman, Charles. *Work Incentive Practices and Policies in the People's Republic of China, 1953-1965.* New York: State University of New York Press, 1967.

Howe, Christopher. *Wage Patterns and Wage Policy in Modern China, 1919-1972.* London: Cambridge University Press, 1973.

Hsia Tsi-an. *The Gate of Darkness: Studies in the Leftist Literary Movement in China.* Seattle: University of Washington Press, 1968.

Hsiao Tso-liang. *The Land Revolution in China, 1930-1934.* Seattle: University of Washington Press, 1969.

Hsiao Tso-liang. *Power Relations within the Chinese Communist Movement, 1930-1934.* Seattle: University of Washington Press, 1961.

Hsü Yung-ying. *A Survey of Shensi-Kansu-Ninghsia Border Region.* New York: Institute of Pacific Relations, 1945.

Huang, Philip C. C., Lynda Schaefer Bell, and Cathy Lemons Walker. *Chinese Communists and Rural Society, 1927-1934.* China Research Monographs, no. 13. Berkeley: Center for Chinese Studies, University of California, 1978.

International Press Correspondence (Vienna). Vols. 1-18. 1921-38.

Isaacs, Harold R. *The Tragedy of the Chinese Revolution.* 2d rev. ed. Stanford: Stanford University Press, 1961.

Johanson, J., and O. Taube. "The Soviet Movement in China." Introductory essay in *Räte China.* Moscow-Leningrad: USSR Foreign Workers Publishing House, 1934.

Johnson, Chalmers A. *Peasant Nationalism and Communist Power.* Stanford: Stanford University Press, 1962.

Kataoka, Tetsuya, *Resistance and Revolution in China: The Communists and the Second United Front.* Berkeley: University of California Press, 1974.

Kim, Ilpyong J. *The Politics of Chinese Communism: Kiangsi Under the Soviets.* Berkeley: University of California Press, 1974.

Klein, Donald W., and Anne B. Clark. *Biographic Dictionary of Chinese Communism, 1921-1965.* 2 vols. Cambridge: Harvard University Press, 1971.

Kon Sin [K'ang Sheng]. "The Political Situation in China and the Tasks of the Communist Party in China." *Communist International* 10, no. 18 (15 September 1933):612-20.

Kraus, David Curt. *Class Conflict in Chinese Socialism.* Studies of the East Asian Institute, Columbia University. New York: Columbia University Press, 1981.

Kuchumov, V. "The Struggle for the Bolshevization of the Communist Party of China." *Communist International* 8, no. 6 (15 March 1931):162-67.

Kuo, Warren. *Analytical History of the Chinese Communist Party.* 4 vols. Taipei: Institute of International Relations, 1968-71.

Labour Laws and Regulations of the People's Republic of China. Peking: Foreign Languages Press, 1956.

Landman, Lynn, and Amos Landman. *Profile of Red China.* New York: Simon and Schuster, 1951.

Lardy, Nicholas R., and Kenneth Lieberthal, eds. *Chen Yun's Strategy for China's Development: A Non-Maoist Alternative.* Translated by Mao Tong and Du Anxia. Armonk, N.Y.: M. E. Sharpe, 1983.

Lewis, John W., ed. *The City in Communist China.* Stanford: Stanford University Press, 1971.

Li Li-san. *Report on the Trade Union Movement in China.* Bombay: People's Publishing House, 1950. Report delivered at Asian and Australian Trade Union Conference, Peking, November 1949.

Li Ming. "Some Experiences of the Communist Party of China in Organizing and Leading Strike Struggles." *Communist International* 11, no. 10 (20 May 1934):335-39.

Lieberthal, Kenneth. "Mao versus Liu? Policy Towards Industry and Commerce: 1946-1949." *China Quarterly* 47 (July-September 1971):494-520.

Lindsay, Michael. "The Taxation System of the Shansi-Chahar-Hopei Border Region, 1938-45." *China Quarterly* 42 (April-June 1970):1-15.

Liu Shao-ch'i. *Collected Works of Liu Shao-ch'i: Before 1944.* Hong Kong: Union Research Institute, 1969.

Lötveit, Trygvie. *Chinese Communism 1931-1934: Experience in Civil Government.* Monograph Series, no. 16. Copenhagen: Scandinavian Institute of Asian Studies, 1973.

Lowe Chuan-hua. *Facing Labor Issues in China.* Shanghai: China Institute of Pacific Relations, 1933.

Lowe Chuan-hua. *Labor Conditions in China.* Nanking: Council of International Affairs, 1937.

Ma Ch'ao-chün. *History of the Labor Movement in China.* Translated by Peter Min-chi Liang. Taipei: China Cultural Service, 1955.

Mao Tse-tung. *On the New Stage.* Chungking: New China Information Committee, 1938.

Mao Tse-tung. *Our Tasks in 1945.* NCNA, 1945.

Mao Tse-tung. *Red China.* Report to the Second National Soviet Congress, 22 January 1934. London: Martin Lawrence, 1934.

Mao Tse-tung. "Reply of the Chinese Soviets to Program of the National Salvation Union." *China Today* 3, no. 4 (January 1937):40-44.

Mao Tse-tung. *Selected Works of Mao Tse-tung.* 5 vols. Peking: Foreign Languages Press, 1965-77.

Mao Tse-tung, Wang Ming, Georgi Dimitroff, I. Jack, and Edgar Snow. *China: The March Toward Unity.* New York: Workers Library, 1937.

"Mao Tse-tung's Speech to the First Plenary Session of the CCP's Ninth Central Committee." *Issues and Studies* (Taipei) 6, no. 6 (March 1970): 92-93. Speech delivered 28 April 1969.

McDonald, Angus W., Jr. "Reflections on Divided Elites, Social Cleavages, and Rural Revolution in Hunan." Paper delivered at Harvard Workshop on the Chinese Communist Rural Base Areas, Cambridge, August 1978.

Meyer, Alfred G. *Leninism.* New York: Praeger, 1962.

Mif, P[avel]. *Heroic China.* New York: Workers Library, 1937.

Mif, P[avel]. "New Developments in the Revolutionary Crisis in China." *Communist International* 10, no. 9 (15 May 1933):302-10.

Mif, P[avel]. "Only the Soviets Can Save China." *Communist International* 11, no. 11 (5 June 1934):366-76.

Miscellany of Mao Tse-tung Thought (1949-1968). 2 vols. Arlington, Va.: Joint Publications Research Service, 1974.

Muramatsu, Yuji. "Revolution and Chinese Tradition in Yenan Communism." Paper delivered at Seminar on East Asian Thought and Society, Stanford University, November 1957. Mimeographed (1958).

Myers, Ramon H. *The Chinese Farm Economy: Agricultural Development in Hopei and Shantung, 1890-1949.* Cambridge: Harvard University Press, 1970.

New China News Agency. *Daily News Release.* Peking, 1949.

Pak, Hyobom, ed. and trans. *Documents of the Chinese Communist Party, 1927-1930.* Hong Kong: Union Research Institute, 1971.

Pen Deh-hwai [P'eng Te-huai]. "Political Mass Work and the Mass Organizations in North China." *Communist International* 16, no. 6 (June 1939):494-500.

Pepper, Suzanne. *Civil War in China: The Political Struggle, 1945-1949.* Berkeley: University of California Press, 1978.

Perkins, Dwight H. *Agricultural Development in China, 1368-1968.* Chicago: Aldine, 1969.

Perkins, Dwight H., ed. *China's Modern Economy in Historical Perspective.* Stanford: Stanford University Press, 1975.

Räte China [Soviets in China]. Moscow-Leningrad: USSR Foreign Workers Publishing House, 1934. Documents of the Chinese Revolution.

"Resolution on the Land Question." *Chinese Studies in History* 4, nos. 2-3 (Winter-Spring 1971):76-101. Resolution of Sixth CCP Congress, Moscow, 1928.

"Resolution on the Trade Union Movement in China." *Chinese Studies in History* 4, no. 1 (Fall 1970):50-70. Resolution of Sixth CCP Congress, Moscow, 1928.

Richman, Barry M. *Industrial Society in Communist China.* New York: Random House, 1969.

Roy, M. N. *Revolution and Counter-Revolution in China.* Calcutta: Renaissance Publishers, 1946.

Rue, John E. *Mao Tse-tung in Opposition, 1927-1935.* Stanford: Stanford University Press, 1966.

Schram, Stuart, ed. *Authority, Participation and Cultural Change in China.* Cambridge: Cambridge University Press, 1973.

Schram, Stuart, ed. *Mao Tse-tung Unrehearsed, Talks and Letters: 1956-71.* London: Penguin, 1974.

Schran, Peter. *Guerrilla Economy: The Development of the Shensi-Kansu-Ninghsia Border Region, 1937-1945.* Albany: State University of New York Press, 1976.

Schwartz, Benjamin I. *Chinese Communism and the Rise of Mao.* Cambridge: Harvard University Press, 1961.

Schwarz, Henry G. *Liu Shao-ch'i and "People's War": A Report on the Creation of Base Areas in 1938.* Research Publication, no. 3. Lawrence: Center for East Asian Studies, University of Kansas, 1969.

Selden, Mark. *The Yenan Way in Revolutionary China.* Cambridge: Harvard University Press, 1971.

Shaffer, Lynda. *Mao and the Workers: The Hunan Labor Movement, 1920-1923.* Armonk, N.Y.: M. E. Sharpe, 1982.

Shen Hsi-meng, Mo Yen, and Lu Hsing-chen. *On Guard Beneath the Neon Lights.* Peking: Foreign Languages Press, 1966.

Sheng Yüeh. *Sun Yat-sen University in Moscow and the Chinese Revolution: A Personal Account.* Lawrence: University of Kansas Press, 1971.

Smedley, Agnes. *China Fights Back.* London: Victor Gollancz, 1938.

Snow, Edgar. *Random Notes on Red China, 1936-1945.* Cambridge: Harvard University Press, 1957.

Snow, Edgar. *Red Star Over China.* New York: Random House, 1938.

Snow, Helen Foster [Nym Wales]. *The Chinese Communists: Sketches and Autobiographies of the Old Guard.* Westport, Conn.: Greenwood Press, 1972.

Stein, Gunther. *The Challenge of Red China.* New York: McGraw-Hill, 1945.

Strong, Anna Louise. *The Chinese Conquer China.* New York: Doubleday, 1949.

"The Struggle Between Two Lines in China's Trade Union Movement." *Peking Review* 11, no. 26 (28 June 1968):17-21.

Swarup, Shanti. *A Study of the Chinese Communist Movement, 1927-1934.* London: Oxford University Press, 1966.

Tawney, R. H. *Land and Labour in China.* New York: Harcourt, Brace, 1932.

Teng Fa. "Trade Unions in Liberated Areas." *New China Review* (Manila) 1, no. 10 (February 1946). English-language supplement to *Chinese Guide.*

Thomas, S. Bernard. *"Proletarian Hegemony" in the Chinese Revolution and the Canton Commune of 1927.* Michigan Papers in Chinese Studies, no. 23. Ann Arbor: Center for Chinese Studies, The University of Michigan, 1975.

Thornton, Richard C. *China, the Struggle for Power, 1917-1972.* Bloomington: Indiana University Press, 1973.

Thornton, Richard C. *The Comintern and the Chinese Communists, 1928-1931.* Seattle: University of Washington Press, 1969.

Ting, Leonard G. "The Coal Industry in China," Part 1. *Nankai Social and Economic Quarterly* (Tientsin) 10, no. 1 (April 1937): 32-74.

Trade Unions in People's China. Peking: Foreign Languages Press, 1956.

Tung Pi-wu. "Memorandum on China's Liberated Areas." Document circulated at United Nations Conference on International Organization, San Francisco, 25 April-26 June, 1945.

U.S. Central Intelligence Agency, Foreign Broadcast Information Branch. *Daily Report, Far Eastern Section* (February 1947-December 1949).

U.S. Consulate, Peiping. *Translations of Radio Broadcasts of Hsin-hua, North Shensi* (November 1947-July 1949).

U.S. Department of Commerce, National Technical Information Service, Foreign Broadcast Information Service. *Daily Report, People's Republic of China* (1975-81).

U.S. Federal Communications Commission, Foreign Broadcast Intelligence Service. *Radio Report on the Far East* (August 1942-August 1945).

U.S. Information Service, Shanghai. *Yenan Broadcasts* (January 1946-January 1947).

Van Slyke, Lyman P. *Enemies and Friends: The United Front in Chinese Communist History.* Stanford: Stanford University Press, 1967.

Van Slyke, Lyman P., ed. *The Chinese Communist Movement.* Stanford: Stanford University Press, 1968. Report of the U.S. War Department, July 1945.

Vladimirov, Peter. *The Vladimirov Diaries: Yenan, China, 1942-45.* New York: Doubleday, 1975.

Wagner, Augusta. *Labor Legislation in China.* Peking: Yenching University, 1938.

Wales, Nym. *The Chinese Labor Movement.* New York: John Day, 1945.

Wales, Nym. *Inside Red China.* New York: Doubleday, Doran, 1939.

Wales, Nym. *My Yenan Notebooks.* Madison, Conn.: Privately published, 1961.

Wales, Nym. "Notes on the Beginnings of the Industrial Cooperatives in China." Unpublished, undated paper at the Hoover Institution, Stanford. Mimeograph.

Wales, Nym, and Kim San. *Song of Ariran: A Korean Communist in the Chinese Revolution.* Rev. ed. San Francisco: Ramparts Press, 1972.

Wan Min [Wang Ming], and Kang Sin [K'ang Sheng]. *Revolutionary China Today.* New York: Workers Library, 1934. Speeches of Wang and K'ang to the ECCI Thirteenth Plenum, December 1933.

Wang Ming. *China Can Win!* New York: Workers Library, 1937.

Wang Ming. "The Revolutionary Movement in the Colonial and Semi-Colonial Countries and the Tactics of the Communist Parties." *Communist International* 12, no. 18 (20 September 1935):1323-33.

Watson, Andrew. *Mao Zedong and the Political Economy of the Border Region.* Cambridge: Cambridge University Press, 1980.

Whitson, William W. *The Chinese High Command: A History of Communist Military Politics, 1927-71.* New York: Praeger, 1973.

Who's Who in Communist China. Rev. ed. 2 vols. Hong Kong: Union Research Institute, 1969.

Wilbur, C. Martin. "The Influence of the Past: How the Early Years Helped to Shape the Future of the Chinese Communist Party." *China Quarterly* 36 (October-December 1965):23-44.

World News and Views. London, vols. 18-30, 1938-50. Successor to *International Press Correspondence.*

Wu Tien-wei. *Mao Tse-tung and the Tsunyi Conference: An Annotated Bibliography.* Washington, D.C.: CCRM, 1974.

Wylie, Raymond F. *The Emergence of Maoism: Mao Tse-tung, Ch'en Po-ta, and the Search for Chinese Theory, 1935-1945.* Stanford: Stanford University Press, 1980.

Yakhontoff, Victor A. *The Chinese Soviets.* New York: Coward-McCann, 1934.

Yao Wen-yuan. "On the Social Basis of the Lin Piao Anti-Party Clique." *Peking Review* 18, no. 10 (7 March 1975):5-10.

Young, Marilyn B., ed. *Women in China.* Michigan Papers in Chinese Studies, no. 15. Ann Arbor: Center for Chinese Studies, The University of Michigan, 1973.

chan-tou tung-yüan [zhandou dongyuan]
战斗动员

ch'en-chiu ssu-hsiang-ti kung-hui tso-yung
[chenjiu sixiangdi gonghui zuoyong]
陈旧思想地工会作用

cheng-feng [zhengfeng] 整风

chiao-ch'a lei-chin kung-tzu chih-tu
[jiaocha leijin gongzi zhidu]
交叉累进工资制度

chien-jui chieh-chi tou-cheng fang-shih
[jianrui jieji douzheng fangshi]
坚锐阶级斗争方式

ch'ih-ti k'u, tso-ti to [chide ku, zuode duo]
吃得苦，作得多

chin [jin] 斤

chin-kung [jingong] 进攻

ching-chi chu-i [jingji zhuyi] 经济主义

ch'ing-ch'iu [qingqiu] 请求

ch'ing-shih-ti t'ai-tu [qingshide taidu]
轻视的态度

ch'ing-suan tou-cheng [qingsuan douzheng]
清算斗争

ch'iu-kuo [qiuguo] 救国

ch'ü [qu] 区

Chung-hua ch'üan-kuo tsung chih-kung hui
[Zhonghua quanguo zong zhigong hui]
中华全国总职工会

Chung-kuo chieh-fang ch'ü chih-kung lienho
hui [Zhongguo jiefang qu zhigong lianhe
hui] 中国解放区职工联合会

fa-pi [fabi] 法币

fan-tui t'e-ch'üan chieh-chi tou-cheng
[fandui tequan jieji douzheng]
反对特权阶级斗争

feng-fu [fengfu] 丰富

hang-hui chu-i che [hanghui zhuyi zhe]
行会主义者

ho-hsin [hexin] 核心

ho-li ti kung-tzu chih-tu [helide gongzi
zhidu] 合理的工资制度

ho-li-ti kung-tzu [helide gongzi]
合理的工资

hsi-wang [xiwang] 希望

hsiang [xiang] 乡

hsiao tzu-ch'an chieh-chi hua [xiao zichan
jiejihua] 小资产阶级化

hsien [xian] 县

hsin lao-tung t'ai-tu [xin laodung taidu]
新劳动态度

huo-pi yü wu-p'in kung-tzu chih-tu [huobi
yu wupin gongzi zhidu]
货币与物品工资制度

jen-t'ung fu-kung [rentong fugong]
忍痛复工

"kan pu kan, i chin pan" ["gan bu gan, yi jin
ban"] 干不干，一斤半

ku-chu [guzhu] 雇主

ku-kan [gugan] 骨干

ku-kan tso-yung [gugan zuoyong]
骨干作用

kuan-men chu-i [guanmen zhuyi]
关门主义

kung-ch'ang kuan-li wei-yüan-hui
[gongchang guanli weiyuan hui]
工厂管理委员会

kung-nung tui-li-ti li-ch'ang [gongnong
duilide lichang] 工农对立的立场

kung-ssu liang-li [gongsi liangli]
公私两利

kung-tsei [gongzei] 工贼

lan-to fen-tzu [landuo fenzi] 懒惰分子

lao-pan [laoban] 老板

lao-tung pao-hu fa [laodong baohu fa]
劳动保护法

lao-tzu cheng-i [laozi zhengyi] 劳资争议

lao-tzu hu-hsiang kuan-hsi [laozi huxiang
guanxi] 劳资互相关系

lao-tzu liang-li [laozi liangli] 劳资两利

lao-tzu shuang-fang-ti li-i [laozi
shuangfangde liyi] 劳资双方的利益

lao-tzu shuang-fang yu-hao kuan-hsi [laozi
shuangfang you hao guanxi]
劳资双方友好关系

lao-tzu t'o-hsieh [laozi tuoxie] 劳资妥协

nong-min cheng-ch'üan [nongmin
zhengquan] 农民政权

nung ts'un lao-tzu kuan-hsi [nongcun laozi
guanxi] 农村劳资关系

pa-kung [bagong] 罢工

pien-pi [bienbi] 边币

p'in-k'u ch'ün-chung [pinku qunzhong]
贫苦群众

p'ing-chün chu-i [pingjun zhuyi] 平均主义

p'o-huai fen-tzu [pohuai fenzi] 破坏分子

pu wang tsu-kuo [buwang zuguo]
不忘祖国

p'u-t'ung [putong] 普通

Shen-Kan-Ning pien-ch'ü tsung kung-hui
[Shen-Gan-Ning bianqu zong gonghui]
陕甘宁边区总工会

sheng [sheng] 省

sheng-ch'an t'u-chi tui [shengchan tuji dui]
生产突击队

shih-ho chan-cheng-ti hsu-yao [shihe
zhanzhengde xuyao] 适合战争的需要

shih-tang [shidang] 适当

t'iao-cheng [tiaozheng] 调整

t'iao-chieh [tiaojie] 调解

tou-cheng [douzheng] 斗争

ts'un [cun] 村

ts'ung-ch'ien [congqian] 从前

tu-li lao-tung-che [duli laodongzhe]
独立劳动者

t'u-hao [tuhao] 土豪

t'ui-kung [tuigong] 退工

tui-li ti-wei [duili diwei] 对立地位

yu ch'ien ch'ü ch'ien, yu li ch'u li [you qian
chu qian, you li chu li]
有钱出钱,有力出力

yu-min [youmin] 愚民

MICHIGAN MONOGRAPHS IN CHINESE STUDIES

No. 45. *Chinese Social and Economic History from the Song to 1900*, edited by Albert Feuerwerker.

No. 46. *China's Universities: Post-Mao Enrollment Policies and Their Impact on the Structure of Secondary Education*, by Suzanne Pepper.

No. 47. *Songs from Xanadu*, by J. I. Crump.

No. 48. *Social Organization in South China, 1911-1949: The Case of The Kuan Lineage of K'ai-p'ing County*, by Yuen-fong Woon.

No. 49. *Labor and the Chinese Revolution*, by S. Bernard Thomas (cloth only).

No. 50. *Soviet Studies of Premodern China: Assessments of Recent Scholarship*, edited by Gilbert Rozman.

No. 51. *Career Patterns in the Ch'ing Dynasty: The Office of the Governor-General*, by Raymond W. Chu and William G. Saywell.

MICHIGAN ABSTRACTS OF CHINESE AND JAPANESE WORKS ON CHINESE HISTORY

No. 1. *The Ming Tribute Grain System*, by Hoshi Ayao, translated by Mark Elvin.

No. 2. *Commerce and Society in Sung China*, by Shiba Yoshinobu, translated by Mark Elvin.

No. 3. *Transport in Transition: The Evolution of Traditional Shipping In China*, translated by Andrew Watson.

No. 4. *Japanese Perspectives on China's Early Modernization: A Bibliographical Survey*, by K. M. Kim.

No. 5. *The Silk Industry in Ch'ing China*, by Shih Min-hsiung, translated by E-tu Zen Sun.

No. 6. *The Pawnshop in China*, by T. S. Whelan.

Michigan Papers and Abstracts available from:

Center for Chinese Studies
The University of Michigan
104 Lane Hall (Publications)
Ann Arbor, Michigan 48109 USA

Printed and bound by CPI Group (UK) Ltd, Croydon, CR0 4YY

13/04/2025

14656508-0003